GANDHI AS A
POLITICAL STRATEGIST

GANDHI AS A POLITICAL STRATEGIST

with Essays on Ethics and Politics

by GENE SHARP

Introduction by
CORETTA SCOTT KING

Extending Horizons Books
PORTER SARGENT PUBLISHERS, INC.
11 Beacon St., Boston, MA 02108

Copyright © 1979 by Gene Sharp
Manufactured in the United States of America
Library of Congress Catalog Card Number: 79-84497
International Standard Book Number: 0-87558-090-4 (cloth)
International Standard Book Number: 0-87558-092-0 (paper)

Book design by Patricia E. McGauley

The intellectual and moral satisfaction that I failed to gain from the utilitarianism of Bentham and Mill, the revolutionary methods of Marx and Lenin, the social contracts theory of Hobbes, the "back to nature" optimism of Rousseau, and the superman philosophy of Nietzsche, I found in the nonviolent resistance philosophy of Gandhi. I came to feel that this was the only morally and practically sound method open to oppressed people in their struggle for freedom.

Dr. Martin Luther King, Jr.
Stride Toward Freedom

Contents

vi

Contents

Introduction

by Coretta Scott King

It is often said of leaders like Mohandas K. Gandhi and
Martin Luther King, Jr. that they were those rare individuals who
were "ahead of their time." But, this is only a half-truth. Both men
were indeed rare individuals, but not because they were ahead of
their time.

Rather, Gandhi and Martin *caught up* with their time because
they discovered a peaceful means for advancing both the material
and spiritual progress of humanity.

They discovered an idea whose time had long since come. It is
an idea that my good friend Gene Sharp has traced as far back as
the early days of the Roman Republic in the fifth century B.C., when
the plebians first challenged the authority of the patricians. It is the
idea that, if it is properly planned, persistent nonviolent action can
achieve significant social progress, however formidable the opposition may appear to be.

While many people share an awareness of this truth, Martin
Luther King, Jr. and Mahatma Gandhi were rare individuals
because they both chose to accept the challenge of socially responsible leadership and act to bring about nonviolent social change.

Martin's journey to awareness of Gandhian strategy and

tactics began in 1949 when he attended a World Pacifist Meeting at Fellowship House in Philadelphia not long after Gandhi's assassination. One of the speakers, Dr. Mordecai W. Johnson (President of Howard University) delivered a ringing sermon on the life and work of Mahatma Gandhi that Martin would later describe as "profound and electrifying." The curiosity that was sparked in my husband that day was, at first, tempered with a healthy skepticism but gradually gave way to a realization that Gandhi was, in fact, right. As Martin wrote in his first book, *Stride Toward Freedom:*

> It was in this Gandhian emphasis on love and nonviolence that I discovered the method for social reform that I had been seeking for so many months. The intellectual and moral satisfaction that I failed to gain from the utilitarianism of Bentham and Mill, the revolutionary methods of Marx and Lenin, the social contracts theory of Hobbes, the "back to nature" optimism of Rousseau and the superhuman philosophy of Nietzsche, I found in the nonviolent resistance philosophy of Gandhi. I came to feel that this was the only morally and practically sound method open to oppressed people in their struggle for freedom.

Martin had the great advantage of drawing from Gandhi's historical legacy. But Gandhi had no such body of recorded experience because the rich, though hidden, heritage of nonviolent struggle had not yet been systematically documented. Indeed, it was not until 1973, when Gene Sharp published his trilogy, *The Politics of Nonviolent Action,* that the definitive historical analysis became available for the first time.

Professor Sharp brings an all too rare combination of scholarly precision and readability to *Gandhi as a Political Strategist.* And just as *The Politics of Nonviolent Action* should be required reading for all serious students of the nonviolent method, this volume fills a tremendous void in the literature about Gandhi and the movement he led.

There is a vast literature on the life and work of Mahatma Gandhi, but it is only with the publication of *Gandhi as a Political Strategist* that we have, for the first time, a single volume which provides an in-depth analysis of Gandhi's political strategy and its relevance for social struggle today. Previous works have tended to concentrate on Gandhi's personal morality in a kind of "great man" interpretation of India's successful struggle for independence or alternatively on Gandhi as a leader who was drafted by the "zeitgeist" of historical circumstances (there is some truth in both views). But, Professor Sharp makes clear once and for all that the driving force in the movement for Indian independence was Gandhi's creative synthesis of India's cultural and historical traditions with a unique interpretation of the principle of militant, nonviolent resistance to all forms of institutional evil.

It is Gene Sharp's contention that the effectiveness and future potential of nonviolent resistance in India has been underestimated by many because of a basic ignorance of its history. In the opening chapter, "Gandhi's Political Significance," the author defines and thoroughly refutes six counterproductive "realist" myths about Gandhian nonviolence, demonstrating beyond any doubt that they are based on false assumptions.

Subsequent sections include enlightening essays on topics as diverse as Erik Erikson's psychohistory of Gandhi, the Indian constructive program (which became the manifesto of the movement for social reform and independence), Gandhi's personal view of *satyagraha's* successes and setbacks and his ideas for a defense policy during World War II. In addition, there is a useful typology of nonviolent strategies and two fascinating discussions on a difficult subject, the relationship of Gandhi's morality of nonviolence to concrete political techniques.

In the pages that follow, the careful reader will find a lucid, compelling case for nonviolent direct action as the most effective means for advancing social change that humankind has ever known. *Gandhi as a Political Strategist* is, as the critics say, the book Gene Sharp had to write. It is a book that should be read by scholars, students, political activists, and everyone who seeks the progress of humanity.

Preface

From the early 1920s to his death in 1948 the name "Gandhi" was often on the front pages of newspapers throughout the world as he challenged the then all-powerful British Empire. That Empire stretched literally around the world—the sun never set on it, it was said. Millions of people of many cultures, languages, colors, and conditions were ruled from London.

Mohandas K. Gandhi—often called Mahatma (great souled one) —held office in no government, and led no terrorist gang or rebel military army. Yet his intentions and actions aroused the millions of Indians, shook the Empire, and provoked both ridicule and admiration among people throughout the world. This strange man for nearly fifty years challenged, first, the European masters of South Africa, then, the British masters of India, and, finally, even the basic tenets of orthodox politics.

Gandhi was the contemporary of Tsar Nicholas, Lenin, and Stalin, of Kaiser Wilhelm and Adolph Hitler, of Woodrow Wilson and Franklin Roosevelt, of the last Emperor of China, Sun Yat Sen, Chiang Kai Shek, and Mao Tse Tung. He bridged the span between the time when wars were fought by armies with rifles to the time when they were fought with atomic bombs.

Gandhi saw millions living under oppression, starvation, and self-degradation. During those decades armies swept across continents, and millions were deliberately exterminated. Racism ran rampant; women, untouchables, and many others were denied dignity and opportunities. These were among the social and political evils for which he sought solutions.

Now, the British Empire is gone, along with many once-entrenched governments and powerful rulers. Certain victories for human dignity and improvements in the conditions of human beings have been achieved. Yet, problems not only remain but some of them are more grave than during Gandhi's lifetime. Poverty and starvation are common conditions in much of the world. The technical capacities of dictators to control individuals and whole societies have increased. The ability of modern governments espousing conflicting ideologies to annihilate human beings has multiplied beyond the most pessimistic predictions.

Today, Gandhi and his ideas rarely receive attention. Many who know the name dismiss him as a strange religious "kook" of some kind, or a prudish ascetic because of his views on sex and pleasures. Others, often condescendingly, view him as someone who was once important due to a unique set of historical circumstances but who is no longer relevant. Many of the people born in the West since 1940 or so have little idea who Gandhi was, and do not even recognize the "Indian National Congress" as the name of the political party which led the independence struggle, sometimes with Gandhi as its strategist and general.

Gandhi has lasting significance, however, not only for his role in the history of India and the world, but also for his challenge to established political tenets. In addition, he contributed to the refinement and application of a different type of struggle than that for which the violent twentieth century is most famous. With deliberate calculation, Gandhi challenged domestic conditions and Imperial rule by nonviolent struggle, when others submitted or used violence. Gandhi called his version of nonviolent action *satyagraha.*

We now know that in this respect he was not so original as we once assumed. Gandhi did not create mass nonviolent resistance. He did not even introduce nonviolent struggle into South Africa, let alone India. But his application and refinement of this technique remain highly important. Significant lessons are still to be learned from them, as Dr. King reminded us not so very long ago.

Although Gandhi was not a systematic social analyst, he developed a conceptual framework and outline of a comprehensive program—implemented by various organizations for particular tasks—to reconstruct society by voluntary self-help outside the dominating institutions and the State apparatus. This he called the constructive program.

The thesis of the chapters of this book is that Gandhi was an extraordinary political strategist, and that an appreciation of this is necessary to understand the man and the movements with which he challenged the most vast Empire which the world had ever seen, and contributed significantly to its dissolution. But there is more to his significance.

This book also suggests that we need to continue to consider Gandhi's challenge to established political tenets, his refinements of nonviolent struggle, and his perceptions of requirements for ending oppression, reconstructing society, and lifting dependency on political violence.

The chapters of this book were originally written and published separately between 1959 and 1970, while I was variously living in England, Norway, and the United States. They were published in journals, weeklies, or books, in England, Norway, India, and the United States, as is specified in detail in Appendix G. They appear here in edited forms, some with only minor editing to improve readability, to remove repetition, or to correct errors in the published versions, and others with more extensive rewriting and additions.

While these chapters do not cover all important aspects of Gandhi's thought and activities, together they offer important insights into his thought and practice as a political strategist, and are much more integrated than might be expected from their separate origins. They offer certain fresh insights, and develop others more fully than do other presentations of them. These essays present new information on the origins of Gandhi's use of nonviolent struggle in South Africa, and offer full treatments of his theory of political power, his evaluation of Indian nonviolent struggle, and his formulation of a broad alternative national defense policy.

This book does not include a presentation of Gandhi's perceptions of the dynamics of nonviolent struggle in open conflict with a repressive opponent. For that aspect, the reader is referred to Gene Sharp, *The Politics of Nonviolent Action,* Part III, "The Dynamics of Nonviolent Action" (Boston: Porter Sargent Publisher, 1973, 1974), in which Gandhi's insights are extensively quoted and cited.

Part Two of this volume includes four essays on ethics and politics, the first three of which do not focus primarily on Gandhi. They deal with the problem of how people can live in the real world and deal responsibly with its acute political conflicts without violation of their ethical principles. Chapter Ten presents the characteristics of six types of principled nonviolence, including Gandhi's *satyagraha*. (The word has come to be used both for his technique of struggle and for his combined personal and social philosophy.) Chapter Eleven examines the views of Max Weber, the important German sociologist, on the crucial role of violence in creating some of the most serious ethical problems for those who seek to influence political events. Chapter Twelve is an attempt to persuade believers in nonviolence as a moral principle that they have a responsibility to help develop the technique of nonviolent action which can be used by people who do not share their convictions. Chapter Thirteen again draws very heavily on Gandhi's thought, utilizing his comments and insights for an exploratory discussion of the relationship between attempts to deal with and to remove violence in society by living according to an ethic of nonviolence and by practicing the technique of nonviolent action on the grounds that it "works." It raises the question whether in the long run behavior which is normative and behavior which is practical are perhaps very close to being identical.

Gandhi was neither the first nor the last important nonviolent leader. As knowledge of nonviolent struggle increases and spreads, and as people become more aware of their capacities and more capable of self-reliance, their dependency on leaders is likely to shrink.

Gandhi offered his views for consideration by others who should independently evaluate them, and then reject, accept, or modify his ideas and proposals as they might find appropriate. Although he was at times followed and revered by millions, he wanted each person to develop his or her own capacities and judgement. He insisted that his was not the last word.

In many ways, we have already moved beyond Gandhi. Yet, we will be able to do so far more ably if we seek to learn as much as possible from the thought and experiences of this man, who was without doubt one of the most remarkable political strategists of this century.

G.S.

Cambridge, Massachusetts
August, 1978

Acknowledgements

It is impossible adequately and completely to acknowledge all the people who have directly and indirectly helped in the preparation and original publication of the chapters of this book over so many years. In addition to those who are specifically mentioned here, the editors and staff members of the journals, books, and other publications in which these chapters originally were published merit acknowledgement. These publications are listed in Appendix G.

Appreciation is also due to the institutions which provided an academic home while these chapters were being written: the Institute of Philosophy and the History of Ideas of the University of Oslo, Norway; the Institute for Social Research, Oslo; St. Catherine's College, Oxford; and Harvard University's Center for International Affairs. Without the financial support of various institutions and individuals, some of them too modest to encourage mention of their assistance, the original research and writing, and the considerable editorial work in transforming the individual essays into this book would have been impossible.

The annotated bibliography on Gandhi and related topics which appears here as Appendix D "Sources for Further Study" is a small portion of a much larger bibliographical project on nonviolent struggle which has been in preparation for several years. Most of this work has been done under my direction by several university students or recent graduates, usually volunteers, including Jane Casey, William Vogele, William Wylie, and most especially Robert Cucci and Lisa Foley. Robert Cucci and Lisa Foley spent months of tedious work in libraries and in development of the classified bibliography. In this preparation the librarians of the Widener Library of Harvard University have been most helpful and patient. Dennis Dalton kindly examined the provisional entries of this section on Gandhi, and suggested some important additional titles which have been added. The full annotated classified bibliography on nonviolent struggle is intended for inclusion in my forthcoming basic introductory book *Beyond Violence: Exploring Nonviolent Alternatives.*

Agnes Brophy, my Assistant, has rendered most valuable help and advice in innumerable ways, from the exploration of the original idea of bringing these independently written essays together into a book, and the evaluation of which to include, on through the various stages of editing and production.

Julie Kittross assisted the preparation of the final manuscript in various ways, most especially in checking the accuracy and sources of almost all of the quotations from Gandhi which appear in this book—and they are many!

Nancy A. Tramontin has spent many hours of most skillful work in helping to locate and correct editorial and stylistic problems, in order to make this book as readable as possible. In this she often had to exercise great patience with me since I never seemed able to stop making revisions and additions to the manuscript! Agnes Brophy and Lisa Foley have assisted ably in the long and tedious proofreading.

Two of my earlier academic mentors merit special mention: Professor Kurt H. Wolff of Brandeis University, who encouraged my studies of Gandhi and the general field of nonviolent struggle when I was a graduate student at Ohio State University; and Arne Næss, formerly Professor of Philosophy at the University of Oslo, who brought me from London to the University of Oslo and, along with Erik Rinde, to the Institute for Social Research, Oslo, to continue my research and writing on Gandhi and nonviolent struggle generally on a full time basis for the first time.

Porter Sargent Publishers, Inc., has made it possible for this book and its companion *Social Power and Political Freedom* to be published. I am grateful for their continuing recognition of the importance of this field, following the foresight of the late F. Porter Sargent in publishing my earlier much larger *The Politics of Nonviolent Action* when other publishers were unwilling to be so adventurous. J. Kathryn Sargent, President, Jennie B. Fonzo, Vice President, and Susan Scown, Editorial Assistant have been very helpful in various ways. Patricia E. McGauley, Coordinator of Porter Sargent's Extending Horizons Series, has supervised the entire production of this book and dealt effectively with a somewhat perfectionist author who repeatedly demonstrated an incapacity to estimate remotely accurately the amount of work required and the time needed to transform the original independent chapters into this book.

The editing of this book has been done at Harvard University's Center for International Affairs while I have been a Research Associate. During this period I have also continued as Professor of Political Science and Sociology at Southeastern Massachusetts University.

Coretta Scott King has been most kind and generous with her time to prepare her Introduction to this volume. My visits to the Martin Luther King, Jr., Center for Social Change in Atlanta, and especially the people I have met at its past three summer Institutes on Nonviolence have enriched my appreciation of the power of nonviolent struggle and my respect both for Dr. King himself and for the many less famous or little known heroes of the struggles for equality in this country.

Copyrights are acknowledged separately in Appendix H.

The quotation from Gandhi which appears following the last chapter was originally published in *Harijan,* 20 March 1937, and reprinted in M.K. Gandhi, *Non-violence in Peace and War* (Ahmedabad: Navajivan, 1948) vol. I, p. 132.

PART ONE

Gandhi as a Political Strategist

1

Gandhi's Political Significance

On 30 January 1948 on his way to prayers Gandhi was assassinated, killed by three bullets in his abdomen and chest. The young assassin was a fanatical Hindu who among others had been inflamed by Gandhi's efforts to bring reconciliation between Hindus and Muslims in riot-torn independent India. After a year of bloody strife, Gandhi's fast had brought peace to Calcutta and all Bengal. Later, sensing an incendiary situation under the surface, he fasted the last time in Delhi and restored an atmosphere of peace. For these and similar acts, he was not loved by all. In Calcutta a mob attacked his residence, a brick was thrown at him, and someone swung a heavy bamboo rod *(lathi)* at his head. Both narrowly missed. During his Delhi fast some shouted outside his quarters, "Let Gandhi die!" A week before his death, a small homemade bomb was thrown at him from a nearby garden during afternoon prayers.

With those three bullets came the bitter fruit of the murder of an important political leader. India and the world were saddened. Political leaders and ordinary people alike felt a personal loss.

In the years which have passed since that January day, many important events have taken place which have altered the world significantly: the death of Stalin, the Communist victory in China, the development of the hydrogen bomb and intercontinental missiles, the Hungarian Revolution, the trial of Eichmann, the end of the British and French colonial empires, President Kennedy's assassination, and the civil rights struggles in the United States, to list only a few.

After such events in a world in which history now moves so quickly, does Gandhi still have any political significance? With the passing of years and the opportunity for a more distant perspective, how is Gandhi to be evaluated? Are there points at which our earlier judgment must be revised?

DIFFICULTIES IN UNDERSTANDING GANDHI

For a Westerner—and perhaps particularly for an American— Gandhi poses special problems in such an evaluation. His eccentricities often get in the way so that it is difficult to get beyond them, or to take other aspects of his life seriously. Even for religious people in the West, his constant use of religious terminology and theological language in explanation or justification of a social or political act or policy more often confuses than clarifies.

The homage which most pay to him by calling him "Mahatma"—the great-souled one—usually becomes a kind of vaccination against taking him seriously. If he was such a saint and holy man, it is thought, this is a full explanation of his accomplishments; we need investigate no further. As a Mahatma, he can be revered while being placed in that special category of saints, prophets, and holy persons whose lives and actions are believed to be largely irrelevant to ordinary people.

It is sometimes the case that Gandhi's own candid evaluations of himself and his work now appear to be more accurate than the opinions of some of his followers and the homage-bearers. "I claim," he once wrote, "to be no more than an average man with less than average ability."[1] Indeed, in important respects this was probably true. He went to South Africa only after having failed in his attempt to be a lawyer in India. Nor was he pleased at the homage given him, although he cherished the affection of people where it was genuine. "My Mahatmaship is worthless," he once wrote.[2]

> I have become literally sick of the adoration of the unthinking multitude.[3]

> I lay no claim to superhuman powers. I want none. I wear the same corruptible flesh that the weakest of my fellow-beings wears, and am, therefore, as liable to err as any.[4]

There are further difficulties in evaluating Gandhi. These include widespread misrepresentations of Gandhi and his political opinions. These misrepresentations are not usually deliberate, but are often made by people who have not made a detailed study of Gandhi's views on the point in question. It has, for example, been widely claimed that Gandhi approved of Indian military action in Kashmir, that he would have approved of the Indian invasion of Goa, and even that he would have supported development of Indian nuclear weapons.

Such misrepresentations are not only made by Westerners, but commonly by educated Indians who often assume, because they are Indians, and have read newspaper reports and repeatedly discussed Gandhi, that they know what they are talking about. Gandhi's own skepticism about the degree of understanding of his nonviolence and views among Western-educated Indians continues to be verified.

Some of the difficulties encountered in understanding Gandhi's views on such questions have roots in the attempt to fit Gandhi into our usual categories. It is, for example, assumed often that he must fit the traditional view of a pacifist or that he is a supporter of military action. When he asserted the existence of political evil which had to be resisted, many people assume that he thereby "of necessity" had supported violence.

Gandhi's thinking was constantly developing. Early in his career he did give certain qualified support to war. By the end of his life he no longer did so. But this did *not* mean he favored passivity to foreign invasions. While believing the Allies to be the better side in the Second World War, he did not support the war. Similarly in Kashmir while believing the Pakistanis to be the aggressors, and believing that India must act, he did *not* favor military action. Instead, he placed his confidence in the application of an alternative nonviolent means of struggle to fight political evil. Here he was constantly experimenting, and his advocacy of the efficacy of nonviolent action in crises was not always convincing to the hard-headed realists. This sometimes meant—as at the time of Kashmir —that he was not politically "effective," but that was quite different from claiming that he had rejected his own nonviolent means. As we shall note later in more detail, it was Gandhi's primary contribution, not only to argue for, but to develop practical nonviolent means of struggle in politics for those situations in which war and other types of political violence were usually used. His work here was pioneering, and sometimes inadequate, but it was sufficient to put him outside the traditional categories: Gandhi was neither a conscientious objector nor a supporter of violence in politics. He was an experimenter in the development of "war without violence."

A final confusion handicaps our attempt to evaluate Gandhi. His politics are sometimes assumed to be identical with those of the independent Indian government under Prime Minister Jawaharlal Nehru. Although Nehru had long had a deep regard for Gandhi, and although Gandhi cooperated with the Indian National Congress in the long struggle for independence, the policies which Gandhi favored are not necessarily those of the Congress government under Nehru and his successors.

Indeed, saddened by the riots between Hindus and Muslims and busy in Calcutta seeking to restore peace, Gandhi refused to attend the independence ceremony and celebrations on 15 August 1947.[5] The riots saddened him both for their own sake and because he believed they reflected a weakness in Indian society which could bring India again under foreign domination by one of the Big Three (which included China).[6]

Gandhi had opposed partition of the whole country into Pakistan and India. Congress leaders had accepted it. His plea for nonviolent resistance in Kashmir with nonviolent assistance from India was ignored. Gandhi had dreamt that a free India would be able to defend her freedom without military means. Yet in the provisional government before independence, and in the fully independent government, military expenditure and influence increased, while Gandhi warned of the danger of military rule and of India's possible future threat to world peace. Her freedom could be defended nonviolently, Gandhi insisted, just as nonviolent means had forced the great British Empire to withdraw.

Political independence had not brought real relief to the peasants, who Gandhi had said ought nonviolently to seize and occupy the land, and even to exercise political power.

Gandhi's picture and name were widely used by the Congress Party in election campaigns. Yet Gandhi had written: "We must recognize the fact that the constitution we want or the social order of our dreams cannot come through the Congress Party of today. . . ."[7] The day before his assassination he drafted a proposal for abolishing the Congress as it existed and suggested a constitution for converting it into an association for voluntary work to build a nonviolent society and guide India's development from outside the government.

Gandhi must be evaluated on the basis of his own outlook and his own policies, not those of others. It is also important that we reexamine some of those views about Gandhi and the nonviolent struggle he led which are widespread in the West. In large degree these are views which have masqueraded as "realistic" assessments. I suggest, however, that these views are often contrary to the facts and may be more akin to rationalizations which help one to avoid considering Gandhi and the Indian experiments seriously. Let us look at six of these a bit more closely.

"INHERENTLY NONVIOLENT" INDIANS

Outside of India, during and for some years after the Indian nonviolent liberation struggle, it was widely said that such nonviolence was simply a characteristic of Indians who were presumed to be, for various reasons, incapable of violence. The implication of this was that the Indian experiments with nonviolent action deserved very little further analysis. For fairly obvious reasons the assumption that Indians were incapable of violence for political ends is almost never heard any longer. But the implications of this altered view are likewise almost never explored.

It is forgotten (except in India) that the 1857–59 Indian War of Independence—which the English called the "Mutiny"—ever occurred, and this included not only guerrilla campaigns but full-scale battles. In the late nineteenth and early twentieth centuries a terrorist movement developed among Indian nationalists (especially in Maharashtra, Bengal, and the Punjab) which was responsible for a number of assassinations by bombings and shootings. Even after Gandhi was actively on the scene, the terrorists continued their actions. For example, as late as 1929 bombs were thrown and shots were fired in the Legislative Assembly in New Delhi. At the end of that year a bomb exploded under the train carrying the Viceroy, Lord Irwin (later known as Lord Halifax when he was British Foreign Secretary and Ambassador to the United States). Even that was not the end of the terrorist movement.

Subhas Chandra Bose by 1928 had achieved an impressive following with his cry of "Give me blood and I promise you freedom." That year both he and Jawaharlal Nehru (later a supporter of Gandhi's methods) favored an immediate declaration of independence to be followed by a war of independence. Bose was President of the Indian National Congress in 1938 and was again elected to that position at the 1939 convention though he already had resigned under pressure from Gandhi. During World War II, Bose headed the "Indian National Army" and fought on the side of the Japanese, capturing the imagination of a significant section of the Indian public.

The religious riots prior to and after Independence are well known. Thousands were killed. Five millions migrated across the new borders of India and Pakistan. There were well-grounded fears of war—first civil war, and later war between the newly independent countries. Troops faced each other in Kashmir.

During the Sino-Indian border conflict, it became unmistakably clear that when faced with a crisis affecting its frontiers the Indian Government was prepared to involve itself in large-scale military preparations. The Indian people shared this reaction by and large: indeed, the most vocal critics of the government felt that it was not sufficiently ready to go to war. The implications of the Indian invasion of Goa and the war in Nagaland, that the Indian government was ready to use military force, were emphatically confirmed. This was as Gandhi had expected. The Indian Government had demonstrated that when it came to military defense, it differed little in its basic approach from other governments.

All these facts should make it quite clear that the Indians have always been quite capable of using violent means, and that there must have been something special which led them to rely on nonviolent struggle as the main strategy for achieving independence.

It is of course true that there were elements in Indian religions and traditions which were conducive to Gandhi's approach, and that as Gandhi drew upon these and spoke in their language, the religious peasants understood him. The most important of these was probably the principle of *ahimsa,* which roughly meant noninjury to living things in thought, word, and deed. These elements were doubtless important, but, as we shall note later, when Gandhi drew upon them, he always gave them new and vital interpretations.

Just as there are in Western civilization traditions and principles counteracting the Christian principle of love for one's enemies, so in Indian religions and traditions there were also counteracting principles. Sikhs and Muslims, for example, believed in military prowess. And the Hindu caste system itself provided for a warrior caste. The *Bhagavad Gita*—which Gandhi so revered and which he reinterpreted symbolically—related the story of physical warfare and dwelt upon the justification for fighting.

In light of these various demonstrations of the Indians' willingness to use violence in political struggles, the view that the Indian independence struggle was predominantly nonviolent because Indians were incapable of approving of violence collapses.

While for strategic reasons a full-scale war with traditional front-lines might not have been possible, a major guerrilla war certainly would have been feasible. (Assuming that the percentage of casualties in proportion to the total population would have been about the same in such a struggle in India as later proved to be the case in Algeria, that would have meant between 3,000,000 and 3,500,000 Indians dead. The estimated number of Indians killed or mortally wounded while participating in the nonviolent struggle given by Richard Gregg is about 8,000.[8] One cannot claim that the

French are by nature proportionally that much more cruel than the English!)

Rather than Indian nonviolence being entirely natural and inevitable, it is clear that Gandhi deserves considerable credit in getting nonviolent action accepted as the technique of struggle in the grand strategy for the liberation movement. It is clear that this acceptance by the Indian National Congress was not a moral or religious act. It was a political act made possible because Gandhi offered a course of action which was nonviolent but which above all was seen to be practical and effective.

DEFYING TRADITIONS

It is widely believed that Gandhi was simply a personification of Indian traditions. As we have pointed out, however, and as has been amply demonstrated by Dr. Joan V. Bondurant, wherever Gandhi drew upon traditional Indian concepts, he gave them a fresh and vital interpretation which differed significantly from the original.[9] At the same time, it is usually forgotten how un-Indian Gandhi was in many ways. He openly, in words and actions, defied widely accepted traditions and orthodoxies. His fight against untouchability, which he undertook several decades ago when it was many times more entrenched than today, is simply an example. His whole experimental approach to life and to politics (he called his autobiography, *The Story of My Experiments with Truth*) has overtones of influence by Western science.

Gandhi's basic assumption that one must not "accept" or "understand" evil but *fight* it, although supported by some, was also in diametrical opposition to other schools of Hindu philosophy which held that one must not fight evil, but transcend it, seeing the conflict between good and evil as something which ultimately contributes to a higher development, and hence about which one ought not to be particularly concerned.

Gandhi's activity and sense of struggle not only challenged or ignored those schools of Hindu thought, they were contrary to widely established patterns of actual behavior. Passivity and submission were such common traits among Indians of his day that Gandhi frequently found that these qualities, not the British, were the main enemy blocking the way to independence. Gandhi is

widely credited with being a major influence in their reduction and replacement by action, determination, and courageous self-reliance.

> Non-violence [wrote Gandhi in 1920], does not mean meek submission to the will of the evil-doer, but it means the pitting of one's whole soul against the will of the tyrant. . . . And so I am, not pleading for India to practise non-violence because she is weak. I want her to practise non-violence being conscious of her strength and power.[10]

appeal.
Many.
Symbols

PROFITS AND STRUGGLE

A third popular view of Gandhi and the Indian struggle has been especially expounded by Marxists. They have frequently argued that Gandhi's nonviolent action had little or nothing to do with the British leaving India, but that they did so because it was no longer profitable for them to hold on to the subcontinent.

These Marxists often demonstrate their ignorance of Gandhi and his nonviolent action by their assumption that these had nothing to do with reduced economic benefits to the British rulers. This assumed separation is manifestly untrue. The new spirit of resistance and independence among the Indians to which Gandhi contributed, in turn increased the difficulties and expense of maintaining the British *Raj,* especially during the major non-cooperation and civil disobedience campaigns.

Even in purely economic terms of trade with India, Gandhi's program had a significant impact. This is particularly demonstrated by the impact of the boycott during the 1930–31 civil disobedience campaign. This coincided with the world-wide depression, but the drop in purchases of British goods by India was not solely the result of that depression but significantly also attributable to the boycott program.

The British Secretary of State for India, in the House Commons in late 1930, (according to J.C. Kumarappa) credited t general depression with a 25 per cent fall in the export trade India, and credited the balance of 18 per cent in the fall directly the boycott program carried on by the Indian National Congress

Total British exports to India according to statistical abstr declined (in millions of pounds sterling) from 90.6 in 1924, to by 1927, then to 78.2 in 1929 and in the boycott year, 1930, to

The total import of cotton piece-goods by India from all countries rose from 1.82 billion yards in 1924 to 1.94 billion yards in 1929 and declined only to 1.92 billion yards in 1930. However, the *British* export of the same commodity to India fell from 1.25 billion yards in 1924 to 1.08 billion yards in 1929—a decline of 14 per cent. Then it fell to 0.72 billion yards in 1930—a decline of 42.4 per cent. Between October 1930 and April 1931, when the boycott was at its height, there was a decline of 84 per cent.[12]

This chapter is not, of course, an attempt to evaluate the variety of specific factors influencing the achievement of political independence by India. But this should make it clear that the Marxist view that economic factors were completely separate from Gandhi's nonviolent action is not based on facts.

WIELDING POWER

A fourth view, often expressed by political "realists," is that Gandhi's nonviolent action is incapable of wielding effective political power, and is hence irrelevant for practical politicians. This view frequently presumes both naiveté on Gandhi's part and that the kind of action he proposed was impotent and posed no real threat to a political opponent. Neither of these presumptions is borne out by the facts.

Some of Gandhi's statements at the beginning of the 1930–31 civil disobedience campaign are enlightening.

> The British people must realize that the Empire is to come to an end. This they will not realize unless we in India have generated power within to enforce our will.[13]

> It is not a matter of carrying conviction by argument. The matter resolves itself into one of matching forces. Conviction or no conviction, Great Britain would defend her Indian commerce and interests by all the forces at her command. India must consequently evolve force enough to free herself from that embrace of death.[14]

> The English nation responds only to force.[15]

> I was a believer in the politics of petitions, deputations and friendly negotiations. But all these have gone to dogs. I know that

these are not the ways to bring this Government round. Sedition has become my religion. Ours is a nonviolent battle.[16]

Rather than being ignorant of the need to wield political power, Gandhi sought to exercise it in ways which maximized the Indian strength and weakened that of the British. By withdrawing the cooperation and obedience of the subjects, Gandhi sought to cut off important sources of the rulers' power. At the same time, the noncooperation and disobedience created severe enforcement problems. In this situation, severe repression against nonviolent people would be likely, not to strengthen the government, but to alienate still more Indians from the British *Raj* and at the same time create —not unity in face of an enemy—but dissent and opposition at home.

This was thus a kind of political *jiu-jitsu* which generated the maximum Indian strength while using British strength to their own disadvantage. "I believe, and everybody must grant," wrote Gandhi, "that no Government can exist for a single moment without the cooperation of the people, willing or forced, and if people suddenly withdraw their cooperation in every detail, the Government will come to a standstill."[17]

The view that Gandhi was ignorant of the realities of political power and that his technique of action was impotent would have been vigorously denied by every British Government and Viceroy that had to deal with Gandhi and his movement.

In a most revealing address to both Houses of the Indian Legislative Assembly in July 1930, the Viceroy, Lord Irwin, declared:

> In my judgment and in that of my Government it [the civil disobedience movement] is a deliberate attempt to coerce established authority by mass action, and . . . it must be regarded as unconstitutional and dangerously subversive. Mass action, even if it is intended by its promoters to be nonviolent, is nothing but the application of force under another form, and when it has as its avowed object the making of government impossible, a Government is bound either to resist or abdicate . . . .
>
> So long as the Civil Disobedience Movement persists, we must fight it with all our strength.[18]

Apparently the political "realist" who has dismissed Gandhi and his technique has some rethinking to do.

ONLY GENTLEMEN AND GENTLE MEN?

A fifth very common view, especially prevalent in Britain and among some Indians, is that Gandhi's nonviolent campaigns were only possible because the opponent was a British Government which was, of course, made up of only gentlemen. While this has an element of truth in it, the degree of validity is almost always exceeded so that rather than the argument providing a useful contribution to an analysis of the events, it becomes a means of dismissing those events without thought.

Admittedly, the British were not nearly so ruthless as Hitler or Stalin would have been, but they were far more brutal in repression than is today remembered. People not only suffered in foul prisons and prison camps, but literally had their skulls cracked in beatings with steel-shod bamboo rods (*lathis*) and were shot while demonstrating. In a more famous and grave case, the 1919 shooting at Jalianwala Bagh in Amritsar, unarmed Indians holding a peaceful meeting were without warning fired upon. According to the Hunter Commission 379 were killed and 1,137 wounded.

If the British exercised some restraint in dealing with the nonviolent rebellion, this may be related more to the peculiar problems posed by a nonviolent resistance movement and to the kind of forces which the nonviolent action set in motion, than to the opponent being "British." The same people showed little restraint in dealing with the Mau Mau in Kenya, or in the saturation bombings of German cities.

It is interesting that Hitler saw no chance of a successful nonviolent or violent revolt in India against British rule. "We Germans have learned well enough how hard it is to force England," he wrote in *Mein Kampf*.[19]

The view that nonviolent action could only be effective against the British was more credible in the days when the Indian experiments were believed to be the main example of nonviolent action for political objectives. Now that this is no longer true and the technique has spread to other parts of the world under a variety of political circumstances—as we shall shortly note—including Nazi and Communist rule, more careful examination of the circumstances for effectiveness is required.

The last popular view which we shall examine is this: nonviolent action for political ends is only practical under the particu-

CONTEXT

lar set of circumstances which prevailed in India during Gandhi's
time. People outside India interpret this to mean that nonviolent
action is impractical for them, and Indians mean that whereas it
once was practical for them, it no longer is so. Sometimes, the view
is even more specific: such nonviolent action is only possible for
people who share the Hindu religious outlook.

This last view is repudiated by the Indian experience itself.
Among the most courageous and consistent of the nonviolent
Indian freedom fighers were the *Muslim* Pathans of the rebellious
and never fully conquered North-West Frontier Province. These
men, with a long tradition of military prowess and skill in war,
quickly became expert and brave practitioners of nonviolent struggle under the leadership of Khan Abdul Ghaffar Khan.

Although this is not our main concern, it should be noted that
there are Indians who believe that nonviolent action is still possible
in India. There has been a considerable use of the technique
domestically since independence, and there are exponents of its use
in place of military resistance in dealing with any possible invasion,
as by China or Pakistan, although it is true that detailed preparations have not been completed for meeting such an eventuality.

GANDHI'S CONTRIBUTION

One of the most remarkable developments of the twentieth
century has been the development and spread of the technique of
nonviolent action. Nonviolent action includes the types of behavior
known as nonviolent resistance, *satyagraha,* nonviolent direct
action, and the large variety of specific methods of action, such as
strikes, boycotts, political noncooperation, civil disobedience, nonviolent obstruction, and the like. This technique has a long history,
but because historians have been more concerned with violent
conflicts and wars than with nonviolent struggles, much information has been lost.

In modern times the technique initially received impetus from
three main groups: (1) social radicals, such as trade unionists,
anarchists, syndicalists, and socialists, who sought a means of
struggle—largely strikes, general strikes, and boycotts—for use
against what they regarded as an unjust social system; (2) nationalists who found the technique useful in resisting a foreign

enemy (such as the Hungarian resistance vs. Austria, 1850–1867, and the Chinese anti-Japanese boycotts); and (3) individuals, both pacifist and nonpacifist, who were pointing a way by which a new society might be achieved (such as Leo Tolstoy in Russia, Henry David Thoreau in America, and Gustav Landauer in Germany).

Little serious attention was given, however, to refining and improving the technique, to the development of its strategy, tactics, and methods of action. Neither was it linked with a general program of social change. The technique remained essentially passive, the action being in most cases a reaction to the initiative of the opponent.

While religious groups, such as the early Quakers, had practiced nonviolent action as a reaction to persecution, the link between the moral qualities of nonviolence and the technique of action in social and political struggles was rarely made, except by individuals such as Tolstoy, and even then remained on the level of ideas.

It remained for Gandhi to make the most significant political experiments to that time in the use of noncooperation, disobedience and defiance to control rulers, alter policies, and undermine political systems. With Gandhi's experiments with the technique, its character was broadened and refinements made. Conscious efforts were made in developing the strategy and tactics. The number of specific forms or methods of action was enlarged. He linked it with a program of social change, and the building of new institutions.

Nonviolent action became not passive resistance, but a technique capable of taking the initiative in active struggle. A link was forged between a means of mass struggle and a moral preference for nonviolent means, although for participants this preference was not necessarily absolutist in character.

This technique Gandhi called *satyagraha,* which is best translated as the firmness which comes from reliance on truth, and truth here has connotations of essence of being. A rather philosophical term, perhaps, but this technique was in Gandhi's view based on firm political reality and one of the most fundamental of all insights into the nature of government—that all rulers in fact are dependent for their power on the submission, cooperation, and obedience of their subjects. "In politics, its use is based upon the immutable maxim that government of the people is possible only so long as they consent either consciously or unconsciously to be governed."[20] Following the widespread experiments under Gandhi, this technique of nonviolent action spread throughout the world at a rate previously unequalled. In some cases this was directly and indirectly stimulated by the Gandhian experiments. Where this was so, it was often modified in new cultural and political settings. In these cases, the technique has already moved beyond Gandhi.

One of the most important instances of this development is of course the adoption of nonviolent action in the Afro-American struggle against racial segregation and discrimination in the United States. This was a possibility envisaged by Gandhi, as he revealed in conversations with visiting Afro-Americans. In 1937 Dr. Channing Tobias and Dr. Benjamin Mays visited Gandhi, and asked him what advice they might relay from him to the American Negroes, and what he saw as the outlook for the future of their struggle.

Gandhi called nonviolent action the way "of the strong and wise," and added: "With right which is on their side and the choice of non-violence as their only weapon, if they will make it such, a bright future is assured."[21]

Earlier, in 1936, Gandhi told Dr. and Mrs. Howard Thurman that "it may be through the Negroes that the unadulterated message of non-violence will be delivered to the world."[22]

AGAINST TOTALITARIANISM

Contemporaneously with the spread of Gandhi-inspired nonviolent action in other parts of the world, there emerged in Communist countries and Nazi-occupied countries independent demonstrations of the technique under exceedingly difficult circumstances.

While no totalitarian system has been overthrown by nonviolent action, there has been more such resistance than is generally recognized. In these cases the fact that the resistance was nonviolent often seemed almost an accident, often without any conscious choice and certainly not the result of moral or religious qualms about violence. Often the nonviolent action even accompanied violence or was tinged with violence, but nevertheless remained basically dependent upon the nonviolent solidarity in noncooperation and defiance of men and women acting without external arms.

The Norwegian resistance during the Nazi occupation is one of the most significant cases. It was largely through such resistance that Quisling's plans for establishing the Corporate State in Norway were thwarted. The heroism of the Norwegian teachers in refusing to indoctrinate school children with the National Socialist ideology or to become part of the fascist teachers' "corporation" is perhaps the best known part of this resistance. But it is by no means the only one. Clergymen, sportsmen, trade unionists, and others played their part too.

Other important cases include: major aspects of the Danish Resistance, 1940–45, including the successful general strike in Copenhagen in 1944; major parts of the Dutch Resistance, 1940–45, including large-scale strikes in 1941, 1943 and 1944; the East German Rising of June 1953, in which there was massive non-violent defiance which included women in Jena sitting down in front of Russian tanks; strikes in the political prisoners' camps (especially at Vorkuta) in the Soviet Union in 1953, which are credited with being a major influence for improving the lot of the prisoners; and major aspects of the Hungarian Revolution, 1956–57, in which in addition to the military battles there was demonstrated the power of the general strike, and large-scale popular nonviolent defiance. The impact of popular pressure in Poland for liberalizing the regime has also been considerable, despite the difficulties. Czechoslovakia in 1968–69, though ultimately defeated, also provided powerful examples against the Soviet invasion and occupation.

The degree of "success" and "failure" varies in such cases. These instances have occurred without advance preparations, with neither serious thought, nor training, nor preparations for such action. These cases are nevertheless significant, for they prove something that is often denied: that nonviolent action is possible under at least certain circumstances against a totalitarian system, and that in certain conditions such action can force concessions and win at least partial victories.

In some circumstances such action may lead—and has led in Denmark, East Germany, and Hungary, for example—to increasing unreliability of the regime's own troops, administration and other agents. Mutiny is simply the extreme form of this.

Other significant developments of nonviolent action have taken place in various parts of Africa, Japan, South Vietnam, and elsewhere. The process is continuing.

Already this technique has moved far from its role in politics when Gandhi first began his experiments with it in South Africa, and later in India. Contrary to the former situation, now for the first time people and some social scientists operating as yet with the most meager resources are attempting to study this technique, and to learn of its nature, its dynamics, the requirements for success with it against various types of opponents, and to examine its future potentialities.

OF WORLD SIGNIFICANCE

The view that this technique can only be used in the peculiar Indian circumstances at the time of Gandhi is thus seen also to be one which has little basis in fact. Indeed, it was argued long ago by an Indian sociologist, Krishnalal Shridharani, in his doctoral thesis at Columbia University (and later in his book, *War Without Violence*) that the West was more suitable than India for the technique:

> My contact with the Western world has led me to think that, contrary to popular belief, Satyagraha, once consciously and deliberately adopted, has more fertile fields in which to grow and flourish in the West than in the Orient. Like war, Satyagraha demands public spirit, self-sacrifice, organization, endurance and discipline for its successful operation, and I have found these qualities displayed in Western communities more than my own. Perhaps the best craftsmen in the art of violence may still be the most effective wielders of nonviolent direct action.[23]

This view has in the intervening years become not only more credible but one for which there is increasing supporting evidence. It is supported by an elementary examination of a large number of cases of nonviolent action which reveals that, contrary to popular belief and the rather conceited assumption of pacifists, in an overwhelming number of such cases leaders and followers have both been nonpacifists who have followed the nonviolent means for some limited social, economic, or political objective. This has profound implications.

Thus Gandhi emerges, along with the technique of action, to the development of which he contributed so significantly, as being important for the world as a whole. Gandhi and nonviolent action clearly can no longer be pigeon-holed and dismissed without serious consideration by informed people.

Gandhi's role in politics was rather peculiar. He was not a student of politics, as we would think of one. He was not a political theoretician or analyst. Nor was he inclined to write, and perhaps not capable of writing, a systematic treatise on his approach to politics. Indeed, he admitted that he could not lay claim to "much book knowledge." These were serious weaknesses and have continued to have important consequences.

Yet, despite these shortcomings, Gandhi was an innovator in politics. He often demonstrated that in spite of his lack of political "book knowledge" he had a very considerable understanding of political realities. He relied upon this and his intuition, as well as his constant "experiments." He had a capacity to sense the feelings and capacities of ordinary people about political issues, clearly understanding the peasants better than his more intellectual fellow nationalists.

His capacity to inspire people to act bravely and to gain a new sense of their capacities was combined with great organizational ability and attention to details. The combination of these various factors resulted in his important contributions to the development of "the politics of nonviolent action."[24]

This development which has taken place side by side with the most extreme forms of political violence—typified by the Hitler and Stalin regimes and by nuclear weapons—has led some people to ask whether the solution to such violence is developing while the problem is becoming more acute.

NONVIOLENT POLICIES FOR INDIA?

After the achievement of political independence, the new Indian Government did not—as Gandhi had hoped—assert its confidence in nonviolent means to defend the newly won freedom. The assumption of some pacifists that after experience with nonviolent action people would rather easily adopt the whole "gospel" was not borne out. Although Gandhi had expected independent India to have an army, he had hoped it would not happen. The Indian nationalists were willing to adopt the nonviolent course of action which Gandhi proposed to achieve political freedom, but when the struggle was won, they did not automatically continue their adherence to nonviolent means. This was a somewhat natural and predictable development.

This is because the adoption by India of the nonviolent struggle to deal with British imperialism was not a doctrinal or a moralistic act. It was a political act in response to a political program of action proposed to deal with a particular kind of situation and crisis. The distinguished Muslim President of the Indian National Congress, Maulana Abul Kalam Azad, once said: "The Indian National Congress is a political organization pledged to win the political independence of the country. It is not an institution for organizing world peace."[25] Thus, for most Indian nationalists, it happened, almost parenthetically, that this nonviolent program offered by Gandhi was morally preferable to violent revolutionary war.

In addition to strategic and tactical advantages, this choice of nonviolent means in some ways increased the strength of the movement by giving it an aura of moral superiority. It was also probably psychologically and morally more uplifting to the society as a whole and to individual participants. But these were certainly not the prime factors determining its acceptance.

In this new situation in which independent India no longer followed his nonviolence, Gandhi was unsure about the best way to proceed, except that he was convinced of the importance of having people who believed in "the non-violence of the brave and the strong" out of moral convictions. He was so busy with the riots and other problems that he did not work out a satisfactory solution to the new problem before his assassination.

The Indian Government sought to pursue a "neutralist" foreign policy while continuing a conventional military defense policy. Inevitably this meant that if confronted with international dangers the Indian government would demonstrate in action the same faith in military defense as other countries.

If this were not to be, someone would have had to formulate at least the framework for a consciously adopted, carefully prepared, systematically trained program for the nonviolent defense of India's newly gained freedom. No one did this, including Gandhi.

The problem of tyranny and the problem of war are problems not only of India, but of the whole world. Even if one thinks the chances of nonviolent action being made into an effective substitute for war are very small, the desperate nature of our situation requires that even such a small chance deserves full investigation.

This is the kind of tribute and remembrance which Gandhi would have appreciated. He was never one to claim to have all the answers or the final truth. He did not want people to be thinking always of him, but of the task which he had undertaken.

"I am fully aware that my mission cannot be fulfilled in India alone," Gandhi once wrote to an American correspondent. "I am pining for the assistance of the whole world. . . . But I know that we shall have to deserve it before it comes."[26]

The quest for an alternative to war is now our common task in which Gandhi pioneered so significantly. Is it not now time that a full investigation into the potentialities of nonviolent action is deserved and required?

NOTES TO CHAPTER ONE

1. Harijan (hereafter cited as H.), 3 Oct. 1936, p. 268; R. K. Prabhu and U. R. Rao, compilers, The Mind of Mahatma Gandhi (London and Bombay: Humphrey Milford, Oxford University Press, 1945), p. 2. Original source given as well as immediate source.
2. Young India (hereafter cited as YI), 27 Oct. 1921, p. 342; Prabhu and Rao, comps., The Mind of Mahatma Gandhi, p. 7.
3. YI, 21 May 1925, p. 176; Prabhu and Rao, comps., The Mind of Mahatma Gandhi, p. 7.
4. YI, 16 Feb. 1922, p. 102; Prabhu and Rao, comps., The Mind of Mahatma Gandhi, pp. 9–10.
5. D. G. Tendulkar, Mahatma: Life of Mohandas Karamchand Gandhi, vol. VIII, 1947–1948 (New edition; New Delhi: Publications Division, Ministry of Information and Broadcasting, Government of India, 1963), pp. 56 and 80.
6. H., 1 Dec. 1946; M. K. Gandhi, Non-violence in Peace and War (hereafter cited as NVPW; 2 vols.; Ahmedabad: Navajivan Publishing House, [1942] 1948 and 1949), vol. II, p. 188.

7. Pyarelal (Nair), **Mahatma Gandhi: The Last Phase** (2 vols.; Ahmedabad: Navajivan Publishing House, 1956 and 1958), vol. II, pp. 664.
8. Richard Gregg, **The Power of Non-violence** (Second rev. ed.; New York: Schocken, 1966, and London: James Clarke, 1960), p. 100.
9. Joan V. Bondurant, **Conquest of Violence: The Gandhian Philosophy of Conflict** (Princeton, N. J.: Princeton University Press, 1958, and Berkeley: University of California Press, 1965), pp. 105–145, esp. pp. 105–108.
10. **YI**, 11 Aug. 1920; **NVPW**, I, p. 2. See Chapter Nine, n 6.
11. J.C. Kumarappa, writing in **YI**, no. 50, 11 Dec. 1930; quoted in Gene Sharp, **Gandhi Wields the Weapon of Moral Power: Three Case Histories** (Ahmedabad: Navajivan Publishing House, 1960), p. 195.
12. Krishnalal Shridharani, **War Without Violence: A Study of Gandhi's Method and Its Accomplishments** (New York: Harcourt, Brace & Co., 1939, and London: Victor Gollancz, 1939), p. 24. Shridharani based these figures on the **Statistical Abstract for the United Kingdom**, no. 74, and **Trade and Navigation, the U.K.**
13. **YI**, 23 Jan. 1930, p. 28; quoted in Gene Sharp, **Gandhi Wields the Weapon of Moral Power: Three Case Histories** (Ahmedabad: Navajivan, 1960), p. 52.
14. Gandhi's letter to Lord Irwin, the Viceroy, 2 March 1930, **Congress Bulletin**, no. 5 (7 March 1930); Sharp, **Gandhi Wields the Weapon of Moral Power**, p. 64.
15. Bhogaraju Pattabhi Sitaramayya, **The History of the Indian National Congress**, vol. I, (1885–1935) (Madras: Working Committee of the Congress, 1935), p. 638.
16. Gandhi, during the 1930 March to the Sea to commit civil disobedience, Pattabhi Sitaramayya, **The History of the Indian National Congress**, vol. I, p. 650.
17. **YI**, 18 Aug. 1920; M.K. Gandhi, **Satyagraha** (Ahmedabad: Navajivan, 1951), p. 157.
18. Lord Irwin's address of 9 July 1930, in Government of India, **India in 1930–31, A Statement prepared for Presentation to Parliament in accordance with the requirements of the 26th section of the Government of India Act (5 & 6 Geo. V, Chap. 61)** (Calcutta: Government of India, Central Publication Branch, 1932) pp. 80–81; quoted in Sharp, **Gandhi Wields the Weapon of Moral Power**, pp. 168–169.
19. Adolph Hitler, **Mein Kampf**. Trans. by Ralph Manheim. (New York: Reynal & Hitchock, 1940), p. 965.
20. **YI**, 3 Nov. 1927, p. 369; Gandhi, **Satyagraha**, p. 35.
21. **H.**, 20 Mar. 1937; **NVPW**, I, p. 128.
22. **H.**, 14 Mar. 1936; **NVPW**, I, p. 116.
23. Shridharani, **War Without Violence**, p. 19.
24. See the survey of the historical development of nonviolent struggle in Gene Sharp, **The Politics of Nonviolent Action** (Boston: Porter Sargent Publisher, 1973). Chapter Two.
25. Nirmal Kumar Bose, **Studies in Gandhism** (Calcutta: Indian Associated Publishing Co., 1947), p. 311.
26. **YI**, 17 Sept. 1925; **NVPW**, I, pp. 35 and 37.

2

Origins of Gandhi's Use of Nonviolent Struggle

A Review–Essay on Erik Erikson's Gandhi's Truth*

One of the most unusual of the national liberation leaders and social revolutionaries of the first half of the twentieth century was one M.K. Gandhi. He struggled against the racist European regime in South Africa at a crucial stage of its development. Back in India, his own country, he led a struggle against the most vast empire the world had ever seen. And even late in life he sought a social revolution which would bring food, justice, and power to the poorest of India.

Gandhi the man, his outlook, and activities were all extremely complex. Honest to the subject and to Professor Erikson's own

---

* Erik Erikson. *Gandhi's Truth: On the Origins of Militant Nonviolence*. New York: W.W. Norton & Co., 1969.

approach, *Gandhi's Truth* neither simplifies nor dismisses Gandhi, as many do. Instead, the author grapples with his lasting significance and relevance for our future.

The only way to "hear" what Professor Erikson says in this study is to read it yourself. This chapter is neither a summary of the book nor a critique of his psychoanalytic examination, for that is not my field. Instead this essay is a parallel exploration of political and historical origins of Gandhi's use of nonviolent struggle, and is intended to supplement Professor Erikson's analysis. Erikson instead uses the term "militant nonviolence."

Professor Erikson has told me that he intended the subtitle "militant nonviolence" to provide a substitute clear English term for Gandhi's word "*satyagraha.*" The subtitle then really means "On the Origins of *Satyagraha*"—a limited theme. The concentrated focus of the book was necessary to make possible the detailed analysis by a Western psychoanalyst into "how the boy and the man grew into his historical role, and . . . into the personal origins of [Gandhi's] militant nonviolence." (p.97)

While primarily describing and analyzing the life and actions of Gandhi which belong to history, Professor Erikson is also clearly pointing toward the future:

> Gandhi's instrument itself . . . now exists . . . It now calls for leaders who will re-innovate it elsewhere . . . but recombining this motivation with totally new elements. For if the instrument once was "the truth," it can and must become actual in entirely different settings. . . . (pp. 435–436)

THE OVERLOOKED HISTORY OF NONVIOLENT STRUGGLE

Erikson's study does not, in my view, give sufficient weight to the impact on Gandhi and the South African Indian community of other cases of nonviolent struggle, but the previous authoritative literature on Gandhi and *satyagraha* to my knowledge has never done so either.

Until recently, in common with other writers about Gandhi, I accepted that his development of nonviolent action in South Africa was largely or completely an independent achievement, inspired by the interaction of his beliefs and personality with the need of the Indian community for some practical means of struggle against the racist European regime. Earlier, I even believed that Gandhi had introduced nonviolent struggle into politics. I rejected that belief several years ago as I became aware that there had historically been diverse cases of political nonviolent struggle used for practical rather than ethical reasons. These cases seemed more similar to the Indian struggles than they were different from them. Placing Gandhi within this wider history of nonviolent action did not belittle Gandhi, nor the Indian "experiments" as he called them; both he and the campaigns contributed significantly to nonviolent action.

I still believed that Gandhi's *satyagraha,* as a technique of struggle, remained predominantly an independent development. He may have drawn on the thinking of others, such as Tolstoy, but I believed he, and he alone, had without major stimulus from other nonviolent struggles, conceived of nonviolent defiance to provide the Indian community in South Africa with effective means of resistance. There is now sufficient reason to conclude that this assumption was, in fact, not true.

GANDHI IN SOUTH AFRICA

There is agreement among writers on Gandhi that the meeting of three thousand Indians, which Gandhi helped to convene in protest against the draft Asiatic Law Amendment Ordinance, held on 11 September 1906 at the Empire Theatre in Johannesburg, South Africa, was crucial for the development of *satyagraha.* A mass pledge was taken at that meeting to disobey nonviolently the pending registration legislation. (The actual struggle did not occur until months later when the bill became law in July 1907.) The accounts of that meeting in standard biographies vary in detail, but in them, and Gandhi's own account in *Satyagraha in South Africa,* (written sixteen or so years later), Gandhi is clearly credited with the central role in that meeting.

The accounts of this event which Gandhi himself published at the time in *Indian Opinion* present a very different view of what occurred at that meeting, and of Gandhi's role in it. Whatever may have happened before, Gandhi did not introduce the theme of disobedience and jail-going to the meeting. The reports indicate that the audience seems to have been thoroughly familiar with the idea already. The chairman spoke ably on the proposal in his introductory remarks, and Gandhi neither introduced nor seconded the "Jail Resolution." Gandhi was, in fact, the eleventh and final speaker on it, probably a key and predetermined position. Muslims were extremely prominent among the advocates of nonviolent resistance by civil disobedience. Gandhi's speech implies that he had proposed in the earlier discussions this method of resisting the proposed discriminatory law. The common assumption that this was a new and novel approach for the Indian minority in South Africa can no longer be accepted.

Gandhi had already been highly influenced by Leo Tolstoy's writings on nonviolence, but it is no longer clear to me that Gandhi reasoned from the ethical to the political. There has never been, to my knowledge, a major claim that Gandhi's development of nonviolent struggle in politics was directly stimulated by other historical and contemporary cases of nonviolent struggle. It now appears that this is true, and that to a considerable extent Gandhi reasoned directly from the political to the political.

INFLUENCE OF THE 1905 RUSSIAN REVOLUTION

In early February, 1970, while attending the International Gandhi Seminar in New Delhi, one of the delegates from the Soviet Union, Dr. E. N. Komarov showed me an unpublished paper he had written which included discussion on Russian contributions to Gandhi's nonviolence. This was not surprising, as Gandhi's study of Tolstoy's writings, and correspondence with him, are very well known. What was startling to me was a section quoting from Gandhi's writings, in *Indian Opinion,* about the Russian 1905 Revolution—an overwhelmingly nonviolent struggle—which was then in full swing. This one case led me to keep my eyes open, as I recently looked through Volumes IV and V of the *Collected Works of Mahatma Gandhi.* The result of even this preliminary examination is sufficient to call into question some basic conceptions about Gandhi's role in the development of nonviolent struggle.

Whatever may be added or modified by additional and more detailed research, it is now clear that the Indian campaigns in South Africa, and Gandhi's own conceptions of appropriate means of struggle, were inspired or influenced by other recent cases of nonviolent resistance and revolution, including events in China, Russia, India, and South Africa. It is also clear that by 1905 Gandhi had already grasped the essentials of the theory of power which views all governments as constantly dependent upon the obedience and cooperation of the ruled. These political and ideational factors need to be taken into account as origins of Gandhi's *satyagraha* in addition to the psychological factors which Professor Erikson analyzes. Those factors are still very important. In fact a great deal of this historical material provides supporting evidence for the accuracy of much of Erikson's interpretation of Gandhi's sense of his own importance.

It is difficult or impossible without much further historical and biographical research to place in clear chronological order Gandhi's acquaintance with various cases of nonviolent action, and his first contact with the theory of power upon which it is based. The evidence, however, shows overwhelmingly that Gandhi knew both of such cases and of this view of power well *before* the Empire Theatre meeting. The years 1905–1906 were "good years" for nonviolent action. Three cases which attracted Gandhi's attention in South Africa during this period were the Chinese boycott of American goods against United States anti-Chinese legislation, the Russian 1905 Revolution, and the boycott movement in Bengal against British partition of that Indian state. Gandhi seems also to have known of other cases, certainly of individual nonviolent action by three Englishmen as well as of group resistance in South Africa itself by Indians and by Africans.

CHINESE NONVIOLENT STRUGGLE

Gandhi first referred to the Chinese boycott in his *Indian Opinion* on 19 August 1905 in an article concerning Lord Curzon's proposal for the partition of Bengal. When the news had reached India that the Secretary of State for India had approved the plan for partition, protest meetings were held in almost every village of Bengal with participation by members of all communities, including Chinese merchants in Bengal, Gandhi reported. Speeches had suggested that if government policy were not changed, Gandhi continued: *"Indian merchants should stop all trade with Great Britain. We must admit that our people have learnt these tactics from China."* Gandhi saw this type of action as powerful and potentially effective:

> But if the people really act accordingly, there would be nothing surprising if our troubles came to a speedy end. For, if this is done, Great Britain will be put to great loss; and the Government can have no means of dealing with it. They cannot compel the people to carry on trade. The method is very straight and simple. But will our people in Bengal maintain the requisite unity? Will the merchants suffer for the good of the country? If we can answer both these questions in the affirmative, India can be said to have truly woken up.[1]

On 30 September 1905 Gandhi published another short article on the Chinese boycott, this time without reference to Bengal. He reported that the boycott had already cost the Americans £5,000,000 (at the time about $24,000,000). This, Gandhi reported, had led American traders and merchants to urge the United States Government to repeal laws intended to exclude Chinese from entering the country. However, American "working classes" had held large meetings and passed resolutions to retain the anti-Chinese laws, regardless of losses to the businessmen. Cablegrams from China showed, Gandhi reported, that the Chinese boycott was gathering strength:

> In all this commotion one thing stands out clear, namely, that where there is unity, there alone is strength, and also victory. This deserves to be carefully borne in mind by every Indian. The Chinese, though weak, appear to have become strong on account of their unity, thereby bearing out the truth of the Gujarati verse, "Thus do ants when united take the life of a fierce snake."[2]

Gandhi referred to the Chinese boycott again in *Indian Opinion,* on 26 May 1906.[3]

"THE RUSSIAN REMEDY"

The year-long Russian 1905 Revolution was predominantly, but not completely, nonviolent. On 11 November 1905 in *Indian Opinion* Gandhi wrote: "The present unrest in Russia has a great lesson for us." He called the Tsar the most autocratic ruler in the world and recounted the sufferings of the Russian people who had "now reached the limit of their patience." He mentioned how the Russian people had risen in rebellion before and assassinated earlier Tsars, "but they could not secure justice."

> *This time they have found another remedy which, though very simple, is more powerful than rebellion and murder. The Russian workers and all the other servants declared a general strike and stopped all work.* They left their jobs and informed the Czar that, unless justice was done, they would not resume work. What was there even the Czar could do against this? It was quite impossible to exact work from people by force. It is not within the power of even the Czar of Russia to force strikers to return at the point of the bayonet.

The Tsar had, therefore, proclaimed that the people would be granted a share in the government and that their consent would be required in the making of laws (presumably referring to the promise of a *Duma*). The Tsar might not keep his word, Gandhi acknowledged, but if it were possible for him to break it, it would show that the people had not been firm enough in applying their remedy, for no one could rule without the cooperation of the ruled. If successful, that revolution would be the greatest victory and event of the twentieth century. Gandhi compared the conditions of India and Russia, finding the only difference to be that power was "more brusquely exercised in Russia than in India." Significantly, he then wrote: *"We, too, can resort to the Russian remedy against tyranny."* He compared the Russian movement to the movement in Bengal.

> Our shackles will break this very day, if the people of India become united and patient, love their country, and think of the well-being of their motherland disregarding their self-interest. *The governance of India is possible only because there exist people who serve. We also can show the same strength that the Russian people have done.*[4]

INDIAN NONVIOLENT STRUGGLE BEFORE GANDHI

In India itself, in Bengal, a major nonviolent resistance movement concentrating on economic boycotts had begun, apparently
directly inspired by the Chinese boycott of American products. In
addition to Gandhi's testimony to this, his faithful secretary and
biographer Pyarelal described this movement as undertaken "after
the manner of the successful Chinese boycott of American goods."[5]
L.S.S. O'Malley in his account of Bengal under British rule said:
"The idea of a boycott of British goods may have been borrowed
from the Irish or from the Chinese, who in May 1905 boycotted
American imports as a protest against an exclusion treaty proposed
by the United States."[6] The Bengali struggle was important in
India's struggle for independence. B. Pattabhi Sitaramayya reported that this partition "broke the back of loyal India and roused
a new spirit in the Nation."[7] Pyarelal cited the partition as "the
beginning of the end of British rule in India."[8]

On 7 August 1905, Bengali leaders met in the Calcutta Town
Hall and resolved to declare a "general boycott of British goods as
practical protest against the proposed Partition."[9] When the partition went into effect, on 16 October 1905, millions throughout the
whole of Bengal observed a day of mourning. Millions fasted,
kitchen fires remained unlit, men, women, and children demonstrated in mammoth processions, black sashes of mourning were
worn on arms, people paraded bare headed and bare footed, sang
patriotic songs, and shouted "Vande Mataram" ("Hail, Mother,"
that is, Mother India). In addition to the boycott of British goods,
a movement of *swadeshi* (use of Indian-made products) became
strong. Students played a very important role in this campaign.
Hartals (limited shut-downs of all economic activities) and picketing took place. The response was government repression, as
processions, meetings, and demonstrations were banned. Students
were prohibited from any participation in nationalist activities.
Students boycotted government educational institutions. "National" schools outside government control were started. Volunteer
organizations sprang up. Additional national educational institutions developed, plans for a national college and a university were
prepared, various newspapers were established. Often only illegal
Indian salt was available, because salt from the British monopoly

was boycotted.[10] (These activities are remarkably similar to those of the 1930–31 struggle which Gandhi planned.) The Lieutenant-Governor, Sir Bampfylde Fuller, of newly created East Bengal (where the boycott and *swadeshi* movements were at their height) was determined to smash the movement by violence.

On 16 September 1905 Gandhi reported in *Indian Opinion* that the "strong movement" in Bengal was of "no mean significance."[11] On 7 October, he commented that the Bengali boycott could only produce good for India, especially by stimulating the Indian industries, which had suffered drastically under British rule. The use so far as possible of only Indian goods *(swadeshi)*, would help in developing India's national spirit.[12] Gandhi continued to report and comment on the Bengal movement in November and December 1905. While writing about the Russian 1905 Revolution and the general strike, Gandhi observed on 11 November: "The movement in Bengal for the use of *swadeshi* goods is much like the Russian movement."[13]

IRISH INFLUENCES

There is a possibility that there were Irish influences on Gandhi in the development of his insight into nonviolent action; firm evidence is lacking thus far, but there are suggestions for research here too. In the late nineteenth century a great deal of nonviolent resistance was practiced in Ireland. The very term "boycott" has an Irish origin, coming into the language after a famous case of noncooperation by Irish peasants with one Captain Boycott in 1880. A very important peasants' rent strike was going on in 1879 and 1880 with the active assistance of Irish nationalist leaders, including Thomas Parnell. Irish rent strikes and tax refusals, mixed with limited violence, occurred all the time from 1879 to 1886.

After Gandhi began studying law in London in November 1888, Pyarelal reported:

> He began to take keen interest in current events. The struggle for Irish Home Rule was in full swing. Parnellism had touched the high-water mark of its success. He studiously followed from day to day the proceedings of the Commission on Irish crimes and

Lord Russell's brilliant cross-examination that exposed the Pigott letters as clumsy forgeries and vindicated Parnell.[14]

There is evidence that Indian leaders, including Gandhi, in South Africa in 1894 had continued to follow Irish developments, and Gandhi specifically referred to Parnell as a leader whose thinking was crucial for the whole of Ireland.[15]

It is doubtful that Gandhi knew any details of the American colonial nonviolent struggles against the British government, but he did at least have some general idea of American colonial resistance to British taxation. In an article on George Washington published in *Indian Opinion* on 30 September 1905, Gandhi mentioned that while under British rule: "quarrels were going on between England and the American people. The people in America did not like certain taxes imposed on them by England."[16]

Gandhi was also familiar with several cases of individual nonviolent action. When Gandhi's own father was seeking release from service to the *Raja* of Vankaner, he gave notice that he would refuse to touch any food or water until arrangements had been completed for him to leave. The *Raja* then let him go.[17] Gandhi was at the time nine years old. Although it appears that he remained at this time in school at Rajkot, he certainly must have known of this fast.

ENGLISH PRECEDENTS

Gandhi knew of certain prominent cases of individual nonviolent action by Englishmen. In early October, 1906, about a month after the Empire Theatre meeting, Gandhi referred in *Indian Opinion* to Wat Tyler, John Hampden, and John Bunyan as Englishmen whose self-sacrifice had in earlier years laid the foundations of England's political supremacy, and as examples whom the Indians should follow.[18] Two weeks later Gandhi wrote an article about these men, summarizing what they had done and commenting on their political significance. Two had refused to pay taxes and Bunyan had refused to obey bishops. From their examples, Gandhi concluded that if the Transvaal Indians were willing to go to jail or suffer economic loss, "their chains will break."[19] It is highly probable that Gandhi had become acquainted with this background while studying law in London. He clearly had known of Hampden for sometime, as he had earlier also referred to Hampden in an article on "Self-Sacrifice" published in January 1904.[20]

PRE-GANDHI MOVEMENTS IN AFRICA

The final examples of nonviolent action which were background for the decision taken at the Empire Theatre in 1906 to practice civil disobedience against discriminatory legislation are South African. I am not at all clear what role, either direct or indirect, Gandhi may have played in any of these cases; the facts of these instances and even dates are not readily available in the Gandhian literature; perhaps they exist elsewhere. Furthermore, the descriptions which Gandhi and occasionally others offered of these cases are very general, and sometimes subject to differing interpretations. Nevertheless, even this slight evidence is sufficient to suggest that the 1906 decision at the Empire Theatre meeting may have been in part rooted in earlier South African experience with nonviolent action.

Some of this Indian nonviolent action in South Africa apparently went back some years. Mr. Hajee Habib referred to such a case in his speech on jail-going at the Empire Theatre meeting:

> We tried this method in the days of the Boer Government also. Some 40 of our men were once arrested for trading without licenses. I advised them to go to gaol [jail] and not to seek release on bail. Accordingly, they all remained there without offering bail. I immediately approached the British Agent, who approved of our action and ultimately secured justice for us.[21]

Gandhi referred to this case also in *Indian Opinion* on 6 October 1906, and also cited the failure of the Government's attempt to send Indians to the Locations.[22] This may or may not be the same case which he cited in the previous paragraph:

> When President Kruger proposed to remove the Indians from the Malay Location and send them to the Tobianski Farm, Mr. Emrys Evans, the British Agent, gave Indians the specific advice that they should on no account submit to President Kruger's order. Hence, despite police investigations and detectives entering their homes, the people remained firm, and they won.[23]

Gandhi in October 1906 reminded Indians of their earlier resistance, not only concerning their refusal to go to the Location, but concerning passes: "The Indian people refused to accept the passes bearing their photographs that Mr. Moore had issued, and the Regulation had to be withdrawn."[24]

The extent to which such activities were deliberate resistance, the details of these struggles, and whether and how Gandhi may have been involved in any of them, are difficult points to determine without considerable research. The one thing that is clear is that Gandhi did know about them, and related those cases to the current need for means of struggle.

Gandhi was also familiar with instances of African non-cooperation. During the objections to an impending new "poll-tax" (not a voting tax, but a "head tax"), Gandhi reported in *Indian Opinion* on 25 November 1905 that one of the African speakers at a "meeting recently held by the Chief Magistrate" had said: "The Government will have to line the roads of the Colony with gaols for the accommodation of the defaulters."[25] In a speech given two days before the Empire Theatre meeting, Gandhi told the Hamidiya Islamic Society that disobedience of the discriminatory Draft Ordinance if it became law would be justified and imprisonment should be cheerfully suffered:

> If therefore we also unite and offer resistance with courage and firmness, I am sure there is nothing that the Government can do. Even the half-castes and Kaffirs, who are less advanced than we, have resisted the Government. The pass law applies to them as well, but they do not take out passes.[26]

In the 6 October 1906 article Gandhi also cited African precedents:

> We can easily find such examples among other communities too. The Pass Law applies to Hottentots, but they oppose it and do not take out passes and the Government is powerless to do anything. A house tax is levied on the Kaffirs of Natal; but some of the Zulu tribes do not pay the tax at all. It is an open secret that the Government does not collect the tax from them.[27]

The "Zulu Rebellion," began in April 1906; during it Gandhi organized an Indian ambulance corps to assist the British. The Rebellion was in part a resistance against that same poll-tax. In addition to direct tax resistance, however, there was significant Zulu violence with highly disproportionate British repression.[28]

PRIOR KNOWLEDGE OF NONVIOLENT STRUGGLE

Gandhi and the Indian minority in South Africa clearly knew of all these cases of nonviolent struggle well before the important Empire Theatre meeting. Gandhi's own article in *Indian Opinion* referred to the nonviolent resistance and revolutionary movements in China on 19 August 1905, in Russia on 11 November 1905, in Bengal on 16 September 1905, in the American colonies on 30 September 1905, and in South Africa by Africans on 25 November 1905. These references range between nine-and-a-half and thirteen months *before* the Empire Theatre meeting of 11 September 1906. Knowledge of the other cases also was clearly antecedent to calculations by the Indians on how to respond to the draft Asiatic Law Amendment Ordinance.

All of this indicates that both Gandhi and other Indians in South Africa were aware of a variety of cases on nonviolent action in their contemporary world and in history well before the Empire Theatre meeting. These had either occurred or had been called to their attention recently enough to be remembered. Such cases served to some degree at least as stimuli and inspiration for the Indian struggles in South Africa which Gandhi later led. Furthermore, these cases were an important factor in the choice and practice of nonviolent struggle by the Indian minority at the time Gandhi began to play a significant role in it. They not only provided general examples of struggle without violence, but also demonstrations of the use of specific methods of nonviolent action which could be imitated, as Gandhi's own comments establish.

The psychological origins of Gandhi's choice of nonviolent struggle and of his leadership in such campaigns are highly important. Here Professor Erikson has made a monumental contribution. It is also clear that the political and historical factors in Gandhi's choice of nonviolent struggle are also highly important.

On the basis of Gandhi's own accounts he possessed some knowledge of contemporary and earlier nonviolent struggles well before the Empire Theatre meeting. From these he already had developed a basic conception of a broad technique of action which included a variety of different specific methods, which had been independently applied in diverse cultural and political conditions. He did this at a time at which (so far as is now known) no theoretical or social scientific studies existed which provided that conceptual framework. Such studies did not appear in European and American literature in even undeveloped forms until the 1930s.

INTERRELATED SPECIFIC METHODS

In 1905 and 1906 Gandhi saw quite different specific methods of action to be related to each other. Gandhi's own father had gone on a fast against an Indian ruler who was his employer. The *hartal,* Gandhi said, went back to very early Indian history, and continued to be often used in India, especially in the Native States. He saw certain similarities between a *hartal* and deliberate breaking of a law with willingness to go to jail.[29] He knew of the nature of ostracism, or social boycott.[30] Gandhi said the Bengali movement of using only *swadeshi* goods, not foreign imports, was similar to "the Russian movement" of 1905, almost certainly meaning the general strike.[31] In the article on Tyler, Hampden, and Bunyan, Gandhi grouped together the two cases of tax refusal with one of religious disobedience. In the comments on African resistance, he implied similarities between nonpayment of taxes and nonregistration for passes. The previous activities of South African Indians which he cited included jail-going, refusal to move to Locations, and refusal to accept passes. He also knew of various other nonviolent methods, such as the economic boycott from China and Bengal.

All this establishes not only that nonviolent action as a broad technique did not originate with Gandhi, but that he knew that it did not, and that Gandhi neither introduced it into South Africa nor India. Instead, he sought deliberately to learn from known examples of its use elsewhere to assist the struggles of the Indians, and developed a conceptual understanding of the broad nonviolent technique and its methods.

NEITHER PASSIVE NOR HOSTILE

In this very broad technique of action there were many possible variations, not only in specific methods, but also in the degree of dynamism, aggressiveness, attitudes to the opponent, and other points. Some of Gandhi's views and measures therefore differed from the extreme other possible responses within the technique. Gandhi soon found that he wished to separate the Indians' attempts to use this technique from both the most passive and also the most personally hostile forms of nonviolent action. Gandhi later often emphasized the conversion aspects of *satyagraha:* users of *satyagraha* did not wish injury to the opponent, but sought "the conquest of the adversary by suffering in one's own person." Gandhi emphasized very strongly, however, that this was not a description of "Satyagrahis as they are." Instead, that passage set forth "the implications of Satyagraha and the characteristics of Satyagrahis as they ought to be."[32] (In fact, as indicated in other chapters in this volume, Gandhi often stressed the "compelling" effects of nonviolent struggle, although he disliked the term "coercion.") Elsewhere in *Satyagraha in South Africa,* Gandhi characterized a *satyagraha* movement as one without hatred, with self-reliance, without leaders, where death of fighters only intensifies the struggle.

> Such is the pure and essential nature of Satyagraha, not realized in practise. . . . Again as Tolstoy observed, the Transvaal struggle was the first attempt at applying the principle of Satyagraha to masses or bodies of men. I do not know of any historical example of pure mass Satyagraha. I cannot however formulate any definite opinion on the point, as my knowledge of history is limited. But as a matter of fact we have nothing to do with historical precedents.[33]

Professor Erikson's study sheds some light on Gandhi's claims to uniqueness for his *satyagraha* movement on the basis of what Gandhi thought it *should* be. If compared to certain other cases of nonviolent action on the basis of the *actual* characteristics of the movement as a whole, much of the uniqueness is not so obvious. Certainly Gandhi made highly important contributions to the development of nonviolent action. These include: bringing the political technique closer to the ethic, still on a relative basis; development of its strategy and tactics; making it more active and dynamic; combining personal good will with realistic and militant struggle; applying it in highly important conflict situations; and making the choice of nonviolent action more intentional and deliberate.

THE THEORY BEHIND THE TECHNIQUE

Gandhi's expressions of friendship and concern for his antagonists, and his emphasis on suffering to convert them may both lead us into exploration of the ethical or psychological ramifications of Gandhi's approach. However, neither of these ought to be allowed to blind us to the fact that even at this very early period Gandhi was clearly operating on the basis of a theory of political power. *"For even the most powerful cannot rule without the cooperation of the ruled,"*[34] Gandhi wrote in November 1905. He continued: "The governance of India is possible only because there exist people who serve."[35]

This view of power claims that all governments depend on sources of power which come from the society, and are made available because of the assistance, cooperation, and obedience of members of that society. When such assistance, cooperation, and obedience are withdrawn effectively the government's power is weakened, and when the sources of power are severed permanently, the government's power is destroyed. Hence, all government, no matter how tyrannical, is potentially subject to control by the citizenry if they are willing to withhold their support despite repression until the regime, with no further sources of power available, disintegrates. Gandhi clearly held this view almost three years before he read Tolstoy's "A Letter to a Hindu," written in 1908, which I had previously assumed to have been the source of Gandhi's view of power. Did he get it from Indian sources, writings of Tolstoy, or while studying law in London?

THE POTENTIAL OF VIOLENCE

The view of the power of rulers as being dependent on the ruled continued throughout his life to be the fundamental political insight upon which Gandhi's struggle rested.[36] This is also the theory of power upon which the whole technique of nonviolent struggle is based.[37] And it is crucial. Someone said the other day that the relationship of that theory of power to nonviolent struggle is, and will one day be recognized as comparable to Einstein's theory of relativity for nuclear energy. Once grasped, and when the associated corollaries of nonviolent discipline, the necessity of wise choice of methods, strategy and tactics, preparations and training, development of internal strength, and persistence in face of repression are also understood and implemented, it becomes possible to end both war and oppression in our lifetimes.

Perhaps Professor Erikson will accept it as a compliment that his study has stimulated me to reexamine my preconceptions of how Gandhi's South African struggles began. It has been a surprising experience. Gandhi's struggles are especially important in the history of "peaceful militancy," but are by no means the only ones. If they had never taken place, there would still be abundant political evidence to justify research and planning into the possibilities of developing and extending the political use of nonviolent action in place of violence and war, in struggles for justice, liberation, and even national defense.

MEETING THE NEEDS

Professor Erikson is actively concerned with how we face the future, profiting from the Gandhian experiments:

> Gandhi could sympathize with proud and violent youth; but he believed that violence breeds violence from generation to generation and that only the combined insight and discipline of Satyagraha can really disarm man, or rather, give him a power stronger than all arms. (p. 438)

> Gandhi's instrument itself . . . now exists. . . . It now calls for leaders who will re-innovate it elsewhere . . . For if the instrument once was "the truth," it can and must become actual in entirely different settings, in which the necessary toolmaking may be based on a different and yet analogous tradition, and where the toolmakers come from different vocations and yet share converging goals. If truth is actuality, it can never consist of the mere repetition of ritualized acts or stances. It calls for a reconstitution

by a new combination of universal verities and social disciplines. (pp. 435–436)

Surely the needs of the people of this country, and of the world, are deep enough, the sufferings and dangers imposed by violence sharp enough, the pains of injustice cutting enough, the cruelties and threats of tyrannies real enough, that the fullest possible research and investigation into the nature of potentialities of nonviolent struggle should soon be launched.

NOTES TO CHAPTER TWO

1. Indian Opinion, 19 August 1905; M.K. Gandhi, The Collected Works of Mahatma Gandhi, (hereafter cited as The Collected Works; Delhi: Publications Division, Ministry of Information and Broadcasting, Government of India, 1961), vol. V, p. 44. Italics added.
2. Indian Opinion, 30 Sept. 1905; Gandhi, The Collected Works, vol. V, pp. 82–83.
3. Indian Opinion, 26 May 1906; Gandhi, The Collected Works, vol. V, p. 329.
4. Indian Opinion, 11 Nov. 1905; Gandhi, The Collected Works, vol. V, pp. 131–132. Italics added.
5. Pyarelal (Nair or Nayar), Mahatma Gandhi: The Early Phase (first vol. of a projected series; Ahmedabad: Navajivan Publishing House, 1965), Vol. I, p. 152.
6. L.S.S. O'Malley, History of Bengal, Bihar & Orissa under British Rule (Calcutta: Bengal Secretariat Book Depot, 1925), p. 496.
7. B. Pattabhi Sitaramayya, The History of the Indian National Congress, 1885–1935 (two vols. Bombay: Padma Publications, [1935] 1946), vol. I, pp. 60–61.
8. Pyarelal, Mahatma Gandhi, vol. I, p. 137
9. Ibid., p. 152.
10. Ibid., pp. 153–155; and Pattabhi Sitaramayya, The History of the Indian National Congress, 1885–1935, vol. I, p. 68.
11. Gandhi, The Collected Works, vol. V, p. 65.
12. Ibid., p. 92.
13. Ibid., p. 132.
14. Pyarelal, Mahatma Gandhi, vol. I, p. 232.
15. Ibid., 420; and Gandhi, The Collected Works, vol. I, pp. 105 and 142.
16. Ibid., vol. V, p. 85.
17. Pyarelal, Mahatma Gandhi, vol. I, pp. 182–183; and Erik Erikson, Gandhi's Truth: On the Origins of Militant Nonviolence (New York: W.W. Norton & Co., 1969), p. 114.
18. Indian Opinion, 6 Oct. 1906; Gandhi, The Collected Works, vol. V, p. 462.
19. Indian Opinion, 20 Oct. 1906; Gandhi, The Collected Works, vol. V, pp. 476–477.
20. Indian Opinion, 21 Jan. 1904; Gandhi, The Collected Works, vol. IV, p. 113.

21. **Indian Opinion,** 22 Sept. 1906; Gandi **The Collected Works,** vol. V, p. 422.
22. Ibid., pp. 461–462.
23. Ibid., p. 461.
24. **Indian Opinion,** 6 Oct. 1906; Gandhi, **The Collected Works,** vol. V, p. 462.
25. Ibid., pp. 140–141.
26. **Indian Opinion,** 22 Sept. 1906; Gandhi, **The Collected Works,** vol. V, p. 418.
27. **Indian Opinion,** 6 Oct. 1906; Gandhi **The Collected Works,** vol. V, p. 462.
28. See ibid., pp. 266–267, 281–282, and 290–291; and D.G. Tendulkar, **Mahatma: Life of Mohandas Karamchand Gandhi** (8 vols. Delhi: Publications Division, Ministry of Information and Broadcasting, Government of India, 1960), vol. I, p. 76.
29. **Indian Opinion,** 6 Oct. 1906; Gandhi, **The Collected Works,** vol. V, p. 461.
30. **Indian Opinion,** 20 Oct. 1906; Gandhi, **The Collected Works,** vol. V, p. 475.
31. **Indian Opinion,** 11 Nov. 1905; Gandhi, **The Collected Works,** vol. V, p. 132.
32. M.K. Gandhi, **Satyagraha in South Africa** (trans. from the Gujarati by Valji Govindji Desai, Revised Second Ed.; Ahmedabad: Navajivan, 1950), pp. 114–115.
33. Ibid., pp. 187–188.
34. **Indian Opinion,** 11 Nov. 1905; Gandhi, **The Collected Works,** vol. V, p. 132. Italics added.
35. Ibid., p. 132.
36. See Chapter Three, "Gandhi on the Theory of Voluntary Servitude."
37. See Gene Sharp, **The Politics of Nonviolent Action** (Boston: Porter Sargent Publisher, 1973), Chapter One.

3

Gandhi on the Theory of Voluntary Servitude

While many of Gandhi's views were constantly developing and changing, his conception of the source of political power remained throughout his active political life essentially the same. It does not appear to have changed basically from the time he developed *satyagraha*, his version of the political technique of nonviolent action, in South Africa until his death. This view was that hierarchical social and political systems exist because of the essentially voluntary submission, cooperation, and obedience of the subordinate group. This submission, with its psychological roots and its practical political manifestations, was regarded by Gandhi as the root cause of tyranny.*

* For a fuller exposition of this theory of power, drawing on Western theorists, see Gene Sharp, *The Politics of Nonviolent Action* (Boston: Porter Sargent Publisher, 1973), Chapter One, written after this chapter.—G.S. 1978.

He granted that rulers use various means to obtain this submission, and that the price of its withdrawal is often harsh repression and extreme suffering aimed at forcing a resumption of cooperation. This fact, however, did not, in his view, invalidate the theory. It remained true, he was convinced, that hierarchical systems ultimately depend upon assistance of the underlings.

This chapter has a very limited objective: to present Gandhi's views on this theory, largely in his own words; there is no attempt here to analyze or criticize this aspect of Gandhi's thought. Ideas must be first understood.

THE BASIC IDEA

". . .[N]o Government—much less the Indian Government—can subsist if the people cease to serve it."[1]

Even the most despotic government cannot stand except for the consent of the governed which consent is often forcibly procured by the despot. Immediately the subject ceases to fear the despotic force, his power is gone.[2]

I believe, and everybody must grant, that no Government can exist for a single moment without the co-operation of the people, willing or forced, and if people suddenly withdraw their co-operation in every detail, the Government will come to a standstill. . . . It remains to be seen whether their [the masses' and the classes'] feeling is intense enough to evoke in them the measure of sacrifice adequate for successful non-co-operation.[3]

The popular saying, as is the king, so are the people, is only a half-truth. That is to say, it is not more true than its converse, as are the people, so is the prince. Where the subjects are watchful a prince is entirely dependent upon them for his status. Where the subjects are overtaken by sleepy indifference, there is every possibility that the prince will cease to function as a protector and become an oppressor instead. Those who are not wide awake, have no right to blame their prince. The prince as well as the people are mostly creatures of circumstance. Enterprising princes and the peoples mould circumstances for their own benefit. Manliness consists in making circumstances subservient to ourselves. Those who will not heed themselves perish. To understand this principle is not to be impatient, not to reproach Fate, not to blame others. He who understands the doctrine of self-help blames himself for failure. It is on this ground that I object to violence. If we blame others where we should blame ourselves and wish for or bring about their destruction, that does not remove the root cause of the disease which on the contrary sinks all the deeper for the ignorance thereof.[4]

As the 1930–31 civil disobedience campaign for Indian independence was about to begin Gandhi wrote: "The spectacle of three hundred million people being cowed down by living in the dread of three hundred men is demoralizing alike for the despots as for the victims."[5]

This conception of the relation between the dominate group and subordinate group, in Gandhi's view, applied to economic exploitation as well as political domination. "No person can amass wealth without the co-operation, willing or forced, of the people concerned."[6]

The rich cannot accumulate wealth without the cooperation of the poor in society. If this knowledge were to penetrate to and spread amongst the poor, they would become strong and would learn how to free themselves by means of non-violence from the crushing inequalities which have brought them to the verge of starvation.[7]

All exploitation is based on cooperation, willing or forced, of the exploited. However much we may detest admitting it, the fact remains that there would be no exploitation if people refused to obey the exploiter. But self comes in and we hug the chains that bind us. This must cease.[8]

INDIA'S SUBJECTION VOLUNTARY

This basic view about the nature of hierarchical systems was reflected in Gandhi's belief that India's subordination to British rule was basically voluntary. This conception was expressed clearly in his 1906 pamphlet, "Hind Swaraj or Indian Home Rule."

The English have not taken India; we have given it to them. They are not in India because of their strength, but because we keep them. Let us now see whether these propositions can be sustained. They came to our country originally for purposes of trade. Recall the Company Bahadur.* Who made it Bahadur? They had not the slightest intention at the time of establishing a kingdom. Who assisted the Company's officers? Who was tempted at the sight of their silver? Who bought their goods? History testifies that we all did this. In order to become rich all at once we welcomed the Company's officers with open arms. We assisted them. If I am in the habit of drinking *bhang*† and a seller thereof sells it to me, am I to blame him or myself? By blaming the seller, shall I be able to avoid the habit? And, if a particular retailer is driven away, will not another take his place? A true servant of India will have to go to the root of the matter.[9]

. . . [T]he English merchants were able to get a footing in India because we encouraged them. When our Princes fought among themselves, they sought the assistance of Company Bahadur. That corporation was versed alike in commerce and war. It was unhampered by questions of morality. Its object was to increase its commerce and to make money. It accepted our assistance, and increased the number of its warehouses. To protect the latter it employed an army which was utilized by us also. Is it not then useless to blame the English for what we did at that time? The Hindus and the Mahomedans [sic] were at daggers drawn. This, too, gave the Company its opportunity and thus we created the circumstances that gave the Company its control over India. Hence it is truer to say that we gave India to the English than that India was lost.[10]

The causes that gave them India enable them to retain it. Some Englishmen state that they took and they hold India by the sword. Both these statements are wrong. The sword is entirely useless for holding India. We alone keep them.[11]

Then it follows that we keep the English in India for our base self-interest. We like their commerce; they please us by their subtle methods and get what they want from us. To blame them for this

---

* This is a reference to the East India Company whose economic activities, leading to political activities, considerably preceeded active involvement of the British Government in India. The meanings of *bahadur* include "brave," "brave people," and "Englishmen." This is important for understanding Gandhi's meaning. Hence, in the quotation from Gandhi, the reference to "the Company Bahadur" refers to "the English Company" or "the Company of brave men." When Gandhi then asks, "Who made it Bahadur?" he returns to the original meaning of *bahadur,* "Who made it brave?"

† An intoxicating drink made from a type of hemp.

is to perpetuate their power. We further strengthen their hold by quarrelling amongst ourselves. If you accept the above statements, it is proved that the English entered India for the purposes of trade. They remain in it for the same purpose and we help them to do so. Their arms and ammunition are perfectly useless.[12]

In 1921 Gandhi still held the view that "it is not so much British guns that are responsible for our subjection as our voluntary co-operation."[13] Twenty-five years later he still insisted:

The only constituted authority is the British. We are all puppets in their hands. But it would be wrong and foolish to blame that authority. It acts according to its nature. That authority does not compel us to be puppets. We voluntarily run into their camp. It is, therefore, open to any and everyone of us to refuse to play the British game.[14]

There is evidence that, while Gandhi came upon this concept independently,* he was later influenced highly in this line of thought by Henry David Thoreau, especially his "Essay on the Duty of Civil Disobedience," and by Count Leo Tolstoy both in correspondence and in Tolstoy's "A Letter to a Hindu."† It is significant that in his introduction to an edition of Tolstoy's essay, Gandhi wrote, in Johannesburg in 1909:

If we do not want the English in India we must pay the price. Tolstoy indicates it. "Do not resist evil, but also do not yourselves participate in evil—in the violent deeds of the administration of the law courts, the collection of taxes, and, what is more important, of the soldiers, and no one in the world will enslave you," passionately declares the sage of Yasnaya Polyana [Tolstoy's home]. Who can doubt the truth of what he says in the following: "A commercial company enslaved a nation comprising two hundred millions. Tell this to a man free from superstition and he will fail to grasp what these words mean. What does it mean that thirty thousand people, not athletes, but rather weak

---

* Research has not yet been done on the possibility that Gandhi encountered the theory while studying law in London in assigned readings on political philosophy and jurisprudence, as by John Austin.—G.S. 1978

† Chapter Nine, "Gandhi as a National Defense Strategist," includes passages from Gandhi's pamphlet "Hind Swaraj," which he wrote in 1908, the year he read Tolstoy's "A Letter to a Hindu."

and ordinary people, have enslaved two hundred millions of vigorous, clever, capable, freedom-loving people? Do not the figures make it clear that not the English, but the Indians, have enslaved themselves?" One need not accept all that Tolstoy says . . . to realize the central truth of his indictment of the present system.[15]

In consequence of this view, Gandhi concluded: "It is my certain conviction that no man loses his freedom except through his own weakness."[16]

OBTAINING SUBMISSION

There were, Gandhi recognized, a number of means which regimes and ruling classes used to obtain and maintain the populace's acquiesence and cooperation. The threat of violent repression and punishment was one of these. This and other needs required the creation of a class of subordinates to assist the regime in carrying out its various functions and in enforcing its will upon the populace. Gandhi wrote, for example, in 1930:

> From the village headmen to their personal assistants these satraps [petty officials] have created a class of subordinates who, whilst they cringe before their foreign masters, in their constant dealings with the people act so irresponsibly and so harshly as to demoralize them and by a system of terrorism render them incapable of resisting corruption.[17]

As an example of this, Gandhi cited the political function served by Indian lawyers operating within the British system:

> But the gravest injury they [the lawyers] have done to the country is that they have tightened the English grip. Do you think that it would be possible for the English to carry on their Government without law courts? It is wrong to consider that courts are established for the benefit of the people. Those who want to perpetuate their power do so through the courts. If people were to settle their own quarrels, a third party would not be able to exercise any authority over them.[18]

> The chief thing . . . to be remembered is that without lawyers courts could not have been established or conducted and without the latter the English could not rule. Supposing that there were

only English judges, English pleaders and English police, they could only rule over the English. The English could not do without Indian judges and Indian pleaders.[19]

Gandhi roundly condemned the behavior of such an intermediate class of Indians subservient to British interests:

> It is worth noting that, by receiving English education, we have enslaved the nation. Hypocrisy, tyranny, etc., have increased; English-knowing Indians have not hesitated to cheat and strike terror into the people. Now, if we are doing anything for the people at all, we are paying only a portion of the debt due to them. . . . It is we, the English-knowing Indians, that have enslaved India. The curse of the nation will rest not upon the English but upon us.[20]

A system of education which inculcated respect and attachment for the culture, traditions and political system of the foreign occupation authority and contributed to the reduced respect and attachment to the Indian counterparts of these, in Gandhi's view, increased submission to the British system: "To give millions a knowledge of English is to enslave them."[21]

A resolution, drawn up by Gandhi, approved by the Congress Working Committee, and then passed by public meetings throughout India on 26 January 1930 included the sentence: "Culturally, the system of education has torn us from our moorings, our training has made us hug the very chains that bind us."[22]

POWER IN POLITICAL CHANGE

Gandhi saw this view of the basis of the regime's power as fully compatible with a recognition of the importance of wielding power of some type in order to change relationships between the rulers and the ruled. Some of his clearest statements on this were made during the early days of the 1930–31 independence struggle. In early January 1930, he declared: "England will never make any real advance so as to satisfy India's aspirations till she is forced to it."[23] Later the same month he wrote in *Young India:*

> The British people must realise that the Empire is to come to an end. This they will not realise unless we in India have generated power within to enforce our will. . . . The real conference therefore has to be among ourselves.[24]

In a letter to the Viceroy in March, just before the beginning of the campaign, Gandhi said:

> It is not a matter of carrying conviction by argument. The matter resolves itself into one of matching forces. Conviction or no conviction, Great Britain would defend her Indian commerce and interests by all the forces at her command. India must consequently evolve force enough to free herself from that embrace of death.[25]

In the same letter, referring to the economic motives for maintaining British rule and the coming resistance he observed: "If the British commerce with India is purified of greed, you will have no difficulty in recognizing our Independence."[26] Commenting on the Viceroy's terse rejection of Gandhi's effort to find a settlement acceptable to the Indian nationalists without resort to nonviolent resistance, Gandhi said: "The English nation responds only to force, and I am not surprised by the Viceregal reply."[27] As the movement began, Gandhi declared:

> I regard this rule as a curse. I am out to destroy this system of Government. I have sung the tune of "God Save the King" and have taught others to sing it. I was a believer in the politics of petitions, deputations, and friendly negotiations. But all these have gone to dogs. I know that these are not the ways to bring this Government round. Sedition has become my religion.[28]

SOCIAL DETERMINANTS OF POLITICAL STRUCTURES

Gandhi at this time believed genuine and lasting freedom to be based upon "a craving for human liberty which prizes itself above mere selfish satisfaction of personal comforts and material wants and would readily and joyfully sacrifice these for self-preservation."[29]

The 1930–31 campaign was, in Gandhi's view, aimed not so much at forcing the granting of specific political demands, as at raising the quality and stature of the Indian people, so that no one for long could deny them their rights. "The present campaign is not designed to establish Independence but to arm the people with the power to do so."[30] "Civil disobedience is the method whereby the nation is to generate the strength to reach her formulated goal."[31]

If they are successful in doing away with the salt tax and the liquor trade from India, there is the victory for *ahimsa* [nonviolence]. And what power on earth is there then, that would prevent Indians from getting Swaraj [self-rule]? If there be any such power, I shall like to see it.[32]

Gopi Nath Dhawan, one of Gandhi's interpreters, wrote:

The idea that underlies non-co-operation is that even the evil-doer does not succeed in his purpose without carrying the victim with him, if necessary, by force, and that it is the duty of the *satyagrahi* to suffer for the consequences of resistance and not to yield to the will of the tyrant. If the victim continues to tolerate the wrong by passive acquiescence, if he enjoys benefits accruing from that wrong or wrong-doer directly or indirectly, the victim is an accessory to the tyrant's misdeeds.[33]

Satyagraha was, then, aimed at influencing the power relationships between the British *Raj* and the Indian nation by (1) the introduction of psychological and moral pressures by the people's determined defiance of British rule coupled with nonretaliatory acceptance of the repression and suffering imposed by the regime; (2) the political impact of a large section of noncooperating disobedient subjects on the functioning and maintenance of the regime; and (3) the improvement of the moral stature of the Indian people through their self-suffering, defiance without retaliation, and their casting off of the attitude of submission. These three factors would in the long run contribute to increased self-reliance and to reduced submission to the British *Raj*. The constructive program for producing social and economic changes without the assistance of the government was also a continuing means for producing self-rule and a weakening of the ties to the British *Raj*.

Gandhi thus shared Godwin's view that the outward political forms and structure are a reflection of and dependent upon certain other qualities of the society. They both were convinced that if freedom is to be genuine and lasting, changes must be made on a deeper level than simply the constitution or the institutional forms at the top of the society.

In this context one can see why Gandhi emphasized the moral improvement of the Indian people and the constructive program as politically relevant. These efforts contributed to increased ability to noncooperate with the British *Raj*. In turn, such noncooperation and voluntary suffering constituted also a means of moral improvement for the Indian people, by making amends for their previous submission to foreign domination. When noncooperation is practiced against a government,

> . . . the primary motive of non-co-operation is self-purification by withdrawing co-operation from unrighteous and unrepentant Government. The secondary object is to rid ourselves of the feeling of helplessness by being independent of all Government control or supervision, i.e., to govern ourselves in all possible affairs; and, in fulfilling both the objects to refrain from doing or promoting injury, or any violence, to individual or property.[34]

This combined program of moral improvement, resistance, and constructive work would, in Gandhi's view, lead to genuine self-rule which was beyond political independence alone. "When India was ready, neither the British nor the *Rajahs,* nor any combination of the Powers could keep India from her destined goal, her birthright. . . ."[35]

Because of these views, Gandhi emphasized moral improvement as a contribution to political change:

> . . . [R]ulers, if they are bad, are so, not necessarily or wholly by birth, but largely because of their environment, that I have hopes of their altering their course. It is perfectly true that the rulers cannot alter their course themselves. If they are dominated by their environment, they do not surely deserve to be killed, but should be changed by a change of environment. But the environment are we—the people who make the rulers what they are. They are thus an exaggerated edition of what we are in the aggregate. If my argument is sound, any violence done to the rulers would be violence done to ourselves. It would be suicide. And since I do not want to commit suicide, nor encourage my neighbours to do so, I become non-violent myself and invite my neighbours to do likewise.
>
> Moreover, violence may destroy one or more bad rulers, but, like Ravana's heads, others will pop up in their places, for, the root lies elsewhere. It lies in us. If we reform ourselves, the rulers will automatically do so.[36]
>
> Like every other Indian, he [a wealthy man] will know that to

blame the English is useless, that they came because of us, and remain also for the same reason, and that they will either go or change their nature only when we reform ourselves. . . ."[37]

The responsibility is more ours than of the English for the present state of things. The English will be powerless to do evil if we will but be good. Hence my incessant emphasis on reform from within.[38]

CHANGE OF ATTITUDE

There must then, Gandhi insisted, be a psychological change from passive submission and acceptance of the rule of the existing powers-that-be to a determination to be self-reliant and to resist all that is regarded as unjust and tyrannical:

The way of peace insures internal growth and stability. We reject it because we fancy that it involves submission to the will of the ruler who has imposed himself upon us. But the moment we realize that the imposition is only so-called and that, through our unwillingness to suffer loss of life or property, we are party to the imposition, all we need to do is to change that negative attitude of passive endorsement. The suffering to be undergone by the change will be nothing compared to the physical suffering and the moral loss we must incur in trying the way of war.[39]

The bond of the slave is snapped the moment he considers himself to be a free being. He will plainly tell the master: "I was your bondslave till this moment, but I am a slave no longer. You may kill me if you like, but if you keep me alive, I wish to tell you that if you release me from the bondage, of your own accord, I will ask for nothing more from you. You used to feed and clothe me, though I could have provided food and clothing for myself by my labour. . . ."[40]

The achievement of this change in the attitude toward the existing regime was an important preliminary step in producing social and political change. "My speeches are intended to create 'disaffection' as such, that people might consider it a shame to assist or coöperate with a government that had forfeited all title to respect or support."[41]

POLITICAL IMPLICATION

In Gandhi's view, if the maintenance of an unjust or non-democratic regime is dependent upon the cooperation, submission, and obedience of the populace, then the means for changing or abolishing it lies in the area of noncooperation, defiance, and disobedience. These forms of action, he was convinced, could be undertaken without the use of physical violence, and even without hostility toward the members of the opponent group. On this basis, he formulated the technique of action, *satyagraha.*

> This force is to violence, and, therefore, to all tyranny, all injustice, what light is to darkness. In politics, its use is based upon the immutable maxim, that government of the people is possible only so long as they consent either consciously or unconsciously to be governed.[42]

Gandhi regarded it as both unmanly and immoral to submit to injustice, even though the consequences for refusal to submit were severe punishment. Speaking to a crowd of Muslims in Bombay in 1920 Gandhi said:

> It was a sign of religious atrophy to sustain an unjust Government that supported an injustice by resorting to untruth and camouflage. So long therefore as the Government did not purge itself of the canker of injustice and untruth, it was their duty to withdraw all help from it, consistently with their ability to preserve order in the social structure.[43]

In "Hind Swaraj" he wrote: "If man will only realize that it is unmanly to obey laws that are unjust, no man's tyranny will enslave him. This is the key to self-rule or home-rule."[44]

When the resister was ready to cast off fear, he could then undertake the noncooperation with the regime which would lead to its downfall. He must, however, be prepared for imprisonment and perhaps even death in the course of the struggle:

> It is a fundamental principle of satyagraha that the tyrant whom the satyagrahi seeks to resist has power over his body and material possessions but he can have no power over the soul. The soul can remain unconquered and unconquerable even when the body is imprisoned. The whole science of satyagraha was born from a knowledge of this fundamental truth.[45]

NONCOOPERATION

The main course of action then lay in the field of noncooperation. Speaking to a group of West African soldiers in 1946 on the means of achieving freedom, Gandhi said:

> The moment the slave resolves that he will no longer be a slave, his fetters fall. He frees himself and shows the way to others. Freedom and slavery are mental states. Therefore, the first thing is to say to yourself: "I shall no longer accept the role of a slave. I shall not obey orders as such but shall disobey them when they are in conflict with my conscience." The so-called master may lash you and try to force you to serve him. You will say: "No,.I will not serve you for your money or under a threat." This may mean suffering. Your readiness to suffer will light the torch of freedom which can never be put out.[46]

Referring to the British *Raj*, Gandhi wrote:

> You have great military resources. Your naval power is matchless. If we wanted to fight with you on your own ground, we should be unable to do so, but if the above submissions be not acceptable to you, we cease to play the part of the ruled. You may, if you like cut us to pieces. You may shatter us at the cannon's mouth. If you act contrary to our will, we shall not help you; and without our help, we know that you cannot move one step forward.[47]

The resolution, drafted by Gandhi, approved by the Congress Working Committee and passed by public meetings on Independence Day, 26 January 1930 contained this statement on noncooperation and the withdrawal of voluntary submission to the British *Raj:*

> We hold it to be a crime against man and God to submit any longer to a rule that has caused this fourfold disaster to our country. We recognize, however, that the most effective way of gaining our freedom is not through violence. We will therefore prepare ourselves by withdrawing, so far as we can, all voluntary association from the British Government, and will prepare for civil disobedience, including non-payment of taxes. We are convinced that if we can but withdraw our voluntary help and stop payment of taxes without doing violence, even under provocation, the end of this inhuman rule is assured.[48]

In an article published in late March, 1930, on "The Duty of Disloyalty," Gandhi wrote:

> It is then the duty of those who have realized the awful evil of the system of Indian Government to be disloyal to it and actively and openly preach disloyalty. Indeed, loyalty to a State so corrupt is a sin, disloyalty a virtue. . . . It is the duty of those who have realized the evil nature of the system, however attractive some of its features may, torn from their context, appear to be, to destroy it without delay. It is their clear duty to run any risk to achieve the end.

> But it must be equally clear that it would be cowardly for three hundred million people to seek to destroy the three hundred authors or administrators of the system. It is a sign of gross ignorance to devise means of destroying these administrators of their hirelings. Moreover they are but creatures of circumstance. The purest man entering the system will be affected by it, and will be instrumental in propagating the evil. The remedy therefore naturally is not being enraged against the administrators and therefore hurting them, but to non-co-operate with the system by withdrawing all the voluntary assistance possible and refusing all its so-called benefits.[49]

Writing in 1920 on noncooperation, Gandhi said:

> What then is the meaning of non-co-operation in terms of the law of suffering? We must voluntarily put up with the losses and inconveniences that arise from having to withdraw our support from a Government that is ruling against our will. Possession of power and riches is a crime under an unjust Government, poverty in that case is a virtue, says Thoreau. It may be that in the transition state we may make mistakes; there may be avoidable suffering. These things are preferable to national emasculation.

> We must refuse to wait for the wrong to be righted till the wrong-doer has been roused to a sense of his iniquity. We must not, for fear of ourselves or others having to suffer, remain participators in it. But we must combat the wrong by ceasing to assist the wrong-doer directly or indirectly.

> If a father does an injustice it is the duty of his children to leave the parental roof. If the headmaster of a school conducts his institution on an immoral basis, the pupils must leave the school. If the chairman of a corporation is corrupt the members thereof

must wash their hands clean of his corruption by withdrawing from it; even so if a Government does a grave injustice the subjects must withdraw co-operation wholly or partially, sufficiently to wean the ruler from his wickedness. In each case conceived by me there is an element of suffering whether mental or physical. Without such suffering it is not possible to attain freedom.[50]

The following year he declared: "Non-coöperation, though a religious and strictly moral movement, deliberately aims at the overthrow of the Government and is therefore legally seditious in terms of the Indian Penal Code."[51]

Faced with a demand, backed by the threat of violence, regarded as unjust, the nonviolent man "was not to return violence by violence but neutralize it by withholding one's hand and, at the same time, refusing to submit to the demand."[52] The means of noncooperation were regarded by Gandhi as applicable to social and economic conflicts as well as to political ones. During his stay in London in 1931, some young Communists asked how Gandhi actually proposed to bring the new order into being if he abjured the use of violence. Was it to be by persuasion? Gandhi answered:

Not merely by verbal persuasion. I will concentrate on my means... My means are non-co-operation.[53]

In 1940, Gandhi wrote:

If however, in spite of the utmost effort, the rich do not become guardians of the poor in the true sense of the term and the latter are more and more crushed and die of hunger, what is to be done? In trying to find out the solution of this riddle I have lighted on non-violent non-cooperation and civil disobedience as the right and infallible means.[54]

Other advocates of the theory that governments and other hierarchical systems can be modified or destroyed by a withdrawal of submission, cooperation and obedience have indicated certain lines along which such withdrawal might be practiced. However, Gandhi was probably the first consciously to formulate over a period of years a major system of resistance based upon this assumption. We have as yet seen only the initial stages of the political application of this theory.

NOTES TO CHAPTER THREE

1. **Young India,** 5 May 1920; quoted in M.K. Gandhi, **Satyagraha** (Ahmedabad: Navajivan Publishing House, 1951), p. 116.
2. **Young India,** 30 June 1920; quoted in Nirmal Kumar Bose, **Selections from Gandhi** (Ahmedabad: Navajivan, 1948), p. 116.
3. **Young India,** 18 August 1920; quoted in Gandhi, **Satyagraha,** p. 157.
4. **Young India,** 8 January 1925; quoted in N. K. Bose, **Studies in Gandhism** (Calcutta: Indian Associated Publishing Co., Ltd., 1947), pp. 93–94.
5. **Young India,** 27 March 1930; quoted in Gene Sharp, **Gandhi Wields the Weapon of Moral Power: Three Case Histories** (Ahmedabad: Navajivan, 1960), p. 82.
6. **Young India,** 26 November 1931, p. 369.
7. **Harijan,** 25 August 1940, p. 260; quoted in Bose, **Selections from Gandhi,** p. 79.
8. **The Amrita Bazar Patrika,** 3 August 1934; quoted in Bose, **Selections from Gandhi,** p. 91.
9. Gandhi, "Hind Swaraj or Indian Home Rule" (pamphlet; Ahmedabad: Navajivan, 1958), pp. 38–39.
10. Ibid., pp. 39–40.
11. Ibid., p. 40.
12. Ibid., pp. 40–41.
13. **Young India,** 9 February 1921; quoted in Bose, **Selections from Gandhi,** p. 116.
14. **Harijan,** 19 September 1946; quoted in Gandhi, **Non-violence in Peace and War** (Ahmedabad: Navajivan, 1949), vol. II, p. 148.
15. Quoted in Kalidas Nag, **Tolstoy and Gandhi** (Patna, Pustak Bhandar, 1950), pp. 79–80.
16. Gandhi, **India's Case for Swaraj;** edited and compiled by W.P. Kabadi, 1932, p. 209; quoted in Bose, **Selections from Gandhi,** p. 116.
17. **Young India,** 27 March 1930, p. 103; quoted in Sharp, **Gandhi Wields the Weapon of Moral Power,** p. 82.
18. Gandhi, "Hind Swaraj," p. 56.
19. Ibid., p. 57.
20. Ibid., pp. 90–91.
21. Ibid., p. 90.
22. All-India Congress Committee, **Congress Bulletin,** 17 January 1930, no. 2, Allahabad; quoted in Sharp, **Gandhi Wields the Weapon of Moral Power,** p. 54.
23. Louis Fischer, **The Life of Mahatma Gandhi** (New York, Harper and Bros., 1950), p. 258.
24. **Young India,** 23 January 1930, p. 28; quoted in Sharp, **Gandhi Wields the Weapon of Moral Power,** p. 52.
25. A.I.C.C., **Congress Bulletin,** 7 March 1930, No. 5; quoted in Sharp, **Gandhi Wields the Weapon of Moral Power,** p. 64.
26. Ibid., p. 65.
27. B. Pattabhi Sitaramayya, **History of the Indian National Congress, 1885–1935** (Madras, Working Committee of the Congress, 1935), vol. I, p. 638.
28. Ibid., pp. 649–651.
29. A.I.C.C., **Congress Bulletin Supplement,** 19 September 1931; quoted in Sharp, **Gandhi Wields the Weapon of Moral Power,** p. 212.

30. **Young India**, 24 April 1930, p. 137; quoted in Sharp, **Gandhi Wields the Weapon of Moral Power**, p. 100.
31. **Young India**, 20 March 1930, p. 137; quoted in Sharp, **Gandhi Wields the Weapon of Moral Power**, p. 72.
32. Pattabhi Sitaramayya, **History of the Indian National Congress, 1885–1935**, vol. I, p. 654.
33. Gopi Nath Dhawan, **The Political Philosophy of Mahatma Gandhi** (Third rev. ed.; Ahmedabad, Navajivan 1962), p. 144.
34. **Young India**, vol. I, p. 42; quoted by Dhawan, **The Political Philosophy**, p. 228.
35. **Harijan**, 2 March 1947; quoted in Gandhi, **Non-violence in Peace and War** (Ahmedabad: Navajivan, 1949), vol. II, p. 223.
36. **Harijan**, 21 September 1934, p. 250; quoted in Bose, **Studies in Gandhism**, p. 94.
37. Gandhi, **Hind Swaraj**, p. 103.
38. **Young India**, 21 May 1925, p. 178; quoted in Bose, **Selections from Gandhi**, p. 157.
39. **Young India**, 20 May 1926; quoted in Gandhi, **Non-violence in Peace and War**, vol. I, p. 57.
40. Gandhi's address to A.I.C.C., 8 August 1942; quoted in Joan V. Bondurant, **Conquest of Violence: The Gandhian Philosophy of Conflict** (Princeton: Princeton University Press, 1958), p. 30.
41. Quoted in Clarence Marsh Case, **Non-violent Coercion: A Study in Methods of Social Pressure** (New York: The Century Co., 1923), pp. 391–392.
42. **Indian Opinion**, Golden Number, 1914; quoted in Gandhi, **Satyagraha**, p. 35.
43. **Young India**, 4 August 1920; quoted in Gandhi, **Satyagraha**, pp. 126–127.
44. Gandi, "Hind Swaraj," p. 81.
45. **Young India**, 21 May 1931; quoted in Gandhi, **Satyagraha**, p. 289.
46. **Harijan**, 24 February 1946; quoted in Gandhi, **Non-violence in Peace and War**, vol. II, p. 10.
47. Gandhi, "Hind Swaraj," p. 100.
48. A.I.C.C. **Congress Bulletin**, 17 January 1930, no. 2; quoted in Sharp, **Gandhi Wields the Weapon of Moral Power**, p. 54.
49. **Young India**, 27 March 1930, p. 108; quoted in Sharp, **Gandhi Wields the Weapon of Moral Power**, p. 82.
50. **Young India**, 16 June 1920; quoted in Gandhi, **Satyagraha**, pp. 114–115.
51. **Young India**, 29 September 1921; quoted in Case, **Non-violent Coercion**, p. 392.
52. **Harijan**, 30 March 1947; quoted in Gandhi, **Non-violence in Peace and War**, vol. II, p. 234.
53. **Young India**, 26 November 1931, p. 369; quoted in Bose, **Studies in Gandhism**, p. 92.
54. **Harijan**, 25 August 1940, p. 260; quoted in Bose, **Selections from Gandhi**, p. 79.

4

Satyagraha and Political Conflict

A Review of Joan V. Bondurant's Conquest of Violence*

This is the first book by a Western political scientist on the significance of Gandhi and *satyagraha* for problems of Western political theory and practice. Dr. Bondurant has abstracted from the Gandhian experiments with *satyagraha* "a theoretical key to the problem of social and political conflict." (By *satyagraha*, the author means, not Gandhi's over-all belief system, but the version he developed of the technique of nonviolent action, including certain basic attitudes to the opponent and to the conflict.)

That "key" to the problem of conflict does not lie in some distant scheme for eliminating social and political conflict, although the author would support efforts to remove nonrealistic

---

* Joan V. Bondurant. *Conquest of Violence: The Gandhian Philosophy of Conflict*. Princeton, N.J.: Princeton University Press, 1958, and Berkeley: University of California Press, 1965.

conflicts and to change social conditions giving rise to realistic conflicts. The "key" lies, rather, in a peaceful method of responding to and conducting the conflict once it exists. Dr. Bondurant's analysis is most relevant for all who are concerned with the peaceful resolution of social and political conflicts and especially for readers who are interested in social research toward this end. This review will first present a summary of the contents of the book, followed by some critical remarks. Special attention will be given to the book's relevance for social research on the peaceful resolution of potentially violent conflicts.

TECHNIQUE OF ACTION

Satyagraha was the most potent legacy Gandhi left to India, writes the author. It is also the key to his political philosophy. The heart of *satyagraha* as an ethical principle is a technique of social action which has been used as a means of struggle for humanitarian goals and for basic change. The author maintains that this technique of action does not depend upon Gandhi's teachings on such matters as vegetarianism, sexual continence, or nonpossession. *Satyagraha,* despite its fairly wide application, remains inadequately understood and in need of testing in action. Gandhi was concerned with practical philosophy and with solving pressing social, political, and economic problems. He could never be called a theoretician. Despite this, Gandhi and his *satyagraha* are "immensely significant" for Western political theory and practice.

In the second chapter Dr. Bondurant reviews the principles of Truth, nonviolence (*ahimsa*), and self-suffering as the basic precepts of *satyagraha.* For Gandhi, absolute Truth exists, but man's knowledge of it is always relative. The "quest for Truth" meant for Gandhi, not withdrawal from the world, but active participation in society. Man's relative knowledge of Truth rules out all right to use violence in its fulfillment. Truth can be reached only by adhering to *ahimsa,* which is defined as "action based on the refusal to do harm" (p. 23). Relative truths can be tested through this nonviolence, which becomes the supreme value and the standard for determing whether actions are consistent with Truth. This union of Truth and *ahimsa* (related to *agapé*, "charity" and "love") is the heart of Gandhi's solution to the problem of means. This type of nonviolence is not passivity: Gandhi said it "means the pitting of one's whole soul against the tyrant" (p. 26). Self-suffering becomes a means for removing social evils. Sincerity, courage, and fearlessness are qualities the resister needs in order to use voluntary self-suffering as a method to achieve the moral persuasion of the opponent.

Ours is increasingly an age of manipulation of people, disregard for the individual, and mass control. Yet in *this* age Gandhi insisted that the individual can refuse to be coerced and that social and political change can be effected by the will and reason of individuals. To turn individual moral indignation and resistance into an active social and political force, Gandhi developed his technique of *satyagraha.* The individual has a social responsibility. He or she should recognize the opponent's individuality. The objective of *satyagraha* is a victory over the conflict *situation,* increasing insight into Truth, and persuasion of the opponent.

Satyagraha can be viewed as "applied sociopolitical action," used within a conflict situation. Dr. Bondurant argues that *satyagraha,* as all methods for effecting change, employs force—a force, however, essentially different from the conventional, violent, conflict behavior. A variety of forms of nonviolent action are open to practitioners of *satyagraha,* including civil disobedience, fasting (under strict conditions), and a number of types of noncooperation (such as economic boycott, variations of the strike, and resignation of offices).

In outline form the author presents some of the essentials of *satyagraha* in action: fundamental rules, a code of discipline, and steps in a *satyagraha* campaign. There are several qualities of "true *satyagraha*" which distinguish it from other types of nonviolent action. Generally speaking, the former is more considerate of the opponent as an individual. Five accounts of *satyagraha* campaigns are presented, which combine brevity with a multitude of facts and which, with the accompanying short analyses, give the reader a good grasp of this method of sociopolitical action. *Satyagraha,* as applied sociopolitical action, is not something which can be left to spontaneity. It requires comprehensive planning, preparation, and studied execution, for which the strategy and tactics vary with the situation.

LIMITED TO HINDUS?

Contrary to the view of some, *satyagraha* is not simply a recent manifestation of the Hindu tradition and, therefore, irrelevant for the problems of Western political theory and practice. One cannot, says the author, overemphasize the importance of differentiating between traditional and Gandhian philosophy. Both traditional Indian and modern Western thought have influenced the theory and philosophy of *satyagraha*. Gandhi introduced interpretations reminiscent of Western rationalism and humanism into traditional Indian precepts. Transformed, the precepts were extended beyond individual salvation to become important parts of a technique of action applied in facing practical social and political problems.

The Indian culture was admittedly highly receptive to the principles of *satyagraha,* but religious or philosophical compatibility do not alone explain Gandhi's success. He combined an appeal to India's spiritual heritage with a perception of her social and political problems and also an awareness of the needs, wants, and capabilities of the masses. Gandhi had some of, but not all, the qualities of the charismatic leader, as described by Max Weber, Leadership qualities, however, do not alone explain his achievements either. The type of sociopolitical action which he forged forms part of that explanation.

Gandhi was not blindly "religious" in the narrow sense of the term. He was willing to accept the results of empirical tests, and he highly valued reason. His technique of action is both human-controlled and nondeterministic. In support of the view that is has an appeal to persons adhering to a variety of religions or philosophies, Dr. Bondurant cites the *Khudai Khitmatgar* ("Servants of God") movement in the North-West Frontier Province of British India. This movement, led by Khan Abdul Ghaffar Khan (the Frontier Gandhi), was, in contrast to the Indian National Congress, based upon nonviolence as a principle. By 1938, the movement had over one hundred thousand members. Its adherents had become among the bravest and most daring of the nonviolent revolutionaries in the Indian struggle.

Yet this movement developed among the Muslim Pathans, a people known as brave warriors who could justly be described as "masters in the art and science of violence" (p. 132), a people trained in the use of military arms and with access to such arms. The practice of *satyagraha* by these Pathans was equally successful and more consistent than that in predominantly Hindu India. An abrupt religious, social, and cultural reorientation had been required and was achieved. This is proof, says the author, that the Hindu milieu is not needed for the acceptance and application of *satyagraha*, for the Pathans were unfamiliar with a tradition of philosophy enjoining nonviolence.

RELEVANCE FOR POLITICAL THEORY

It is difficult to place Gandhi within the traditional schools of political thought. There are some grounds for calling him a conservative, a philosophical anarchist, a socialist, a pro-capitalist, and a primitive communist. Although his thought has all these qualities, he does not really belong to any of these schools. Gandhi was primarily concerned with means, not ideal systems. When he saw inequality, oppression, and exploitation, Gandhi asked *how* this could be changed rather than what the ideal ultimate form of social and political organization was. His means, *satyagraha,* possessed such qualities that its introduction into any system would modify that system along lines of redistributing and resettling power and authority.

It is Dr. Bondurant's contention that "in the Gandhian development lies a contribution of great significance for political philosophy. The contribution centers upon the role which satyagraha as a technique of action, together with the philosophy of conflict which lies behind it, may play in a social and political system based upon them" (p. 147). Gandhi's "inestimable" contribution to political theory extends beyond social and political methodology into the realm of political thought. There it challenges the basic assumptions of the main stream of political theory which has assumed a separation of means and ends. The significance of *satyagraha* here is that it points to the necessity of bringing means and ends together through a philosophy of action.

In the book's last chapter, "The Gandhian Dialectic and Political Theory," Dr. Bondurant presents a theoretical framework for the Gandhian philosophy of conflict as a point of departure for the concluding critical remarks on the failure of traditional political theory. The "Gandhian dialectic" views means as "ends-in-the-making." In contrast to the Hegelian and Marxian dialectics, the Gandhian dialectic is not descriptive of society but is a process to be applied by human beings in resolving basic conflicts and in producing an entirely new total circumstance. This method differs radically from compromise, although the *satyagrahi* may use compromise where matters of principle are not involved. Instead, to achieve agreement, the *satyagrahi* uses nonviolent persuasive action, possibly involving aggressive nonviolent action, which must continue until the process has carried the conflict into a "higher" level of adjustment mutually agreeable to the respective parties. This method, in common with violent conflict, requires the willingness to sacrifice one's life in the struggle.

The author considers the relevance of *satyagraha* to contemporary political theory and problems. In an analysis of anarchist thought, she finds its main weakness to be the absence of a constructive technique whereby the anarchist can struggle toward the avowed goals. In contrast, she argues, it is precisely in the area of means, of social techniques, that *satyagraha* is distinctly superior. She observes that, in general, political theory has failed to deal adequately with the question of means, the point at which the challenge of *satyagraha* is most serious, and cites this failure in conservatism and authoritarian idealism (Hegel's metaphysical theory of the State and history).

This failure to deal adequately with the question of means is true even of liberal democratic theory, although it constitutes the heart of the answer to the ends-means question offered by Western theory. A comparison of liberal democratic method and *satyagraha,* therefore, most sharply reveals the latter's significance for Western political thought. We can only sketch the outline of her analysis here. Where extensive fundamental agreement does not exist, the regulative device of majority decision and the unrefined method of compromise as liberal democracy's one technique for adjusting conflicting interests are inadequate. Compromise may break down into barter and may distort basic convictions and principles; a better technique is then crucially needed, or compromise may be rejected by groups prepared to use violence to achieve their ends. When challenged by aggression or subversion, says the author, liberal democracy differs little from other systems. Instead of challenging violence, liberal democracy ultimately relies upon it to maintain its very foundations. Violence is the operative sanction provided in its basic law, and violent revolution is regarded as the ultimate sanction in face of undemocratic usurpation of power. The liberal democrat has tried only to mitigate, but not to supplant, violence. Device, the author maintains, is not a substitute for technique.

Satyagraha is relevant for meeting these weaknesses in liberal democracy, Bondurant continues, for it provides a new technique of revolution, a means for adjusting persisting conflicts, and a possible answer to the means-ends problem in political theory and practice, most serious in the conduct of conflict. *Satyagraha* may even have a degree of effectiveness against a totalitarian regime, and nonviolent resistance may in this technological age be the only possible alternative to submission open to an oppressed people.

Means, the author insists, must be understood and designed to be not simply instrumental but creative. Not until then will the next step be taken in developing a constructive philosophy of conflict. The Gandhian approach can be regarded as little more than a beginning point by the political philosopher searching for an adequate technique of action. The findings of colleagues in other disciplines regarding all types of human conflicts must also be brought to bear upon the problem. But the problem of violence itself must be tackled. It is not enough to flee from it. "The Gandhian experiments suggest that if man is to free himself from fear and threat alike, he pause in his flight from violence to set himself to the task of its conquest" (p.232).

CRITIQUE OF THE BOOK

A number of criticisms of this book need to be made, although they ought not to obscure its merits. A minor point—but regrettable in light of the need for clarity in terminology in this field—is the author's use of the term "non-resistance." Dr. Bondurant correctly contrasts this with *satyagraha,* but ignores the several existing uses of the term to describe various schools of pacifist thought. Her own use of the term is a bit ambiguous. It is first used undefined but with a meaning approximate to "submission" and "obedience." It is then indicated that "non-resistance" "describes only a step in a civil disobedience effort" (p.37), by which she probably means voluntary submission to arrest after willful disobedience of the law. Later, the term is defined as "obedience to established law and consent to traditional rule" (p. 207). The confusion probably arose from descriptions of the nonresistant Christian pacifist sects as law-abiding and submissive to established civil authority and then identifying the quality of submission as the definition of the term without realizing that this was only a particular quality of a whole belief pattern to which the term referred.

There are two points in which the author's pioneering theoretical analysis of apsects of *satyagraha* may still require refinement. First, in the discussion of the "Gandhian dialectic" Dr. Bondurant emphasizes that the conclusion of a conflict in which one side relies upon *satyagraha* is a "synthesis"—not a blatant triumph of one side over the other. This analysis is very worthwhile (although it is possible to overemphasize the likelihood of *satyagrahis'* becoming convinced that at least parts of the opponent's case are superior to their own). It seems, however, to the reviewer that the author weakens this analysis, and at this point misrepresents *satyagraha,* when she says: "The *satyagrahi* must recognize that elementary to his technique is the first step of a full realization that his immediate goal is not the triumph of his substantial side of the struggle—but, rather, *the synthesis of the two opposing claims*" (p. 196) (italics added). The use of "claims" here is out of keeping with the earlier analysis of the value of *satyagraha* in conflict situations in which there is no ethical middle ground between the goals of the respective groups. Are we now to suppose that the use of *satyagraha* by South African opponents of color oppression will produce a synthesis between apartheid and equality? In the reviewer's opinion, the author states the *satyagrahi's* aim more correctly when she writes on the same page that "he seeks a victory, not over the opponent, but over the situation in the best (in the sense of the total human needs of the situation) synthesis possible" (p.196).

Second, Dr. Bondurant has made a significant contribution in her analysis of Gandhi's reliance upon taking "one step" at a time, being prepared to let the ends emerge from the morally correct means. Hence his views about an ultimate social structure were vague and undogmatic. As the author points out, he was flexible concerning the ends when he was certain concerning the means, for they would lead to ends consistent with the means used. Her analysis here is fresh and revealing. It seems to the reviewer, however, that Dr. Bondurant has used this to explain, for example, contradictions in Gandhi's statements concerning economic systems when these may have arisen instead from the evolving nature of Gandhi's thinking. Concerning the systems of capitalism and landlordism, Gandhi was considerably more critical and radical in his later years than earlier. Contradictions between early and later statements concerning economic systems, therefore, may also be due to a genuine change in views concerning the desired ends rather than to flexibility concerning them.

The author's claim that the introduction of *satyagraha* into any political system will inevitably change it and lead to something "out of and beyond" (p. 172) is valid. She slips a bit, however, in stating that its introduction into a "Gandhian conservatism" might lead to something "very much like the welfare state" (p. 172). As she has already pointed out, *satyagraha* contributes to decentralizing power in society; the Western conception of the welfare State, however, concentrates power in the State, which is the opposite.

Dr. Bondurant usefully distinguishes between persuasion through reason and persuasion through *satyagraha*. The latter, making more social impact, can function successfully where the former is ineffective. She accepts Clarence Marsh Case's term "non-violent coercion" to describe aspects of *satyagraha;* "coercion" being "the application of either physical or moral force to induce another to do something against his will" (p. 10). Yet the difference between violent coercion and nonviolent coercion is "of such great degree that it is almost a difference of kind" (p.9). This whole analysis is of considerable value, especially in a consideration of the social and political potentialities of *satyagraha*. The present reviewer, however, is left with a feeling that a more detailed analysis of the relation of persuasion and coercion, in nonviolent action in general and in *satyagraha* in particular, is still needed. A greater refinement in terminology and concepts may still be necessary before our understanding can be considerably increased. Further attention must be paid to the relative influence of (*a*) the voluntary self-suffering, per se and (*b*) the difficulties of maintaining the status quo which follow from the numerical multiplication of non-cooperating, defiant subjects prepared to accept the punishments which are expected to insure obedience.

SOCIAL SCIENCE STUDIES

It is difficult to compare *Conquest of Violence* with other books in the field because this field has very little really good analytical literature, and because Dr. Bondurant's study is unique in the existing literature. Its main objective is to analyze the significance of *satyagraha* for political theory and to find a solution to the problem of conflict. No other writer has yet tackled this aspect of *satyagraha* with comparable thoroughness. The author would not claim that this study has exhausted the subject. Rather, she has opened up a whole new field which ought now to be explored by social scientists. We now turn our attention to those aspects of the book which are most relevant for social science, especially for research.

In the Preface Dr. Bondurant writes:

> It is hoped that the following pages will raise many questions and suggest certain challenges to students of psychology and sociology and to those working in the intensive areas where two or more such fields of inquiry impinge—such, for example, as communications and propaganda, and politics and anthropology. Indeed, as I have pursued the implications of the Gandhian experiments for political philosophy, suggestions for exploration in many other areas have pressed in upon the mind with great insistence. The further delineation of the Gandhian technique and its adaptation to different levels of conflict in differing cultural settings; the design of a procedure making full use of the latest findings in sociology and psychology; the implication of aspects of satyagraha techniques by bringing to bear upon them what can be learned from developing psychoanalytic method—these, and many other areas await exploration by those who would know more of the potential suggested by the Gandhian experience and its significance for formulating an adequate theory for the constructive conduct of conflict [p. viii].

Very few social scientists have turned their attention to this field. There have been a few such studies,* such as Clarence Marsh Case's *Non-violent Coercion*,[1] Krishnalal Shridharani's *War without Violence*,[2] David Spitz's more recent essay, "Democracy and the Problem of Civil Disobedience,"[3] and Leo Kuper's *Passive Resistance in South Africa*.[4] But these have scarcely scratched the surface of this large area of social behavior.

Beginnings are being made in correcting this disproportionate inattention. A number of Master's and Doctor's theses have been or are being written in the field. Steps have been taken in formulating research problems. For example, Professor Arne Næss has offered a systematization of Gandhian methods of conflict behavior in which the normative power of the system rests on only one norm: "Act in group struggle in a way conducive to long-term universal reduction of violence;" the validity of every other statement in the system is seen as testable by social-science techniques.[5] Irving L. Janis and Daniel Katz, after examining studies in this field by Næss and others, prepared a paper on the types of variables that might yield pertinent data and samples of the kind of hypotheses which could be empirically tested.[6] They are almost entirely concerned with theoretical analysis and empirical testing to make possible an evaluation of the social and psychological consequences of various ethical means of social action contained in Næss' analysis of the Gandhian ethical system. These consequences refer to the psychological effects of such means on the respective groups, to the changes in attitudes by third parties, and to the achievement or nonachievement of the avowed objectives.

There are important areas for research on *satyagraha* and other types of nonviolent resistance which Janis and Katz do not touch upon, or do not discuss in detail. For example, there is the area of psychological and sociological mechanisms of nonviolent struggle and that of analysis of such conflicts with a view to obtaining optimal future operation of the methods. In addition, there is the area of exploration of the long-term social consequences of the use of nonviolent action instead of either violent conflict or passive acquiescence, and of a comparison between long-term and

* This particular discussion is on the basis of the literature at the time of writing in 1959.

short-term consequences. The conditions contributing to the substitution of nonviolent for violent conflict ought also to be explored, including examination of the limitations of such methods. Dr. Bondurant's study demonstrates that there is a large area for theoretical analysis in light of the Gandhian and other nonviolent methods of sociopolitical action; existing social and political theory has largely been formulated without considering them. Dr. Bondurant's analysis of *satyagraha* and the means-end problem, for example, ought to be followed up by further related studies on the subject. Her analysis has implications for a revision of the theoretical power of the means-end scheme as it exists in contemporary social science. On this revision, either its theoretical power is likely to be much diminished as compared with that which it enjoys at the present time in much social science or the scheme will be radically changed.

Katz, writing on "Consistent Reactive Participation of Group Members and Reduction of Intergroup Conflict"[7] has pointed out the way in which the lack of effective power to make and implement decisions leads to apathy and how apathy in turn leaves the leaders, without check on their power drives, free to lead their people more readily into violent conflicts. The point on which Katz is silent, however, is *how* the group members are to participate effectively in making social decisions and checking power drives. C. Wright Mills has pointed out some of the realities of the present American power structure which operate to negate the traditional machinery of democratic control.[8] These traditional means being largely blocked, it may be necessary to explore others that are likely to restore or establish effective popular control over major social decisions, especially those related to war and peace. It is here that Joan Bondurant's call for an examination of *satyagraha* as a technique by which individual citizens can meet some of the weaknesses of liberal democracy becomes most relevant.

Satyagraha, unlike the more conventional political approaches in practice, operates from the assumption that the genuine source of social and political power lies in fact at the grass roots and not at the pinnacle of the State or ruling elite. It is the cooperation and obedience of the subjects which permit elites to wield power. Hence their power can be curtailed by the withdrawal of such cooperation and obedience. Accordingly, on the question of how to achieve social and political changes, *satyagraha* differs fundamentally from those political philosophies which accept the need for a seizure of power (whether by violence, majority decision, or other means) in order to use the State to effect the desired change.

The theory of social and political power basic to *satyagraha*— the theory of "voluntary servitude"—was absorbed by Gandhi even before he read Tolstoy and Thoreau.* Tolstoy had been influenced in this view by an essay, "*Discours de la servitude volontaire,*" by the sixteenth century writer Estienne de la Boëtie. This concept is present with variations in the writings of thinkers as widely divergent as the Greek Stoics, Gustav Landauer, Niccolo Machiavelli, William Godwin, and even Adolph Hitler. In an age when mankind is threatened both by powerful tyrannies and by the very means which had commonly been used to abolish them, a serious investigation is merited of the validity and implications of this theory which is basic to *satyagraha*.

A SUBSTITUTE FOR VIOLENCE?

Without necessarily intending to do so, Dr. Bondurant has, in this reviewer's view, pointed to the solution of a problem which has long plagued social scientists interested in research for promoting peace: on what problems and phenomena, if any, should research concentrate in order best to use available resources and make the greatest contribution? Parsons,[9] Shils,[10] Merton,[11] Coser,[12] and others have discussed the nature of functional alternatives, sometimes called "functional substitutes" or "functional equivalents." Is not this theory applicable to methods of social conflict as well as to other forms of social action?

Merton has pointed out that, "just as the same item may have multiple functions, so may the same function be diversely fulfilled by alternative items."[13] Relating the analysis of functional alternatives to conscious efforts to produce social change, Merton offers the following as "a basic theorem":

---

* It is also possible that Gandhi encountered the theory in other forms while studying law in London. For a presentation of Gandhi's insights into this theory, see Chapter Three.

> . . .*[A]ny attempt to eliminate an existing social structure without providing adequate alternative structures for fulfilling the functions previously fulfilled by the abolished organization is doomed to failure.*[14]

Violent conflict, including war, seems to have served the function, among others, of providing a means of conducting acute conflicts which have not proved resolvable by talking, negotiation, conciliation, or compromise of principles. A basic element in conscious efforts to eliminate major instances of violent social conflict would thus seem to be the substitution in its place of a nonviolent technique of conflict, assuming the existence of a technique that is socially adequate.

Students of *satyagraha* and other types of nonviolent action—Ranganath R. Diwakar, Homer Jack, Nirmal Kumar Bose, Krishnalal Shridharani, Gopi Nath Dhawan, Richard Gregg, for example—have repeatedly claimed that this technique does in fact constitute a socially adequate functional substitute for violent conflict. Dr. Bondurant quotes Prime Minister Jawaharlal Nehru, who referred to the "new dynamic that Gandhi brought into the political and social field." He continued: "I feel more and more convinced that it offers us some key to understanding and to the proper resolution of conflict" (p. x).

Dr. Bondurant herself, although not specifically referring to the theory of functional alternatives, says that the Gandhian dialectical approach "provides dynamic control on the field of action through the fashioning of techniques for the creative resolution of conflict" (p. 199). She writes:

> . . .[T]here is rapidly developing a demand hitherto neglected by social and political theory. This is the demand for solutions to the problem of conflict—not for theoretical systems of end structure aimed at ultimately eliminating conflict, but for ways of conducting conflict when it arises: ways which are constructive and not destructive. Such a demand must be met by a theory of process and of means, and not of further concern for structure, for pattern, and for ends. Basic to such a theory is a philosophy of action [p. v].

> The problem of human conflict is perhaps the most fundamental problem of all time. . . . This essay on satyagraha and political thought is an effort to focus attention on yet another direction in which solutions might be sought [pp. vii–viii].

There seems to be sufficient evidence—and Dr. Bondurant's study provides part of it—to justify focusing research on examining whether or not *satyagraha* and other forms of nonviolent action are in fact an adequate functional substitute for violent conflict, and, if so, under what conditions this is true, how nonviolent confict operates, and related questions.

The time has passed when nonviolent methods of action could be viewed by intelligent people as "esoteric," "typically Indian," or "irrelevant" to the modern world. A scientific attitude requires an impartial study of these phenomena and an examination of their possible application. Dr. Bondurant's book is an illustration from a particular discipline of the richness of the new field. Unfortunately, in this chapter, the reviewer has not been able to discuss all the aspects of this study which merit attention, but a review, or even a review article, is never a substitute for reading the book itself. *Conquest of Violence* is a "must" for all interested in social research to promote peace. No sociologist, psychologist, political scientist, or social and political philosopher ought to miss it.

NOTES TO CHAPTER FOUR

1. Clarence Marsh Case, **Non-violent Coercion: A Study in Methods of Social Pressure** (New York: Century Co., 1923).
2. Krishnalal Shridharani, **War Without Violence: A Study of Gandhi's Method and Its Accomplishments** (New York: Harcourt, Brace and Co., 1939 and London: Victor Gollancz, 1939).
3. David Spitz, "Democracy and the Problem of Civil Disobedience," **American Political Science Review,** vol. XLVII, no. 2 (June, 1954), pp.386–403.
4. Leo Kuper, **Passive Resistance in South Africa** (New Haven: Yale University Press, 1957).
5. Arne Næss, "A Systematization of Gandhian Ethics of Conflict Resolution," **Journal of Conflict Resolution,** vol. II, no. 2 (1958), pp.140–155.
6. Irving L. Janis and Daniel Katz, "The Reduction of Intergroup Hostility: Research Problems and Hypotheses," **Journal of Conflict Resolution,** vol. III, no. 1 (March, 1959), pp. 85–100.
7. Daniel Katz, "Consistent Reactive Participation of Group Members and Reduction of Intergroup Conflict," **Journal of Conflict Resolution,** vol. III, no. 1 (March, 1959), pp. 28–40.
8. C. Wright Mills, **The Causes of World War Three** (New York: Simon & Schuster, 1958).
9. Talcott Parsons, **Essays in Sociological Theory, Pure and Applied** (Glencoe, Ill.: Free Press, 1949).

10. Talcott Parsons and Edward A. Shils, **Toward a General Theory of Action** (Cambridge, Mass.: Harvard University Press, 1951).
11. Robert K. Merton, **Social Theory and Social Structure** (Glencoe, Ill.: Free Press, 1949).
12. Lewis A. Coser, **The Social Functions of Conflict** (New York: Free Press, 1956, and London: Routledge & Kegan Paul, 1956).
13. Merton, **Social Theory and Social Structure**, p. 35.
14. Ibid., p. 79.

The original version of this article appeared under the title "A Review of Joan V. Bondurant's *Conquest of Violence: The Gandhian Philosophy of Conflict*" by Gene Sharp published in *Journal of Conflict Resolution,* vol 3, no. 4, December 1959, pp. 401–410 and is reprinted herewith by permission of the Publisher, Sage Publications, Inc.

5

The Theory of Gandhi's Constructive Program

Whenever people conclude that their social order must be either reformed or replaced in order to meet human needs more adequately, the problem arises as how best to bring about the change. In the past at least four approaches to this problem have been proposed:

(1) Reliance solely upon changing individuals, often including a personal withdrawal from the social evil, and sometimes attempts to influence others (including those in positions of authority) by speeches, letters, conversations, admonitions, articles, and books;

(2) Reliance on "good works" including social work and programs for the relief of human suffering, without a serious attempt to produce major institutional changes;

(3) Reliance on attempts to reform the social order gradually (including political and economic institutions) through the State by legislation, executive orders, and judicial decisions, and similar means, (sometimes accompanied by support for cooperatives, for example, which are relatively independent of the State); and

(4) Reliance upon an extensive program of institutional changes to be effected through the State following the seizure of power by the group believing in such a policy (for example, a Communist Party).

THE INADEQUACIES OF THE TRADITIONAL APPROACHES

Each of these traditional approaches, however, has certain inadequacies. Individual change and example, the first approach, has a powerful effect upon others and must be viewed as important in a balanced program of social change. It must be recognized, however, that much of what is regarded as evil by such persons is embodied in powerful social institutions which aid both its continuation and growth. A program of dealing with such institutions would have to be found if the evil is to be removed. Even if people believing in this approach do not recognize the need for changing institutions when they still are few in numbers, it would force itself to their attention when their numbers grew significantly larger. They would then have to face the problem of developing alternative social institutions if they were not as a group to support the continuation of the evil they rejected. They would also at that point have to face the problem of how to dispose of , or combat, the old institutions which violated their principles.

It is important to relieve human misery, need, and unhappiness. This has been the object of social work and relief activities, the second approach we have listed. We need to recognize, however, that such programs ignore the institutions which often are in large measure responsible for the creation of the needs in the first place. If left to function as they have previously done, they will create misery and need more rapidly than programs of social work and relief can hope to relieve them.

The third aproach, reliance upon a gradual reform of existing social institutions by the intervention of the State through legislation, executive orders or judicial decisions, is the policy generally practiced in liberal democratic countries. These measures of reform have contributed to improved social conditions without, however, making basic social changes. These improvements have been accompanied by the preservation of political democracy and civil liberties relatively well, certainly as compared with totalitarian countries. However, that preservation ought not to blind us to some associated long-term dangers.

The growing reliance upon the State in social and economic matters inevitably leads to more and more centralization of power within the society. Decisions are made increasingly by officials, experts, and heads of bureaus, resulting in less genuinely popular control. As such reforms continue, there is a progressive reduction of local control and an increase in centralization. In those countries —such as in Scandinavia—where independent efforts, such as the cooperative movement, have been strong, freedom has a more real content than where the State has been relied upon more exclusively. The general trend of reliance on the State to achieve reforms has neither produced basic social changes, nor contributed to self-reliance and the diffusion of power within the society.

The reliance upon the State to effect major institutional changes in a relatively brief space of time—as has been the case in the Soviet Union—has led to extreme centralization of power over the whole social, economic, and political order. This fourth approach has been associated with an absence of political democracy and civil liberties. Instead of the new order putting more real power and control into the workers' and peasants' hands, such power has been further taken away, and given to centralized bureaus and other organs of the State. The opportunities for those who do not support either the objectives or the methods of the State to seek a change of policies by legal means are virtually nonexistent. The "new order" produced by reliance on the State to effect the revolution has thus resulted in a new and more powerful master.

Another criticism of reliance upon the State to effect either reforms or major institutional changes is that advocates of change cannot demonstrate in action their program until they are able to control the State. Furthermore, the persons most qualified to lead social change do not always win the elections. In making vast social changes it is essential to experiment, suspend judgement during the experimentation, and willingly learn from the results. A large scale

State program cannot provide the diversified social experimentation required to learn the best means.

AN ALTERNATIVE CONCEPTION

Since each of these four means has proven to be inadequate, and often worse, the question arises as to whether there is an alternative aproach. Gandhi sought to develop another option. He assumed that a just social order characterized by self-reliance and freedom must be produced by a movement with those same characteristics. Gandhi therefore developed the idea of creating a new social order through a voluntary constructive program functioning independently of the State and other institutions of the old order. His efforts were experimental; he would be the last to call them adequate. His thinking about the theory of the constructive program was only suggestive of a direction; he was never a theoretician. Yet it does seem a direction which deserves a serious effort to understand it and explore its problems and possibilities. Perhaps the thinking upon which it is based can best be made clear by a story:

If a person's house is in dangerous condition, inadequate, and its foundations are shattered, then he or she needs to build a new one. Mere patchwork on it will not be sufficient. Simply tearing down the old building is not enough. Nor will an appeal to someone to abandon a dangerous structure be heeded if there is nowhere else to live. It is difficult to persuade the person who has no safe bedroom to sleep in the snow rather than remain in the old room which might—but only *might*—collapse in a storm.

Instead, while the old house still exists, the wise person will lay the foundation of the new one, raise the framework and walls, lay the roof, and then complete one room after another, perhaps even reusing suitable materials and fixtures from the old house in the new structure.

The person will then have a place to live during the construction (assuming none other is available). As the new structure rises, and is ready for occupation, it is possible to withdraw from section after section of the old one, which finally stands deserted and unneeded. The new improved way to meet the need for shelter has made it possible to abandon the old structure.

No longer of use, the old weak structure can be dismantled. The new, strong house remains, still needing refinement and finishing touches, but structurally capable of providing safe shelter and withstanding what storms may come.

BUILDING A NEW SOCIAL ORDER

An advocate of basic nonviolent social change—such as Gandhi—claims that we face a somewhat comparable situation in opposing an old inadequate social order which is dangerous to the development of human personality and indeed even to the continued existence of humanity. A new social order needs to be built, that advocate believes. The old one is no longer acceptable. But the people must have a genuine alternative order.

A comprehensive program of nonviolent social change is viewed as having three main parts: (1) improvement of individuals in their own lives and ways of living; (2) a constructive program to begin building a new social order even as the old one still exists; and (3) the practice of various forms of nonviolent action against specific social evils. It is a constructive program with which we are here concerned.

The nonviolent civilization is envisaged by its advocates as one in which most of the services performed by the State and large corporations will be carried out by cooperatives and voluntary associations with decentralized control. Many of these institutions can be begun now, it is reasoned, alongside the old structures. To the extent that these new institutions succeed, they may gradually replace the former system. Or, when the advantages of the new ways are demonstrated, the more flexible of the old institutions may be changed, adopting the new orientation.

The constructive program is an attempt to build the beginnings of the new social order while the old society still exists. The nonviolent revolutionary—which Gandhi claimed to be—thus begins to build the new even while struggling against the old. One does not need to wait for the capture of the State machinery to begin. The constructive program has been described as the scaffolding upon which the structure of the new society will be built.

ASPECTS OF THE INDIAN CONSTRUCTIVE PROGRAM

Accordingly, Gandhi developed a constructive program specifically designed to meet India's needs, one which reflected his personal outlook. This program included the following seventeen aspects:

1) **Communal unity:** Working to establish unity of the various religious and ethnic groups in India, and the removal of the prejudices and segregation among them.

2) **Removal of untouchability:** Gandhi called for the abolition of "this blot and curse upon Hinduism."

3) **Prohibition:** The removal of "the curse of intoxicants and narcotics" was to be accomplished through the help of medical people, acts of loving service and "recreation booths where the tired labourer will rest his limbs, get healthy and cheap refreshments, and find suitable games."

4) **Khadi:** This hand-spun and hand-woven cloth symbolized to Gandhi the "unity of Indian humanity, ...its economic freedom and equality." Its village production helped decentralize production and distribution, enabled the poor and unemployed to help themselves, and helped to free India from foreign economic exploitation and control by ending dependence on foreign manufacturers.

5) **Other village industries:** These include such essentials in the village economy as hand-grinding, hand-pounding, soap-making, paper-making, match-making, tanning, and oil-pressing. ". . .[W]e will develop a new national taste in keeping with the vision of a new India in which pauperism, starvation and idleness will be unknown." Gandhi claimed that nonviolent life necessarily implies decentralized cottage industries and self-sufficient and self-sustaining rural communities.

6) **Village sanitation:** "A sense of national or social sanitation is not a virtue among us," Gandhi declared, urging positive action to remedy this defect.

7) **New or basic education:** "Basic education links the children, whether of the cities or the villages, to all that is best

and lasting in India. It develops both the body and mind, and keeps the child rooted to the soil with a glorious vision of the future in the realization of which he or she begins to take his or her share from the very commencement of his or her career in school."

8) **Adult education:** "My adult education means ... true political education of the adult by word of mouth ... Side by side. ... will be the literary education ... this ... only points the way."

9) **Women:** "In a plan of life based on non-violence, woman has as much a right to shape her own destiny as man has to shape his ... rules of social conduct must be framed by mutual co-operation and consultation."

10) **Education in health and hygiene:** *"Mens sana in corpore sano* [a healthy mind in a healthy body] is perhaps the first law for humanity." He emphasized several laws of health and hygiene such as pure thoughts, fresh air, balance between bodily and mental work, good posture, neatness, cleanliness, and simple food.

11) **National language:** For discourse among all Indians speaking diverse languages a national language was needed, preferably one which the largest numbers of Indians already knew and which others could easily learn. This was Hindi, also called Urdu when written with the Urdu characters, and its use was urged by Gandhi.

12) **Economic equality:** This Gandhi called "the master key to non-violent Independence." This included, according to Gandhi, "abolishing the eternal conflict between capital and labour," "leveling down of the few rich" and "levelling up of the semi-starved naked millions." He stressed the idea of trusteeship. Economic equality, he concluded, "has to be built up brick by brick by corporate self-effort."

13) **Peasantry:** Those 80 percent of the Indian people must be helped, but not used for power politics.

14) **Labor:** Gandhi advocated the establishment of more labor unions like the Ahmedabad Labour Union, whose strikes were "wholly non-violent" in attitude and action.

15) **Hill tribes:** Gandhi advocated working with these people to help them. Such work would not be only humanitarian but would make a contribution to the national welfare.

16) **Lepers:** These people were as much a part of society as anyone. Their neglect was heartless. If India were truly pulsing with a new life, all the lepers and beggars would be cared for.

17) **Students:** While calling them "the hope of the future," Gandhi regretted their general lack of concern with non-violence and offered a list of eleven suggestions for improving their lives, education and contribution to their people.*

These seventeen items were based on Gandhi's interpretation of the needs of India and the means of meeting those needs. This program was not intended for automatic adoption in other countries, where very different constructive programs might be developed.

CARRYING OUT THE CONSTRUCTIVE PROGRAM

The constructive program, in Gandhi's opinion, was to be carried out in a spirit of service. The volunteers who stimulate participation in the work in India were to serve as full time volunteers, receiving only sufficient income to meet their barest needs. Their living was to be extremely simple and on the level of voluntary poverty.

In a sense the constructive program was a social implementation of Gandhi's essentially individualistic philosophy. He felt that to bring about basic changes, people should emphasize quality rather than numbers. Workers for social change should concentrate their efforts on a particular locality, as a town or village, and there on certain individuals. Such work would leave no room for hypocrisy, violence, or compulsion, because it is entirely voluntary and often difficult, requiring undramatic day-by-day efforts.

* All quotations above are from M.K. Gandhi, "Constructive Programme: Its Meaning and Place," (pamphlet; 32 pp. Ahmedabad: Navajivan Publishing House, 1948).

The constructive program work, Gandhi insisted, was to be undertaken for its own sake and not with the aim of exploiting the people by gaining their sympathies and thus control over them. Such work would establish living contact with large numbers of people. It would convince one's opponents of the peaceful intentions and sincerity of the people participating in the constructive work. The work would elevate the status of the masses, and also show them something of the potency of the way of nonviolent social change for the ending of exploitation. The work was also intended to inspire the people with faith and strengthen their determination. The contact with the people during the constructive program work would prove invaluable in times of direct action.

The various aspects of the constructive program were conceived to form an inter-knit program of social reconstruction, rather than their being simply piecemeal efforts at reconstruction. This program was seen to be unified by the fundamental principles of the new society and by the interrelatedness of the specific tasks. By operating under an overall plan—subject to revision if needed as work proceeded—it would be possible to proceed with its specific components so that they would contribute to an integrated whole.

CONSTRUCTIVE PROGRAM AND NONVIOLENT ACTION

Constructive program work, Gandhi recommended, generally ought to proceed, accompany, and follow nonviolent action. Such work was seen to be the constructive aspect; the nonviolent action was the cleansing aspect. He also felt that the constructive program was more important than direct action and regretted the fact that it had never received the full backing in action of many Indians, including the Indian National Congress. Gandhi argued that, theoretically, if the effort of the whole nation were secured for the constructive program, nonviolent action would not be needed. However, in application that situation would not occur and direct action would still be needed. In any program which envisages the building of a new society, opposition can be expected to arise at various stages and to specific parts of the program, Gandhi argued. It is then necessary to take direct action to remove the obstacle to enable the constructive work to proceed.

Such work also served, he believed, as a preparation and training of the individuals for participation in nonviolent action. By doing constructive work the nonviolent volunteer would become trained and disciplined. New recruits would be trained, tested, and strengthened, and would develop discipline in the course of the hard everyday work involved in the constructive program.

Gandhi felt that training was necessary for civil disobedience, just as it was for violent revolt. Training for violent revolt meant learning the use of military weapons; training for civil disobedience meant the constructive program. "My handling of civil disobedience without the constructive programme would be like a paralysed hand attempting to lift a spoon." He recognized that previous constructive program work would not always be needed for local specific direct action where the common grievances are tangible, and limited to a specific locality. However, Gandhi was convinced that such work was necessary whenever one sought to achieve such large and vague aims as "independence" or "a new society."

Many questions could be raised in relation to the theory of Gandhi's constructive program; its potentialities and limitations; and the role of past constructive program work in India. Those deserve careful thought and investigation. Also, exploratory analysis may be merited on development of constructive programs based on this broad theory for other countries including those in the industrialized West. The limited purpose of this chapter has been to present the basic conception of the constructive program as Gandhi saw it.

6

Gandhi's Evaluation of Indian Nonviolent Action

Opinions about Gandhi the man, his philosophy, and his political activities are easy to find and vary widely. Gandhi has been regarded as a great independence leader and also a tool of the British; as a Mahatma and also a shrewd political manipulator; as a muddling fool in politics and also an accomplished strategist and political innovator. His "nonviolence" and its role in the Indian independence movement are considered by some as completely successful, by others as total failure, and by still others as once useful but now irrelevant.

Unfortunately, these opinions are rarely based upon deep knowledge of the subject, careful analysis, and critical judgement. It is now time for serious scholars to undertake careful research and evaluation of Gandhi, his beliefs, political technique, and actions. These studies are important, not only for Indian history, biographical studies, and political philosophy, but also for facing the problems of our contemporary world of unrest, conflict, oppression, and violence.

In examining Gandhi's work, it is essential to be familiar with his own evaluations both of the "nonviolence" which he preached and also of that which he led in local and national uprisings. It is important to know his own views of the merits and achievements of the Indian experiments in nonviolent political struggle. This chapter is focused only on these evaluations and views.

It is widely believed that Gandhi finally concluded that the only worthwhile "nonviolence" was that which was based on faith and religious belief, and that Indian nonviolent action had been a failure. Such simplistic summaries of his views could impede fresh scholarly examination and evaluation of Gandhi's work, philosophy, and accomplishments. This chapter will show that these representations are distortions of his own complex evaluations. Here we have two limited purposes: 1) to establish Gandhi's own conclusions about what type of "nonviolence" was worth developing and 2) to establish his own evaluations of the nonviolent campaigns which he led or inspired in South Africa and India.[1] Last, we will critically examine some of his own comments and observations.

GANDHI'S CHANGING VIEWS

The usual—and inaccurate—version of Gandhi's changing views on the relationship between the principle and the technique reads roughly like this: In the early stage of his career Gandhi advocated the adoption of nonviolent action as a practical means of struggle, to achieve certain objectives by people who would otherwise have used violence or passively submitted. This expedient nonviolence Gandhi often called the "nonviolence of the weak." Later, however, especially from the 1930s on, the argument continues, Gandhi became dissatisfied with the results of this; instead, he then emphasized the importance of accepting nonviolence as a comprehensive principle, which he often called "the nonviolence of the brave," or "the nonviolence of the strong." It seems quite simple. It is therefore often concluded that Gandhi's final view of how to relate nonviolence as a moral principle to its application in society was roughly approximate to that of Western pacifists (with the proviso that believers in principled nonviolence ought to seek actively to improve their society).

This conclusion is quite in error, however. Gandhi's views of the problem of how to relate the nonviolent ethic to social and political realities were far more complex than the above version of them would suggest. He often seemed torn in two or more directions at the same time, and some of his statements were in clear contradiction to others. Although he was dissatisfied with his experiments in nonviolent action, Gandhi neither concluded that in the past he ought not to have made them, nor that in the future he ought to renounce political nonviolent action in favor of a "fellowship of believers." If, then, the usual simple version of Gandhi's views on this problem is erroneous and distorts Gandhi's own views, we need to examine in detail Gandhi's thinking on these matters.

SOME POSSIBLE RELEVANT FACTORS

When evaluating Gandhi's views in this field it may help to keep them within the perspective of his world-view and his political life. A few specific factors are especially important here.

The first is Gandhi's growing sense of alienation from the course of political events as independence approached and in the months afterwards. This alienation stemmed in part from: the offer by the Indian National Congress to fight militarily on the side of the British during World War II in a bargain for independence; the continued communal tensions; the Congress' rejection of his concept of national defense by nonviolent resistance coupled with an increase in the military budget and military preparations before and after full independence; the plight of the peasants; the development of Western-type industrialization; the partition of the country into India and Pakistan; and the Hindu-Muslim riots.

Second, in reacting to this situation Gandhi became hypercritical of himself and of the movement which he had led. He sought to justify this reaction with his own philosophy of non-violence, which began and ended by self-examination and self-criticism. This he applied both to himself and to others. Instead of concentrating on condemnation of the brutality of the military in trying to stop the riots, for example, Gandhi felt that the people ought to examine their own behavior in the riots.[2] "The golden rule in life," he said on another occasion, "was to exaggerate one's own faults and belittle those of others. That was the only way to self-purification."[3] In commenting on Indian political events, Gandhi emphasized his own shortcomings and felt his personal inadequacy acutely:

> It is as likely as not that a fitter instrument will be used to carry it [the divine purpose] out and that I was good enough to represent a weak nation, not a strong one. May it not be that a man purer, more courageous, more far-seeing is wanted for the final purpose?[4]

Gandhi's strong dislike of anything which might be understood as hypocrisy must be kept in mind as the third relevant factor. Thus Gandhi, in 1946, pressed for the removal from an Indian National Congress policy document of the words "peaceful and legitimate" from the description of the means Congress would use, because he thought others no longer accepted such limits.[5] Sometimes Gandhi applied the term hypocrisy to behavior which was not necessarily hypocritical. During the very periods of his career in which he argued for the adoption of nonviolent struggle as a practical substitute for violence to achieve Indian political independence, Gandhi at times equated expediency with hypocrisy and therefore rejected it. He made this equation especially during the anguish he felt at the course of events taking place in India in the 1940s. It was in 1946 that he sought to remove the words "peaceful and legitimate" from the Congress document: "To take the name of non-violence when there is sword in your heart, is not only hypocritical and dishonest but cowardly."[6] Such circumstances do not, however, explain similar statements which he made in 1926:

> Time for expedient non-violence passed away long ago.

> A sense of self-respect disdains all expedience.

> Let there be no cant about non-violence. It is not like a garment to be put on and off at will. Its seat is in the heart, and it must be an inseparable part of our very being.[7]

Another factor should be kept in mind when evaluating Gandhi's thinking about expedient and principled nonviolence. In his distress and sense of failure, he may well have been more inclined to accept the criticisms of Western pacifists at least in a modified form than he would have at other times. Gandhi's whole approach differed radically from Western pacifism, and the pacifists clearly recognized this. Not only did Gandhi's attitude to war differ sharply from simple conscientious objection or war resistance,[8] but his attempt to apply nonviolence in mass political struggle seemed to some pacifists dangerous because he accepted the need for conflict and struggle. This attempt also offended many pacifists because Gandhi did not simply seek converts to the nonviolent ethic but tried to apply nonviolent action with the participation of multitudes who would never share that total belief. When things seemed to be going well, it must have been easier for Gandhi to dismiss the pacifists' criticisms. But when his use of expedient nonviolence was followed by undesirable events, Gandhi must have wondered whether the pacifist critics might after all be right. Once during this period he publicly mentioned the earlier criticisms by pacifists. In late 1947, in a talk with students, *Harijan,* Gandhi's own small weekly paper, reported: "Gandhiji then proceeded to say that it was indeed true that many English friends had warned him that the so-called non-violent non-cooperation of India was not really non-violent."[9] This does not establish anything substantive, but does suggest a possible association between the criticisms made by pacifists and some of Gandhi's more sweeping statements on the problem.

IMPOSSIBLE PERFECTION AND CORPORATE STRENGTH

A last general factor which should be kept in mind is that Gandhi neither demanded perfect nonviolence nor thought that it was possible to attain. When asked in 1940, "Does anyone know true nonviolence?" Gandhi replied:

Nobody knows it, for nobody can practise perfect non-violence.[10]

Perfect non-violence is impossible so long as we exist physically . . . but we have to endeavour every moment of our lives.[11]

Gandhi insisted that although imperfection and inconsistencies were inevitable, one's duty was to strive constantly toward the least imperfection and the least inconsistency.

> Let us be sure of our ideal. We shall ever fail to realize it, but should never cease to strive for it.[12]

> ...[B]etween the ideal and practice there must always be an unbridgeable gulf. The ideal will cease to be one if it becomes possible to realize it.[13]

Inevitably then, the exponent of nonviolence would have to operate in the ordinary world of human beings; such a person would have to choose as best he or she could the most appropriate means to serve one's fellow human beings and fulfill one's principles; in this choice, one would have always to operate with a degree of inconsistency and imperfection. This difficulty was more severe for Gandhi than for exponents of other types of principled nonviolence, such as the Christian nonresistant sects, for Gandhi insisted that nonviolence was not to be simply an individual virtue, nor even that of a small group of believers.

Nonviolence for Gandhi was not only personal but also social and political. Even in his moments of sharpest anguish he never altered this view.

> Non-violence is not an individual virtue but a course of spiritual and political conduct both for the individual and the community.[14]

> Non-violence is not meant to be practised by the individual only. It can be and has to be practised by society as a whole.[15]

> That non-violence which only an individual can use is not of much use in terms of society. Man is a social being.[16]

While Gandhi believed that "pure" nonviolent individuals could wield immense power which could make organized mass nonviolent struggle unnecessary, he was also convinced that the community as a whole ought to learn how to use nonviolent action. This would make the community conscious of its collective strength and enable it to solve problems through its own efforts. True, one perfect *satyagrahi* could "defy the whole might of an unjust empire ... and lay the foundation for that empire's fall or regeneration."[17] Organized action was theoretically not needed, *if* a perfect *satyagrahi* existed. "A man or woman who is saturated with *ahimsa* [nonviolence] has only to will a thing and it happens."[18] Such a perfect *satyagrahi* was, however, in Gandhi's view not possible, and even if such a person were, the greatest utility which could be made of such powers would be to educate the masses in *satyagraha*.[19]

> In this age of democracy . . . it is essential that desired results are achieved by the collective effort of the people. It will no doubt be good to achieve an objective through the effort of a supremely powerful individual, but it can never make the community conscious of its corporate strength.[20]

> Anything that millions can do together becomes charged with a unique power.[21]

In response to critics who blamed Gandhi for not personally going to Sindh in 1942 to resolve a dangerous situation, Gandhi wrote:

> I have not conceived my mission to be that of a knight-errant wandering everywhere to deliver people from difficult situations. My humble occupation has been to show people how they can solve their own difficulties.

> If I had adopted the role my critic has suggested, I would have helped people to become parasites. Therefore it is well that I have not trained myself to defend others. I shall be satisfied if at my death it could be said of me that I had devoted the best part of my life to showing the way to become self-reliant and cultivate the capacity to defend oneself under every conceivable circumstance. My correspondent has committed the grave error of thinking that my mission is to deliver people from calamities. That is an arrogation only claimed by dictators.[22]

MASS NONVIOLENT ACTION AFFIRMED

Gandhi's insistence that his important contribution was that of offering people a technique with which they could cope themselves with their social and political problems was not reversed when he became dissatisfied with the Indian practice of nonviolent action and when he increasingly emphasized the importance of the "non-violence of the brave." Looking at the surface of some of his statements, one would expect that his conclusion was that mass application of nonviolent action was either itself the fault or impossible to achieve with sufficient quality. The dates of some of the above statements clearly contradict that interpretation however. In fact Gandhi explicitly refuted the view that the riots brought into question "the efficacy of non-violence in matters political. What was the people's fight against the foreign power, if it was not a political matter?"[23] In facing the difficulties of applying nonviolent means in the real world, Gandhi therefore declined to follow the earlier examples of believers in some types of principled nonviolence who had attempted to withdraw from the problems of social and political life. Instead, he confirmed his confidence in the role of collective nonviolent popular action to solve problems.

Not only was Gandhi convinced that people *ought* to be able to help themselves by using the technique of *satyagraha*, but he also believed that the masses of people were *capable* of doing so. Much of Gandhi's political life is a testimony to that conviction, but he also made the view explicit in his speeches and writings. For example, in 1934 he was asked whether he thought the masses could remain nonviolent in thought and action despite provocations. His questioner suggested that an individual could attain such a standard, but not the masses. Gandhi replied:

> This is a strange question . . . , for the entire course of our nonviolent fight bears testimony to the fact that wherever violence has broken out it has broken out not on the part of the masses but . . . was manipulated by the intellectuals . . . There is no *prima facie* reason why under non-violence the mass, if disciplined, should be incapable of showing the discipline which in organized warfare a fighting force normally does . . . But . . . non-violence in action cannot be sustained unless it goes hand in hand with nonviolence in thought.[24]

Gandhi had by this time already begun to emphasize the "nonviolence of the brave." In fact within seven weeks of the above statement, on 17 September 1934, he announced his withdrawal from the Indian National Congress. ". . . [T]here is a growing and vital difference of outlook between many Congressmen and myself."[25] Very prominent among these differences, Gandhi listed the divergence between his own and the Congressmen's approach to nonviolence and civil resistance.[26] Later he stated that he severed the connection with the Congress then because he considered himself "a confirmed representative of *ahimsa* . . . ."[27] The 1934 affirmation of the possibility of mass nonviolent action for political ends was therefore made at the very time when he was acutely dissatisfied with the Congress' attitude toward, and practice of, nonviolent action, and only shortly before his withdrawal from the Indian National Congress. This indicates that his desire for an improved quality of nonviolence did *not* mean the rejection of mass nonviolent action. This is confirmed by a similar statement in 1939. Gandhi was asked:

> How do you think that the masses can practise non-violence, when we know that they are all prone to anger, hate, ill-will? They are known to fight for the most trivial things.

Gandhi replied: "They are, and yet I think they can practise non-violence for the common good." He cited as examples of mass action without ill will the instance of women collecting illegal salt during the 1930–31 independence campaign and the behavior of the peasants in Champaran in 1917.[28] In neither case did the *satyagrahis* have any real intellectual understanding of the nonviolent means. "But their belief in their leaders was genuine, and that was enough."[29]

MORAL PROBLEMS OF INACTION

Today it is often forgotten that Gandhi did not begin his political career with a fully developed outlook or political program. Both his political philosophy and his political technique were, to a considerable degree, worked out and developed in response to immediate social needs and in the fire of political struggle. Gandhi's version of the technique of nonviolent action, *satyagraha*, was born in the midst of the conflict between the Indian minority and the South African government. There was for Gandhi no simple tug between the nonviolent ethic and the imperfections of an individual seeking to live by it. He also faced social and political problems and the need for effective means of struggle.[30]

Gandhi was confronted with both the ethical problems of *acting* in such a situation, and also those of *not* acting. He often found the latter to be more dangerous. Gandhi resolved that he must act, that the victims of the injustice or oppression ought to be offered means of action to right the wrong, and that such means on ethical and practical grounds ought to be nonviolent. Nor could he wait until he had converted the oppressed group, or even a significant section of it, to a belief in nonviolence as a moral principle. Had he waited—as he later said—his attempt to relate nonviolence to politics would never have been initiated, and waiting for conversions to the ethic among the oppressed would likely have resulted in passivity or violence.

"NONVIOLENCE AS A POLICY"

Gandhi's approach could be described as opposing spiritual strength to physical might, he thought. But had he presented it solely in those terms it would have gained few adherents. Consequently, he did not wait, but countered India's feelings of powerlessness and paralysis "before the machine-guns, the tanks and the aeroplanes of the English," with a practical strategy of noncooperation. If applied by enough people it could bring deliverance from "the crushing weight of British injustice," he said in 1920.[31]

Gandhi at times explained his advocacy of limited nonviolence for achieving political objectives in those terms. At other times, as in 1925, he explained it partly in terms of his own spiritual imperfections:

> I have not the capacity for preaching universal non-violence to the country. I preach, therefore, non-violence restricted to the purpose of winning our freedom and therefore perhaps for preaching the regulation of international relations by non-violent means. But my incapacity must not be mistaken for that of the doctrine of non-violence. I see it with my intellect . . . My heart grasps it. But I have not yet the [spiritual] attainments of preaching universal non-violence with effect.[32]

Gandhi called this nonviolent action adopted for limited political objectives "non-violence as a policy."[33] "A policy may be changed, a creed cannot. But either is as good as the other whilst it is held."[34] But while it was maintained as a policy, Gandhi insisted, it had also to be applied consistently and honestly—and with full confidence in the policy itself.

> I cannot get rid of the conviction, that the greatest obstacle to our progress toward Swaraj [self-rule] is our want to faith in our policy.[35]

This statement raises the question of whether he saw the difficulties to be rooted, in part at least, not in the failure to promote nonviolence as a creed for the whole of life, but in inadequacies in the application of nonviolent action *within the context of nonviolent action as a policy*. This interpretation is supported by statements in a letter written by Gandhi to the British Government of India, refuting certain charges made against himself and the Congress. Gandhi wrote:

> ... I have also said that for my movement I do not at all need believers in the theory of non-violence, full or imperfect. It is enough if people carry out the rules of non-violent action.[36]

This statement was made as late as July 1943.

The practical application of nonviolent action, however, had to be honest and the maintenance of nonviolence had to be thorough. Members of the Indian National Congress who did not really believe in the organization's policy of nonviolent means ought either to have the policy changed or resign.[37] "If they do not believe in the expedient of non-violence, they must denounce it but not claim to believe in the expedient when their heart resists it."[38] While the policy was accepted, however, it must be thoroughly implemented.

> I want complete obedience to the policy of non-violence. While the policy lasts, it is the same as ... a creed. ... [39]

Even for nonviolent actionists who practiced the technique as a measure of sound policy, attitudes as well as actions were important.

> But even policies require honest adherence in thought, word and deed ....[40]

> Non-violence to be a potent force must begin with the mind. Non-violence of the mere body without the co-operation of the mind is non-violence of the weak or the cowardly, and has therefore no potency. If we bear malice and hatred in our bosoms and pretend not to retaliate, it must recoil upon us and lead to our destruction. For abstention from mere bodily violence not to be injurious, it is at least necessary not to entertain hatred if we cannot generate active love.[41]

Both in South Africa and in India Gandhi presented *satyagraha* as a practical technique of action to the masses of people who needed one; and it was accepted as such. In both situations, means of parliamentary action were either not open at all or were so only to a limited degree. In each case the people were poorly equipped to use violent resistance. Nonviolent action, if developed practically, therefore, had significant advantages if the people were to resist at all. In both countries Gandhi offered and argued for nonviolent action in such practical terms. Later, however, Gandhi sometimes deprecated this expedient acceptance and application of the nonviolent technique. He sometimes did so while confirming that his approach had been accepted for these practical reasons and not because of "religious" or other grounds.[42]

MAINTAINING NONVIOLENT STANDARDS

With nonviolent action adopted as a practical technique of action, conscious steps were needed to maintain the highest possible standards of nonviolence, and the required coherence and direction in the movement, and hence the greatest effectiveness. Gandhi instituted, therefore, a system of strong leadership in the initial stages of such campaigns and also required effective discipline among the actionists. A leader or leaders carefully planned the general course of the struggle and the detailed opening phases. After some experience Gandhi became convinced that in order to reduce the possible temptation to introduce violence, and to apply the nonviolent technique most effectively, this leadership should be limited to persons believing in nonviolence as an ethic. With this restriction, the leader was nonviolent "out of choice and moral strength."[43] (At a later stage of the struggle, with arrests, increased repression, and interference with communications, central leadership tended to become impossible, and leadership became highly diffused and not restricted to persons with such a belief).

An example of Gandhi's insistence on such an arrangement was the 1930–31 campaign. The Indian National Congress had decided upon the struggle and it was conducted as its campaign; Gandhi was chosen to lead and initiate it. However, after such decisions were taken by the Congress, Gandhi insisted on having full authority to make the basic decisions in the planning and initial stages of the struggle. [44] The Working Committee of the Congress authorized Gandhi and those working with him to begin the campaign "as and when they desire and in the manner and to the extent they decide."[45] Later when Gandhi was in prison, leadership shifted to Congressmen who did not share his beliefs. As repression increased and the struggle deepened, leadership diffused still more and became decentralized down to the village level. Often all identifiable leaders were in prison.

As another tool used to assist the practical operation of nonviolent action, Gandhi insisted upon discipline within the movement and often formal pledges of appropriate behavior by the nonviolent volunteers. The precise form of such pledges differed with the specific conditions of the campaign, but they generally pledged the actionist to disciplined behavior in harmony with the plan of the struggle, to the maintainance of nonviolence, and to persistence in face of repression.[46]

"A WEAPON OF THE WEAK"

At various points, and especially later in his career, Gandhi saw the expedient use of the nonviolent technique in an unfavorable light.

> But their nonviolence, I must confess, was born of their help-lessness. Therefore, it was the weapon of the weak.[47]

> I have frankly and fully admitted that what we practised during the past thirty years was not non-violent resistance but passive resistance which only the weak offer because they are unable, not unwilling, to offer armed resistance.[48]

It was thus not moral conviction which had ruled out violence, but the incapacity to use violence effectively. Therefore people had accepted the alternative nonviolent means of struggle which Gandhi had proposed. This would make it less powerful, in Gandhi's view, because he had laid down as an axiom of non-violence the principle that "man for man the strength of non-violence is in exact proportion to the ability, not the will, of the non-violent person to inflict violence."[49] Their moral influence on the opponent would be much greater if he saw clearly that their nonviolence was not based upon an inability to use violence. Hence,

Gandhi's emphasis on appropriate attitudes in addition to outward nonviolent behavior. This view is also related to Gandhi's general opinion that in *satyagraha* quality is more important than numbers (even if only for the sake of long-term numerical strength).[50]

Gandhi even repeatedly described the Indian practice by the derogatory term "passive resistance." It implied weakness, passivity, hatred, and a willingness to use violence when it might win.[51] "I thought our struggle was based on non-violence," Gandhi wrote in 1947, "whereas in reality it was no more than passive resistance which essentially is a weapon of the weak."[52] According to a report of a talk by Gandhi,

> He confessed that . . . what he had mistaken for Satyagraha was not Satyagraha but passive resistance—a weapon of the weak. Indians harboured ill-will and anger against their erstwhile rulers, while they pretended to resist them non-violently. Their resistance was, therefore, inspired by violence and not by regard for the man in the British, whom they should convert through Satyagraha."[53]

> ". . . [W]hat I had mistaken for *ahimsa* was not *ahimsa*, but passive resistance of the weak, which can never be called *ahimsa* even in the remotest sense."[54]

Speaking to students in Peshawar in 1938 Gandhi had discussed the same theme.

> Well, we may be weak and oppressed, but non-violence is not a weapon of the weak. It is a weapon of the strongest and the bravest. Violence may well be the weapon of the weak and the oppressed. Being strangers to non-violence, nothing else is open to them. It is, however, true that passive resistance has been regarded as weapon of the weak. That was why the name "satyagraha" was coined in South Africa to distinguish the movement there from passive resistance.[55]

Because Gandhi's various evaluations of the Indian struggles differ so widely, citation of only his harsher views can give quite a distorted impression. We shall, therefore, present his views in their variety, beginning in this section with his more critical judgements, and continuing in the remaining sections with those less critical.

> As a matter of fact, [Gandhi wrote in late 1947] in the name of non-violence people observed the outward peace of the impotent. They had never even attempted to drive violence from their hearts.[56]

This reference to the "outward peace of the impotent" indicates Gandhi was talking about passivity, *not* nonviolent action. This was not simply an ethical compromise in Gandhi's view, but could have serious social consequences:

> If this weakness continues we shall have to go through rivers of blood once the British rule goes.[57]

> There is nothing more demoralizing than fake non-violence of the weak and impotent.[58]

> [The] non-violence of the weak and the helpless . . . will never take us to our goal and, if long practised, may even render us for ever unfit for self-government.

Gandhi wrote this last statement at the time of the 1938 riots in Allahabad. After advocating the use of "non-violent army of volunteers" to quell the riots, Gandhi continued:

> It has been suggested that when we have our independence riots and the like will not occur. This seems to me to be an empty hope, if in the course of the struggle for freedom we do not understand and use the technique of non-violent action in every conceivable circumstance.

Reliance on the police and the military in such situations constituted, in his view, an admission of failure.[59] Nonviolence "in the hands of the weak" could work "to a certain extent." "But when it becomes a cloak for our weakness, it emasculates us."[60]

By 1947 Gandhi's uneasiness and forebodings had heightened and he often saw connections between the riots and the inadequacy of the nonviolence used in the Indian independence struggle. Not always, but often, he saw the hatred which had been felt but denied outward expression during the period of nonviolent struggle as a *cause* of the riots. At other times, however, he said it was the absence of a different type of nonviolence which made the riots *possible*, although they had *other* causes. In late May 1947 Gandhi apparently did not think that the rioting in Bengal, Bihar, and the Punjab was caused by the independence struggle itself. He wrote: "it is just an indication that as we are throwing off the foreign yoke all the dirt and froth is coming to the surface."[61]

In late July, however, he connected the independence struggle and the riots:

The British Government's imminent withdrawal had set free the
bottled violence which was finding free vent against their own
kith and kin.[62]

It was because their struggle was not non-violent that they today
witnessed loot, arson and murder.[63]

Now that the British were voluntarily quitting India, apparent
non-violence had gone to pieces in a moment. The attitude of
violence which we had secretly harboured, in spite of the restraint
imposed by the Indian National Congress, now recoiled upon us
and made us fly at each other's throats when the question of the
distribution of power came up.[64]

On New Year's Day, 1948, he returned to the theme, writing: "The
internecine feud that is going on today in India is the direct
outcome of the energy that was set free during the thirty years'
action of the weak."[65]

The "nonviolence of the brave," he had written earlier, would
have led to different results.

If we had the requisite non-violence in us, our public life would be
characterized by utmost toleration.[66]

Had it been the non-violence of the strong, the practise of a
generation would have made the recent orgies of destruction of
life and property impossible.[67]

If we knew the use of non-violent resistance which only those with
hearts of oak can offer, we would present to the world a totally
different picture of free India instead of an India cut in twain, one
part highly suspicious of the other, and the two too much engaged
in mutual strife to be able to think cogently of the food and
clothing of the hungry and naked millions . . . .[68]

These interpretations left, of course, a lot of unanswered
questions. Gandhi generally did not ask these questions, and it is
not known what answers he might have offered. The questions are,
however, important in evaluating his work, and we shall return to
them.

INDIAN ACHIEVEMENTS

Gandhi's more self-critical statements and harsher judgements
concerning the Indian practice of nonviolent action need to be

balanced against (1) his success in the refinement and application of the technique of nonviolent action which could be used in political conflicts in place of violence; and (2) his own acknowledgement of beneficial results from the Indian practice. The type of nonviolent action applied in India was still useful, Gandhi said, "as a substitute of terrorism . . . . "[69]

It was in a large degree precisely that substitute which Gandhi had sought to develop. He claimed "no newness or merit" for such a substitute.[70] Nonviolent action had been practiced long before Gandhi. He made, however, significant modifications and refinements in the nonviolent technique, including bringing it into closer association with the ethic of nonviolence. In contrast to the simplistic black and white picture often presented by some believers in Western pacifism, Gandhi recognized degrees not only of violence, but also of nonviolence.[71]

Focusing only on Gandhi's deprecation of Indian nonviolent action, it is easy to conclude that he regretted having advocated and led expedient nonviolent action in South Africa and India. That conclusion, however, is quite inaccurate. One ought not be disheartened or give up because one's nonviolence is not perfect, he believed. Indeed it could not be. "We may not be perfect in our own use of it, but we definitely discard the use of violence, and grow from failure to success."[72]

In 1947 he said that had he in advance known its inadaquacies, from personal motives he would not have launched the struggle. But he added that the struggle had been in accordance with God's will, implying that his personal wishes were wrong and that the experiment had in fact been beneficial:

> Intoxicated with his success in South Africa, he came to India. Here too the struggle bore fruit. But he now realized that it was not based on non-violence. If he had known so then, he would not have launched the struggle. But God wanted to take [obtain] that work from him. So He blurred his [Gandhi's] vision.[73]

> Yes, I adhere to my opinion that I did well to present to the Congress non-violence as an expedient, [he wrote in 1942]. I could not have done otherwise, if I was to introduce it into politics. In South Africa too I introduced it as an expedient. It was successful there because resisters were a small number in a compact area and therefore easily controlled. Here we had numberless persons scattered over a huge country. The result was that they could not

be easily controlled or trained. And yet it is a marvel the way they have responded. They might have responded much better and shown far better results. But I have no sense of disappointment in me over the results obtained. If I had started with men who accepted non-violence as a creed, I might have ended with myself. Imperfect as I am, I started with imperfect men and women and sailed on an uncharted ocean. Thank God that, though the boat has not reached its haven, it has proved fairly stormproof.[74]

Gandhi told students in late 1947 that:

He had all along laboured under an illusion. But he was never sorry for it. He realized that if his vision were not covered by that illusion, India would never have reached the point which it had today.[75]

Our *ahimsa* was imperfect because we were imperfect, because it was presented to you by an imperfect being like myself. If then, even in the hands of imperfect instruments it could produce such brilliant results, what could it not achieve in the hands of a perfect Satyagrahi?[76]

The use of nonviolent action had resulted in a considerable strengthening both of the Indian National Congress and of the people as a whole. "It is my conviction," Gandhi wrote in 1938, "that the phenomenal growth of the Congress is due to its acceptance and enforcement, however imperfect, of the policy of non-violence."[77] He wrote on this theme several times during 1946.

It is my conviction that the whole mass of people would not have risen to the height of courage and fearlessness that they have but for the working of full non-violence. How it works we do not yet fully know. But the fact remains that under non-violence we have progressed from strength to strength even through our apparent failures and setbacks.[78]

For the past 25 years, willingly or unwillingly, the Congress has spoken to the masses in favour of non-violence as against violence for regaining our lost liberty. We have also discovered through our progress that in the application of non-violence we have been able to reach the mass mind far more quickly and far more extensively than ever before.[79]

Later that year, Gandhi wrote that "our *ahimsa* was lame. It walked on crutches." But he added: "Even so it has brought us to our present strength."[80]

India's experience in the application of nonviolent struggle, Gandhi said, had been "a very imperfect experiment" in the use of the technique by the masses of mankind. Keeping in mind both the achievements and the inadequacies, in the new situation it was, "the duty of Free India to perfect the instrument of non-violence for dissolving collective conflicts, if its freedom was going to be really worth while."[81]

"NONVIOLENCE OF THE BRAVE"

Gandhi long insisted—especially in his later years—that the "nonviolence of the brave" did not contain the weaknesses he saw in the Indian practice. The impression is widespread that this type of nonviolence can be equated with belief in nonviolence as an ethical or religious principle. An examination of Gandhi's own descriptions of the "nonviolence of the brave" does not confirm this simple interpretation, however, True, one of the important qualities of the "nonviolence of the brave," is that it is a "creed" and not a "policy." That is, it is accepted as a permanent approach to life including the problems of society and politics.

> With the Congress non-violence was always a policy. It was open to it to reject it if it failed. If it could not bring political and economic independence, it was of no use. For me non-violence is a creed. I must act up to it whether I am alone or have companions.

> Non-violence of the strong cannot be a mere policy. It must be a creed, or a passion, if "creed" is objected to.[82]

In summer 1947 Gandhi cited the "one fundamental difference" between him and his friends and former colleagues:

> Non-violence is my creed. It never was of the Congress. With the Congress it has always been a policy. A policy takes the shape of a creed while it lasts, no longer. The Congress had every right to change it when it found it necessary. A creed can never admit of any change.[83]

Gandhi maintained that nonviolence as a creed should be expressed "in every little act" of the adherent to the doctrine. "Therefore he who is possessed by non-violence will express it in the family circle, in his dealings with neighbours, in his business, in Congress meetings, in public meetings, and in his dealings with his opponents."[84]

Gandhi also called this "the enlightened non-violence of resourcefulness"[85] which indicates another of its qualities. Belief in the nonviolent ethic was not by itself in Gandhi's view sufficient to qualify one as a votary of the nonviolence of the brave. Creativity and the use of the intellect were also needed in the application of nonviolence in meeting the problems of personal and social life.

> A mere belief in *ahimsa* . . . will not do. It should be intelligent and creative. If intellect plays a large part in the field of violence, I hold that it plays a larger part in the field of non-violence.[86]

Gandhi also called the "non-violence of the brave" the "non-violence of the strong" and the "non-violence of the stout in heart."[87] These three terms together describe two other qualities of this type as Gandhi viewed it. First, the *satyagrahi* with such confidence in the nonviolent course would be both willing to act, and to persist in the action even in face of severe repression and danger.

> Let me say in all humility that *ahimsa* belongs to the brave . . . *Ahimsa* calls for the strength and courage to suffer without retaliation, to receive blows without returning any.[88]

> Given the unquenchable faith in the law, no provocation should prove too great for the exercise of forbearance.[89]

> . . .[W]e must do our duty and die in the course of performing it if necessary. To die without killing is the battle of a Satyagrahi. If we had lived up to that ideal we would have won Swaraj by now.[90]

In summary then, the "nonviolence of the brave," required (1) adherence to nonviolence even in crises; (2) application in all areas of life; (3) resourcefulness; (4) creativity; (5) use of the intellect; and (6) bravery in face of severe repression. Although this type of nonviolence superficially gave less attention to expediency than the nonviolent action as a policy, Gandhi was convinced that its tenacity gave it a greater social and political impact. "Non-violence of the strong is any day stronger than that of the bravest soldier fully armed or a whole host."[91]

ITS DIFFERING RESULTS

Had Indian nonviolent action been the "nonviolence of the brave," the social and political consequences would, in Gandhi's opinion, have been quite different. ". . . [W]e would present to the world a totally different picture of free India . . . ." [92]

In 1938 Gandhi had expressed "the fear that our non-violence is not of the kind required." [93] Were it instead the nonviolence of the strong, "we should be able to deal with riots and stop the increasing tension between Hindus and Mussalmans." [94] By 1947 Gandhi was even more firmly convinced of the validity of this viewpoint. The past type of nonviolence could "have no play in the altered circumstances." [95] "Hence, during the Hindu-Muslim quarrel it proved a failure on the whole." [96] In the midst of intense hatreds and blood-thirsty atrocities only nonviolence of the strongest and bravest type could bring people to their senses and halt the riots. The "nonviolence of the weak" would not "serve the purpose in communal strife. For that was required pure nonviolence of the brave." [97] In the riots "only non-violence of the strong could prove really effective." [98]

The distrust and violence between Hindus and Muslims was closely related to the partition of India. Here, too, "there was only one way to avoid the calamity and that was by the non-violence of the brave." [99]

Gandhi also discussed the differing political consequences of the "nonviolence of the weak" and the "nonviolence of the brave." He pointed to the relation between the type of independence achieved and the general means by which it was obtained (as violence, political bargaining, or nonviolent struggle). [100] He perceived differences in consequences following from the use respectively of different techniques of action, and also from different types of nonviolent action. The various resulting differences were associated with his perception that nonviolent action effectively diffuses power throughout the society. [101] In Gandhi's experiences, nonviolent struggle strengthened individuals and also increased the vitality of social groups and institutions. "Non-violent Swaraj cannot be won except by non-violence." [102] Expedient nonviolent action consistently applied could achieve political independence.

From that point one could seek by nonviolent means to strengthen the democracy and improve the society.

> While it has not yet been tested for a whole nation, [Gandhi wrote in 1938] I believe that disciplined *satyagraha* by a considerable number of people in a nation can win its freedom, and with that method can go on to build better civilization for mankind to emulate and thereby save the world.[103]

The higher the quality of nonviolence, however, the better the consequent democracy: ". . . as can be definitely proved, no perfect democracy is possible without perfect non-violence at the back of it."[104] Gandhi believed that the quality of the nonviolent action was also relevant for its world-wide acceptance.

> Not until the Congress or a similar group of people represents the non-violence of the strong, will the world catch the infection.[105]

> It is easy enough to see that non-violence required here is of a wholly different type from what the Congress has known hitherto. But it is the only non-violence that is true and that can save the world from self-destruction. This is a certainty . . . if India cannot deliver the message of true nonviolence to a world which wants to be saved from the curse of wars and does not know how to find the deliverance.[106]

Despite Gandhi's depression, disappointment, and lack of ready-made answers, he maintained his determination to press on with the development of a nonviolent way out of the difficulties faced by India and the world. "We cannot remain static. We must move forward or we shall slide back." [107] In this effort, Gandhi believed that India had a special responsibility:

> India was now free. . . . Now that the burden of subjection had been lifted, all the forces of good had to be marshalled in one great effort to build a country which forsook the accustomed method of violence in order to settle human conflicts whether it was between two States or two sections of the same people. He had yet the faith that India would rise to the occasion. . . .[108]

DEVELOPING NONVIOLENCE OF THE BRAVE

Gandhi confessed that his effort to discover a way to cultivate the "nonviolence of the brave" had been rather "desultory." In 1940, he wrote:

I have not concentrated upon it, or given it the weight I might have. This was all right while I was devoting all my energy to forging means to give battle to the government. But it had the result of retarding the growth of pure *ahimsa*, so that today we are not even within ken of the *ahimsa*, of the strong.[109]

In later years, Gandhi thought more on the question. The development of this nonviolence would take time, and "weak people" could not "develop it all of a sudden."[110] He suggested a variety of means to help cultivate this "nonviolence of the brave." The person seeking to develop this quality would base his relationships with people in his personal and domestic life upon nonviolence.[111] "Selfless service" of one's fellow human beings, the casting off of fear, and the earned capacity to risk one's life "at the time of political or communal disturbances or under the menace of thieves and dacoits [bandits],"[112] were part of its development. "So long as we have not cultivated the strength to die with courage and love in our hearts, we cannot hope to develop the *ahimsa* of the strong."[113] Gandhi also emphasized the importance of belief: "Consciousness of the living presence of God within one was undoubtedly the first requisite,"[114] Gandhi's conception of God was, of course, extremely catholic, and he identified Truth with God.[115] (This statement therefore does not imply a theological belief as a prerequisite for the "nonviolence of the brave.") A close relationship therefore exists between this emphasis on "the living presence of God" and the discussion by one of Gandhi's interpreters Ranganath R. Diwaker on the role of truth in *satyagraha:*

The basic preparation in Satyagraha is the inculcation of faith in truth and its ultimate triumph . . . the people concerned must be sure that truth, as they see it, is on their side. Then only can they have sufficient determination and moral strength to stake for it everything they possess. [116]

Although Gandhi's prescriptions on the development of the "non-violence of the brave" remained in very general terms, he said in 1947 that "it was truer (if it was a fact) to say that India was not ready for the lesson of the *ahimsa* of the strong than that no programme had been devised for the teaching."[117]

Even when the development of this type of nonviolence was adequately solved, there remained another problem: how to apply the "nonviolence of the brave." There was a strong tendency in Gandhi's discussions of this concept to revert to greater reliance on individuals and small groups. However, only some few weeks before his assassination he explicitly rejected any interpretation which limited nonviolence to personal, and not group or political, relationships:

> That non-violence which only an individual can use is not of much use in terms of society. Man is a social being. His accomplishments to be of use must be such as any person with sufficient diligence can attain. That which can be exercised only among friends is of value only as a spark of non-violence. It cannot merit the appellation of *ahimsa*.[118]

How then to act? Gandhi did not know. "If Satyagraha is a universal principle of universal application, I must find an effective method of action even through a handful," Gandhi wrote in 1939. He added: ". . . I have not yet found with certainty how a handful can act effectively."[119] Having taken some experienced nonviolence workers with him to East Bengal in late 1946 in an effort to stop the riots, Gandhi admitted: "I myself don't know what the next step is and cannot guide them."[120] This was a "new experiment" in "the nonviolence of the strong."[121]

The tendency in Gandhi's thinking toward reliance on perfection of individuals is perhaps most strongly expressed in a letter written to Amiya Chakravarty. Even here, however, Gandhi did not reject corporate resistance. He wrote:

> Of course there must be organized resistance to organized evil. The difficulty arises when the organizers of Satyagraha try to imitate the organizers of evil. I tried and failed hopelessly. The way of organizing forces of good must be opposite to the evil way. What it exactly is I do not yet know fully. I feel that it lies, as far as may be, through perfection of individuals. It then acts as the leaven raising the whole mass. But I am still groping.[122]

At a later date, 1 January 1948, Gandhi confirmed his failure to find an answer to the problem: ". . . the technique of unconquerable non-violence of the strong has not been at all fully discovered as yet."[123]

UNASKED QUESTIONS ON THE RIOTS

It may be helpful now to look critically at certain elements of Gandhi's own evaluations and comments recounted above. Not all of these may be equally valid or equally helpful in reaching our own conclusions. Some of Gandhi's opinions seem either to be invalid, unfair, or cannot be accepted without considerably more investigation. The first of these views of dubious validity is that the later Hindu-Muslim riots were caused by expedient nonviolent action against British rule. It is not possible, for several reasons, to accept this view without a considerable amount of evidence.

While the possibility of a causal connection cannot be dismissed, it would only be valid if the rioters and the nonviolent resisters were in fact the same persons. Gandhi never said that they were, and we have no evidence to that effect. Indeed, it is highly unlikely that the rioters and the resisters were the very same persons, partly because India has such a vast and heterogeneous population and also because the *active* participants of the non-violent struggles were always a clear minority of the whole population. In addition, the worst of the Hindu-Muslim riots to which Gandhi referred occurred in 1946 and 1947, whereas the major nonviolent struggles which Gandhi led took place in the 1920s and 1930s. If the rioters were *not* the former nonviolent resisters, but others who participated little or not at all in the resistance to the British, the suggestion of a direct causal relationship collapses.

There might still be an indirect relationship, if a connection were established between the aggressiveness released in the riots and a build-up of frustration and hostility during the nonviolent campaigns among the *nonparticipants* in the struggle (who used neither violent nor nonviolent resistance). Yet, even if that possible connection were established the causal relationship would be only between the *inaction of nonparticipants* in nonviolent struggle and *their* later use of violence—*not* between the use of nonviolent action and later social violence. A series of research questions arise from these possible interrelationships.

The second point about the riots is this: simply because riots followed the use of nonviolent struggle, it cannot be assumed that nonviolent struggle caused the riots. In India especially, the causes of the riots may have had little or nothing to do with prior nonviolent action by the independence movement. (The question whether, once the riots began, nonviolent action could or could not have halted them is separate from the problem of determining their cause.) A reverse proposition is also plausible: would the riots and other violence have been worse if there had been no earlier nonviolent campaigns? Neither proposition can be answered without more information. One would need to determine, for example, the intensity of general hostility and communal hatreds over the years and whether these increased or declined because of the nonviolent struggles before attempting to answer the question. Any possible view that communal riots are caused only by nonviolent struggles, or that those alone increase the hostilities and violence in such riots, seems to be refuted by the Cyprus experience. Increased hostilities and violence there between the Turkish and the Greek communities followed guerrilla warfare (in the form of terrorism) against British rule.

Third, the suggested direct causal connection between nonviolent action and communal riots in India is less plausible since the most serious riots occurred fifteen or more years after the most significant mass nonviolent struggles of the early 1920s and 1930s. It would be at least as logical to connect the riots with something else, such as the *absence* of recent nonviolent struggles; Congress parliamentary activity after the early 1930s; or the 1942 campaign with its underground activities. These are at least as plausible, since some evidence exists that at times participants in nonviolent struggles experience both a release of internal aggressiveness and frustration and a reduction of personal hostility toward members of the opponent group.

These three points make it impossible to accept, without much further support, certain of Gandhi's more severe deprecations of the Indian use of nonviolent action.

Sometimes a very different point is argued: that the type and quality of nonviolent action used against the British *Raj* was not strong enough to prevent or halt the communal riots (caused by other factors) with their greater intensity of hatred, bitterness, and atrocities. Gandhi at times suggested this, but that is a very different question.

FURTHER RESERVATIONS ON GANDHI'S VIEWS

There seems to be built into Gandhi's terminology an invalid preconception which, if accepted, may interfere with reasonable and objective analysis. The main term involved is "the nonviolence of the weak." Its characteristics as perceived by Gandhi have been recounted above. At times he said: "When it becomes a cloak for our weakness, it emasculates us." It is relevant to ask: *When* does nonviolence become a cloak for weakness? Does it *any* time people use nonviolent action as an expedient? Or, does it do so when they plead reasons of nonviolence to justify *inaction* in crisis situations? If not, when? Gandhi was not clear. Quite different conclusions would follow from such alternative answers, and the answer and conclusion would prove to be important in evaluating some of Gandhi's extreme statements on the Indian struggles.

To the degree that Gandhi identified the "nonviolence of the weak" with use of nonviolent action as an expedient technique, we need to ask why such use can be described as based upon weakness. In at least two passages which we have cited Gandhi identified the source of this "weakness." In one he said: ". . . their non-violence. . . was born of their helplessness. Therefore, it was the weapon of the weak." In the other, the Indian practice had been "passive resistance which only the weak offer because they are unable, not unwilling, to offer armed resistance."

If these were Gandhi's reasons for choosing the term the "nonviolence of the weak," it is a highly questionable term. Not only has it strong emotional overtones, it seems to be based on two *non sequiturs*. They need to be examined separately.

If people in a difficult political or social situation have felt themselves to be helpless, and then resort to nonviolent action in an attempt to cope with their problem, is not the earlier condition of helplessness changed? One of the basic characteristics of nonviolent action, in both theory and practice, is that resort to the technique makes people able to cease being the helpless victims of forces beyond their control, and instead able to act to influence the course of their own lives and society. This view was firmly supported by Gandhi. If the condition of helplessness is ended through use of nonviolent action, and replaced by self-reliance and corporate action, Gandhi's statement that "their non-violence. . . was born of their helplessness" is invalid. Their earlier inaction and passivity, instead, were born of their helplessness. But their later nonviolent action was instead born of a new determination and ability to control their own fate. Therefore, it would *not* follow that their expedient nonviolent action was the "weapon of the weak."

Gandhi's second point cited above was that weakness in nonviolent action is traced to the inability, not unwillingness, to use violent resistance. Why should a condition of *military* weakness be reason to describe the users of substituted nonviolent action as "weak"? The condition of military weakness is quite different from a condition of weakness in nonviolent action, due to the radical differences in the two techniques. Gandhi himself repeatedly said that the Indian use of nonviolent action as an expedient had considerably strengthened the Indian people as a whole and the Indian National Congress. He said (as cited above), "under non-violence we have progressed from strength to strength even though our apparent failures and setbacks." In 1925 he wrote:

> The non-violence I teach is active non-violence of the strongest. But the weakest can partake in it without becoming weaker. They can only be the stronger for having been in it. The masses are far bolder today then they ever were.[124]

If military weakness is not a justification for labeling the substitute nonviolent action as weak, and if nonviolent struggle often increases the strength of the resisting population, there is little justification here for labeling the expedient use of nonviolent action as the "nonviolence of the weak." Gandhi's choice of terminology in this particular case seems inaccurate, and if not replaced it is likely to distort both perception and analysis.

In two other cases Gandhi's criticisms of Indian nonviolent action seem unfair in light of his own recommendations and actions. He had recommended nonviolent action as a practical technique of struggle for use by people who did not believe in nonviolence as a moral principle. Is it not unreasonable for him later to criticize their expedient use of the technique as "hypocritical," "dishonest," and "cowardly," or to deprecate it as simply action taken by people when they saw no other effective way to resist? Is it really hypocrisy when people deliberately and bravely practice nonviolent action only to achieve a limited political objective (provided that they do not pretend that they would never use violence in other situations)? Gandhi's occasional deprecation of the use of nonviolent action simply as a substitute for violence in conflicts is not really fair when Gandhi had himself advocated, developed, and urged others to adopt precisley such as substitute.

It is evident that as his focus or mood shifted, Gandhi applied different criteria in his criticisms of Indian nonviolent action and in his evaluation of what was needed in the future. In the perspective of his whole outlook and program, these criteria were not necessarily ultimately inconsistent with each other. But he did not always make clear that the use of one criterion did not necessarily mean rejection of another. Nor did he make clear their interrelationships. The results often are apparent flat contradictions between his own views, often held simultaneously, on the same subject.

MASS POLITICAL ACTION AFFIRMED

Despite these several criticisms, there is a great deal which is important and stimulating in Gandhi's evaluations of Indian nonviolent action. Some of the difficulties with Gandhi's evaluations are rooted in the same source as that which makes his approach to nonviolence important and provocative.

For Gandhi, moral principles and religion could not be separated from social and political life.

> I claim that human mind or human society is not divided into watertight compartments called social, political and religious. All act and react upon one another.[125]

Inevitably, then, evaluations of nonviolence in the context of these interrelating factors are complex and difficult.

Significantly, despite his most extreme criticisms of Indian nonviolent action, Gandhi did not recommend withdrawal from political nonviolent action. There are a series of statements made as late as 1940 to the end of 1947—during the period of his greatest depression over the course of events in India—in which he categorically affirmed the relevance of nonviolent action to society as a whole, and to politics in particular. At a meeting of the All-India Congress Committee in January 1942, for example, Gandhi insisted with no regrets on the political nature of nonviolent action as he had presented it to India. He also rejected the views of those who dismissed his policy as being "religious":

> I placed it before Congress as a political method, to be employed for the solution of the political questions. It may be it is a novel method, but it does not on that account lose its political character . . . As a political method, it can always be changed, modified, altered, and even given up in preference to another. If, therefore, I say to you that our policy should not be given up today, I am talking political wisdom. It is political insight. It has served us in the past, it has enabled us to cover many stages toward independence, and it is as a politician that I suggest to you that it is a grave mistake to contemplate its abandonment. If I have carried the Congress with me all these years, it is in my capacity as a politician. It is hardly fair to describe my method as religious, because it is new.[126]

Despite Gandhi's dissatisfaction with the Indian practice of nonviolent action, he did not revert to a "fellowship of true believers" who, despite their small numbers, would save the world by the purity of their doctrine and practice. Instead, Gandhi affirmed the importance of corporate and mass action, by which ordinary people could themselves correct the problems they faced, and thereby achieve a sense of their own strength and power.

NOTES TO CHAPTER SIX

1. This is closely related to, but not identical with, the question of whether Gandhi finally saw "nonviolence" to be a moral principle, a political technique, or some combination of these. This article is largely based upon some sections of a long paper prepared at the Institute of Philosophy and the History of Ideas of the University of Oslo in 1965, on "Nonviolence: Moral Principle or Political Technique? Clues from Gandhi's thought and experience." Complementary aspects to those discussed here are analysed in Chapter Thirteen, with the same title. There is a limited over-lapping of these two discussions, since they are very closely related.

2. **Harijan** (hereafter cited as H.), 24 Mar. 1946; M.K. Gandhi, **Non-violence in Peace and War** (hereafter cited as NVPW. The original source and date are

given, in addition to the book in which it is reprinted), (2 vols. Ahmedabad: Navajivan, 1948-1949), vol. II, p. 64.

3. H., 8 Feb. 1948; NVPW, II, p. 382.
4. H., 12 Oct. 1947; NVPW, II, p. 321. See also H.; 21 July 1940; NVPW, I, pp. 290-292.
5. H., 6 Oct. 1946; NVPW, II, p. 153.
6. H., 6 Oct. 1946; NVPW, II, p. 153.
7. Young India (hereafter cited as YI) 12 Aug. 1926; NVPW, I, pp. 59-61.
8. See Chapter Eight, "Gandhi's Defense Policy."
9. H., 31 Aug. 1947; NVPW, II, p. 289.
10. H., 21 July 1940; NVPW, I, p. 292.
11. H., 21 July 1940; NVPW, I, p. 292.
12. M.K. Gandhi, Speeches and Writings of Mahatma Gandhi (Madras: 1922), p. 301; Gopi Nath Dhawan, The Political Philosophy of Mahatma Gandhi (Third rev. ed.; Ahmedabad: Navajivan, 1962), p. 107.
13. H., 14 Oct. 1939; Dhawan, The Political Philosophy of Mahatma Gandhi, pp. 107-108.
14. H., 29 Sept. 1940; Dhawan, The Political Philosophy of Mahatma Gandhi, p. 165.
15. H., 12 Jan. 1947; NVPW, II, p. 190.
16. H., 14 Dec. 1947; NVPW, II, p. 339.
17. YI, I, p. 262; Dhawan, The Political Philosophy of Mahatma Gandhi, p. 165.
18. H., 18 Aug. 1940; Dhawan, The Political Philosophy of Mahatma Gandhi, p. 165.
19. Sarvodaya (Hindi), April 1940; Dhawan, The Political Philosophy of Mahatma Gandhi, pp. 165-166.
20. H., 8 Sept. 1940; Dhawan, The Political Philosophy of Mahatma Gandhi, p. 166. See also H., 19 May 1946.
21. H., 7 Apr. 1946; Dhawan, The Political Philosophy of Mahatma Gandhi, p.166.
22. H., 28 June 1942; Gandhi, In Search of the Supreme (Ahmedabad: Navajivan, 1961), vol. II, p. 42.
23. H., 2 Nov. 1947; NVPW, II, p. 329.
24. The Amrita Bazar Patrika, 3 Aug. 1934; Nirmal Kumar Bose, Selections from Gandhi (Ahmedabad: Navajivan, 1948), p. 196.
25. D.G. Tendulkar, Mahatma: Life of Mohandas Karamchand Gandhi, (First ed.; 8 vols. Bombay: Jhaveri & Tendulkar, 1952) vol. III, p. 362.
26. Ibid., p. 364.
27. H., 21 July 1940; NVPW, I, p. 290.
28. For accounts of both such cases see Gene Sharp, Gandhi Wields the Weapon of Moral Power: Three Case Histories (Ahmedabad: Navajivan, 1960).
29. H., 4 Nov. 1939; NVPW, I, p. 245.
30. For further discussion of this point see Chapter Thirteen, "Nonviolence: Moral Principle or Political Technique?"
31. YI, 11 Aug. 1920; NVPW, I, p. 3.
32. YI, 7 May 1925; NVPW, I, p. 28.
33. YI, 30 July 1931; Bose, Selections from Gandhi, p. 123.
34. YI, 30 July 1931; Bose, Selections from Gandhi, p. 124.
35. Ibid. It is clear from the context that Gandhi indeed meant policy here, both from the distinction in the previous quotation between policy and creed and

from his putting "policy" in italics two sentences prior to that.

36. M.K. Gandhi, **Correspondence with the Government, 1942–1944** (Second ed.; Ahmedabad: Navajivan, 1957), p. 138.

37. See YI, 31 July 1931; Bose, **Selections from Gandhi,** p. 124, and H., 29 Sept. 1940; NVPW, I, p. 353.

38. YI, 2 Mar. 1922; Bose, **Selections from Gandhi,** pp. 123–124.

39. H., 29 Sept. 1940; NVPW, I, p. 353.

40. YI, 2 Mar. 1922; Bose, **Selections from Gandhi,** p. 123.

41. YI, 2 Apr. 1931; Bose, **Selections from Gandhi,** p. 154.

42. See discussion on this point in Chapter Thirteen, "Nonviolence: Moral Principle or Political Technique?"

43. YI, 2 Feb. 1930; Dhawan, **The Political Philosophy of Mahatma Gandhi,** pp. 122–123.

44. YI, 20 Feb. 1930; Sharp, **Gandhi Wields the Weapon of Moral Power,** pp. 57–58.

45. All-India Congress Committee, **Congress Bulletin,** 21 Feb. 1930, no. 4; quoted in Sharp, **Gandhi Wields the Weapon of Moral Power,** p. 57.

46. For a variety of these pledges, see Ranganath R. Diwakar, **Satyagraha: Its Technique and History** (Bombay: Hind Kitabs, 1946), Appendices III and IV, pp. 188–194, and Sharp, **Gandi Wields the Weapon of Moral Power,** pp. 67–69 and 80–81.

47. H., 4 Aug. 1946; NVPW, II, p. 132.

48. H., 27 July 1947; NVPW, II, p. 281. See also H., 29 June 1947; NVPW, II, p. 266.

49. Dhawan, **The Political Philosophy of Mahatma Gandhi,** p. 72.

50. See M.K. Gandhi, **Satyagraha** (Ahmedabad: Navajivan, 1951) pp. 33, 87, 292, 294, 295 and 347.

51. See M.K. Gandhi, **Satyagraha in South Africa** (Second rev. ed.; Ahmedabad: Navajivan, 1950), pp. 111–115, and M.K. Gandhi, **An Autobiography or the Story of My Experiences with Truth** (Ahmedabad: Navajivan, 1956), p. 138.

52. H., 27 July 1947; NVPW, II, p. 276.

53. H., 31 Aug. 1947; NVPW, II, p. 289.

54. H., 11 Jan. 1948; NVPW, II, pp. 327–328. See also H., 14 Oct. 1939 (NVPW, I, p. 235); H., 9 Dec. 1939 (NVPW, I, p. 250); H., 13 July 1947 (NVPW, II, p. 272); H., 16 Nov. 1947 (NVPW, II, p. 323); and Gandhi, **Delhi Diary** (Ahmedabad: Navajivan, 1948), p. 280.

55. Tendulkar, **Mahatma** (new ed.), vol. IV, p. 258.

56. H., 2 Nov. 1947; NVPW, II, p. 328. See also H., 3 Aug. 1947; NVPW, II, p. 279, and H., 24 Feb. 1946; NVPW, II, p. 30.

57. H., 28 Apr. 1946; NVPW, II, p. 84.

58. H., 6 Oct. 1946; NVPW, II, p. 153.

59. H., 26 Mar. 1938; NVPW, I, pp. 133–135.

60. H., 2 Apr. 1938; NVPW, I, p. 136.

61. H., 8 June 1947; NVPW, II, p.258.

62. H., 3 Aug. 1947; NVPW, II, p. 279.

63. H., 27 July 1947; NVPW, II, p. 277.

64. H., 31 Aug. 1947; NVPW, II, p. 289.

65. H., 11 Jan. 1948; NVPW, II, p. 328.
66. H., 6 Oct. 1946; NVPW, II, pp. 153–154.
67. H., 13 July 1947; NVPW, II, p. 272.
68. H., 27 July 1947; NVPW, II, p. 281.
69. H., 9 Dec. 1939; NVPW, I, p. 250.
70. H., 9 Dec. 1939; NVPW, I, p. 250.
71. See H., 30 Sept. 1939; NVPW, I, p. 230.
72. H., 21 July 1940; NVPW, I, p. 292.
73. H., 27 July 1947; NVPW, II, p. 277.
74. H., 12 Apr. 1942; NVPW, I, p. 396.
75. H., 31 Aug. 1947; NVPW, II, 290.
76. H., 21 July 1946; NVPW, II, p. 109.
77. H., 26 Mar. 1938; NVPW, I, p. 133. See also H., 14 Oct. 1939; NVPW, I, p. 236.
78. H., 10 Feb. 1946; NVPW, II, p. 2.
79. H., 24 Feb. 1946; NVPW, II, p. 30.
80. H., 21 July 1946; NVPW, II, p. 109.
81. H., 31 Aug. 1947; NVPW, II, pp. 289–290.
82. H., 29 June 1940; NVPW, I, pp. 275–276.
83. H., 27 July 1947; NVPW, II, p. 280.
84. H., 29 June 1940; NVPW, I, p. 276.
85. Dhawan, The Political Philosophy of Mahatma Gandhi, p. 70.
86. H., 21 July 1940; NVPW, I, pp. 290–291.
87. H., 12 May 1946; NVPW, II, p. 91, and H., 31 Aug. 1947; NVPW, II, p. 289.
88. H., 7 Apr. 1946; NVPW, II, p. 57.
89. H., 8 Sept. 1946; NVPW, II, p. 146.
90. H., 21 July 1946; NVPW, II, p. 109.
91. H., 12 May 1946; NVPW, II, p. 91.
92. H., 27 July 1947; NVPW, II, p. 281.
93. H., 9 Apr. 1938; NVPW, I, p. 140.
94. H., 2 Apr. 1938; NVPW, I, p. 137.
95. H., 29 June 1947; NVPW, II, p. 265.
96. H., 31 Aug. 1947; NVPW, II, p. 289.
97. H., 29 June 1947; NVPW, II, p. 266.
98. H., 30 Mar. 1947; NVPW, II, p. 238.
99. H., 27 July 1947; NVPW, II, p. 276.
100. See, for example, Bose, Selections from Gandhi, pp. 42–43; Bose, Studies in Gandhism (Calcutta: Indian Associated Publishing Co., 1947), pp. 15, 65 and 71; and Tendulkar, Mahatma: Life of Mohandas Karamchand Gandhi (New ed.), vol. VI, p. 41.
101. See Gene Sharp, "Social Power and Political Freedom," in Social Power and Political Freedom. Boston: Porter Sargent Publishers, Inc., 1979.
102. H., 22 Sept. 1940; NVPW, I, p. 470.
103. H., 24 Dec. 1938; NVPW, I, p. 437.
104. H., 2 Mar. 1947; NVPW, II, p. 218. See also Dhawan's discussion, The Political Philosophy of Mahatma Gandhi, p. 130.
105. H., 4 May 1940; NVPW, I, p. 267.

106. H., 29 June 1940; NVPW, I, p. 277.
107. H., 10 Feb. 1946; NVPW, II, p. 3.
108. H., 31 Aug. 1947; NVPW, II, p. 290.
109. H., 21 July 1940; NVPW, I, p. 300.
110. H., 6 Jan. 1940; NVPW, I, pp. 252–253.
111. H., 21 July 1947; NVPW, I, p. 302.
112. H., 21 July 1947; NVPW, I, p. 302.
113. H., 15 Sept. 1946; NVPW, II, p. 136.
114. H., 29 June 1947; NVPW, II, p. 267.
115. See Bose, Selections from Gandhi, pp. 3–7.
116. Diwakar, Satyagraha, pp. 73–74.
117. H., 29 June 1947; NVPW, II, p. 267.
118. H., 14 Dec. 1947; NVPW, II, p. 339.
119. H., 24 June 1939; Gandhi, Satyagraha, p. 296.
120. H., 12 Jan. 1947; NVPW, II, p. 196.
121. H., 26 Jan. 1947; NVPW, II, p. 207.
122. Amiya Chakravarty, A Saint at Work: A View of Gandhi's Work and Message (pamphlet; William Penn Lecture 1950. Philadelphia: Young Friends Movement of the Philadelphia Yearly Meetings, 1950), p. 20.
123. H., 11 Jan. 1948; NVPW, II, p. 328.
124. YI, 12 Feb. 1926; Bose, Selections from Gandhi, p. 160.
125. YI, 2 Mar. 1922; Bose, Selections from Gandhi, p. 26.
126. Tendulkar, Mahatma (new ed.), vol. VI, pp. 40–41.

7

India's Lesson for the Peace Movement

The Indian Government and people have [1963] responded to the Chinese use of military force to adjust the border between their countries with war preparations and reliance upon military means to deal with the foreign threat. This Indian reaction has, for many people in the peace movement, and pacifists in particular, been something of a shock. Many of these people believe that India has somehow let them down, that she has failed to live up to the moral challenge which has been imposed in different ways both by Gandhi and by the nature of modern war.

Yet India's reaction should not have surprised anyone because her reaction could have been predicted. Similarly the response of pacifists and other peace workers could have been anticipated. This attitude seems to me to be the wrong reaction to the Indian situation, a reaction which has its roots more clearly in the Western peace workers than in the Indian situation itself.

There are doubtless a variety of interpretations of the Indian response, all of which may have some truth in them. The interpretation presented here may not be the only credible one, but it contains important insights which are missing in the other explanations.

PACIFIST DEPRECATION

Pacifists in particular have rarely responded to the challenge of the Indian nonviolent struggle for freedom on the level which those struggles demanded. Initially many pacifists in Europe opposed Gandhi and regarded his nonviolent struggles as being rather violent at heart. As the years went by, however, Gandhi's movement began to be regarded in two other ways. On the one hand a considerable number of individual pacifists and peace workers began to champion the Indian cause and to work very hard for Indian freedom. On the other hand, the example of nonviolent mass revolutionary action in India began to be used by pacifists as an argument in support of the practicality of their own doctrine and program. Yet in my opinion the peace and pacifist movements did not appreciate at that time, and have not since adequately appreciated, some of the peculiar lessons which the Indian nonviolent struggles have for the peace movement.

This is particularly true of those sections of the peace movement, principally pacifist organizations, whose approach has been largely a doctrinal one, that is, they have been more concerned with a message or doctrine than they have been with developing practical political courses of action which could be supported by the vast number of people who are not, and probably never will be, doctrinal pacifists.

These lessons of the Indian movement, and probably of other nonviolent movements in other parts of the world in more recent years, can perhaps be described as lessons concerning the technique approach to nonviolent action. This approach has long been strongly deprecated by large numbers of personal pacifists and particularly by religious pacifists.

This deprecation however, is extremely undesirable. In particular it fails to consider why more people have not accepted the doctrines of nonviolence which their exponents have preached. One of the most important reasons why these doctrines have been rejected is that most people have not believed that they were realistic, that is, that they could deal with serious political conflicts and threats to freedom. These people have rejected the philosophies of nonviolence because they believe them not to include an effective technique of struggle with which to deal with crises.

The Indian experience, both under Gandhi and in face of the Chinese situation, has a considerable amount to teach us about the doctrinal approach. This lesson is not, however, the one which many pacifists are expounding; that if one does not accept the full pacifist dogma one will eventually fall prey to human weakness and resort again at a later stage to war in a new situation. The lesson is a quite different one.

A POLITICAL ACT

The adoption by India of nonviolent struggle under Gandhi to deal with British imperialism was not a doctrinal or a moralistic act. It was a political act in response to a political program of action proposed to deal with a particular kind of situation and crisis. It also happened, almost parenthetically, that this nonviolent program was morally preferable to violent revolutionary war, and this in some ways increased the strength of the movement by giving it an aura of moral superiority. The nonviolent course of action was only possible in India because people could be brought to see that the nonviolent way of acting was the practical course of action which would enable them to achieve their goals. It was also probably psychologically and morally more uplifting to the society as a whole and to individual participants, but this was certainly not the primary factor determining its acceptance.

The Indian nationalists, when faced with foreign oppression and exploitation, were willing to consider and adopt the course which Gandhi proposed for achieving their political freedom. It is quite true, particularly in his later years, that Gandhi felt there had been inadequacy in the movement, but this does not alter or invalidate the interpretation which is offered here.*

The overwhelming percentage of people throughout the world are not, and never will be, predominantly doctrinally minded in situations in which they do not understand how pressing practical problems can be faced and resolved satisfactorily if they continue to adhere to the particular doctrine in question. They are concerned predominantly in such situations with the questions of how to act in a crisis and how to solve the problem. They are not primarily concerned with how *not* to face problems and how *not* to act. Yet the pacifists have predominantly concentrated on the latter, that is how *not* to act and how *not* to solve problems. (Some may remember A.J. Muste's old pamphlet, *How to Deal with a Dictator.* In it he was almost exclusively concerned with how *not* to deal with a dictator.)

The Indian nationalists when faced with foreign oppression and exploitation were willing to consider and to adopt a nonviolent course of action which Gandhi proposed in order to achieve political freedom. When that struggle was won, however, Indians did not automatically continue their adherence to nonviolent means. This was a natural and predictable consequence.

THE REAL CHOICE

In a multitude of situations throughout the world, people have used and will continue to use the technique of nonviolent action for certain limited objectives. As they do so, they will not limit themselves to the same nonviolent means in all other current situations. Nor will they in advance reject the option of violence in all conceivable future situations. There are many people, particularly doctrinal and religious pacifists, who deprecate most strongly this adoption of the nonviolent technique without the nonviolent creed or philosophy or doctrine as well. This response is based on a totally misleading understanding of the situation and the possible choices before the people.

---

* See Chapter Six, "Gandhi's Evaluation of Indian Nonviolent Action."

In India and in these other situations, the choice has not been one of adopting on a limited scale the nonviolent technique as against adopting a whole nonviolent philosophy or creed. For most of these people it was inconceivable that this full doctrinal change could take place within the context and limits of the time in which the problem was going to be faced and solved in one way or another. The choice in this situation and for that political society was instead one between the nonviolent technique and the violent technique, that is, war.

It is true that every case of nonviolent action in which the technique is widely and successfully practiced by ordinary people is an important contribution to the wider adoption of nonviolent means in place of war and other types of political violence. But one must not expect that the same people who have used nonviolent action on one occasion will automatically continue sole reliance upon that technique in new situations in place of violence.

Very little consideration has yet been given to the whole phenomenon of widespread adoption of the nonviolent technique for political ends and of the role which this adoption may have in the removal of political violence from modern society. Much serious work is needed here.

In the United States, particularly in the civil rights struggles, certain American pacifists have made important contributions to the nonviolent struggle movements, and have fully appreciated the importance of the adoption by the Afro-Americans of nonviolent action to deal with the segregation situation (even though this did not in most cases mean adoption of nonviolence as a way of life). The choice there was again between nonviolent action and violent action. The lessons of this situation seem to be similar to those of the Indian situation.

Those pacifists and peace workers who have been surprised with the Indian reliance upon military means in facing the Chinese border conflict ought not to have been surprised. Gandhi repeatedly warned in his later years that India was trying to continue with the British-initiated military defense policy and that she might even become a major world military power. But we have rarely examined the reasons why India has behaved in this way.

The Indians' own experience with nonviolent struggle is an important potential contribution to their capacity to see its power and its relevance to any new situation. There is, however, no automatic transference as so many pacifists have assumed.

PRACTICAL POLICY REQUIRED

The answer in a new situation must also be an answer in practical terms, for it is because of the lack of confidence in the practicality of nonviolent action, that confidence is in turn shifted to, or continues to lie with, violent courses of action—either of military action in war or as strong military preparation as a deterrent. If people had in the past believed that nonviolent means of action were effective and practical for meeting severe threats, then the nonviolent philosophies and creeds, with their moral principles condemning violence, would not have been so often abandoned or so drastically compromised.

Simple moral exhortations are in the present situation in India inevitably going to have next to no impact. Faced with what they believe to be unjustified military invasion and threat of invasion, the Indians have turned to the only means they believe to be effective in *this* situation—that is, to military might.

Gandhi frequently stated his belief that a free India should be able to defend her freedom nonviolently.* When the Japanese approached India, for example, he thought of ways of resisting that invasion nonviolently, just as he had resisted the British occupation. However, no one in the days immediately preceding or following independence to the present day has, to my knowledge, formulated even the framework for a consciously adopted, carefully prepared, systemically trained program of nonviolent defense of India's newly gained freedom: neither Gandhi nor his associates, nor Vinoba Bhave, nor Jayaprakash Narayan, nor Rammanohar Lohia, nor any of the visiting Western pacifists.

This is not surprising, but it was fatal. For it meant that in the absence of a practical alternative course of action, India's defense effort became totally military. And it meant that despite the superiority of India's nonalignment policy, she continued all the

* See Chapter Eight, "Gandhi's Defense Policy."

time to combine an idealistic international policy with a conventional military program. In a crisis this would inevitably mean that to the maximum of her capacity, she would fight in the same way as any other country would have fought—just as without Gandhi's earlier practical program India's revolution would have been a bloody one (witness 1857-1859 or the twentieth century Indian terrorists for example).

Viewed in this light, the Indian shift in the Chinese crisis to open war, and major war preparations on a larger scale than before it, is neither surprising nor a phenomenon which requires great pondering over India's so-called betrayal. It is the inevitable consequence of the lack of any preparation of an alternative practical nonviolent defense policy. The problem, therefore, is not to be met by private pleas to Prime Minister Nehru or other government leaders to be nonviolent in the situation. Nor is it to be met by exhortations calling for Indians to be true to Gandhi, or to save the world. It can only be met with the development of a realistic powerful alternative way of maintaining one's national freedom in face of external threats—as well as against internal threats to freedom.

It is hardly surprising that Western pacifists do not see the Indian situation in the same light as this analysis. Over past decades they have made precisely the same mistake as that which has been made by the Indian Gandhians. That is, Western pacifists have not sought to substitute a nonviolent way of meeting potential aggression or of discouraging it by a capacity to resist, but have been largely concerned with moralizing about what *not* to do, and in action they have been concerned often with quite incomplete and sometimes naive proposals.

THE CHALLENGE

The challenge of the Indian crisis today is, therefore, not simply one of how to help India to save her notion of nonviolence. Instead, the challenge is as much to us as to the Indians. It is to offer an alternative practical course of action upon which people can rely to deal with those rulers who seek by military means to impose their will upon their neighbors.

Hitherto, the problem of war and the problem of tyranny have usually been viewed as separate problems. This has been an error. Both war and tyranny can be described as efforts by rulers to impose their will upon people by the threat of political violence and armed oppression. Hence, from a point of view which rejects major violence for political ends, war and tyranny fall in the same category.

Let us look at it another way. Past efforts to preserve or achieve peace have rarely been seriously concerned with the preservation and achievement of freedom as well. Indeed, some peace proposals in the past have often been at the price of acquiescence or inaction against modern tyrants. On the other hand, those people who have been most concerned with freedom, have usually axiomatically assumed that this freedom could only be achieved or guaranteed by some type of violence, that is, by armed insurrection or by international war or preparations for war. Thus both of these groups of people—those who have favored peace and those who have favored freedom—have tended to support courses of action which have in fact acted against the achievement of the other objective.

WHAT ANSWER?

It may be that our whole analysis has been wrong. It may be that war and tyranny are intimately related. It may also be that the vast majority of mankind is more concrned with freedom than with peace, even in a nuclear age. It may be that people will never be able to give up war until they have confidence in a substitute way of dealing with threats to their liberty. As Hannah Arendt has suggested in her book, *On Revolution,* the problems of modern war and of modern tyranny must, if either is to be solved, be faced simultaneously.* This is a departure from the traditional peace and

* New York: Viking Press, 1963, and London: Faber and Faber, 1963. See Gene Sharp, "Freedom and Revolution: A review-essay on Hannah Arendt's *On Revolution"* in Sharp, *Social Power and Political Freedom* (Boston: Porter Sargent Publishers, Inc., 1979). Several additional chapters in *Social Power and Political Freedom* develop the theme of this chapter in considerably greater detail.

pacifist movement and its programs. It is, however, the lesson which we have to learn not only from the Indian crisis but also from a perceptive look at the failure of the Western peace and pacifist movements.

We still must face that disturbing question: Why is it that when most of the people of the literate world at least agree that war must be abolished and know that another world war may end everything, does almost everybody continue to support preparations for war? The answer, I suggest, is that they will continue to do so until they have the confidence in an alternative way of dealing with those crises for which they have traditionally relied upon war.

The answer to our problem, therefore, is not one of reasserting this dogma or that, but of developing a course of action in which ordinary people as well as political leaders can have confidence, a course of action which can preserve and extend freedom in the face of modern tyranny but which can do this without the necessity of military means.

8

Gandhi's Defense Policy

Gandhi was neither a supporter of violence in politics nor a conscientious objector. He was an experimenter in the development of "war without violence"—as Shridharani called it.* Gandhi's work here was pioneering, and not always adequate, but it represents a major development of historical significance both in ethics and in politics. With the deliberate refinement of nonviolent means of struggle it became possible for one to act effectively in conflict situations against political injustices and oppression while applying only nonviolent means of action. Many problems in the further development and application of this approach of course remained,

* See Appendix A, "Shridharani's *War Without Violence*."

and will continue to arise in the use of those means in facing new difficulties and new situations. But in words and action Gandhi pointed toward what may be the key to the resolution of the dilemma of how one can behave peacefully and at the same time actively and effectively oppose oppression and injustice. He believed that he had a solution for the conflicting demands of peace and national defense.

Naturally—as Gandhi insisted—we must all think for ourselves. It would not be right for us simply to repeat parrot-like what Gandhi or anyone else has said. (Gandhi would be horrified if we did.) But if we are to decide that we do not share the views of such men as Gandhi, it is important that we reject them partially or fully only after having fairly considered them. There is, remarkably, a great deal of ignorance and misrepresentation of Gandhi's opinions and beliefs, especially concerning the question of violence, resistance, and national defense. If we are to be able to make our own evaluation of their relative merit and validity, therefore, it is very important that the widespread lack of understanding and misunderstandings on Gandhi's views be corrected.[1]

DISTORTIONS OF GANDHI'S VIEWS

Two widespread distortions of Gandhi's views became prevalent in India during the first two decades after his death. If not examined critically these may prevent us from seeing Gandhi's potential relevance to the resolution of the dilemma about peace and defense.

The first was a tendency among some exponents of nonviolence in India to dismiss Gandhi's contribution to the development of nonviolent struggle for use in place of political violence. It was now possible, it was said, to develop a so-called "higher" type of nonviolence in which struggle and resistance have little or no role. It is incumbant upon such exponents,* if they are to maintain their position, to show in detailed political analyses either that major conflicts over important issues do not exist today, or that no alternative to political violence is in fact needed (because it is either best *not to resist* evil *at all*, or because it is right to use violence for

---

* This referred especially to Vinoba Bhave.

political ends). Careful analyses of such questions have not, however, been offered. Unless these questions (and the questions they raise) are carefully faced, this position leads inevitably to a withdrawal from some of the most crucial problems of the modern world, and to a position very similar to the politically-irrelevant nonresistant Christian sects.[2] In the absence, therefore, of a carefully reasoned explanation of *why* Gandhi's most important contribution to the development of nonviolence and politics is to be dismissed as lower or inferior, this first tendency deserves in my view very little serious consideration. As it stands, the view arrogantly belittles Gandhi and his contribution, and diverts us from seeing Gandhi's immense contribution to the resolution of the dilemma of how one can simultaneously promote peace and oppose injustice and oppression.

A second distortion of Gandhi's opinions about violence and defense became much more widespread and accepted. On the basis that he said violence is better than cowardly submission to evil, it has been insisted that Gandhi supported military defense for India. Therefore, it is concluded, Gandhi's blessing rests on India's preparations for and use of war, and his name must not be invoked in criticism of that policy or in favor of any other possible policy. One hears this view almost endlessly from Indians. Perhaps none of the people using this argument would change his or her personal views if this representation of Gandhi's opinions were disproved. Nevertheless, this invocation of Gandhi's blessing is based on such a gross misunderstanding that it ought never to be allowed to be repeated without challenge, not only for the sake of accuracy, but also because it blinds us to Gandhi's quite different view of India's defense policy.

Another general source of misunderstanding is rooted in the tendency to force Gandhi's views into the mold of our own assumptions and patterns of thinking, when in fact they often do not fit at all. This response may be quite unconscious, but the results are just as distorted as if it were deliberate. We tend to assume, for example, that Gandhi must fit the general pattern of a Western pacifist, war resister, or conscientious objector, or if he does not, that he was at least a qualified supporter of political violence and war. Also, at times we bring to this discussion the unstated assumption that, despite certain limited exceptions, it is the person who uses violence who is *really* courageous and effective, and that rejection of violence has within it, to some degree at least, aspects of cowardice, naiveté and ineffectiveness. If such unexamined assumptions are in the backs of our minds, they are likely to lead us to commit distortions or major misrepresentations when we discuss Gandhi's views.

In order to understand Gandhi's views, therefore, and to correct these distortions of them, let us look in detail at what Gandhi did in fact say about cowardice, violence, nonviolent action, defense against aggression, and India's defense policy. The bulk of this chapter is devoted to a systematic presentation of Gandhi's views in this field.

COWARDICE AND VIOLENCE

Gandhi *did* repeatedly say that resistance by violence was morally better than cowardice, submission and impotence when faced with violent attack, suppression, and political evil. The distortion arises because most of the exponents of such misunderstandings have not read Gandhi's statements on the subject, and especially the additional passages in them which contain rejection of that same violence. Nor do they go on to recount Gandhi's explicit views on war and defense.

His actual statements make it quite clear that Gandhi was not endorsing violence. He was instead condemning cowardice, passivity, and submissiveness to evil, saying that people ought not to be personal hypocrites if they believed in violence. But he added that there was a superior alternative nonviolent way of acting, which was the course in which he believed and which he recommended to others. There is no sin like cowardice, in Gandhi's view.[3] Cowardice is "violence double distilled."[4] There were some who sought to justify their passivity and inaction in times of crisis by pleading they were being "nonviolent." Gandhi wrote, however,

> We have always proclaimed from the housetops that non-violence is the way of the brave but there are some amongst us who have brought *ahimsa* [nonviolence] into disrepute by using it as a weapon of the weak. In my opinion, to remain a passive spectator of the kind of crimes that Bombay has witnessed of late is cowardice.[5]

Non-violence is not a cover for cowardice, but it is the supreme virtue of the brave. Exercise of non-violence requires far greater bravery than that of swordsmanship. Cowardice is wholly inconsistent with non-violence. Translation from swordsmanship to non-violence is possible and, at times, even an easy stage.[6]

But cowards cannot for ever remain cowards. You do not know what a coward I was when young, and you will agree that I am not quite a coward today. Multiply my example and you will have one whole nation shaking off its cowardice.[7]

Gandhi's condemnation of cowardice thus had a political as well as a moral intention. Such a national change from passivity and submission to defiance and self-reliance was crucial in Gandhi's thinking because of his view that it was the Indian's submission and cooperation which made the British *Raj* possible.[8]

People ought not, Gandhi insisted, pretend that they are abstaining from violence because of moral reasons when in fact they are afraid to take part in *any* kind of struggle, even less courageous violent struggle.

. . .[I]t is better to be violent, if there is violence in our breasts, than to put on the cloak of non-violence to cover impotence. Violence is any day preferable to impotence. There is hope for a violent man to become non-violent. There is no such hope for the impotent.[9]

Far better than emasculation would be the bravery of those who use physical force. Far better than cowardice would be meeting one's death fighting.[10]

There should be no camouflage.[11]

For, under *Swaraj* [self-rule] too I would not hesitate to advise those who would bear arms to do so and fight for the country.[12]

If an individual or a group of people are unable or unwilling to follow this great law of life [nonviolence], . . . retaliation or resistance unto death is the second best, though a long way off from the first. Cowardice is impotence worse than violence. The coward desires revenge but being afraid to die, he looks to others, maybe the Government of the day, to do the work of defence for him. A coward is less than a man.[13]

It is clear from several statements that in these and some of the following quotations Gandhi was looking at the problem in terms of the effects of the various possible courses of action on the integrity of the individual carrying them out, rather than at the social and political results of such violence, which he discusses elsewhere. Various statements also make it clear that in such violence it is not the willingness to *kill* which Gandhi finds admirable, but the willingness to risk one's own death fighting for one's beliefs. It is in this context that his admiration can be best understood for instances of men fighting tenaciously to the last man against overwhelming odds without any hope of victory. "If a man fights with his sword single-handed against a horde of dacoits [bandits] armed to the teeth, I should say he is fighting almost non-violently."[14]

> If Poland has that measure of uttermost bravery and an equal measure of selflessness, history will forget that she defended herself with violence. Her violence will be counted almost as non-violence.[15]
>
> ... [Y]ou must understand the meaning at the back of my mind. There is the refusal to bend before overwhelming might in the full knowledge that it means certain death. The Poles knew that they would be crushed to atoms, and yet they resisted the German hordes. That was why I called it almost non-violence.[16]

These statements, however, do not mean that Gandhi viewed violence, even for a good objective, as an unmixed expression of bravery. Violence, too, contained a significant element of fear and weakness.

> ... [V]engeance is any day superior to passive, effeminate and helpless submission. Forgiveness is higher still. Vengeance too is weakness. The desire for vengeance comes out of fear of harm, imaginary or real.[17]

Men who "believed in war" ought not to avoid taking part in it because of "cowardice," "base motives," or "anger," and Gandhi had therefore advised on occasion that such men who did not share his approach to nonviolence ought, for example, to enlist in the army or "to defend the honour of their womenfolk and their property by force of arms." This was simply because they ought not to be cowards but should be true to their own beliefs. The nonviolent way was better, and was the one Gandhi pursued. He made it clear in that discussion that "I do not believe in the use of arms, and ... it is contrary to the religion of *ahimsa* which I profess. ..." He added that it was difficult to practice that doctrine "in the midst of a world full of strife, turmoil and passions ... And yet the conviction too that without it life is not worth living is growing daily deeper."[18] In 1928 Gandhi wrote:

> I do not believe in short-cuts to success. ... However much I may sympathize with and admire worthy motives, I am an uncompromising opponent of violent methods even to serve the noblest of causes.[19]

A WEAPON OF THE STRONG

One of the statements by Gandhi concerning cowardice and violence which is often quoted or paraphrased comes from his 1920 article "The Doctrine of the Sword": "I do believe that, where there is only a choice between cowardice and violence, I would advise violence." Gandhi continued immediately with some specific examples:

> Thus when my eldest son asked me what he should have done, had he been present when I was almost fatally assaulted in 1908, whether he should have run away and seen me killed or whether he should have used physical force which he could and wanted to use, and defended me, I told him that it was his duty to defend me even by using violence. Hence it was that I took part in the Boer War, the so-called Zulu Rebellion and the late War. Hence also do I advocate training in arms for those who believe in the method of violence. I would rather have India resort to arms in order to defend her honour than that she would, in a cowardly manner, become or remain a helpless witness to her own dishonour.[20]

It is not usual for the next paragraph which follows immediately in the original text and also certain other passages in the article to be quoted, for they challenge the comforting view that the passage establishes that Gandhi was a supporter of war and military defense:

> But I believe that non-violence is infinitely superior to violence, forgiveness is more manly than punishment. Forgiveness adorns a soldier. But abstinence is forgiveness only when there is the power to punish; it is meaningless when it pretends to proceed from a helpless creature. A mouse hardly forgives a cat when it

allows itself to be torn to pieces by her. I therefore appreciate the sentiment of those who cry out for the condign punishment of General Dyer* and his ilk. They would tear him to pieces, if they could. But I do not believe India to be helpless. I do not believe myself to be a helpless creature. Only I want to use India's and my strength for a better purpose.[21]

The remaining three-quarters of the article is largely a continuous plea for India to practice nonviolence because she realizes her strength and because "she has a mission for the world."[22] Various other passages of the article will be included in this chapter at a later point. A reading of the whole text thus gives a totally different view than that which is often implied by a citation of only the first sentence of the article.

Gandhi did not want simply an abstention from violence for whatever reason. He wanted men to give up violence because they were strong enough not to feel the need for it and because they had a better way of facing serious conflicts.

What is wanted is a deliberate giving up of violence out of strength. To be able to do this requires imagination coupled with a penetrating study of the world drift.[23]

Strength does not come from physical capacity. It comes from an indomitable will.[24]

. . . [India] has no consciousness of strength. She is conscious only of her weakness. If she were otherwise, there would be no communal problems, nor political. If she were non-violent in the consciousness of her strength, Englishmen would lose their role of distrustful conquerors. We may talk politically as we like and often legitimately blame the English rulers. But if we, as Indians, could but for a moment visualize ourselves as a strong people disdaining to strike, we should cease to fear Englishmen whether as soldiers, traders or administrators, and they to distrust us.[25]

"We are regarded as a cowardly people," Gandhi said in 1918.[26] And he saw nonviolent resistance as a technique which not only did not make cowards of men, but which "infused courage" into them. He recommended nonviolent action because "it was the weapon of the really brave."[27]

---

* General Dyer had ordered the shooting without warning of people at a peaceful meeting in 1919, the "Massacre of Jallianwala Bagh" in Amritsar. See Chapter One.

The bravery of the non-violent is vastly superior to that of the violent. . . . there is no comparison between the two types of bravery. The one is limited, the other is limitless.[28]

"And it is wrong to say that a person is unarmed in the sense of being weak who has *ahimsa* as his weapon."[29] There was no passive submission here. The use of nonviolent action "does not mean meak submission to the will of the evil-doer, but it means the pitting of one's whole soul against the will of the tyrant."[30] "In the code of the Satyagrahi there is no such thing as surrender to brute force."[31]

It never implied that a non-violent man should bend before the violence of an aggressor. . . . He was not to return violence by violence but neutralize it by withholding one's hand and, at the same time, refusing to submit to the demand. This was the only civilized way of going on in the world.[32]

Courage and fearlessness were essential for nonviolent struggle.[33] In fact, Gandhi insisted, it required more courage than did violence.[34]

I present Dr. Benes [President of the Czechoslovak Republic at the time of the Nazi invasion] with a weapon not of the weak but of the brave. There is no bravery greater than a resolute refusal to bend the knee to an earthly power, no matter how great, and that without bitterness of spirit and in the fullness of faith that the spirit alone lives, nothing else does.[35]

A SUBSTITUTE FOR VIOLENCE

Gandhi's view was, therefore, not that violence and military defense were necessary and right because the alternative was cowardice and submission to evil. A nonviolent alternative existed which he supported and sought to develop. "Satyagraha is always superior to armed resistance . . . It is the weapon that adorns the strong."[36] "Non-violence is without exception superior to violence, i.e. the power at the disposal of a non-violent person is always greater than he would have if he was violent."[37]

Gandhi's nonviolent alternative was "designed to be a complete and effective substitute" for the means of violence in political conflicts.[38] *Satyagraha* was, he said, "the real sanction."[39] In his testimony before the Hunter Committee in 1920, Gandhi declared that the *satyagraha* movement was "intended to replace methods of violence. . . ." "It is conceived entirely with the object of ridding the country of the idea of violence."[40] In 1933 Gandhi wrote of *satyagraha:* "It was conceived as a complete substitute for violence,"[41] repeating, "Satyagraha has been designed as an effective substitute for violence."[42] Critics, or even smug "believers," might argue that such nonviolence was only suitable for a small moral elite. This was not Gandhi's view:

> Of course the critics can reasonably argue that the non-violence pictured by me is not possible for masses of mankind, it is possible only for the very few highly developed persons. I have combatted that view and suggested that, given proper training and proper generalship, non-violence can be practised by masses of mankind.[43]

There thus existed, in Gandhi's view, two broad sanctions, or techniques of struggle, between which anyone attempting to behave realistically in politics had to choose: the established means of political violence and the developing technique of nonviolent action.

> Non-co-operation may have come in advance of its time. India and the world must then wait, but there is no choice for India save between violence and non-co-operation.[44]

This nonviolent alternative, Gandhi believed, offered the prospect of the capacity to cope with both threatening internal violence and foreign oppression: "The way out of the riots on the one hand and British bayonets on the other is frank acceptance of non-violence."[45] Gandhi's basic approach to the problems of struggle and violence, therefore, was first to try to arouse people from cowardice and submissiveness, to urge them to be true to their convictions and ready to act against injustice, and second to try his best to present and demonstrate the nonviolent alternative technique of struggle which they could use. He could not do everything himself. Others, too, would have to choose between the two techniques and help in their implementation. If people did not choose the nonviolent alternative, then violence became inevitable; in such cases Gandhi often said that it was such, but these statements were descriptions of the situations, and not expressions of Gandhi's moral choice.

GANDHI AND MILITARY DEFENSE

Gandhi's thinking about violence and nonviolence was never static but always developing. This was certainly the case concerning Gandhi's views about war. As noted above, Gandhi did at several points in the early part of his career give a kind of qualified support for war, or at least participated in it to a certain degree—though never to the point of using weapons himself.[46] "My repugnance to war was as strong then as it is today; and I could not then have, and would not have, shouldered a rifle."[47] He did not seek to dismiss his critics by pleading that he had done only noncombatant work, for as he viewed it, even medical help to the wounded constituted participation in war. "There is no defence for my conduct weighted only in the scales of *Ahimsa.*"[48] This is not the place to repeat Gandhi's later explanations for his limited assistance during those wars; they are readily available elsewhere.[49] It is more important to note that Gandhi's thinking about war and the means of removing it developed considerably in his later years.

Gandhi never changed his view that those who believed in violence ought to be willing to take part in violent resistance against oppression and invasion.[50] His 1921 statement remained valid: "For, under Swaraj too I would not hesitate to advise those who would bear arms to do so and fight for the country."[51] But that did not mean that he favored military defense. Violence was "at best a poor weapon of defence."[52] Arms were a symbol of helplessness, not of strength.[53] Contrary to the preponderant view that military defense was necessary to defend democracy, Gandhi believed that democracy and the military way were incompatible with each other. "It will be a poor democracy that depends for its existence on military assistance."[54] "Democracy and the military spirit he held to be a contradiction in terms."[55] ". . .[D]emocracy and dependence on the military and the police are incompatible."[56]

> Peace through superior violence inevitably led to the atom bomb and all that it stood for. It was the completest negation of non-violence and of democracy which was not possible without the former.[57]

This perception of interrelationships between the type of ultimate sanction and the type of political system was based in part on Gandhi's view that under democracy "the weakest should have the same opportunity as the strongest. That can never happen except through non-violence."[58] But this was not the only basis, for Gandhi believed that there also existed a significant interrelationship between modern political violence and extreme dictatorship. The processes operating in modern war strongly tended toward the destruction of genuine political democracy even in the victorious and previously democratic country.[59]

> Science of war leads one to dictatorship pure and simple. Science of non-violence can alone lead one to pure democracy.[60]

> Democracy and violence can ill go together. The States that are today nominally democratic have either to become frankly totalitarian or, if they are to become truly democratic, they must become courageously non-violent.[61]

FIGHTING NAZISM BY WAR

Gandhi was not, however, blind to the realities of the conflicts often involved in wars, and to the fact that one side might well have much more right on its side than the other. In such cases, "neutrality" or "impartiality" played no role in Gandhi's thinking.

> Whilst all violence is bad and must be condemned in the abstract, it is permissible for, it is even the duty of, a believer in *ahimsa* to distinguish between the aggressor and the defender. Having done so, he will side with the defender in a non-violent manner, i.e. give his life in saving him.

Even if the defender continued to struggle by violent means in such an instance, Gandhi believed that such nonviolent intervention and assistance would contribute to a quicker and less vindictive peace.[62] During World War II, therefore, he said, "strange as it may appear, my sympathies are wholly with the Allies. Willy nilly this war is resolving itself into one between such democracy as the West has evolved and totalitarianism as it is typified in Herr Hitler."[63] He reached this view despite an acute awareness that by his standards the Western countries were not "genuine democracies" and that the Soviet Union, too, was a totalitarian system.

> If there ever could be a justifiable war in the name of and for humanity, a war against Germany, to prevent the wanton per-

secution of a whole race, would be completely justified. But I do not believe in any war.[64]

Gandhi, therefore, rejected not only any possible alliance with Germany or Japan, with the aim of defeating the British and achieving independence for India. He also rejected any military alliance with the Allies even as part of a bargain in exchange for India's independence (although he gave them moral support and did not wish to cause them unnecessary embarrassment or difficulties). It is significant that Gandhi's statement on the persecution of the Jews was made before World War II and *before* the Nazis put into operation "the Final Solution," which began *after* the outbreak of the war. He even warned that the outbreak of the war might contribute to the mass murder of the Jews rather than save them from such a fate: "The calculated violence of Hitler may even result in a general massacre of the Jews by way of his first answer to the declaration of such hostilities."[65]

Though Gandhi was opposed to Nazism, and respected the Allies' determination to fight it, he could not approve of the means they used.

> For Britain, so long as she holds to the orthodox method, has to copy the Nazi methods, if she is to put up a successful defence. Thus the logical outcome of the violent method seems to be increasingly to brutalize man including "the weak majority." For it has to give its defenders the required measure of co-operation.[66]

> . . .[C]ounter-violence can only result in further brutalization of human nature.[67]

> After all, what is the gain if the so-called democracies win? War certainly will not end. Democracies will have adopted all the tactics of the Fascists and the Nazis, including conscription and all other forcible methods to compel and exact obedience. All that may be gained at the end of the victory is the possibility of comparative protection of individual liberty. But that protection does not depend upon outside help. It comes from the internal determination to protect it against the whole world.[68]

"What terrifies me," Gandhi wrote in late 1940, "is that as things are going on at present defeat of Nazism will be bought at a terrific price, viz., superior Nazism, call it by any name you like."[69]

In his July 1940 appeal "To Every Briton," Gandhi developed this theme:

I appeal for cessation of hostilities, not because you are too exhausted to fight, but because war is bad in essence. You want to kill Nazism. You will never kill it by its indifferent adoption. Your soldiers are doing the same work of destruction as the Germans. The only difference is that perhaps yours are not as thorough as the Germans. If that be so, yours will soon acquire the same thoroughness as theirs, if not much greater. On no other condition can you win the war. In other words, you will have to be more ruthless than the Nazis. No cause, however just, can warrant the indiscriminate slaughter that is going on minute by minute. I suggest that a cause that demands the inhumanities that are being perpetuated today cannot be called just.[70]

After the war, Gandhi wrote: "The United Nations set out to fight Hitler with his weapons and ended by out-Hitlering Hitler."[71] The Axis Powers were crushed, true, but the result was "an empty victory."[72] The atomic bomb and all that it stood for were a negation not only of nonviolence but also of democracy itself. [73] Liberty and democracy would not be defended "by following totalitarian methods so far as war is concerned," Gandhi warned in 1940. "If liberty and democracy are to be truly saved, they will only be by non-violent resistance no less brave, no less glorious, than violent resistance."[74]

INDIA'S MILITARY PREPARATIONS

Contrary to a widespread opinion, Gandhi's rejection of military defense applied to India also. He recognized often that in the absence of confidence in nonviolent alternatives it was inevitable that India would use violent means of defense. But these were simply acknowledgements of the probable course of events in the situation in which reliance was placed on military means. Gandhi placed *his* confidence elsewhere. One of his post-prayer speeches in New Delhi in 1947 is an example of this:

Gandhiji said . . . that he had been an opponent of all warfare. But if there was no other way of securing justice from Pakistan, if Pakistan persistently refused to see its proved error and continued to minimize it, the Indian Union Government would have to go to war against it. War was not a joke. No one wanted war. That way lay destruction. But he could never advise anyone to put up with injustice. . . . As for Gandhiji himself, his way was different.[75]

The following day he developed that comment:

> Gandhiji said . . . that newspapers had displayed his remarks about war in such a way that there was an enquiry from Calcutta whether he had really begun to advocate war. He was wedded to non-violence for all time and could never advocate war. In a State run by him there would be no police and no military. But he was not running the Government of the Indian Union. He had merely pointed out the various possibilities. . . . That did not mean that his faith in non-violence had weakened in the least degree.[76]

Some weeks earlier Gandhi had said:

> It is true that I do not agree with what many of my closest friends have done or are doing. . .And what are the differences that matter? If you analyse them you would find only one fundamental difference to which all the others could be traced. Non-violence is my creed. It never was of the Congress. With the Congress it has always been a policy. . .The Congress had every right to change it when it found it necessary.[77]

Gandhi hoped that "free India would present to the world a lesson of peace," not the lesson "of hatred and violence of which the world is already sick unto death."[78] ". . . [A]n unwieldly, soulless India would merely be an imitation, and a third rate imitation at that, of the Western military States, utterly powerless to stand up against their onslaught."[79] Even the 1946 level of expenditure for military defense would mean that free India "will bring no relief to the famishing millions."[80]

> Our statesmen have for over two generations declaimed against the heavy expenditure on armaments under the British regime, but now that freedom from political serfdom has come, our military expenditure has increased and still threatens to increase and of this we are proud! There is not a voice raised against it in our legislative chambers. In spite, however, of the madness and the vain imitation of the tinsel of the West, the hope lingers in me and many others that India shall survive this death dance and occupy the moral height that should belong to her after the training, however imperfect, in non-violence for an unbroken period of thirty-two years since 1915.[81]

As early as 1920 Gandhi had spoken of the possibility of India resorting to violence to achieve liberation, and firmly rejected that course:

I believe absolutely that she has a mission for the world. She is not to copy Europe blindly. India's acceptance of the doctrine of the sword will be the hour of my trial. I hope I shall not be found wanting.[82]

Now with India freed from British political rule, Gandhi faced the deliberate increase of India's military might. He warned of dictatorship:

I see clearly that if the country cannot be turned to non-violence it will be bad for it and the world. It will mean goodbye to freedom. It might even mean a military dictatorship.[83]

He warned of war:

When we talk of armed preparation, we contemplate preparation to meet any violent combination with our superior violence. If India ever prepared herself that way, she would constitute the greatest menace to world peace.[84]

If I am in the minority of one, I must try to make converts. Whether one or many, I must declare my faith that it is better for India to discard violence altogether even for defending her borders. For India to enter into the race for armaments is to court suicide. With the loss of India to non-violence the last hope of the world will be gone.[85]

You know I have capitulated on the question of the desirability of maintaining a police force. But. . .I do not want to prepare India for military defence from today. We should never forget that we are not the whole of India. . . . And if the Congress too surrenders, there is no one to represent the no-army mentality.[86]

GANDHI AND KASHMIR

It is often said that Gandhi endorsed India's military action in Kashmir, and general conclusions about his approval of military defense have been drawn from this. A careful examination of Gandhi's various statements on that conflict, especially in the light of his general attitudes to cowardice and violence, and his sense of isolation in independent India, does not confirm the popular impression.[87] In a post-prayer speech in November 1947 Gandhi emphatically rejected any such interpretation about his views on the Kashmir conflict. He had received a letter which recalled his advice to other countries during World War II to adopt nonviolent resistance instead of war. Why then, the letter asked, had he abandoned his nonviolence when his own friends in the Government had sent military aid to Kashmir? How were the Kashmiris to resist nonviolently? Gandhi's views were recorded by an aide:

Replying Gandhiji said that he was sorry for the ignorance betrayed by the writer. The audience would remember that he had repeatedly said that he had no influence in the matter over his friends in the Union Cabinet. He held on to his views on non-violence as firmly as ever, but he could not impose his views on his best friends, as they were, in the Cabinet. He could not expect them to act against their convictions and everybody should be satisfied with his confession that he had lost his original hold upon his friends. The question put by the writer was quite apposite. Gandhiji's answer was quite simple.

His *ahimsa* forbade him from denying credit where it was due, even though the creditor was a believer in violence. Thus, though he did not accept Subhas Bose's belief in violence and his consequent action [Bose organized the "Indian National Army" and fought on the side of the Japanese in World War II], he had not refrained from giving unstinted praise to his patriotism, resourcefulness and bravery. Similarly, though he did not approve of the use of arms by the Union Government for aiding the Kashmiris and though he could not approve of Sheikh Abdulla's resort to arms, he could not possibly withhold admiration for either for their resourceful and praiseworthy conduct, especially, if both the relieving troops and the Kashmiri defenders died heroically to a man. He knew that if they could do so, they would perhaps change the face of India. But if the defence was purely non-violent in intention and action, he would not use the word "perhaps," for, he would be sure of change in the face of India even to the extent of converting to the defender's view the Union Cabinet, if not even the Pakistan Cabinet.

The non-violent technique, he would suggest, would be no armed assistance to the defenders. Non-violent assistance could be sent from the Union without stint. But the defenders, whether they got such assistance or not, would defy the might of the raiders or even a disciplined army in overwhelming numbers. And defenders dying at their post of duty without malice and without anger in their hearts against the assailants, and without the use of any arms including even their fists would mean an exhibition of heroism as yet unknown in history. Kashmir would then become a holy land shedding its fragrance not only throughout India, but the world.[88]

Pyarelal, Gandhi's secretary and biographer, put the situation concisely:

> His fundamental attitude on war had not changed. He was *not* reconciled to war in Kashmir or for that matter anywhere. He *knew* non-violence was more *effective* than armed force. He was engaged in perfecting his weapon—which, though it had demonstrated its efficacy in the struggle for independence, needed to be refurbished and over-hauled—perhaps redesigned for the duty which now awaited it.[89]

GANDHI'S DEFENSE POLICY

Conflicts would continue. Oppression would have to be opposed, and injustices removed. Aggression would have to be resisted. But the military technique, Gandhi believed, was not the way to face these problems, especially in independent India.

> He was convinced that unless India developed her non-violent strength, she had gained nothing either for herself or for the world. Militarization of India would mean her own destruction as well as of the whole world.[90]

Gandhi was asked what scientists should do if asked by the independent Indian Government to engage in research in assisting war and the development of the atomic bomb. Gandhi promptly replied: "Scientists to be worth the name should resist such a State unto death."[91] Gandhi's rejection of the military way while accepting the need for struggle and defense against aggression did not leave him resourceless. There was, he believed, a nonviolent alternative, one which could be adopted and applied successfully even by men who had spent their lives fighting by military methods.[92]

Defense capacity did not in Gandhi's view come from violence. It was rooted, instead, in the capacity to live as, and to remain, free men. If people learned not to live as slaves to anyone, there was no need for an army.[93] Gandhi spoke in 1947 of "the true art of self-defence":

> Violence always thrived on counter-violence. The aggressor had always a purpose behind his attack; he wanted something to be done, some object to be surrendered by the defenders. Now, if the

defender steeled his heart and was determined not to surrender even one inch, and at the same time to resist the temptation of matching the violence of the aggressor by violence, the latter could be made to realize in a short while that it would not be paying to punish the other party and his will could not be imposed in that way. This would involve suffering. It was this unalloyed self-suffering which was the truest form of self-defence which knew no surrender.[94]

Therefore, in the context of this general view, Gandhi at the time of the Italian invasion of Ethiopia expressed his opinion that if Ethiopia had been nonviolent, although not offering military resistance, she would have refused to give the Italians any cooperation even in face of violent sanctions. This noncooperation would thwart Italy's will, because she wanted submission.[95] Under those conditions, Mussolini could have had "no interest in Abyssinia [Ethiopia] . . . . Mussolini wanted submission and not defiance, and if he had met the quiet, dignified and non-violent defiance that I have described, he would certainly have been obliged to retire."[96]

Later he wrote:

. . .[A]t the back of the policy of terrorism is the assumption that terrorism if applied in a sufficient measure will produce the desired result, namely, bend the adversary to the tyrant's will. But supposing a people make up their mind that they will never do the tyrant's will, nor retaliate with the tyrant's own methods, the tyrant will not find it worth his while to go on with his terrorism.[97]

Ironically, Hitler too saw this as a crucial point and argued that it was imperative to reach the minds of the populace and convince them that they were defeated. In ruling conquered people, the impression had to be given that the conquerors were indeed the masters, Hitler told Rosenberg in May 1943. In the occupied East, German policy had to be so tough as to numb the population's political consciousness. Hitler continued:

. . . [R]uling the people in the conquered regions is, I might say, of course a psychological problem. One cannot rule by force alone. True, force is decisive, but it is equally important to have this psychological something which the animal trainer also needs to be master of his beast. They must be convinced that we are the victors. . . .[98]

But Gandhi maintained that men could and ought to refuse to become submissive and defeated subjects. By maintaining their courage, their self-respect and their self-confidence, they had the possibility of throwing off the tyrant. "It is claimed that a State can be based on non-violence, i.e. it can offer non-violent resistance against a world combination based on armed force."[99]

National defense by nonviolent resistance would be, Gandhi was convinced, more powerful and effective than military defense. *Ahimsa* was "a force mightier than the force of arms however powerful."[100] ". . . [T]he power that armaments give to defend right is nothing compared to the power that non-violence gives to do the same thing and that too with better show of reason."[101] Such a means of defense would cost no more lives, and in terms of financial and material cost would be much cheaper.[102] Gandhi believed that "the true democrat is he who with purely non-violent means defends his liberty and therefore his country's and ultimately that of the whole of mankind."[103] This was Gandhi's solution to the conflicting demands of peace and national defense.

In 1947 Gandhi firmly rejected the view that nonviolence was of no present use to India, and that she needed instead a strong army. Only ignorance could make one say "that in this age non-violence has little scope in the face of violence, whereas I make bold to say that in this age of the atom bomb unadulterated non-violence is the only force that can confound all the tricks of violence put together."[104]

Speaking on problems of personal as well as wider conficts, Gandhi wrote:

> For me there can be no preparation for violence. All preparation must be for non-violence if courage of the highest type is to be developed. Violence can only be tolerated as being preferable always to cowardice. . . . the real effective resistance lies in non-violence. . . . [Since the world lacked] the highest courage, namely, courage born of non-violence, it arms itself even unto the atom bomb.[105]

> . . . [I]n this age of the atom bomb there was no weapon like non-violent resistance. It did not make cowards of men. It infused courage even in women. If he recommended non-violence, it was because he was convinced that it was the weapon of the really brave.[106]

. . . [H]owever small a nation or even a group may be, it is able, even as the individual, provided that it has one mind as also the will and the grit, to defend its honour and self-respect against a whole world in arms. Therein consists the matchless strength and beauty of the unarmed. That is non-violent defence which neither knows nor accepts defeat at any stage. Therefore, a nation or a group which has made non-violence its final policy, cannot be subjected to slavery even by the atom bomb.[107]

If my argument has gone home, is it not time for us to declare our changeless faith in non-violence of the strong and say we do not seek to defend our liberty with the force of arms but we will defend it with the force of non-violence?"[108]

FIGHTING NAZISM BY NONVIOLENT RESISTANCE

Gandhi admitted that the nonviolent technique had not been tried on a large scale, but, "In so far as it has been tried, it has shown promising results."[109] These results, combined with his distrust of the efficacy of violent means of conflict, led Gandhi to suggest that the victims and enemies of Nazism use nonviolent resistance instead of war.

Drastic diseases require drastic remedies. In this instance nothing but non-violence can cure Nazi violence.[110]

Gandhi's appeal, significantly, was not simply on abstract moral grounds, but also on grounds of practicality: nonviolent resistance if really applied would be more effective in destroying Nazism and would give better long-term results for both democracy and peace.

The non-violent method would have meant no abject surrender. It would have confounded all modern tactics of war, indeed rendered them of no use. The new world order, which all dream of, would surely have been found.[111]

Herr Hitler can only be confounded by the adoption by Britain of the novel method of fighting. At one single stroke he will find that all his tremendous armament has been put out of action. A warrior lives on his wars whether offensive or defensive. He suffers a collapse, if he finds that his warring capacity is unwanted.[112]

In late 1938 and early 1939 Gandhi appealed to Jews in Germany to resist the Nazi persecutions by nonviolent resistance.[113] From October to December, 1938—after the Munich Agreement (30 September) and before the full German occupation of Czechoslovakia (late March 1939)—Gandhi appealed to the Czechs and Slovaks to resist with his technique of struggle. Their plight had moved him "to the point of physical and mental distress. . . ."[114] He rejected Munich as "a peace that was no peace."[115] British and French intervention could, however, have led only to unprecedented bloodshed and destruction. Yet violent resistance by Czechoslovakia alone was "pure bravado."

> If I were a Czech. . .I would not be a vassal to any nation or body.
> I must have absolute independence or perish.[116]

Resistance by nonviolent means was Gandhi's prescription.

> The Czechs could not have done anything else [other than what they did] when they found themselves deserted by their two powerful allies. And yet I have the hardihood to say that, if they had known the use of non-violence as a weapon for the defence of national honour, they would have faced the whole might of Germany with that of Italy thrown in.[117]

It would have been better, Gandhi wrote in June 1940, if the various European peoples had resisted the Nazis by nonviolent resistance.[118]

In particular, Gandhi appealed to the British peoples to resist Nazism with his technique.

> Herr Hitler. . .contemptuously rejected the way of peace or persuasion and chose that of the sword. Hence my sympathy for the cause of the Allies. But my sympathies must not be interpreted to mean endorsement, in any shape or form, of the doctrine of the sword for the defence even of proved right. Proved right should be capable of being vindicated by right means as against the rude, i.e. sanguinary, means.[119]

> I want you to fight Nazism without arms, or, if I am to retain the military terminology, with non-violent arms.[120]

> The meaning of refusal to own allegiance is clear. You will not bow to the supremacy of the victor, you will not help him to attain his object.[121]

In early 1942, when Nazi armies seemed at times invincible and had conquered vast territories, Gandhi wrote:

> If the Nazis come to India, the Congress will give them the same fight that it has given Great Britain. I do not underrate the power of *satyagraha*. . . .[122]

With the prospect of a Japanese invasion of India, Gandhi counseled nonviolent resistance, although the situation was complicated by India's lack of independence of action and by the presence of British armed forces fighting the Japanese. ". . .[I]t is no part of their [nonviolent resisters'] duty to help anyone to steal their country."[123]

> If the British have retired in an orderly manner, leaving things in Indian hands, the whole thing can work splendidly and it might even be made difficult for the Japanese to settle down in India or any part of it in peace, because they will have to deal with a population which will be sullen and resistant. It is difficult to say what can happen. It is enough if people are trained to cultivate the power of resistance, no matter which power is operating—the Japanese or the British.[124]

DIFFICULTIES ACKNOWLEDGED

Gandhi's general position, strongly in favor of national defense by nonviolent resistance by India and other countries, is quite clear. It must be admitted, however, that when it came to explanations of how his policy would actually operate, or to expositions of detailed courses of action which might be used, Gandhi's appeals and statements were too vague and general to convince the "hardheaded realists." He expressed his general faith, for example, that the self-suffering of *satyagrahis* would convert the Nazis,[125] or at least could influence those Germans who had been duped by Hitler so that they might rebel against him.[126]

At times Gandhi's comments on how to meet an invasion were especially inadequate and unconvincing.[127] In 1940 Gandhi was asked what he thought were the chances of free India adopting a nonviolent defense policy and, in that event, whether resistance would take place at the frontier or would be put into operation only after the physical occupation had taken place. Gandhi discussed the questions only generally, and prefaced his comments by a statement which made it clear that he realized that adequate answers to the practical problems had not yet been developed:

> The questions are admittedly theoretical. They are also premature for the reason that I have not mastered the whole technique of non-violence. The experiment is still in the making. It is not even in its advanced stage.[128]

Congressmen had not learned how they could "defend the country by non-violent means."[129] Gandhi clearly acknowledged the practical difficulties in the implementation of such a policy, saying, "the snag comes in when we consider the ways and means of working the non-violent method."[130] Gandhi occasionally included discussions by others of the problems of a defense policy using nonviolent resistance in his journal *Harijan.*[131]

At times Gandhi seemed to assume that these difficulties would be solved in the course of action (ignoring the possibility that most people probably would not accept the policy unless they saw solutions for such difficulties). Thus he wrote after the war: "If the Government had not arrested me in 1942, I would have shown how to fight Japan by non-violence."[132] In 1940 he voiced the rather extreme view: "A non-violent man or society does not anticipate or provide for attacks from without. On the contrary, such a person or society firmly believes that nobody is going to disturb them."[133] Generally, however, Gandhi demonstrated a fairly realistic anticipation of what the British and other governments might do—such as the above comment on the prospect of a Japanese invasion and the need to resist it. He also frequently emphasized the importance of training for such resistance.

> I have always advised and insisted on non-violent defence. But I recognize that it has to be learnt like violent defence. It requires a different training. . . .[134]

". . . [G]iven proper training and proper generalship, non-violence can be practised by masses of mankind."[135]

Gandhi did not pretend that he had all the answers. He was able only to point the general direction, and to try in a small way to find the answers.

It [the experiment with nonviolence] has entered upon a most interesting, though at the same time a most difficult, stage [concerning its application to the defense problem]. I am myself sailing on uncharted waters. I have to take soundings every half-hour. The difficulty only braces me for the struggle.[136]

"That very few understand how to wield this mighty weapon is true."[137] People would gain an increased understanding of, and confidence in, nonviolent action as they saw it demonstrated in action as a powerful and effective technique.

An ocular demonstration of the success of nation-wide Satyagraha must be a prelude to its world-wide acceptance and hence as a natural corollary to the admission of the futility of armament. The only antidote to armament, which is the visible symbol of violence, is Satyagraha, the visible symbol of non-violence.[138]

India's nonviolence could be "a sendable commodity"—to assist, for example, Norway, Denmark, Spain, and China in their plights —"when India has gained her freedom through non-violence."[139]

Some people argue that nonviolent action could only be applied by the masses of people in a near-perfect society, but Gandhi sought to apply the technique in a society filled with inequality, injustice and oppression. Some insisted that the world being as it is unfortunately necessitated fighting the Nazis or the Japanese by military means, but Gandhi tried to develop a quite different way of fighting. Some maintained that before men can use *satyagraha* they must first seek to perfect themselves, yet Gandhi counseled that no one ought to wait for perfection before trying to deal with oppression and war. His appeal to the British to adopt nonviolent resistance against the Nazi system was met with strong criticism, but Gandhi remained convinced that his basic advice was sound:

In spite of the fierce criticism which has been levelled against my letter "To Every Briton," I adhere to every word of it, and am convinced that posterity will adopt the remedy suggested therein against violence however organized and fierce. And now that the enemy is at the gates of India I am advising my countrymen the same course of action I advised the British people. My advice may or may not be accepted by my countrymen. I would remain unmoved. . . . I would subscribe to the charge of my imperfection.

But a *satyagrahi* does not wait for perfection before he invites others to experiment with him, provided always that his faith is immovable like a mountain . . . If the war is damnable, how can [one] stop the things that go on by taking part in it, even though it may be on the defensive side and at the cost of his own life? For the defence has to resort to all the damnable things that the enemy does, and that with greater vigour if it has to succeed. Such a giving of life is not only not saving it but a mere waste.[140]

But Gandhi did not want people to accept his advice simply because he offered it; everyone had to think for him or herself and not "imitate others sheep-like."[141]

WHICH POLICY FOR INDIA?

The way which Gandhi himself favored and offered to others, however—let there be no mistake—meant active opposition to injustice, oppression, and aggression, not with the means of political violence which he rejected, but, by the use of "nonviolent arms." This advocacy, he made quite clear, was intended for India herself, and for the world as a whole.

In 1939, looking forward to the time of independence, Gandhi foresaw the strong possibility that India would adopt military defense. Even if that were inevitable because most Indians favored it, Gandhi was of the opinion that the Congress at least ought to continue to rely on nonviolent means of struggle in political conflicts, including its use as a defense policy instead of war.

It will make all the difference in the world whether the Congress is party to them [military preparations] or not. The world is looking for something new and unique from India. The Congress will be lost in the crowd, if it wears the same old outworn armour that the world is wearing today. The Congress has a name because it represents nonviolence as a political weapon *par excellence*.[142]

A nation which had won freedom without the force of arms should be able to keep it too without the force of arms. This he said in spite of the fact that India had an army, a navy in the making and an air force and these were being developed still further. He was convinced that unless India developed her nonviolent strength, she had gained nothing either for herself or for the world.[143]

In late 1939 Gandhi discussed with members of the Congress Working Committee the question of defending India against invasion by nonviolent means. The question was no longer "hypothetical."

> . . . [T]he Congress has to declare its policy and say whether it would fight the invading host violently or non-violently. So far as I can read the Working Committee's mind after a fairly full discussion, the members think that congressmen are unprepared for non-violent defence against armed invasion. This is tragic. Surely the means adopted for driving an enemy from one's house must, more or less, coincide with those to be adopted for keeping him out of the house. If anything, the latter process must be easier.

> Free India can have no enemy. And if her people have learnt the art of saying resolutely "no" and acting up to it, I dare say, no one would want to invade her.[144]

In April 1940 Gandhi acknowledged that "the chances of non-violence being accepted as a principle of State policy [by independent India] are very slight, so far as I can see at present."[145] On 21 June 1940 the question of defending India against invasion by nonviolent resistance was again discussed when Gandhi attended the Congress Working Committee. Gandhi later wrote that he had "pleaded hard" with the Committee. They faced the problems both of internal order and external defense. Gandhi advocated meeting the emergency: "by non-violent action. For if all were non-violent, there could be no anarchy and there would be no question of anybody arming for meeting aggression from without."[146] Following this discussion the Working Committee passed a declaration of policy which made it clear that Congress and Gandhi had different views on the means for national defense and that neither was responsible for the views or policy of the other. The Working Committee declaration read in part:

> The war in Europe, resulting from a desire for imperialist domination over other peoples and countries and a suicidal race in armaments, has led to human sorrow and misery on a scale

hitherto unknown. It has demonstrated the inefficacy of organized violence, on however vast a scale, for the defence of national freedom and the liberties of peoples. It has shown beyond a doubt that warfare cannot lead to peace and freedom; and the choice before the world is uttermost degradation and destruction through warfare or the way of peace and non-violence on basis of freedom for all peoples. Mahatma Gandhi has presented to the peoples of the world, crying for relief from the crushing burden of war, a weapon in the shape of organized non-violence designed to take the place of war for the defence of people's rights and freedom against armed aggression. He feels that at this critical phase in the history of man the Congress should enforce this ideal by declaring that it does not want that India should maintain armed forces to defend her freedom against external or internal disorder.

While the Working Committee hold that the Congress must continue to adhere strictly to the principle of non-violence in their struggle for independence, the Committee cannot ignore the present imperfections and failings in this respect of the human elements they have to deal with, and the possible dangers in a period of transition and dynamic change, until the Congress has acquired non-violent control over the people in adequate measure and the people have imbibed sufficiently the lesson of organized non-violence. The Committee have deliberated over the problem that has thus arisen and have come to the conclusion that they are unable to go the full length with Gandhiji. But they recognise that he should be free to pursue his great ideal in his own way, and therefore absolve him from responsibility for the programme and activity which the Congress has to pursue under the conditions at present prevailing in India and the world in regard to external aggression and internal disorder.

Many of the problems which the Working Committee have considered in this connection are not of the present, though they may be of the near future. The Committee wish to make it clear that the methods and the basic policy of non-violence in the national struggle for freedom continue with full force and are not affected in the least by the inability to extend it to the region of national defence.[147]

Gandhi later wrote:

My position was different. . . . And so I asked for absolution from the Committee. Hitherto I have been responsible for guiding the general policy of the Congress. I could no longer do so when fundamental differences were discovered between them and me. They readily recognized the correctness of my attitude. And they gave me the absolution. . . . They had not the confidence in themselves or those whom they represented, that they could express in their actions the required measure of non-violence. And so they made the only choice they could honestly make.[148]

Unable to carry the Congress with him, Gandhi tried to go his own way. The ranks of the "non-violent army" were thinning. That was all right; it would multiply again some day. But this did not mean that only those persons who had become perfectly nonviolent could support and participate in his policy.

Let no one understand from the foregoing that a non-violent army is open only to those who strictly enforce in their lives all the implications of non-violence. It is open to all who accept the implications and make an ever-increasing endeavour to observe them. It will be formed of those who will honestly endeavour to observe non-violence.[149]

Gandhi kept trying. In the midst of the war, in 1942,* Gandhi was asked whether free India would adopt the methods of total war. He replied:

I cannot say whether free India will take part in militarism or choose to go the non-violent way. But I can say without hesitation that if I can turn India to non-violence, I will certainly do so. If I succeed in converting forty crores [400,000,000] of my people to non-violence, it will be a tremendous thing, a wonderful transformation.[150]

Not only did Gandhi not reverse his advocacy of national defense by nonviolent resistance and opposition to military defense, but—as we have seen in various statements—these views seemed to intensify as time passed. Some of the most emphatic such expressions came in the weeks just before his assassination. Bemoan-

---

* For a more detailed discussion of Gandhi's views at that point see Appendix B, "The War in 1942."

ing both the communal riots and the expansion of the armaments program, Gandhi expressed the hope "that this blood-bath will soon end and out of that, perhaps, inevitable butchery, will rise a new and robust India—not warlike, basely imitating the West in all its hideousness, but a new India learning the best that the West has to give and becoming the hope not only of Asia and Africa, but the whole of the aching world."[151]

INDIA'S MISSION

The coming of World War II, the course by which it was waged, and the development of the atomic bomb made Gandhi even more convinced that the only way of avoiding disaster was in the extension of *satyagraha* to the field of national defense. Anticipating the outbreak of major hostilities in Europe, Gandhi wrote in late 1938: "There is no escape from the impending doom save through a bold and unconditional acceptance of the nonviolent method with all its glorious implications."[152] After the war, in 1946, his view was basically the same: "I have no doubt that unless big nations shed their desire of exploitation and the spirit of violence of which war is the natural expression and atom bomb the inevitable consequence, there is no hope for peace in the world."[153] ". . . [T]here is no hope for the aching world except through the narrow and straight path of non-violence."[154]

Gandhi had long believed that India had a special responsibility and duty in the development of a nonviolent alternative means of struggle which would make possible the abolition of war.

And so I am not pleading for India to practise non-violence because she is weak. I want her to practise non-violence being conscious of her strength and power. No training in arms is required for realization of her strength. We seem to need it, because we seem to think that we are but a lump of flesh. I want India to recognise that she has a soul that cannot perish and that can rise triumphant above every physical weakness and defy the physical combination of a whole world. . . . I believe absolutely that she has a mission for the world.[155]

POSTSCRIPT

PRESENT DIFFICULTIES

It must be admitted that Gandhi's challenge has not yet been fully taken up either by India or any other country. Within India there has been a recognition of the task in the concept of the volunteer, privately organized group called *Shanti Sena* (Peace Army), and in the statements of individual Gandhians. Jayaprakash Narayan, for example, has pointed out that the alternative to war is not meek submission: "There is no failure in a nonviolent war and we cannot forget all Gandhi taught us. The alternative to violent war is total disarmament and nonviolent rearmament." This would mean a casting off of fear of invaders and becoming "determined not to bow our head before any aggressor; we will offer nonviolent resistance to them."[156] There have been other statements by Jayaprakash Narayan and others which recognize the need for a substitute for war if India is not to continue to pursue a military policy.

The difficulties have come in at two points. First, it is often assumed axiomatically that such a nonviolent defense policy for India could operate only *after* Indian society has been revolutionized, i.e. after the development of the *Sarvodaya,* or the nonviolent, society. While it cannot be denied that there is a connection between social structure and techniques of conducting conflicts, the above assumption seems to have been accepted too hastily without the kind of careful thought and analysis which are required on such complicated questions as these. While it is not possible here to go into great detail on this problem, it is necessary to offer briefly two or three reasons for suggesting that the assumption is not necessarily a sound one.

Doubtless an ideal decentralized society in which injustice has been removed and which operates as an active participating democracy would be very conducive to the operation of a defense policy relying on nonviolent resistance to defeat foreign invasion. This does not necessarily mean, however, that such a society must be established *before* such a defense policy. That certainly was not

Gandhi's view. While he sought through the constructive program*
to build up the nonviolent social order, he forged the nonviolent
means for freeing India from the occupation under which she was
already living without waiting for the social order of his dreams.
Similarly, in his view that India ought to adopt a nonviolent defense
policy, whether in meeting the Japanese invasion or as a general
defense policy for free India, Gandhi sought to achieve the adoption and implementation of the policy in the immediate or very near
future—rather than at some distant time after most of India's
economic, social and political problems had been solved. One may
differ from Gandhi, but should do so on one's own, not by
representing Gandhi's view as the opposite of what it was.

An additional problem with the assumption that a change in
defense policy must *follow* basic social change, is that the requirements of continuing military defense (in finances, resources, regimentation, and centralization) work *against* the effort to improve
the society. Under those conditions the new society will never be
achieved. Also, there is good reason to believe that the adoption of
a nonviolent defense policy will help the effort to improve the social
order, partly by the absence of the negative military requirements
cited above, partly because decentralization often seems conducive
to increased efficiency in nonviolent resistance (and hence could
receive official impetus), partly because of the importance of
improving the society to make it more worthy of defense in the eyes
of the men and women who will have to carry out the resistance. As
stated, the relationship between social structure and the defense
policy is complicated and requires very careful study. The point
here simply is that the view widely held in India that Gandhi's type
of defense policy cannot be practical until after society has reached
an advanced ideal condition cannot be accepted, especially not in
the form in which it has been thus far presented. We cannot dodge
the defense problem in that way.

The second major difficulty faced especially by Gandhians in
India is that the border conflicts and defense problems are often
very immediate and real, while, as Jayaprakash Narayan wrote:
"Unfortunately, however, the forces of nonviolence are pitifully
unprepared yet to offer effective defence."[157] This situation is

* See Chapter Five, "The Theory of Gandhi's Constructive Program."

especially serious in light of the wider problem we all face, for "the question . . . whether conflicts in human society, including international conflicts, should be settled by the means of violence or nonviolence is no longer a sectarian question, but one that modern weapons of warfare have made relevant to the very survival of the human race."[158] It is reasonable to conclude that this situation is not basically different from the situation which Gandhi himself confronted. His response, as sketched throughout this chapter, was to recognize that while people who had no confidence in nonviolent means could only use violence, the dangers of the military policy must be constantly pointed out, and the main task lay in the formulation and development of an alternative nonviolent defense policy. The response was therefore neither acceptance of military defense, nor simple conscientious objection. It was the formulation and development of an alternative course of action which would make it possible for people to choose between military and nonviolent defense policies.

INVESTIGATION AND DEVELOPMENT

This type of alternative defense policy—which is now also called "civilian defense" or "civilian-based defense"—will not receive serious consideration, much less be adopted by any country, until its practical operation has been worked out carefully and in considerable detail. People must have confidence in the alternative if they are to accept and implement it. Most people will not adopt an abstract dogma of "nonviolence" when they do not see it to "work." It will therefore be necessary to investigate and work out the alternative policy with sufficient objectivity, realism and attention to difficulties and details that people will be able to make a choice. As long as the idea of "nonviolent defense" remains simply a generalization and an abstraction, there is no choice possible for most people. With research, investigation, attention to strategy and tactics, the development of alternative ways of meeting various types of attacks and repression, the broad outline which Gandhi sketched may be filled out so that India and the rest of the world can choose.

Many more people are today willing to investigate and consider a reasonable alternative to war than are yet prepared to adopt only nonviolent means. Jawaharlal Nehru, for example, once spoke to Joan Bondurant of the importance of considering the potentialities of Gandhi's technique: "I do not pretend to understand fully the significance of that technique of action, in which I myself took part. But I feel more and more convinced that it offers us some key to understanding and to the proper resolution of conflict." Gandhi's way showed achievement, he said. "That surely should at least make us try to understand what this new way was and how far it is possible for us to shape our thoughts and actions in accordance with it."[159]

The attempt to formulate, develop and investigate the idea of an alternative defense policy has in the past few years received increased attention in Europe and America. There is considerable evidence that there exists significant real and latent support for the attempt to investigate the difficulties and the potentialities of this policy, to conduct objective research into its nature, and to examine alternative strategies and tactics of this policy of civilian defense. Support for research and investigation now comes from a number of military officers and strategists in several countries. All of these efforts are as yet minute. But a beginning has been made. And I think Gandhi would be pleased.

NOTES TO CHAPTER EIGHT

1. For a brief discussion of some popular misconceptions of Gandhi and his activities, see Chapter One, "Gandhi's Political Significance."
2. See Chapter Ten, "Types of Principled Nonviolence," section on nonresistance.
3. **Harijan** (hereafter cited as **H.**), 3 Nov. 1946; M.K. Gandhi, **Non-violence in Peace and War** (hereafter cited as **NVPW**; original source and date are given in addition to the book in which it is reprinted); (2 vols. Ahmedabad: Navajivan, 1948–1949), vol. II, p. 159.
4. **H.**, 2 Apr. 1946; **NVPW**, II, p. 119.
5. **H.**, 7 Apr. 1946; **NVPW**, II, p. 57.
6. **Young India** (hereafter cited as **YI**), 12 Aug. 1926; **NVPW** (1948 ed.), I, pp. 59–60.
7. **YI**, 15 Oct. 1931; **NVPW**, I, p. 105.
8. See Chapter Three, "Gandhi on the Theory of Voluntary Servitude."
9. **H.**, 21 Oct. 1939; **NVPW**, I, p. 240.

10. **H.,** 2 Apr. 1938; **NVPW,** I, pp. 136–137.

11. **H.,** 8 Sept. 1946; **NVPW,** II, p. 146.

12. **YI,** 17 Nov. 1921; **NVPW,** I, p. 23.

13. **H.,** 15 Sept. 1946; **NVPW,** II, p. 148.

14. **H.,** 25 Aug. 1940; **NVPW,** I, p. 323.

15. **H.,** 23 Sept. 1939; **NVPW,** I, p. 226.

16. **H.,** 8 Sept., 1940; **NVPW,** I, p. 338.

17. **YI,** 12 Aug. 1926; **NVPW,** I, p. 60.

18. **YI,** 5 Nov. 1925; **NVPW,** I, pp. 49–50.

19. **YI,** 15 Nov. 1928; R.K. Prabhu and U.R. Rao, eds., **The Mind of Mahatma Gandhi** (Bombay: Humphrey Milford, Oxford University Press, 1945), p. 126.

20. Gandhi's phrase "took part" (**NVPW,** I, p. 1) must be carefully understood, for it did not mean taking part in the use of weapons or even in training for fighting with weapons. In the Boer War, Gandhi and other Indians, having trained themselves at their own expense as nurses, were finally accepted by Natal as an "Indian Ambulance Corps," which was led by Gandhi. They served in the front lines. During the so-called Zulu Rebellion—actually a punitive expedition—Gandhi with twenty-four Indian volunteers joined the British army as stretcher bearers and sanitary aids and nursed the whipped and wounded Zulus whom the white medical team would not help. Gandhi was then a sergeant major. During World War I, in London in 1914, Gandhi led eighty Indian volunteers in taking a course in first aid, and Indian women made clothes for the soldiers. In 1918 in India Gandhi campaigned for recruitment for the British army among those who believed in violence, and met considerable opposition. See D. G. Tendulkar, **Mahatma: Life of Mohandas Karamchand Gandhi** (Delhi: Publications Division, Ministry of Information and Broadcasting, Government of India, 1960), vol. I, pp. 53–54, 76, 153 and 226–234. See the below discussion of war also.

21. **YI,** 11 Aug. 1920; **NVPW,** I, p. 1.

22. **YI,** 11 Aug. 1920; **NVPW,** I, p. 3.

23. **YI,** 22 July 1929; **NVPW,** I, p. 94.

24. **YI,** 11 Aug. 1920; **NVPW,** I, p. 1.

25. **H.,** 12 Oct. 1935; **NVPW,** I, p. 112.

26. Tendulkar, **Mahatma,** 1, p. 229.

27. **H.,** 8 June 1947; **NVPW,** II, p. 261.

28. **H.,** 1 Sept. 1940; **NVPW,** I, pp. 335–336.

29. **YI,** 7 May 1931; M.K. Gandhi, **Satyagraha** (hereafter cited as S.) (Ahmedabad: Navajivan Publishing House, 1951), p. 286.

30. **YI,** 11 Aug. 1920; **NVPW,** I, p. 2. See Chapter Nine, n. 6.

31. **YI,** 30 Apr. 1931; **S.,** p. 81.

32. **H.,** 30 Mar. 1947; **NVPW,** II, pp. 233–234.

33. See for example, **H.,** 21 July 1940 (**NVPW,** I, p. 302); **H.,** 1 Sept. 1940 (**NVPW;** I, p. 335); and M.K. Gandhi, "Hind Swaraj or Indian Home Rule" (pamphlet; Ahmedabad: Navajivan, 1958), pp. 82 and 85.

34. See for example, Ibid., p. 81; **YI,** 11 Oct. 1928 (**NVPW,** I, p. 76); **H.,** 20 Mar. 1937 (**NVPW,** I, pp. 131–132); **H.,** 29 Sept. 1940 (**NVPW,** I, p. 358); **H.,** 17 Mar. 1946 (**NVPW,** II, p. 59); **H.,** 4 Aug. 1946 (**NVPW,** II, p. 133); **H.,** 30 Mar. 1947 (**NVPW,** II, p. 234).

35. H., 15 Oct. 1938; NVPW, I, p. 154.
36. H., 17 Mar. 1946; NVPW, II, p. 60.
37. H., 12 Oct. 1935; NVPW, I, p. 111.
38. H., 30 June 1946; NVPW, II, p. 16.
39. YI, 2 July 1931; S., p. 83.
40. YI, 21 Jan. 1920; S., pp. 19 and 22.
41. H., 15 Apr. 1933; S., p. 202.
42. H., 6 May 1933; S., p. 320.
43. H., 17 Dec. 1938; NVPW, I, p. 168.
44. YI, 1 June 1921; S., p. 163.
45. H., 9 Mar. 1940; NVPW, I, p. 262.
46. See above n. 17.
47. YI, 5 Nov. 1925; NVPW, I, p. 49.
48. YI, 13 Sept. 1928; NVPW, I, p. 73.
49. See for example, NVPW, I, pp. vi, 21–24, 68–75, and 228–231.
50. N.B. This did not, however, prevent Gandhi from making strong statements against the use of violence by Indian nationalists in the independence struggle. This raises the question as to whether his warnings against such violence in a good cause by people who believed in violence were not motivated by consideration of the probable undesirable political consequences of such violence. See Gene Sharp, **Gandhi Wields the Weapon of Moral Power: Three Case Histories** (Ahmedabad: Navajivan, 1960). pp. 44 and 92. His advice to nuclear scientists (see below) lends credence to this interpretation. Together they give a less tolerant view toward political violence even when used bravely with good intentions.
51. YI, 17 Nov. 1921; NVPW, I, p. 23.
52. H., 27 July 1947; NVPW, II, p. 278.
53. H., 27 Oct. 1946; NVPW, II, p. 159.
54. H., 9 June 1946; NVPW, II, p. 140.
55. H., 13 July 1947; NVPW, II, p. 272.
56. H., 12 Jan. 1947; NVPW, II, p. 192.
57. H., 30 Mar. 1947; NVPW, II, p. 234.
58. H., 18 May 1940; NVPW, I, p. 269.
59. See H., 6 July 1940; NVPW, I, p. 280.
60. H., 15 Oct. 1938; NVPW, I, p. 152.
61. H., 12 Nov. 1938; NVPW, I, p. 159.
62. H., 21 Oct. 1939; NVPW, I, pp. 238–239.
63. H., 30 Sept. 1939; NVPW, I, p. 230.
64. H., 26 Nov. 1938; NVPW, I, pp. 160–161.
65. H., 26 Nov. 1938; NVPW, I, p. 161.
66. H., 11 Aug. 1940; NVPW, I, p. 307.
67. H., 20 Oct. 1940; NVPW, I, p. 365.
68. H., 15 Apr. 1939; NVPW, I, p. 204.
69. H., 22 Sept., 1940; NVPW, I, p. 471.
70. H., 6 July 1940; NVPW, I, pp. 280–281.
71. H., 24 Nov. 1946; NVPW, II, p. 179.
72. H., 2 Mar. 1947; NVPW, II, p. 221.

73. H., 30 Mar. 1947; NVPW, II, p. 234.
74. H., 29 Sept., 1940; NVPW, I, pp. 357–358.
75. H., 5 Oct. 1947; NVPW, II, p. 316.
76. H., 5 Oct. 1947; NVPW, II, p. 317.
77. H., 27 July 1947; NVPW, II, p. 280.
78. H., 8 June 1947; NVPW, II, p. 258.
79. H., 18 Jan. 1948; NVPW, II, p. 342.
80. H., 9 June 1946; NVPW, II, p. 140.
81. H., 7 Dec. 1947; NVPW, II, p. 325.
82. YI, 11 Aug. 1920; S., p. 135.
83. H., 27 July 1947; NVPW, II, p. 277. See also H., 3 Aug. 1947; NVPW, II, p. 279.
84. H., 25 Aug. 1940; NVPW, I, p. 323.
85. H., 14 Oct. 1939; NVPW, I, p. 237. See also H., 5 May 1946; NVPW, II, p. 88.
86. H., 11 Aug. 1940; NVPW, I, p. 312.
87. See Pyarelal, **Mahatma Gandhi: The Last Phase** (2 vols.; Ahmedabad: Navajivan Publishing House, 1958), vol. II, pp. 490–505, and M.K. Gandhi, **Delhi Diary** (Ahmedabad: Navijivan, 1948), pp. 115, 122–123, 128, 131–133, 143–145, 163–164, 212, 282–284, 287, 294–295, 307–308, 364, and 385.
88. Ibid., pp. 144–145.
89. Pyarelal, **Mahatma Gandhi: The Last Phase**, II, pp. 504–505.
90. H., 14 Dec. 1947; NVPW, II, pp. 340–341. See also H., 30 Sept. 1939; NVPW, I, pp. 227–228.
91. H., 24 Aug. 1947; NVPW, II, p. 287.
92. H., 9 June 1946; NVPW, II, p. 39.
93. H., 27 July 1947; NVPW, II, p. 278.
94. H., 31 Aug. 1947; NVPW, II, p. 288.
95. H., 12 Oct. 1935; NVPW, I, pp. 111–112.
96. H., 14 May 1938; NVPW, I, p. 143.
97. H., 24 Dec. 1938; NVPW, I, p. 174.
98. Alexander Dallin, **German Rule in Russia, 1941–1945: A Study of Occupation Policies** (London: Macmillan, 1957), p. 498.
99. H., 12 May 1946; NVPW, II, p. 90.
100. H., 5 May 1947; NVPW, II, p. 251. See also H., 14 Apr. 1946: NVPW, II, p. 35.
101. H., 14 Oct. 1939; NVPW, I, p. 234.
102. H., 13 Apr. 1940; NVPW, I, p. 265.
103. H., 14 Apr. 1939; NVPW, I, p. 204.
104. H., 16 Nov. 1947; NVPW, II, p. 143.
105. H., 9 Feb. 1947; NVPW, II, p. 161.
106. H., 8 June 1947; NVPW, II, p. 261.
107. H., 18 Aug. 1946; NVPW, II, p. 141. See also H., 1 June 1947; NVPW, II, p. 254.
108. H., 22 June 1940; NVPW, I, p. 274.
109. H., 21 July 1940; NVPW, I, p. 296.
110. H., 20 Oct. 1940; NVPW, I, p. 365.
111. H., 21 July 1940; NVPW, I, p. 294.
112. H., 28 July 1940; NVPW, I, p. 305.

113. See H., 12 Nov. 1938 (NVPW, I, pp. 161-163); H., 17 Dec. 1938 (NVPW, I, pp. 167-169); H., 18 Feb. 1939 (NVPW, I, pp. 200-201); H., 27 May 1939 (NVPW, I, pp. 205-206).
114. H., 15 Oct. 1938; NVPW, I, p. 152.
115. H., 8 Oct. 1938; NVPW, I, p. 149.
116. H., 15 Oct. 1938; NVPW, I, p. 152.
117. H., 8 Oct. 1938; NVPW, I, p. 149. See also further comments on pp. 149-151; ref.,n.112, pp. 152-154; H., 12 Nov. 1938 (NVPW, I, pp. 157-158) and H., 24 Dec. 1938 (NVPW, I, pp. 175-176).
118. H., 22 June 1940; NVPW, I, p. 273.
119. H., 14 Oct. 1939; NVPW, I, p. 233.
120. H., 6 July 1940, NVPW, I, p. 281.
121. H., 18 Aug. 1940; NVPW, I, p. 317.
122. H., 15 Feb. 1942; NVPW, I, p. 374.
123. H., 12 Apr. 1942; NVPW, I, p. 397.
124. M.K. Gandhi, quoted in "Armed Invasion and Nonviolent Resistance," Appendix A in Pyarelal, Mahatma Gandhi: The Last Phase, II, p. 818. See also the rest of the discussion between Mirabehn and Gandhi, pp. 815-818.
125. See H., 15 Apr. 1939; NVPW, I, p. 203.
126. See H., 7 Jan. 1939; NVPW, I, p. 180, and H., 18 Aug. 1940; NVPW, I, p. 321.
127. See for example, H., 25 Aug. 1940; NVPW, I, p. 325.
128. H., 13 Apr. 1940; NVPW, I, p. 264.
129. H., 30 Sept. 1939; NVPW, I, p. 230.
130. H., 11 Aug. 1940; NVPW, I, p. 307.
131. See for example, H., 11 Aug. 1940; NVPW, I, p. 306, and H., 26 Apr. 1942; NVPW, I, p. 485.
132. H., 9 June 1946; NVPW, II, p. 39.
133. H., 14 Apr. 1940; S., p. 386.
134. H., 2 Mar. 1940; NVPW, I, p. 260.
135. H., 17 Dec. 1938; NVPW, I, p. 168. (See also H., 30 Sept. 1939; NVPW, I, p. 230, and H., 9 Feb. 1947; NVPW, II, p. 161.
136. H., 11 Aug. 1940; NVPW, I, pp. 307-308.
137. H., 1 June 1947; NVPW, II, p. 254.
138. YI, 2 July 1931; NVPW, I, p. 103.
139. H., 4 May 1940; NVPW, I, p. 267.
140. H., 15 Mar. 1942; NVPW, I, pp. 381-382.
141. H., 29 June 1947; NVPW, II, p. 265.
142. H., 14 Oct. 1939; NVPW, I, p. 237.
143. H., 14 Dec. 1947; NVPW, II, pp. 340-341.
144. H., 14 Oct. 1939; NVPW, I, pp. 235-236. See also Tendulkar, Mahatma (First ed.) V, p. 208.
145. H., 13 Apr. 1940; NVPW, I, pp. 264-265.
146. H., 29 June 1940; NVPW, I, p. 274.
147. Quoted from the full text, NVPW, I, Appendix VI, pp. 445-447, reproduced from H., 29 June 1940. See also Congress President Maulana Abul Kalam Azad's statement to the July 1940 meeting of the All-India Congress Commit-

tee on the series of discussions between Gandhi and the Working Committee on Gandhi's pleas for the Congress to rely upon nonviolent resistance to meet external aggression, in Nirmal Kumar Bose, **Studies in Gandhism** (Calcutta: Indian Associated Publishing Co., 1947), pp. 308–311.

148. H., 29 June 1940; NVPW, I, p. 275.
149. H., 21 July 1940; NVPW, I, p. 300.
150. H., 19 July 1942; Pyarelal, **Mahatma Gandhi: The Last Phase**, II, p. 508.
151, H., 7 Dec. 1947; NVPW, II, p. 325.
152. H., 12 Nov. 1938; NVPW, I, p. 159. See also YI, 13 Sept. 1928; NVPW, I, p. 75.
153. H., 10 Nov. 1946; NVPW, II, pp. 163–164.
154. H., 29 June 1947; NVPW, II, p. 266. See also H., 8 June 1947; NVPW, II, pp. 259–260.
155. YI, 11 Aug. 1920; NVPW, I, pp. 2–3.
156. Jayaprakash Narayan's speech at Tirupathur on 24 May 1963, **Peace News**, 12 July 1963.
157. Jayaprakash Narayan's statement of 3 Nov. 1962, reprinted in **Background**, no. 20.
158. Ibid.
159. Quoted in Joan Bondurant, **Conquest of Violence: The Gandhian Philosophy of Conflict** (Princeton, N.J.: Princeton University Press, 1958), p. x.

9

Gandhi as a National Defense Strategist

The facets and contributions of Gandhi are diverse and many, for he was a complex man, his activities were varied, and he participated actively in public life for over half a century. A single aspect of his thought and life can often be viewed from more than one perspective. For example, Gandhi's *satyagraha* as a type of struggle may be viewed as a contribution to the uniting of religion and politics; as a contribution to the forms of revolutionary struggle; or as a kind of social behavior intended to help the individual achieve greater fulfillment.

It is unusual to view Gandhi as a strategist of national defense. However, many of his activities and policy recommendations for nearly thirty years clearly involved problems of national defense.

National defense in this context includes both preparations and resistance for dealing with new attacks on a country's independence and freedom, as well as efforts to liberate a country already under foreign military occupation and political rule. In this national defense context, then, Gandhi made strategic and tactical recommendations for meeting three defense situations: (1) how to achieve the national liberation of India from British political and military occupation; (2) how to deal with a Japanese invasion during World War II; and (3) how to defend an independent India from future invasion. Of these three defense tasks, Gandhi of necessity primarily concentrated on the first. The breadth of his recommendations encompassing all three defense situations, however, is highly important. His insights, policy judgements, strategic decisions, and recommendations for these defense problems may have significance far beyond the particular political situations and historical contexts in which he operated. The possibility of such significance may, at the least, be worth exploring because the tensions and dilemmas arising from the conflicting demands of world peace and of effective defense against aggression still remain unresolved. Gandhi thought he had found the basis of their resolution.*

COMBATTING FOREIGN OCCUPATION

After he began his political activities in India, a great deal of Gandhi's recommendations and actions falls within the scope of national defense. These recommendations and activities were designed to increase national strength in order to combat British power, to dissolve the foreign control, and to restore national independence. The British did not recognize Gandhi's activities as national defense measures. From the European perspective, India was a colony, a part of the British Empire. In addition, British domination over India had not resulted from the military defeat of India in a conventional war. However, by whatever varied means the British had attained control, they did, as foreigners, rule the

---

* For a detailed treatment of Gandhi's fundamental thinking on this, see Chapter Eight, "Gandhi's Defense Policy."

subcontinent, and they maintained their domination by means which included political, police, and military power. Therefore, India was under foreign occupation. The struggle to bring that occupation to an end fell just as surely within the context of national defense as did the struggles of the resistance movements in the countries of Occupied Europe during World War II. Gandhi's general recommendations for Indian resistance to Japanese invasion forces in 1942 also, and more obviously, fell into the scope of national defense. This was the case even though India was already occupied by the British who were fighting the Japanese; continuing Japanese aggression was reaching toward India.

Both before independence and after, Gandhi's view was that an India which had been able to drive the British out by nonviolent means should also be able to defend that newly won freedom by nonviolent means. Gandhi's way of dealing with violence was very different from the ways of Western pacifists. Although he did not support military means, Gandhi was neither a conscientious objector, nor a war resister. He experimented with what Krishnalal Shridharani called "war without violence."[1] Therefore, when it came to India's national defense policy he did not perceive his role to be one of witnessing or protesting against it. Instead, he had a vision that a *military* defense policy was not needed because people could effectively defend their country's freedom by nonviolent noncooperation. This was clearly a recommendation on the level of national defense policy.

ALTERNATIVE FIGHTING CAPACITY

Viewing Gandhi as a national defense strategist implies a view of Gandhi as a politician, rather than simply as a saint or a Mahatma. Although this is a view which Gandhi himself emphasized,[2] many people continue to approach Gandhi primarily from a religious or philosophical outlook. It is, therefore, relevant to note several of his underlying assumptions which led to his policy recommendations, strategic decisions, and campaign leadership in the field of Indian national defense. It is crucial at this point not to try to force Gandhi into our own preconceptions. Several misunderstandings and misrepresentations of his views are rooted in such attempts; some have even led to the claim that Gandhi approved of political violence and of military defense.[3]

It is true that Gandhi did repeatedly say that violence was better than cowardice, submission, and impotence in face of violence and political evil. In so doing, he did not endorse violence; he condemned weak responses to attack and oppression. He also paid tribute to bravery and sacrifice even when expressed in violence, and especially when the odds were overwhelmingly against the violent resister. He made it clear, however, that his position was different: "However much I may sympathize with and admire worthy motives, I am an uncompromising opponent of violent methods even to serve the noblest of causes."[4]

Gandhi did not want simple abstention from violence without regard for the reason or form of the alternative behavior. He wanted people to give up violence because they were strong enough not to need it, and because they had found a better way to conduct serious conflicts. He recommended nonviolent action because "it was the weapon of the really brave."[5] There was here no passive submission to tyranny, violence or aggression. The use of non-violent action, Gandhi said, "does not mean meek submission to the will of the evil-doer, but it means the pitting of one's whole soul against the will of the tyrant."[6]

> In the code of the Satyagrahi there is no such thing as surrender to brute force.[7]
>
> It [was] never implied that a non-violent man should bend before the violence of an aggressor. . . . but neutralize it by withholding one's hand and . . . refusing to submit to the demand.[8]

Such action required great courage. But this type of nonviolent struggle was, Gandhi believed, the more moral way to behave. Also, in times of severe danger and attack, it made possible a course of action which differed both from the usual military response and, even more, from cowardly submission. Gandhi's nonviolent alternative was "designed to be a complete and effective substitute" for the means of violence in political conflicts.[9] This type of struggle, he was convinced, gave greater power to its users than did violence.[10] Furthermore, he denied that such political nonviolence was only for a very few highly developed individuals: ". . . given proper training and proper generalship, non-violence can be practised by masses of mankind."[11] If implemented, this nonviolent alternative, Gandhi believed, offered the capacity to cope both with threatening internal violence and foreign oppression.

GANDHI AND MILITARY DEFENSE

Gandhi did at several points in the early part of his career give a kind of qualified support to war, or at least participated in it to a certain degree though never to the point of using weapons himself. He never changed his view that people who believed in violence ought to be willing to take part in violent resistance against oppression and invasion, but this did not mean that he favored such violent defense.* Indeed, he found democracy and the military way to be incompatible with each other.[12]

Gandhi realized, however, that crucial issues were often at stake in wars. In such cases, Gandhi rejected neutrality and impartiality. He could approve of a good cause, but without condoning or actually assisting the violence. So in World War II, for example, his sympathies were wholly with the Allies and against the Nazis, but he warned that Allied violence sufficient to defeat the Germans would contribute to the further brutalization of human nature, to increased militarization, to the adoption of fascist methods to enforce obedience, and to Allied slaughter and destruction in excess of that of the Germans. "If liberty and democracy are to be truly saved," he wrote, "they will only be by non-violent resistance no less brave, no less glorious, than violent resistance."[13] Gandhi applied this general view to every people and country, and especially to India.

Gandhi based his view of the practical superiority of non-violent struggle for dealing with oppression and invasion upon the assumption that, ultimately, there is no inconsistency between that course of action which is the most ethical and that which is the most practical.† He identified his type of nonviolent behavior with the

---

* For a more complete discussion of these points, see Chapter Eight, "Gandhi's Defense Policy," pp. 134–137.
† For a discussion of this, see Chapter Thirteen, "Nonviolence: Moral Principle or Political Technique?"

ethical, moral, and religious; at the same time this identical nonviolent behavior was recommended on practical grounds as the most effective response to serious political conflicts.[14] Gandhi here in no way resembles a nonviolent "true believer" who chooses to "witness" in isolation against the evil of the world by withdrawing from its conflicts and from influence on its events. To the contrary, Gandhi felt it impossible to be nonviolent, in the sense in which he understood it, without entering directly into the center of political life and conflict. There, he believed, it was necessary to chart a nonviolent course which ordinary people could follow and by which they could maximize their power to control events. While Gandhi often discussed the spiritual, religious and ethical aspects of *satyagraha,* he made it clear that action based on those principles was simultaneously also *practical:* ". . . Satyagraha is, as a matter of fact and in the long run, the most expeditious course."[15] The *satyagraha* leader, he said, who relies on the strength of God and on the guidance of the "Voice within," and who shuns so-called practical politics, will be in the end shown to have had "the most practical politics."[16]

> If any action of mine claimed to be spiritual is proved to be unpractical, it must be pronounced to be a failure. I do believe that the most spiritual act is the most practical in the true sense of the term.[17]

For Gandhi, then, there was no problem about inconsistencies between ethical and practical politics. Part of Gandhi's genius was that he was able in the national independence struggle, and other social conflicts, to formulate and put into action, strategies of nonviolent struggle which were (and even by skeptics were seen to be) practical means of combat. He did this far more ably in actual struggle against the existing occupation than in formulating future strategies in anticipation of real or potential new invasions. His recommendations for national defense policy for the latter cases were met with infinitely greater skepticism by almost everyone, including his fellow nationalists in the Indian National Congress. This was not without good reason, for his proposals on how to combat British power, although general, were accompanied by specific strategies and organizational work for particular campaigns. His defense recommendations against Japan, on the other hand, were incomplete and lacked the specifics and comprehensiveness of, for example, the 1930-31 struggle against the British. His proposals for the national defense of an independent India were general only and never detailed. The people and government of independent India were therefore offered a choice between an organized and prepared military policy with trained personnel, and Gandhi's vague generalizations about defending India nonviolently. It was not a real choice for people who did not share his religious convictions concerning nonviolence, and only a handful did.

NONVIOLENT NATIONALISM

Along with the need for effective national defense measures, Gandhi also accepted as "good" a type of nationalism which he called "non-violent nationalism." On this, too, he differed from Western pacifists and peace workers, many of whom have decried all nationalism and often deprecated patriotism. This special nationalism also underlay his approach to national defense. Just as one should serve one's family, and through it serve one's community, and through it serve one's country, so, Gandhi argued, one should serve one's country and through that service benefit the whole world. Indeed, one of the reasons why he wanted India to be independent and self-reliant was that she could thereby better benefit the world. This approach differed radically from what was often called nationalism in the West, for it rejected domination, aggression, and exploitation of other nations, and even military power.

> I live for India's freedom and would die for it, because it is part of Truth . . . But my patriotism is not exclusive; it is calculated not only to hurt another nation but to benefit all in the true sense of the word.[18]

> Through the deliverance of India, I seek to deliver the so-called weaker races of the earth from the crushing heels of Western exploitation. . . . India's coming to her own will mean every nation doing likewise.[19]

> . . . [I]t is impossible for one to be an internationalist without being a nationalist. . . . It is not nationalism that is an evil, it is the

narrowness, selfishness, exclusiveness which is the bane of modern nations which is evil.[20]

I want the freedom of my country so that other countries may learn something from my free country, so that the resources of my country might be utilized for the benefit of mankind.[21]

...[T]he adoption of non-violence to the utmost extent possible (by the National Government)... will be India's great contribution to the peace of the world and the establishment of a new world order.[22]

Gandhi thereby made distinctions between home rule and national independence on the one hand, and other less noble policies which had also gone under the name of nationalism, on the other. National independence was positively good; therefore, it was necessary to have effective means of action to restore independence when it had been taken away, and, once achieved, to preserve it against new threats and attacks.

SOCIAL ROOTS OF NATIONAL INDEPENDENCE

Gandhi's view of what made self-reliant national independence possible was more complex than the view of military defense specialists. It was, for Gandhi, far from being simply a matter of the relative balance between military weaponry, size and efficiency of the armed forces, and related factors. Hence, one of his contributions as a national defense strategist was to produce certain underlying conditions in the people and the society which were necessary for national defense. In other words, success or failure of the specific defense strategies in crises would hinge upon whether or not there was sufficient genuine vitality and strength in the country's citizens themselves and in its social institutions to carry out a policy of nonviolent noncooperation.[23]

Although this was a rather complex and sophisticated political view, Gandhi had reached it very early in his life.* He appears to have been influenced highly in the development of this position

* See Chapter Three, "Gandhi on the Theory of Voluntary Servitude."

once he had accepted it by study of Tolstoy's "A Letter to a Hindu," which had been written in 1908 (not to Gandhi, but to an Indian advocate of terrorism against the British as a means to achieve national liberation).[24] That same year Gandhi wrote his pamphlet "Hind Swaraj or Indian Home Rule."[25] In "Hind Swaraj" Gandhi argued that it was the internal weakness of India which had led to British control, especially Indian internal rivalries, quarrels, and greed for British goods.

> The English have not taken India; we have given it to them. They are not in India because of their strength, but because we keep them.[26]

> If man will only realize that it is unmanly to obey laws that are unjust, no man's tyranny will enslave him. This is the key to self-rule or home-rule.[27]

Addressing the English in that booklet he wrote:

> You have great military resources. Your naval power is match-less. If we wanted to fight with you on your own ground, we should be unable to do so, but if the above submissions be not acceptable to you, we cease to play the part of the ruled. You may, if you like cut us to pieces. You may shatter us at the cannon's mouth. If you act contrary to our will, we will not help you; and without our help, we know that you cannot move one step forward.[28]

> We shall get nothing by asking; we shall have to take what we want, and we need the requisite strength for the effort. . . .[29]

He then outlined nineteen ways in which to mobilize that internal Indian strength: ". . .the English . . . will either go or change their nature only when we reform ourselves. . . ."[30]

Most of the remainder of Gandhi's life after writing "Hind Swaraj" was devoted to efforts to strengthen India internally. The aim was to bring her as a nation and her people, individually and collectively, to that greater strength which would make it impossible for any domestic tyrant or foreign conqueror to oppress India. Internal strength was the necessary prerequisite for effective national defense.

MOBILIZING INTERNAL STRENGTH

Gandhi's program for creating, mobilizing and utilizing this internal strength may be roughly divided into five components.

1. A transformation was needed in the Indian people themselves. The needed changes involved increased dignity and self-respect and the reduction and elimination of all feelings of inferiority, especially as regarded the English. Because, Gandhi believed, Indian civilization was superior to that of the Europeans, Indians should be proud of being Indians, and should in no way regard the foreign rulers as their superiors, nor cower in passive submissiveness before them. This renewed self-respect would express itself in minute aspects of individual behavior as well as in major nationalist campaigns of resistance.

2. Dependence of any kind by Indians on the foreign occupation regime helped only to perpetuate it, Gandhi believed. Therefore, deliberate efforts were required to strengthen India's own society, including its economy and its social and political institutions. As the Indians became more self-reliant, and less dependent on the British, the balance of power and control in the country would shift. The development of a strong Indian society outside of British control, and continuing efforts to improve the society and to uplift all sections of the population, would result in greater "Indian power" which meant control of their own destiny. This would be true even while the British remained; it would finally make continued foreign domination impossible. Gandhi therefore pressed various aspects of his constructive program.[31]* Greater economic self-sufficiency was vital; it both reduced British motives for remaining in India and enabled Indians to control and improve their economy.

An India filled with internal injustices and problems was both doomed to weakness and was a violation of the human dignity which its leaders espoused. Therefore, efforts were needed to eradicate untouchability, to achieve communal unity and the rights of women, and to advance the education of both children and

---

* On the constructive program, see Chapter Five, "The Theory of Gandhi's Constructive Program."

adults, through a new Indian approach to education. Various Indian social and political institutions had to be strengthened or revived, and new ones needed to be created. For example, the settlement of civil cases by local *panchayats* (village councils) was to be encouraged because it kept cases out of the British court system, and to that degree thereby reduced the British regime's control over the country. The very growth of the Indian National Congress as a political institution provided the country with a rival national authority and an alternative to the British *Raj*. In certain extreme situations elements of the Congress took on characteristics of a parallel government. In addition, by transforming the Congress from an elitist discussion group into a mass organization, the power of the people (including students, urban poor, and peasants) was mobilized to strengthen the national cause. The constant internal strengthening of Indian society and its institutions was seen by Gandhi as leading to the inevitable end of British rule.

3. Struggle—not petitions and patient pleas—was needed to attain national liberation.

> The matter resolves itself into one of matching forces. Conviction or no conviction, Great Britain would defend her Indian commerce and interests by all the forces at her command. India must consequently evolve enough force to free herself from that embrace of death.[32]

But Gandhi saw no reason to assume that "force" must be violent. To the contrary, in his view the Indians could mobilize much greater power if they waged their struggle by nonviolent action only. Violence was "at best a poor weapon of defence."[33] It was possible for India to replace violence even though the substituted nonviolent action was not of the highest possible quality: "We may not be perfect in our own use of it, but we definitely discard the use of violence, and grow from failure to success."[34]

Gandhi offered India nonviolent struggle as the means with which to combat and disintegrate domination by the British Empire. It is clear that the Indian National Congress' acceptance of this technique as part of the grand strategy for achieving independence was not a moral or religious act. It was a political decision which was possible because Gandhi offered a course of action which was nonviolent but which above all was seen to be practical and effective. Gandhi and others credited this nonviolent action with achieving the extraordinary growth of the Congress, the involvement of the masses in Congress activities, the casting off of submissiveness and passivity in the people, and their replacement with courage and fearlessness. All these instances of the empowerment of India contributed significantly to the achievement of independence.[35]

4. Gandhi also had a distinctive approach to "the enemy." He distinguished between the people on the one hand, and their policies and system on the other. Sometimes he described this as the difference between the evil-doer and the evil itself. The "enemy" was also seen as a victim of his own system, a view which was usually interpreted from a moral perspective. Whatever the origins of this distinction, it is clear that from a strategic point of view it was very effective. This approach deliberately encouraged Britishers to oppose policies of the British Government in India and to work for Indian independence. The nonviolent character of the Indian national struggle made it easier and very much more likely for Indians to receive assistance from within the heart of the Empire itself.

In other words, support for the Indians within Great Britain was not simply a result of special qualities in the British, or even the Labour Party, but at least as much, or more so, the result of the Indian reliance upon the nonviolent technique to fight the British *Raj*. This made it easier for people within the United Kingdom to support the Indians, for they did not then appear unpatriotic or as defenders of murderers of the mother country's sons. In the absence of distracting violence by the Indians, it was easier to keep attention concentrated on injustices in India. And certainly even relatively mild violent repression against disciplined nonviolent men and women aroused sympathy for the Indians and condemnations of British measures, in Britain as well as throughout India and the world. More severe repression against serious nationalist violence would not have had these results. The distinction between individuals and policies, therefore, helped to promote internal opposition in the "enemy's" own country and to encourage help to the Indian cause. (These results are comparable to the results of the nonviolent resistance by American colonists against the Stamp Act in 1765–66.)*

5. Gandhi also sought to mobilize the strength of India by increasing the moral stature of Indians, individually and collectively. He sought to do this in a variety of ways, believing that enhanced moral qualities in individuals would have many beneficial social and political consequences. One of these would be to make the country's freedom invulnerable. If men and women were willing to live and die for Truth, Gandhi believed, and willing persistently to refuse to submit to any tyrant or aggressor no matter what the suffering inflicted, no one could conquer that people. Nonviolent resistance was "the weapon of the really brave."[36] Through it a country could "defend its honor and self-respect against a whole world in arms."

> That is non-violent defence which neither knows nor accepts defeat at any stage. Therefore, a nation or a group which has made non-violence its final policy, cannot be subjected to slavery even by the atom bomb.[37]

STRATEGIES FOR NATIONAL LIBERATION AND DEFENSE

In developing appropriate nonviolent struggle for Indian independence, Gandhi was dealing with a special type of defense situation: the British *Raj* was already established in India, and in his view India was weak and prostrate. In the *satyagraha* campaigns directed against the British, Gandhi always made the objectives limited; they were in fact far short of immediate independence. He appears to have done so both because of the view that it was strategic wisdom to have objectives which could actually be won by a particular campaign, and also because of the view that the

---

* See Walter Conser, Ronald McCarthy, David Toscano, and Kenneth Wadoski, eds., *To Bid Defiance to Tyranny: Nonviolent Action and the Movement for American Independence, 1765–1775* (Boston: Porter Sargent Publishers, Inc., forthcoming). See especially Conser's and Langford's chapters on the Stamp Act resistance.

campaigns were intended at least as much to increase the power of the Indians as they were to undermine that of the British.

The choice of specific issues made it possible often to concentrate resistance efforts on the opponent's weakest points, and often on issues with the potential for the greatest possible support. "Independence" or "freedom" were too vague and elusive to be the sole demands of a struggle. Instead, Gandhi insisted upon making the issue very specific. "The issue must be definite and capable of being clearly understood and within the power of the opponent to yield."[38] A number of specific issues, carefully chosen, could constitute the substance of independence. Or, if they should be granted as a result of nonviolent struggle, the power positions would have been so altered that full independence could not long be withheld.

This was not a case of being moderate in one's aims but of concentrating one's strength in ways which would make victory more likely. Success in such limited campaigns would in turn increase the self-confidence of the nonviolent actionists,[39] and also their ability, with experience, in wielding nonviolent action to gain their larger objectives. The choice of the specific "points" is therefore very important. In the 1930-31 campaign for independence, for example, Gandhi formulated eleven specific demands which if won, would—he believed—constitute the substance of independence.[40] S. Gopal points out that they "were shrewdly chosen to win the sympathy of every social group" in India.[41] The more obviously justifiable were the specific demands, the more likely would be sympathy and wider support for the actionists in times of repression.

Gandhi also placed great importance on the smaller, tactical decisions. These included the choice of the *place* of action. For example, as the place where he would in 1930 break the Salt Laws and spark nationwide civil disobedience, Gandhi chose the little-known Dandi beach on the Gulf of Cambay. The beach was not significant in itself, but it was far enough away from his *ashram* (see glossary) to allow Gandhi and his followers to walk for twenty-six days—the now famous Salt March—while the country and the world watched with increasing suspense.[42] He also had a sense of *timing*. Nehru said of Gandhi: ". . . he knows his India well and reacts to her slightest tremors, and gauges a situation accurately and almost instinctively, and has a knack of acting at the psychological moment."[43] Sometimes Gandhi timed the launching of a campaign to coincide with a significant day or occasion. In 1930, for example, civil disobedience was started on 6 April, the beginning of National Week, which was observed in homage to the victims of the Amritsar Massacre of Jallianwala Bagh in 1919.[44]

Gandhi was also careful in his use of *numbers* of actionists. He frequently used small numbers of highly disciplined *satyagrahis* for very important missions. He rejected large numbers for their own sake for, when undisciplined and unreliable, they weakened the movement. Under necessary standards and discipline, however, large numbers become "irresistible."[45]

To seize and keep the *initiative* was crucial for effective strategy, in Gandhi's view. He wrote:

> An able general always gives battle in his own time on the ground of his choice. He always retains the initiative in these respects and never allows it to pass into the hands of the enemy.[46]

Since there are a multitude of *specific methods* of nonviolent action[47] it was also important, Gandhi felt, to select those nonviolent weapons most suitable for the needs of the particular struggle. The potential of the method of picketing, for example, is very different from that of a fast. Both of these methods differ from civil disobedience and economic boycotts. A nonviolent raid, or establishment of a nonviolent parallel government also have—as two other specific methods—their own particular qualities, dangers, and potentials. There were many others. Gandhi spent much time considering when and how such specific methods should, and should not, be used. Certain classes of methods—such as noncooperation—had requirements for effectiveness which differed from other groups of methods. For example, for effective noncooperation, larger numbers of participants are usually required and the action usually continues over longer periods of time. Gandhi said in 1930 that, whereas the cooperation of three hundred million people would be necessary for the boycott of foreign cloth to be successful, for the civil disobedience campaign, an army of ten thousand defiant men and women would be enough.[48]

The more extreme nonviolent methods had the potential, Gandhi suggested in specific comments, of working faster, but the risks to the *satyagrahis* and the wider political dangers were both greater. Careful preparation, high discipline, higher quality leadership, and often supplementary use of milder methods, were all required. "The quickest remedies are always fraught with the greatest danger and require the utmost skill in handling them."[49] Gandhi frequently utilized the public response to the use of certain specific methods—as the *hartal* (see glossary)—to judge whether it was wise to launch more extreme measures, such as civil disobedience.[50] In the 1930-31 struggle, a varied plan was used, with both mild and strong methods applied during all phases.[51] (Phased campaigns of nonviolent resistance in which it is planned in advance to shift at certain points in the campaign to use of different specific forms of actions, of course, had not been introduced by Gandhi: American colonists had used them in the 1770s and Russian peasants had planned such action during the 1905 Revolution.) For Gandhi, strategic and tactical considerations were vital when the struggle was going against the nonviolent actionists as well as in times of advances.[52] Where there were necessary retreats —as in war—it was necesary to regroup, mobilize new strength, and be ready to launch a new more powerful struggle. When victories occurred, they were to be springboards to greater ones, to full independence, and to a better society.

NONVIOLENT DEFENSE AGAINST JAPAN?

In 1942 India was confronted with an impending foreign military invasion while she was herself living under foreign military and political rule. The existing British occupation situation made it extraordinarily difficult for Gandhi to prepare effectively for defending India nonviolently against the Japanese. Indian non-cooperation could only come into operation if and when British military forces had been driven into retreat or defeated. Even apart from the Japanese threat, the situation was complicated; there were within India at least four groups: (1) the British and the British-commanded Indian army; (2) pro-Japanese Indians hoping the Japanese would drive the British out and then withdraw leaving India liberated; (3) neutrals resolved to help neither the British nor the Japanese; and (4) nonviolent resisters opposed to both the

Japanese invasion and the British occupation.[53] This was a complex situation within which to operate a national defense struggle; one which, many people would say, required very careful strategic planning for any eventuality. Gandhi in March 1942 rejected the British plan for a scorched earth policy in India if the British military forces retreated.[54] The next month, in the 12 April issue of *Harijan,* Gandhi insisted that, "Resistance, violent or non-violent, has to be well thought out."[55] However, in that same issue in a discussion of a possible Japanese invasion, he prescribed simply "determined pursuit of the constructive programme" as "the best preparation" for nonviolent resistance.[56] This was scarcely the presentation of a careful plan for resistance activities, nor the presentation of a thought-out plan for carrying out the needed organizational and training preparations for such resistance.

At times Gandhi appears to have expected very little non-violent resistance if the Japanese should come: ". . . if for want of enough companions non-violent resisters cannot reach the goal, they will not give up their way but pursue it to the death."[57] There should not be any rush of resisters from all over India to the point of Japanese entry; residents of each province should remain for resistance in their own province.[58]

> If we were a free country, things could be done non-violently to prevent the Japanese from entering the country. As it is, non-violent resistance could commence the moment they effected a landing. Thus non-violent resisters would refuse them any help, even water. For it is no part of their duty to help anyone to steal their country. But if a Japanese had missed his way and was dying of thirst . . . a non-violent resister . . . would give water . . . Suppose the Japanese compel resisters to give them water, the resisters must die in the act of resistance. It is conceivable that they will exterminate all resisters.[59]

In May Gandhi acknowledged his absence of detailed strategic planning to deal with the Japanese:

> I have no plan in mind. . . . there should be unadulterated non-violent non-co-operation, and if the whole of India responded and unanimously offered it, I should show that without shedding a single drop of blood Japanese arms—or any combination of arms—can be sterilized. That involves the determination of India not to give quarter on any point whatsoever and to be ready to

risk loss of several million lives. But I would consider that cost
very cheap and victory won at that cost glorious . . . India may
not be ready to pay that price . . . but some such price must be
paid by any country that wants to retain its independence . . .
Therefore, in the non-violent technique I am asking India to risk
no more than other countries are risking and which India would
have to risk even if she offered armed resistance.[60]

In July he affirmed in a letter "To Every Japanese" the intention of
full resistance against the possible Japanese incursion.[61] Later he
told Americans that if India's independence were unconditionally
recognized, India would be able then to offer "irrestible opposition
to Japanese aggression."[62]

DEFENSE FOR INDEPENDENT INDIA

During the years in which he struggled for independence, and
in the short time between that achievement and his death, Gandhi
made it clear in general terms that he favored for his country a
policy of national defense by nonviolent resistance in place of the
usual military defense. Citing the brave struggle of 1930–31, he
wrote: "No different capacity is required from what has been
already evinced, if India has to contend against an invader."[63]
National defense by nonviolent resistance would be, Gandhi was
convinced, more powerful and effective than military defense; it
would cost no more lives, and its material cost would be much
cheaper.[64]

Gandhi acknowledged the practical difficulties in the implementation of such a policy.[65] At times he seemed to assume that
these difficulties did not require prior solutions, but would be
solved in the actual course of struggle (ignoring the possibility that
most people probably would not accept the policy unless they saw
solutions for such difficulties). He even once rejected the idea of
preparations,[66] a view inconsistent with other statements:

> I have always advised and insisted on non-violent defence. But I
> recognize that it has to be learnt like violent defence. It requires
> a different training. . . . [67]

Attempts to apply nonviolent action to the national defense problem of an independent country he compared to "sailing on uncharted waters."[68]

The last years of Gandhi's life were the years of World War II, and then for India the approach to independence and its first months. Gandhi's advocacy of national defense by nonviolent resistance intensified. He made it very clear that he intended this policy seriously both for India and the whole world. In 1939 when he foresaw India as a whole adopting military defense he still wanted the Indian National Congress to reject that course and to continue the development of "non-violence as a political weapon."[69] "A nation that had won freedom without the force of arms should be able to keep it too without the force of arms,"[70] he said in 1947. In late 1939 Gandhi discussed with the Working Committee of the Congress the question—now no longer "hypothetical"—of defending India from invasion by application of nonviolent means of struggle. He reported that their opinion was against his proposal, based on the judgement that Congressmen themselves were unprepared for this type of national defense. Gandhi's view was that the methods they had used to deal with the British more or less coincided with those for use against a new invasion, and perhaps the latter would be easier.[71] The latter suggestion was inconsistent with his later recognition that there might be millions of casualties in the nonviolent defense of India against Japanese invasion. Also, he appears never to have contemplated seriously whether, and if so how, he might have dealt with the objection of Congressmen that they were unprepared for such defense by himself initiating development of a program of preparations for nonviolent defense of India of comparable extent and complexity to that of military defense.

In June, 1940 Gandhi urged the Working Committee to extend the political use of nonviolent action to India's national defense. This the Committee rejected, arguing for several reasons that India was not ready to take that step.[72] Gandhi, however, continued to insist that India for her own sake, as well as that of the world peace, ought to reject military defense and military preparations in favor of defense of her independence by popular nonviolent resistance. This was India's mission.

LEVELS OF STRATEGY

We have argued in this chapter that the struggle against the British regime as an existing foreign occupation, the recommendations for opposing the then threatening Japanese invasion, and advocacy of the general future policy of defense by nonviolent resistance all fall within the realm of national defense. It is, however, quite clear even from this brief survey, that in dealing with the British Gandhi offered to Congressmen and India as a whole more than the general outlines of a possible course of action; he formulated specific campaigns, with particular objectives, strategies, tactics, and methods of action, and topped this off with considerable preparations, organizational work, and specific instructions for the resisters' behavior and discipline. It was all this, it is here argued, which made it *possible* for Indian politicians and others who did not share Gandhi's philosophy nevertheless to accept his plan of nonviolent struggle instead of using violent means. Gandhi's strategies and their detailed development transformed the general conception. It became visibly practicable and workable, and was seen to possess significant advantages over violence.

It is true that it is more difficult to work out in advance comparable detailed plans for implementation against a specific expected invasion. It is even more difficult to make such nonviolent strategies visibly practical for facing *future* potential invasions from uncertain sources, at unspecified times, for unclear objectives. It is also true that Gandhi could not do everything, and that his activities were often controlled either by imprisonment, or by his attempts to respond to immediate desperate human needs, as the communal riots before and after independence. Above all, it is true, as he acknowledged, that in exploration of this new type of national defense he too was not always sure what should be done next.

For whatever reasons, however, Gandhi's recommendations for meeting the Japanese invasion remained general. His call for India, or at least the Congress Party, to adopt nonviolent defense for the country as a whole were even more general, often highly moral in tone, and totally unaccompanied by specifics in any way comparable to those of the struggle against the British *Raj*. Gandhi was convinced that the specifics could be developed, but that remained undone.

Gandhi's expectation that it was possible for Indians to choose his recommended policy was therefore without basis. He offered the people, the Congress, and the Government only generalizations and a vague direction of a possible defense policy in place of the existing, specific, already-organized, military policy. As long as the idea of "nonviolent defense" remains a generalization and an abstraction no choice is possible for most people. Whatever the disadvantages of military means, people and governments are unlikely and even unable to give these up without confidence that they can choose an alternative policy which will be at least as effective as the one they are giving up. This had been the way Gandhi persuaded most Indians to leave violent struggle against the British in favor of nonviolent struggle; it applies even more to defense of an independent country. The precondition which might have enabled India to adopt Gandhi's defense policy was therefore absent. The refinement and evolution of this policy was left as a task for others.

POSTSCRIPT

THE TASK TAKEN UP BY OTHERS

One of the remarkable developments in the field of national defense and international security since 1957 has been the significant development in the West of the policy of national defense by prepared nonviolent resistance. The concept, of course, had not been original with Gandhi. It had been advocated in several European countries and the United States even before World War II. Not only had those advocacies usually been as generalized as Gandhi's; most of them were also tied to doctrines of pacifism or some type of social radicalism, and by and large assumed the abandonment of military defense capacity *before* nonviolent defense measures would be initiated. The beginnings of change in this policy were, however, occurring in the early 1950s in Europe, especially in the direction of separating this national defense concept from pacifism. A lecture by Professor Arne Næss in Norway in 1953 is a case in point, and there were apparently others.

The first major breakthrough occurred in England in 1957–58 when a retired naval Commander, Sir Stephen King-Hall (later Lord King-Hall), aroused considerable public attention and respectful, if skeptical, responses from British military officers and strategists for his proposal that there be an official investigation into the possibility that prepared nonviolent resistance might constitute a better defense policy for Great Britain than military means which included nuclear weapons. Sir Stephen did not know all the answers (no one did), and after some time did not press his proposition so vocally. However, this concept of national defense had been taken out of the exclusive hands of doctrinalists and opened to examination on a strategic basis, of whether it could "work" and if so how. His 1957 lecture on the subject to admirals, generals, field-marshals and other officers at the Royal United Services Institution was an historic occasion. King-Hall's book *Defense in the Nuclear Age*[73] was a milepost if not the definitive work. In the period after its publication, various scholars and exponents of this policy were active in several countries, including Norway and Germany, in achieving a wider hearing for the concept, and the book was published in several countries.

The second major breakthrough occurred in 1964. A few young people (including April Carter, Theodor Ebert, Adam Roberts and the present author) from several countries set themselves the task of developing this policy further. They changed the terminology in order to by-pass preconceptions and complete the severance from doctrinal pacifism. The policy was renamed "civilian defense." The term might confuse and be unclear, but that was preferable to an immediate prejudicial dismissal. Civilian was nonmilitary, and so civilian defense was to be the defense of the country's independence and freedom and chosen social and political institutions by actions of the civilian population themselves, using civilian means of action. This change was no longer associated with "disarmament"—which to many people implied helplessness in face of international dangers. The change-over was to be "transarmament"—the transition from one defense system, or weapons system, to another. In addition, it was emphasized that thorough research, detailed planning, and complex preparations would be necessary in advance of the adoption of this policy. Nor was military defense to be abandoned first—which was viewed as impossible in any case. After the initial introduction of civilian defense into the country's policy along side military defense, the civilian component would be gradually expanded, and as justifiable confidence in it grew, it would be possible to scale down and finally phase out the military component when it became unneeded.

In March 1964 a booklet called "Civilian Defence" was published in London. The publisher was still pacifist—the weekly newspaper *Peace News*—but the Introduction was by the Director of the Institute for Strategic Studies, the Hon. Alastair Buchan.[74]

That September a specialist conference on the nature and problems of civilian defense was held at Oxford. Participants included specialists not only in nonviolent action, but also in resistance movements against the Nazis—M.R.D. Foot; in *coup d'état* —Lt. Col. D.J. Goodspeed of Canada; in Nazi totalitarianism—Professor Ernest K. Bramsted; and in military strategy and international security problems—Sir Basil Liddell Hart, Lt. Col. Alun Gwynne Jones (later Lord Chalfont), and the Hon. Alastair Buchan. The gathering engaged in a common and most serious grappling with the difficult problems of this civilian type of national defense.

From this point on, civilian defense has been recognized as a serious, if unorthodox, proposal in the field of national defense alternatives. Adam Roberts edited the book which was an outgrowth of that 1964 Civilian Defense Study Conference: *The Strategy of Civilian Defense.*[75] The American edition was entitled, *Civilian Resistance as a National Defense,*[76] as was the paperback.[77] Conferences on the subject have been since held in Sweden, Germany, the Netherlands, and Belgium. New books and translations of the above have now been published in Denmark, Sweden, Norway, the Netherlands, Germany, India, Japan and the United States, as well as Britain. Serious interest by individual military officers and strategists has grown, and the first tentative small beginnings of interest have developed by defense departments and governments, especially in Sweden, but also in the Netherlands, Norway, and Denmark. Graduate and undergraduate seminars directly on civilian defense or on closely related maters have already begun at several colleges and universities in Europe and the United States. Quietly, with little fanfare, Gandhi's defense policy has been undergoing extraordinary development. The 1968 invasion and unprepared resistance of Czechoslovakia highlighted several relevant claims of exponents of civilian defense: there is need for national defense; nonviolent resistance has great potential in meeting foreign invasion as well as internal *coups d'état;* and major advance preparations and training are necessary for effectiveness. Public presentation of the essentials of this policy has begun over the media of mass communication.

Difficulties still remain in 1979, some of them major ones. The literature, though vastly expanded since 1964, is still inadequate. Historical studies of unprepared nonviolent struggle against dictators, invasions, and the like, have begun to appear, but many more are needed. The policy of civilian defense—or, as it is increasingly called in the United States, civilian-based defense—still requires major conceptual development and the preparation of feasibility studies for particular societies which may face particular threats with various possible objectives.

In some European countries conceptual confusion has been introduced by those who would use the term "civilian defense" (or the local corresponding term "social defense") to include not only a defense policy but a particular conception of social change. Major efforts have also been made to shift the framework of thought from strategy, calculation of the possible, and effectiveness, to the field of ideology, which has usually proved to be the quicksand of new thought and beneficial change. This is especially grave since the innovations in the policy, and the terminological changes, made around 1964 were specifically intended to extricate the policy conception from the octupus-like grip of doctrine and ideology. Where ideological orientations have taken hold, policy-development and sympathetic public examination of civilian-based defense have been stultified.

Much additional work is still needed in conceptual development and definitions of terms. Nowhere has a major research program been established to explore the nature and potential of civilian-based defense, and almost no research funds are available.

Nevertheless, despite these difficulties, serious thou policy still continues, the idea is spreading, and recogn... growing that this policy probably has *some* role to play in defense, at least as a reserve capacity along side a predominantly military posture. Time schedules are of course dangerous to predict, but there are indications that it is not unreasonable to say that civilian-based defense is likely to be introduced by the first country as a component within the wider predominantly military national defense program within ten years, and possibly by the mid-1980s. At this point it appears that it is likely to be one of the Scandinavian countries, but there could be surprises. Prediction of the time when the first country would complete transarmament to civilian defense must be less reliable, but it could happen within twenty-five years. Civilian-based defense is, of course, neither a panacea, nor without risks and dangers. Nothing is.

Research and analysis of the nature and problems of civilian defense are urgently needed. This requires both funds and scholars. Given a significant influx of these, major steps can be taken within our lifetimes toward the removal of war from human society, while increasing our capacities to destroy dictatorships and provide effective defense against aggressors. When that is accomplished, a great deal of credit will have to go to the insights and actions of Gandhi as a national defense strategist.

NOTES TO CHAPTER NINE

1. Krishnalal Shridarani, **War Without Violence: A Study of Gandhi's Method and Its Accomplishments** (New York: Harcourt, Brace, and Co., 1939, London: Victor Gollancz, 1939).
2. See Chapter Eight, "Gandhi's Defense Policy."
3. See Ibid., pp. 132–134.
4. **Young India** (hereafter cited as YI) 15 Nov. 1928; R.K. Prabhu and U.R. Rao, eds., **The Mind of Mahatma Gandhi** (Bombay: Oxford University Press, 1945), p. 126; also see Chapter Eight, "Gandhi's Defense Policy," pp. 138–148.
5. **Harijan** (hereafter cited as H.), 8 June 1947; M.K. Gandhi, <u>Non-violence</u> in Peace and War (hereafter cited as NVPW. The original source and date are given, in addition to the book in which it is reprinted), (2 vols. Ahmedabad: Navajivan, [1942] 1948–1949), vol. II, p. 261.

6. **YI,** 11 August 1920; **NPVW, I,** p. 2. Apparently as a typographical error the third edition, 1949, of **NVPW, I,** substitutes "putting" for "the pitting." Here I have corrected the quotation, as the text quoted by Joan V. Bondurant, **Conquest of Violence** (Princeton, N.J.: Princeton University Press, 1958), p. 26. She has used a different source.

7. **YI,** 30 Apr. 1931; M. K. Gandhi, **Satyagraha** (hereafter cited as **S.**) (Ahmedabad: Navajivan, 1951), p.81.

8. **H.,** 30 Mar. 1947; **NVPW, II,** pp. 233–234.

9. **H.,** 30 June 1946; **NVPW, II,** p. 16.

10. **H.,** 12 Oct. 1935; **NVPW, I,** p. 111.

11. **H.,** 17 Dec. 1938; **NVPW, I,** p. 168.

12. See Chapter Eight "Gandhi's Defense Policy," pp. 141–142.

13. **H.,** 29 Sept. 1940; **NVPW, I,** pp. 357–358.

14. See Chapter Thirteen, "Nonviolence: Moral Principle or Political Technique."

15. **YI,** 19 Sept. 1924; **S.,** p. 189.

16. **YI,** 2 Aug. 1928; **S.,** p. 216.

17. **YI,** 1 July 1939; Nirmal Kumar Bose, **Selections from Gandhi** (Ahmedabad: Navajivan, 1948), p. 224.

18. **YI,** 3 Apr. 1924; Bose, **Selections from Gandhi,** p. 43.

19. **YI, III,** pp. 548–549; Gopi Nath Dhawan, **The Political Philosophy of Mahatma Gandhi** (Third rev. ed.; Ahmedabad: Navajivan, 1962), p. 326.

20. **YI, II,** p. 1292; Dhawan, **The Political Philosophy of Mahatma Gandhi,** p. 326.

21. Mahadev Desai, **Gandhiji in Indian Villages,** p. 170; Dhawan, **The Political Philosophy of Mahatma Gandhi,** p. 326.

22. **H.,** 21 June 1942, p. 197; Dhawan, **The Political Philosophy of Mahatma Gandhi,** p. 326.

23. See Gene Sharp, "Social Power and Political Freedom," in Sharp, **Social Power and Political Freedom** (Boston: Porter Sargent Publishers, Inc. 1979).

24. Leo Tolstoy, "A Letter to a Hindu: The Subjection of India—Its Cause and Cure," with an Introduction by M. K. Gandhi, in **The Works of Tolstoy,** vol. 21, **Recollections and Essays** (trans. by Aylmer Maude; London: Humphrey Milford, 1937), pp. 413–432.

25. M.K. Gandhi, "Hind Swaraj or Indian Home Rule" (pamphlet; new revised edition; Ahmedabad: Navajivan, 1958).

26. Ibid., p. 38.

27. Ibid., p. 81.

28. Ibid., p. 100.

29. Ibid., p. 101.

30. Ibid., p. 103.

31. See M.K. Gandhi, "The Constructive Programme" (pamphlet; Ahmedabad: Navajivan, 1966).

32. Gene Sharp, **Gandhi Wields the Weapon of Moral Power: Three Case Histories,** (Ahmedabad: Navajivan, 1960), p. 64.

33. **H.,** 27 July 1947; **NVPW, II,** p. 278.

34. **H.,** 21 July 1940; **NVPW, I,** p. 292.

35. **H.,** 26 Mar. 1938 (**NVPW, I,** p. 133); **H.,** 14 Oct. 1939 (**NVPW, I,** p. 236); **H.,** 10 Feb. 1946 (**NVPW, II,** p. 2); **H.,** 24 Feb. 1946 (**NVPW, II,** p. 30).

36. **H.**, 8 June 1947; **NVPW**, II, p. 261.
37. **H.**, 18 Aug. 1946; **NVPW**, II, p. 141. See also, **H.**, 1 June 1947; **NVPW**, II, p. 254.
38. Gandhi, quoted in Nirmal Kumar Bose, **Studies in Gandhism** (Second ed.; Calcutta: Indian Associated Publishing Co., 1947), p. 134.
39. M.K. Gandhi, **Satyagraha in South Africa**, (Ahmedabad: Navajivan, 1950), p. 46.
40. See Sharp, **Gandhi Wields the Weapon of Moral Power**, p. 60.
41. S. Gopal, **The Viceroyality of Lord Irwin, 1926–1931** (Oxford: Clarendon Press, 1957), p. 56.
42. Sharp, **Gandhi Wields the Weapon of Moral Power**, pp. 70–90.
43. Jawaharlal Nehru, **An Autobiography** (New ed.; London: The Bodley Head, 1953), p. 253.
44. Sharp, **Gandhi Wields the Weapon of Moral Power**, p. 84.
45. **S.**, p. 288 and Dhawan, **The Political Philosophy of Mahatma Gandhi**, pp. 224-225.
46. Gandhi, quoted in Bose, **Selections from Gandhi**, p. 202.
47. See Gene Sharp, **The Politics of Nonviolent Action** (Boston: Porter Sargent Publisher, Inc. 1973).
48. Sharp, **Gandhi Wields the Weapon of Moral Power**, p. 72.
49. **S.**, p. 173.
50. See Ibid., pp. 25, 115-116, 127, 151, and 173.
51. Sharp, **Gandhi Wields the Weapon of Moral Power**, pp. 51-206.
52. See Bose, **Selections from Gandhi**, p. 202; Bose, **Studies in Gandhism**, p. 176; and Joan V. Bondurant, **Conquest of Violence: The Gandhian Philosophy of Conflict** (Princeton, N.J.: Princeton University Press, 1958), pp. 38–39.
53. **NVPW**, I, pp. 397–398.
54. **H.**, 22 Mar. 1942; **NVPW**, I, pp. 388–389.
55. **H.**, 12 Apr. 1942; **NVPW**, I, p. 390.
56. **H.**, 12 Apr. 1942; **NVPW**, I, pp. 398–399.
57. **H.**, 12 Apr. 1942; **NVPW**, I, p. 398.
58. **H.**, 12 Apr. 1942; **NVPW**, I, p. 398.
59. **H.**, 12 Apr. 1942; **NVPW**, I, p. 397.
60. **H.**, 24 May 1942; **S.**, pp. 377–378.
61. **H.**, 26 July 1942; **NVPW**, I, p. 410.
62. **H.**, 9 Aug. 1942; **NVPW**, I, p. 415.
63. **H.**, 14 Oct. 1939; **NVPW**, I, p. 236.
64. **H.**, 25 May 1947 (**NVPW**, II, p. 251); **H.**, 14 Apr. 1946 (**NVPW**, II, p. 35); **H.**, 14 Oct. 1939 (**NVPW**, I, p. 234); **H.**, 13 Apr. 1940 (**NVPW**, I, p. 265); **H.**, 16 Nov. 1947 (**NVPW**, II, p. 143).
65. **H.**, 11 Aug. 1940; **NVPW**, I, p. 307.
66. **H.**, 14 Apr. 1940; **S.**, p. 386.
67. **H.**, 2 Mar. 1940; **NVPW**, I, p. 260.
68. **H.**, 11 Aug. 1940; **NVPW**, I, pp. 307-308. For a further description of Gandhi's prescription of a national defense policy by nonviolent resistance for India, see Chapter Eight, "Gandhi's Defense Policy," esp. pp. 148-160.
69. **H.**, 14 Oct. 1939; **NVPW**, I, p. 237.

70. **H.,** 14 Dec. 1947; NVPW, II, pp. 340–341.
71. **H.,** 14 Oct. 1939; NVPW, I, pp. 235–236.
72. See NVPW, I, Appendix VI pp. 445–447; Bose, **Studies in Gandhism,** pp. 308–311; and **H.,** 29 June 1940; NVPW, I, p. 275.
73. Stephen King-Hall, **Defence in the Nuclear Age** (London: Victor Gollancz, 1958, and Nyack, N.Y.: Fellowship, 1959).
74. Adam Roberts, Jerome Frank, Arne Naess, and Gene Sharp, "Civilian Defence" (pamphlet; London: Peace News, 1964).
75. Adam Roberts, ed., **The Strategy of Civilian Defence: Non-violent Resistance to Aggression** (London: Faber & Faber, 1967).
76. Adam Roberts, ed., **Civilian Resistance as a National Defense: Non-violent Action Against Aggression** (Harrisburg, Pa.: Stackpole Books, 1968).
77. Adam Roberts, ed., **Civilian Resistance as a National Defence: Non-violent Action Against Agression** (Harmondsworth, Middlesex; Baltimore, Maryland; Ringwood, Victoria; and Markham, Ontario: Penguin Books, 1969).

PART TWO

Essays on Ethics and Politics

10

Types of Principled Nonviolence

A variety of belief systems exist which reject violence on grounds of principle. The violence rejected may be general or particular, and the principle involved may be a specific imperative against violence. Or the violence may be rejected as the secondary result of the operation of a principle which is not intrinsically related to violence and nonviolence. At first glance, all that is "not violence" may seem to be of a single kind. In a society where such systems of ideas, beliefs, and behavior are usually regarded as esoteric, "crack-pot," impractical, dangerous, or simply strange, few people undertake a sufficiently serious examination of these phenomena to make them aware that quite different types of beliefs are involved. "Pacifism," "nonviolence," and other terms are conmonly used either as broad generalities (glittering, scathing, or just vague), or with a wide variety of more specific meanings for the same word.

This lack of clarity has had its effect on the groups promoting nonviolent approaches, on criticisms by their opponents, and on the thinking of others. The usual degree of misunderstanding which may result from a varied and imprecise use of terms becomes plain confusion when the phenomena concerned are relatively little known. When these phenomena involve unorthodox ideas and beliefs—which may be associated with strong emotions among both proponents and opponents—the confusion may become chaos. A failure to discern the very real differences among the various types of principled nonviolence and to exercise more care in the use of terms may have a number of undesirable consequences. Two of these are that evaluation of the merits and demerits of these approaches will be seriously handicapped, and that research and analysis in this area will face unnecessary difficulties. A typology of the phenomena, therefore, may serve a useful role. Hans Reichenbach has written: "Classification is the first step toward scientific investigation."[1] It should be noted that we are here concerned with belief systems involving the rejection of violence, and not with the technique of nonviolent action (although one of the differences among these belief systems is their attitude toward that technique). A similar classification of the types of nonviolent action and of the types of situations in which it may be applied is also needed, but this is not attempted here.

DISTINCTIONS MADE BY DEVOTEES OF "NONVIOLENCE"

Persons rejecting violence on grounds of principle have rarely analyzed the relation of their particular belief systems to those of others also rejecting violence. They have failed to do this largely because such analysis has seemed to them irrelevant: their duty was to follow the imperatives of their beliefs. However, some of them have recognized differences in motivation and behavior among those rejecting violence.

For example, Guy F. Hershberger, a Mennonite, distinguished between "non-resistance" and "modern pacifism." Non-resistance, he said, describes the faith and life of those "who cannot have any part in warfare because they believe the Bible forbids it, and who renounce all coercion, even non-violent coercion." Pacifism, he said, is a "term which covers many types of opposition to war."[2]

Some Western pacifists[3] have seen Gandhi's approach so sufficiently different from their own that they have felt it was not genuinely "pacifist." Reginald Reynolds wrote:

> A reading of "official" [British] pacifist literature from, say, 1920 onward would reveal some odd things which many pacifists would prefer to forget. People accepted as "leading pacifists" were, as late as 1930, writing abusive articles about Gandhi and defending British Rule in India. Such articles and letters could be found in *The Friend* (weekly unofficial paper of the Quakers), in *Reconciliation* (monthly organ of the Fellowship of Reconciliation), and in *No More War* (the monthly organ of the [No More War] movement).[4]

Western pacifists have sometimes distinguished between the "religious" pacifists and the "nonreligious" pacifists who base their pacifism on "humanitarian" or "philosophical" considerations. This distinction has also been made by nonpacifists.[5] Pacifists have also recognized differences among themselves in their response to military conscription. There have been (1) the "absolutists," who believe in civil disobedience to such laws and refuse cooperation with the administrative agencies for military conscription even to obtain their personal exemption from military duty where the law allows for such exemption; (2) those who refuse entry into the military forces (even as noncombatants) but are willing to cooperate with the conscription system to obtain their exemption from military duty and are willing to perform alternative civilian work where such alternative is allowed; and (3) those who refuse to bear arms but are willing to perform noncombatant (such as medical) duties within the military forces.[6]

Although Gandhi never wrote systematic treatises on "nonviolence," he did distinguish between two or more types of "nonviolence."[7] After first calling his South African protest movements "passive resistance," he discarded the term and adopted a new term, *satyagraha*.[8]

> When in a meeting of Europeans I found that the term "passive resistance" was too narrowly construed, that it was supposed to be a weapon of the weak, that it could be characterized by hatred, and that it could finally manifest itself as violence, I had to demur to all these statements and explain the real nature of the Indian movement. It was clear that a new word must be coined by the Indians to designate their struggle.[9]

Gandhi also seems to have assumed an implicit distinction between Western pacifism and *satyagraha*, although explicit statements to this effect are difficult to find. Bharatan Kumarappa, in an introductory note to a small collection of Gandhi's writings prepared for the World Pacifist Conference in India, December, 1949–January, 1950, wrote:

> It is a far cry ... from pacifism to Gandhiji's idea of non-violence. While pacifism hopes to get rid of war, chiefly by refusing to fight and by carrying on propaganda against war, Gandhiji goes much deeper and sees that war cannot be avoided, so long as the seeds of it remain in man's breast and grow and develop in his social, political and economic life. Gandhiji's cure is, therefore, very radical and far-reaching. It demands nothing less than rooting out violence from one's self and from one's environment.[10]

OTHER CLASSIFICATIONS

The distinctions made by analysts have often included types of nonviolent action as a political technique as well as types of principled nonviolence. The Amercan sociologist Clarence Marsh Case in his study of such phenomena explicitly recognized differences between various types,[11] although he made no attempt to develop a typology. He used the terms "nonviolent resistance" and "passive resistance" interchangeably.[12]

Political scientist Dr. Mulford Sibley distinguished three types of "nonviolence": Hindu pacifism *(satyagraha),* Christian pacifism, and revolutionary secular pacifism.[13] This classification, however, did not purport to encompass the field of "nonviolence" and was limited to those modern types of pacifism containing political theory. Professor Leo Kuper has distinguished between nonviolent resistance movements aimed at achieving their goals by means of embarrassment and conversion of their opponents, respectively,[14] but, again, this does not purport to be a full typology.

Theodore Paullin[15] comes close to developing a typology of "nonviolence," although this was not his main intention. Paullin structured his discussion on the basis of six types resulting from a continuum,

> ... at one end of which we place violence coupled with hatred, and at the other, dependence only upon the application of positive love and goodwill. In the intermediate positions we might place (1) violence without hatred, (2) nonviolence practiced by necessity rather than because of principle, (3) nonviolent coercion, (4) *satyagraha* and nonviolent direct action, and (5) non-resistance.[16]

The nonviolence extremity of his continuum, "active goodwill and reconciliation," becomes the sixth type. Because Paullin's main objective in the booklet was to consider the application of "nonviolent means of achieving group purposes,"[17] his classification has suffered through lack of development and refinement. Some types of "nonviolence" have not been included,[18] and some seem classified incorrectly.[19] Paullin has, however, made a genuine contribution toward the development of a typology.

In this chapter, however, contrary to Paullin (and earlier versions of this typology) we are classifying *only belief systems involving a rejection of violence,* and are not including the various types of nonviolent action. The various types of principled nonviolence differ from each other on a number of points, as we shall see, and have in common only the single point of the rejection of violence because of some principle.[20]

Not included in this broad classification are (1) hermits, (2) cases of cowardice (both involving a *de facto* withdrawal, though for different reasons, from aspects of life involving physical violence rather than offering a nonviolent response in the situation), and (3) legislation, State decrees, etc. (backed by threat of physical violence, such as imprisonment, execution, and so on).

The term "pacifism" as defined here includes the belief systems of those persons and groups who, as the minimum, refuse participation in all international or civil wars or violent revolutions, and base this refusal on moral, ethical, or religious principle. Such persons and groups are here called "pacifists." "Pacifism" is an intermediary classification including several of the types of principled nonviolence described below. These are indicated below after the typology.

In developing this typology, I sought to observe the "natural" groupings or types as they seem to exist rather than preselecting certain criteria and then seeking to fit the phenomena into the predetermined categories. After a classification of the types had been made, I sought to examine what were the intrinsic characteristics possessed by the respective types which distinguished them from the others. The criteria which emerged included such factors as the nature of the principle which leads to abstention from violence; whether the nonviolent group's belief system is "otherworldly" or "this-worldly"; whether or not the nonviolent group has a program of social change; what is the nonviolent group's attitude toward the opponents; whether all or only certain physical violence is rejected; whether the nonviolent group is concerned with its own integrity; and others. Following the description of the types of principled nonviolence, Chart 1 following the text of this chapter lists the main criteria which emerged.

The six types of principled nonviolence described below[21] are nonresistance, active reconciliation, moral resistance, selective nonviolence, *satyagraha,* and nonviolent revolution.[22] These are listed roughly in the order of increasing activity.[23] There is no strict separation between some of these types, and particular cases may not seem to fit exactly into any one of them. This classification should be viewed simply as a tool to facilitate understanding and study of the phenomena, a tool which is neither perfect nor final but may nevertheless be useful.

The examples cited and statements used as illustrations for the respective types have been chosen from those available on the basis of their adequacy as illustrations and because of the presence of suitable documentation. There is no pretense that the examples cited are geographically representative or exhaustive of the cases belonging to each type. Further research on each of these types could provide abundant additional examples and illustrative statements, and new such material from the years since this study was prepared might be added.

NONRESISTANCE

The nonresistants reject on principle all physical violence, whether on an individual, State, or international level. There are various Christian sects of this type, such as the Mennonites and the Amish. They refuse participation in war, and also in the State by holding government office, voting, or having recourse to the courts. They pay their taxes, however, and do what the State demands, as long as it is not inconsistent with what they consider to be their duty to God. They refuse to resist evil situations even by nonviolent methods, and in times of oppression simply hold to their beliefs and follow them—ignoring the evil as much as possible, and suffering their lot as part of their religious duty.

The nonresistants are concerned with being true to their beliefs and maintaining their own integrity, rather than with attempts at social reconstruction, many even opposing attempts to create a good society here on earth. A common belief of the nonresistants is that it is not possible for the world as a whole to become free from sin, and, therefore, the Christian should withdraw from evil. Such influence as they have on society results from their acts of goodwill (such as relief work), their exhortations, and their example.

The nonresistants have their roots in early Christianity. With very few exceptions, the early Christians refused all military service and subservience to the Roman emperor. The crucial change began under the reign of Constantine, who was converted to Christianity in 312 A.D. and who declared it to be the State religion in 324 A.D.[24] After the main Christian groups began to turn to the State for support and no longer refused participation in war, small heretical groups perpetuated the pacifist interpretation of Christianity. They were cruelly persecuted, and some of their names have been lost.

From the Middle Ages on, there were many sects which sought a return to what they believed to be the basic gospel. Among these were the Albigenses or Cathari; "Christ's Poor"; the Waldenses, or "The Poor Men of Lyons"; the "Humilates"; the Bohemian Brethren, of the Church of the *Unitas Fratrum;* the revived *Unitas Fratrum,* or the Moravian Church; the Schwenkfelders; the German Baptists, or Dunkers; the Obbenites; the Mennonites; the Collegiants (which represented a movement for a creedless spiritual worship within the existing denominations); the Simonians; the Socinians; and the Brownists. Some of these were Anabaptist sects. Hershberger described these sects:

> Alongside the medieval church there were certain small, intimate groups of Christians who refused to accept a compromise with the social order. They stood aloof and maintained that indifference or hostility to the world which characterized the primitive church. These groups are known as the sects. They generally refused to use the law, to take the oath, to exercise domination over others, or to participate in war. Theirs was not an ascetic emphasis on heroic and vicarious achievement. It was not an oppositon, in most cases, to the sense life or the average life of humanity, but simply an opposition to the social institutions of the world.
>
> The sects generally emphasized lay religion, personal ethical achievement, religious equality, brotherly love, indifference to the state and the ruling classes, dislike of the law and oath, the ideal of poverty and frugality, direct personal religious relationship, appeal to the primitive church, and criticism of the theologians. They always demanded a high standard of moral performance. This made for small groups, of course, but what they lost in the spirit of universalism, they made up for in intensity of life. This tradition of the sects was carried down from the Montanists and Dontanists through the Waldensians to the followers of Wycliff and Huss to the Anabaptists.[25]

Describing one of the nonresistant sects, the Mennonites, C. Henry Smith wrote:

> They adopted bodily the faith of the peaceful type of Anabaptists, and that was a rejection of all civil and a great deal of the prevailing ecclesiastical government as unnecessary for the Christian. . . . [They] went no further, however, in their opposition to the temporal authority than to declare that the true church and the temporal powers had nothing in common and must be entirely separate; not only must the state not interfere with the church, but the true Christian must be entirely free from participating in civil matters. The temporal authority must needs exist, since it was instituted of God to punish the wicked, but in that work the Christian had no hand. This position they reached from a literal interpretation of the Sermon on the Mount, where Christ taught his disciples, among other things, to "love their enemies" and to "swear not at all." Hence their position involved opposition to the oath, holding of office, and bearing of arms.[26]

In 1917 in America the general conference and various branches of the Mennonite Church united in addressing a signed "Appeal to the President" in which they said:

> Because of our understanding of the teachings of Christ and the New Testament generally against war in any form, we can render no service, either combatant or non-combatant, under the military establishment, but will rather be amenable to any punishment the government sees fit to lay upon us as a penalty.[27]

ACTIVE RECONCILIATION

The nonviolence of the group favoring the use of active goodwill and reconciliation is based upon principle. It refers not only to outward actions but also to personal reconciliation and improvement of one's own life before attempting to change others.

> Its proponents seek to accomplish a positive alteration in the attitude and policy of the group or person responsible for some undesirable situation; but they never use coercion—even nonviolent coercion. Rather they seek to convince their opponent. . . . They place their emphasis on the positive action of goodwill which they *will* use rather than upon a catalogue of violent actions which they will not use.[28]

A large part of the basis of this approach is the importance placed on the worth of every individual and the belief that he or she can change. Direct action and strategy are not involved. Tolstoy and a great number of his followers and many of the present Society of Friends (Quakers) are proponents of this type of principled nonviolence. So also are many other individual pacifists.

Tolstoy rejected the use of violence under all circumstances, and rejected also private property and association with institutions which practice coercion over men. Tolstoy depended upon the power of example and good will to influence men. He sought a regeneration of society as a whole through the practice of love in all one's relationships, simple living, self-service, and the persuasion of others to follow this way of life.[29] In Tolstoy's own words:

> . . . [I]t is this acknowledgement of the law of love as the supreme law of human life, and this clearly expressed guidance for conduct resulting from the Christian teaching of love, embracing enemies

and those who hate, offend, and curse us, that constitute the peculiarity of Christ's teaching, and by giving to the doctrine of love, and to the guidance flowing therefrom, an exact and definite meaning, inevitably involves a complete change of the established organization of life, not only in Christendom, but among all the nations of the earth.[30]

The time will come—it is already coming—when the Christian principles of equality and fraternity, community of property, nonresistance of evil by force will appear just as natural and simple as the principles of family or social life seem to us now.[31]

The Christian will not dispute with any one, nor attack any one, nor use violence against any one. On the contrary, he will bear violence without opposing it. But by this very attitude to violence, he will not only himself be free, but will free the whole world from all external power.[32]

George Fox and the early Quakers recognized religious experience as the final authority in religion, in place of the Scriptures, which were the authority of the nonresistant sects and other Protestants. The Friends believe that the life of every person, however degraded, has worth and is guided by an Inner Light (sometimes called "the spirit of Christ"). This rules out any right to constrain man by means of violence. Also involved is the conviction that men should live the kind of life which removes the occasion for war and builds a world of peace. Friends in general have not completely rejected the use of violence by a civil government[33] and today often work for the adoption of legislation and sometimes hold office (even as judges).

Early Quakers, believing in the imminence of the spiritual regeneration of the world, eventually identified themselves with the civil government, expecting to administer the affairs of State on the principles of love, kindness, and goodwill. With most Quakers there was a fundamental difference between the use of violence in personal relations and by the military on the one hand, and by a civil government on the other. After some years of Quaker administration in Pennsylvania, the Quakers withdrew from the government. There is variation in opinion on the matter among present-day Quakers, many of whom are not pacifists. Quakers have made large efforts at international relief and reconstruction, international conciliation and peace education, social reform activities, and conscientious objection.

Quakers describe their belief in peace in these terms:

The conviction that the spirit of Christ dwells in the souls of all men is the source of our refusal to take part in war, and of our opposition to slavery and oppression in every form. We believe that the primary Christian duty in relation to others is to appeal to that of God in them and, therefore, any method of oppression or violence that renders such an appeal impossible must be set on one side.[34]

There is a right and possible way for the family of nations to live together at peace. . . . It is the way of active, reconciling love, of overcoming evil with good. We feel an inward compulsion, which we cannot disregard, to strive to follow the way of constructive goodwill, despite the sense of our own shortcomings and despite the failure, in which we have shared, to labor sufficiently for the Kingdom of God on earth.[35]

The fundamental ground of our opposition to war is religious and ethical. It attaches to the nature of God as revealed in Christ and to the nature of man as related to Him. . . . The only absolute ground for an unalterable and inevitable opposition to war is one which attaches to the inherent nature of right and wrong, one which springs out of the consciousness of obligation to what the enlightened soul knows ought to be. . . . [This peace testimony] never was "adopted." [For] it is not a policy; it is a conviction of the soul. It cannot be followed at one time and surrendered at another time. . . . The Christian way of life revealed in the New Testament, the voice of conscience revealed in the soul, the preciousness of personality revealed in the transforming force of love, and the irrationality revealed in modern warfare, either together or singly, present grounds which for those who feel them make participation in war under any conditions impossible . . . [Friends] do not rest their case on sporadic texts. They find themselves confronted with a Christianity, the Christianity of the Gospels, that calls for a radical transformation of man, for the creation of a new type of person and for the building of a new social order, and they take this with utmost seriousness as a thing to be ventured and tried.[36]

Persons sharing the "active reconciliation" beliefs often prefer a rather quietist approach to social problems, disliking anything akin to "agitation" or "trouble." Some of them may thus oppose nonviolent action (including strikes, boycotts, etc.), and even outspoken verbal statements, believing such methods to be violent in spirit, perhaps even immoral, and harmful in their effects on the opponent. They would prefer much quieter methods, such as personal representations, letters and private deputations. Others have participated in, led, and made major contributions to the development of nonviolent action.

MORAL RESISTANCE

Believers in "moral resistance"—a matter of principle—are convinced that evil should be resisted, but only by peaceful and moral means. The emphasis on individual moral responsibility is an important part of this approach. "Moral resistance" includes both a personal refusal of individuals to participate in evil—such as war or, earlier, slavery—and an imperative for individuals to do something actively against the evil, such as speaking, writing, or preaching. Nonviolent resistance and direct action are not ruled out, though the major emphasis is usually placed upon education, persuasion, and individual example. Believers in "moral resistance" in Western society, although lacking an overall social analysis or comprehensive program of social change, generally favor gradual social reform through such methods as legislation, education, and efforts to influence government officials.

The pacifism of various peace societies in New England during the middle of the last century was of this type. Adin Ballou and William Lloyd Garrison (of antislavery fame) were well-known spokesmen for these groups.[37] A part of the "Declaration of Sentiments" (written by Garrison) adopted by the Peace Convention, Boston, 18-20 September 1838, read as follows:

> We register our testimony, not only against all wars, whether offensive or defensive, but all preparations for war. . . . Hence we deem it unlawful to bear arms or to hold a military office. . . . As a measure of sound policy . . . as well as on the ground of allegiance to Him who is King of Kings and Lord of Lords, we cordially adopt the Non-Resistance principle, being confident that it provides for all possible consequences, will ensure all

things needful to us, is armed with omnipotent power, and must ultimately triumph over every assailing force. . . .

But while we shall adhere to the doctrine of Non-Resistance and passive submission to enemies, we propose, in a moral and spiritual sense, to speak and act boldly; to assail iniquity, in high places and in low places, to apply our principles to all existing civil, political, legal and ecclesiastical institutions. . . . We shall employ lecturers, circulate tracts and publications, form societies, and petition our state and national governments, in relation to the subject of *universal peace.* It will be our leading object to devise ways and means for effecting a radical change in the views, feelings and practices of society, respecting the sinfulness of war and the treatment of enemies.[38]

Adin Ballou stated:

The term nonresistance . . . requires very considerable quali-ficatons. I use it as applicable only to the conduct of human beings towards human beings—not towards the inferior animals, inanimate things or satanic influences. . . . But I go further, and disclaim using the terms to express *absolute passivity* even towards human beings. I claim the right to offer the utmost moral resistance, not sinful, of which God has made me capable, to every manifestation of evil among mankind. Nay, I hold it my *duty* to offer such moral resistance. In this sense my very nonresistance becomes the highest kind of resistance to evil. . . . There is an uninjurious, benevolent *physical* force. There are cases in which it would not only be allowable, but in the highest degree commendable, to *restrain* human beings by this kind of force . . . as maniacs, the delirious, the intoxicated, etc. And in cases where deadly violence is inflicted with deliberation and malice of forethought, one may nobly throw his body as a temporary barrier between the destroyer and his helpless victim, choosing to die in that position, rather than be a passive spectator. Thus another most important qualification is given to the term nonresistance. . . . It is simply nonresistance of injury with injury—evil with evil.[39]

Garrison stated his interpretation of "nonresistance" in these terms:

Non-Resistance is . . . a state of activity, ever fighting the good fight of faith, ever foremost to assail unjust power, ever struggling for liberty, equality, fraternity, in no national sense, but in a world-wide spirit. It is passive only in this sense—that it will not return evil for evil, nor give blow for blow, nor resort to murderous weapons for protection or defence.[40]

He illustrated the "moral resistance" attitude toward methods to be used in a social struggle in his speech at the New England Abolitionists Convention, Boston, 26 May 1858:

When the anti-slavery cause was launched it was baptized in the spirit of peace. . . . I do not believe that the weapons of liberty ever have been, or ever can be, the weapons of despotism. I know that those of despotism are the sword, the revolver, the cannon, the bombshell; and, therefore, the weapons to which tyrants cling, and upon which they depend are not the weapons for me, as a friend of liberty. I will not trust the war spirit anywhere in the universe of God, because the experience of six thousand years proves it not to be at all reliable in such a struggle as ours. . . . I pray you, Abolitionists, still adhere to that truth. . . . Blood . . . shall not flow through any counsel of mine. Much as I detest the oppression exercised by the Southern slave-holder, he is a man, sacred before me. . . . I have no other weapon to wield against him but the simple truth of God, which is the great instrument for the overthrow of all iniquity and the salvation of the world.[41]

A very large part of contemporary Western pacifists are of this type, although there is variation within the membership of most of the pacifist organizations. The United States Fellowship of Reconciliation (a religious, largely Christian, pacifist organization), for example, contains members sharing the nonresistance and active reconciliation positions, although it is probable that a very large percentage belong in the moral resistance category. The organization's Statement of Purpose largely reflects this position:

Although members do not bind themselves to any exact form of words, they refuse to participate in any war or to sanction military preparations; they work to abolish war and to foster goodwill among nations, races and classes; they strive to build a social order which will suffer no individual or groups to be exploited for the profit or pleasure of another, and which will ensure to all the means for realizing the best possibilities of life; they advocate such ways of dealing with offenders against society as shall transform the wrongdoer rather than inflict retributive punishment; they endeavor to show reverence for personality—in the home, in the education of children, in association with those of other classes, nationalities and races; they seek to avoid bitterness and contention, and to maintain the spirit of self-giving love while engaged in the struggle to achieve these purposes.[42]

A non-Western example of "moral resistance" is the pacifism of the traditional Hopi Indian nation. In the 1950s they sought to spread their views, which they believed to be helpful to other people. Dan Kachongva, leading adviser and spokesman of the traditional Hopis, said that people were turning away from the Life Plan of the Great Spirit. "Each and every human being knows these simple instructions upon which are based all the various Life Plans and religions of the Great Spirit," he said. The laws of the Great Spirit must be followed even though they might conflict with other "laws." All the various instructions of the Great Spirit came from:

> . . . the seed of one basic instruction: "You must not kill; you must love your neighbor as yourself." From this one commandment to respect and reverence life, came all the other commandments: to tell the truth, to share what we have; to live together so we can help each other out; to take care of our children and old people, the sick and strangers, friends and enemies; to not get drunk, or commit adultery, or lie or cheat, or steal, or get rich, because all these negative acts cause fights and struggles which divide the community into groups too small to support and carry on the life stream.[43]

SELECTIVE NONVIOLENCE

The chief characteristic of "selective nonviolence" is the refusal to participate in *particular* violent conflicts, usually international wars. In certain other situations the same persons might be willing to use violence to accomplish the desired ends. Two most important examples are the international Socialists, especially during World War I, and Jehovah's Witnesses. Also included are nonpacifist anarchists, objectors primarily concerned with authoritarianism, and other nonpacifists who believe that the manufacture and use of nuclear weapons can never be justified. Many objectors to the American war effort in Vietnam also came within this class.

The international Socialists object to war because, they declare, it is a product of capitalism, and there is no reason why the workers of one country should fight the workers of another when the real enemy of the workers of all countries is capitalism. Most, but not all,[44] of the Socialist objectors to World War I would have participated in a violent revolution of the working people to abolish capitalism, imperialism, and greed, and to bring in the cooperative commonwealth. Their objections were intimately tied up with their conception of the class struggle. This conception is reflected in the 1917 St. Louis Manifesto, overwhelmingly approved by the Socialist Party, U.S.A.:

> The Socialist Party of the United States in the present grave crisis reaffirms its allegiance to the principle of internationalism and working-class solidarity the world over, and proclaims its unalterable opposition to the war just declared by the government of the United States. . . . The mad orgy of death which is now convulsing unfortunate Europe was caused by the conflict of capitalist interests in European countries. In each of these countries the workers were oppressed and exploited. . . . The ghastly war in Europe . . . was the logical outcome of the competitive capitalist system. . . . Our entrance into the European war was instigated by the predatory capitalists of the United States who boast of the enormous profits of seven billion dollars from the manufacture and sale of munitions and war supplies and from the exportation of American foodstuffs and other necessities. . . . We brand the declaration of war by our government as a crime against the people of the United States and against the nations of the world.[45]

The same majority report also stated: ". . . the only struggle which would justify the workers in taking up arms is the great struggle of the working class of the world to free itself from economic exploitation and political oppression. . . ."[46]

At the party's state convention in Canton, Ohio, Eugene V. Debs declared:

> The master class has always declared the wars; the subject class has always fought the battles. The master class has had all to gain and nothing to lose, while the subject class has had nothing to gain and all to lose—especially their lives.[47]

On trial in 1918 for violation of the U.S. Sedition Act on ten counts allegedly committed during that speech, Debs told the jury:

It [the St. Louis Manifesto] said, in effect, to the people,
especially the workers, of all countries, "Quit going to war. Stop
murdering one another for the profit and glory of the ruling
classes. Cultivate the arts of peace. Humanize humanity. Civilize
civilization."[48]

In Britain, the Independent Labour Party; in the United States,
the Socialist Party, U.S.A., and the Socialist Labor Party; in
Russia, the *Bolsheviki;* and in Germany, the group of Socialists led
by Karl Liebnecht and Rosa Luxemburg all opposed World War I.
Most of the other Socialist groups abandoned the Socialist doctrine
on war at that time. Only a few Socialists opposed World War II on
similar grounds. The Socialist Party, U.S.A. (only a remnant of the
earlier party), for example, tried to maintain a position of "neutrality" on the war, neither supporting nor opposing it, while some of
its members gave full support, some gave critical support, and some
opposed it. In most countries, Socialist groups fully supported the
war.

Jehovah's Witnesses[49] also object to *particular* violent conflicts. They regard all governments that took part in World War II
as being equally guilty. The existing governments of all nations are
regarded as being ruled by Satan; the Witnesses declare that the
existing governments have failed because they merely rendered lip
service to morality. To support any such government is to support
Satan and to deny God. The present wars are regarded as merely a
sign of the end of an age and a preliminary worldly step before the
righteous King Jesus soon returns to establish his heavenly rule on
earth. The people of good will will survive the Battle of Armaged-
don, which will be fought by angels against Satan's organization,
and will "carry out the divine mandate to 'fill the earth' with a
righteous race."[50] The Witnesses are not prohibited from using
violence in their personal relationships or in resisting persecution,
as they once were. If God were concerned with the present wars, as
he was with some earlier ones, they would be willing to fight.
Witnesses were sent to conscientious objector camps, interned,
imprisoned, or sent to concentration camps by both sides during
World War II.[51]

Stroup, in his study of the movement, wrote:

The law of God forbids the Witnesses to engage in war. The view
has commonly been taken that they are pacifists. Such they are

not, for they feel that they must often employ physical force to resist persecution, and they also believe that Jehovah has engaged in and encouraged wars between peoples. The Witnesses will not engage in the present war [World War II] because they think that Jehovah is not concerned with it; otherwise they would be quite willing to fight. Most of them believe that Satan is "running the whole show" and therefore they will have nothing to do with it. This is similar to their attitude towards the first World War. The Witnesss were interned by both sides, because the Society boldly stated that the war was being fought by equally selfish interests and without the sanction of God. Their own fight, they declared, was not fought with "carnal weapons": it was a battle of cosmic proportons with the adversary of every man, Satan.[52]

The position of certain nonpacifist but antiwar anarchists would come under this classificaton also. Their position is similar to that of the international Socialists, in that under certain circumstances they would be willing to use violence to abolish the existing order of society to bring in the classless, stateless, and warless society of their dreams. For example, both the principals charged with murder in the famous Sacco-Vanzetti case had gone to Mexico during World War I to avoid military conscription.[53] In the last interview with W. G. Thompson before their execution, Vanzetti said that he "feared that nothing but violent resistance could ever overcome the selfishness which was the basis of the present organization of society and make the few willing to perpetuate a system which enabled them to exploit the many."[54]

In his speech to the court on 9 April 1927, anarchist Vanzetti said:

> . . . [T]he jury were hating us because we were against the war, and the jury don't know that it makes any difference between a man that is against the war because he believes that a war is unjust, because he hates no country, because he is a cosmopolitan, and a man that is against the war because he is in favor of the other country . . . and therefore, a spy, an enemy. . . . We are not men of that kind. . . . We were against the war because we did not believe in the purpose for which they say that war was fought. We believed that the war is wrong. . . . We believe more now than ever that the war was wrong, and we are against war more now than ever, and I am glad to be on the doomed scaffold if I can say to mankind, "Look out. . . . All that they say to you, all that they have promised to you—it was a lie, it was an illusion,

it was a cheat, it was a fraud, it was a crime. . . ." Where is the moral good that the war has given to the world? Where is the spiritual progress that we have achieved from the war? Where are the security of life, the security of the things that we possess for our necessity? Where are the respect for human life? Where are the respect and the admiration for the good characteristics and the good of human nature? Never before the war as now have there been so many crimes, so much corruption, so much degeneration as there is now.[55]

Also included in the category of "selective nonviolence" are a number of individuals whose objection to participation in modern wars is not essentially an objection to violence per se, but rather to authoritarianism in government, institutions, and even individuals. They have thus refused to cooperate with military conscription and have received the consequences of such noncooperation. Norman Thomas[56] mentioned a type of "conscientious objection by radicals [which] was based rather on an objection to conscription . . . than to killing," and Case says: "A type of objector . . . directs his protest against *conscription* in and of itself, without regard for the right or wrong of war in general or of the particular war in question."[57] Their objection is to ordering individuals around, as contrasted to allowing their free action and development. They may, however, use violence in their personal lives. Some of these oppose participation in modern war because they view it as an extreme development of both regimentation and violence.

Those individulas who now believe that preparations for nuclear war cannot under any conditions be justified, though they believe that war with earlier weapons has, at least at times, been justified, are also included in this category of "selective nonviolence."

SATYAGRAHA

Satyagraha is the type of principled nonviolence developed by Mohandas K. Gandhi. This discussion is focused exclusively on Gandhi's normative approach to nonviolence. The term *satyagraha* is also used to indicate his technique of action suitable for use by people *not* sharing his beliefs. On that focus, see the chapters in this book which discuss *satyagraha* as a technique of struggle.

Satyagraha means (approximately) "adherence to Truth" or "reliance on Truth"—Truth having the connotation of "essence of being," or "reality." The believer in *satyagraha,* a *satyagrahi,*[58] aims at attaining Truth through love and right actions. *Satyagraha* is a matter of principle.[59] It was developed by Gandhi through his searchings and experiments in his personal life and his efforts at combating social evils and building a better social order. The *satyagrahi* seeks to "turn the searchlight inward" and to improve his own life so that he does no harm to others. He seeks to combat evil in the world through his own way of living, constructive work, and resistance and action against what are regarded as evils. He seeks to convert the opponent through sympathy, patience, truthfulness, and self-suffering. He believes that sufficient truthfulness, fearlessness, and deep conviction will enable him to attack that which he regards as evil, regardless of the odds against him. He will not compromise on basic moral issues,though he may on secondary matters. Gandhi left behind no systematized philosophical system. He dealt with practical problems as they arose and sought solutions for them within the context of his basic ethical principles: *satya* (Truth), *ahimsa* (noninjury of living beings in thought, word, and deed), and equality. The *satyagrahi* believes means and ends must be equally pure. Gandhi regarded *satyagraha* as basically a matter of quality rather than quantity. When facing social conflict, he believed the *satyagrahi's* own inner condition was more important than the external situation.

A basic part of *satyagraha* in Gandhi's view was a constructive program to build a new social and economic order through voluntary constructive work. This he regarded as more important than resistance. The Indian constructive program included a variety of specific measures aimed at social improvement, education, decentralized economic production and consumption, and improvement in the lot of the oppressed sections of the population. He believed that such a program would gradually build up the structure of a new nonviolent society, while resistance and direct action would be used to remove parts of the old structure which were obstacles to the new one.

Gandhi believed that when social evils require direct and active challenging, the various methods of nonviolent action provide a substitute for rioting, violent revolution, or war. Gandhi has made a unique contribution in combining nonviolence as a principle with methods and strategy of resistance, forging it into a technique of meeting social conflicts, which was regarded as more influential both than individual example and persuasion without such supporting action, and than the previous forms of nonviolent resistance. Investigation, negotiation, publicity, self-purification, temporary work stoppages, picketing, boycotts, nonpayment of taxes, mass migration from the state, various forms of noncooperation, civil disobedience, and the fast (under strict limitations) are among possible methods of action. The *satyagrahi* is always ready to negotiate a settlement which does not compromise basic principles.

Gandhi became convinced that *satyagraha* based upon an inner conviction was more effective than nonviolence practiced as a temporary policy. He said of the "nonviolence of the brave": "It is such nonviolence that moves mountains, transforms life and flinches from nothing in its unshakable faith."[60] *Satyagraha,* when developed by Gandhi, became unique among the existing types of principled nonviolence by including a program for social reconstruction and an active individual and group technique of attacking what were regarded as social evils.[61]

NONVIOLENT REVOLUTION

"Nonviolent revolution" is the most recent type of principled nonviolence. It is still very much a direction of developing thought and action rather than a fixed ideology and program. "Nonviolent revolutionaries" believe that the major social problems of today's world have their origins at the roots of individual and social life and can therefore be solved only by a basic, or revolutionary, change in individuals and society.

There is general recognition among believers in this approach of four aspects of a nonviolent revolutionary program: (1) the improvement by individuals of their own lives; (2) gaining the acceptance of such principles as nonviolence, equality, cooperation, justice, and freedom as the determining values for the society as a whole; (3) building a more equalitarian, decentralized, and libertarian social order; and (4) combating what are regarded as social evils by nonviolent action.[62] A major objective of nonviolent revolution is to substitute nonviolent, cooperative, equalitarian relationships for such aspects of violence as exploitation, oppression, and war. The nonviolent revolution is to be effected largely (in the view of some) or entirely (in the view of others) without use of the State machinery. Some advocates of this approach place relatively more emphasis on achieving changes in policies, institutions, ownership, power relationships, etc., while others put relatively more emphasis on achieving changes in beliefs and attitudes as a preliminary to such social changes.

The nonviolent revolutionary approach has been developing since about 1945[63] in various parts of the world, including Hong Kong,[64] Germany,[65] the United States, India and England.[66] Nonviolent revolution has mixed origins. These origins may, for the purposes of analysis, be divided roughly into those in which ideological factors are predominant and those in which they are subordinate to "practical" efforts to find solutions to certain pressing social problems. The "ideological" and "practical" factors are, however, never fully separated. On the one hand, the associated ideologies propose solutions for social problems, and on the other, the search for solutions for such problems at some stage usually involves consideration of ideological approaches per se or methods of action which are closely related to them. On the ideological level nonviolent revolution has been developing through the interplay and synthesis of several formerly distinct approaches. These include (1) certain types of pacifism, largely "moral resistance" and the Tolstoyan and Quaker approaches ("active reconciliation"); (2) *satyagraha;* and (3) ideologies of social revolution (that is, basic social change), including the socialist, anarchist, and decentralist approaches.[67] In some ways, *satyagraha* is the most important of these,[68] largely because it combines a "pacifist" position with a technique of resistance and revolution, thus serving as a bridge or catalyst between pacifism and social revolution.

On the "practical" level the nonviolent revolutionary approach has had origins in efforts to effect social, political, or economic changes where parliamentary means are either nonexistent or not responsive to popular control, and where violent means are rejected either because the means of effective violent struggle are predominantly at the disposal of supporters of the status quo, or for other reasons. Nonviolent resistance and intervention have often appeared relevant in such situations. Where nonviolent techniques and methods have been seriously used in such situations, there have often been ideological and programmatic consequences resulting from the combination of nonviolence and revolution. An associated factor in the development of nonviolent revolution is that common concern with pressing social problems (land in India, nuclear weapons in Britain, freedom in South Africa, for example) has brought pacifists, *satyagrahis* and social revolutionaries[69] together to find and apply solutions for such problems. This interaction has contributed to the synthesizing of these approaches.

Because of the recency of this type of nonviolence, it is perhaps desirable to cite at greater length than usual examples of the thought which underlies it. These citations, largely from American and Indian sources, are only illustrative.

Although the nonviolent revolutionary movement has never developed in the United States into anything approaching political significance, some of the clearest ideological statements of this approach came from this country. For example, in 1946 there existed a Committee for Nonviolent Revoluton which issued this policy statement:

> We favor decentralized, democratic socialism guaranteeing worker-consumer control of industries, utilities and other economic enterprises. We believe that the workers themselves should take steps to seize control of factories, mines and shops. . . . We believe in realistic action against war, against imperialism and against military or economic oppression by conquering nations, including the United States. We advocate such techniques of group resistance as demonstrations, strikes, organized civil disobedience, and underground organization where necessary. As individuals we refuse to join the armed forces, work in war industries, or buy government bonds, and we believe in campaigns urging others to do similarly. We see nonviolence as a principle as well as a technique. In all action we renounce the methods of punishing, hating or killing any fellow human beings. We believe that nonviolence includes such methods as sit-down strikes and seizure of plants. We believe that revolutionary changes can only occur through direct action by the rank and file, and not by deals or reformist proposals directed to the present political and labor leadership.[70]

A. J. Muste, in the period following the Committee for Nonviolent Revolution, was the leading exponent of the nonviolent revolutionary approach:

... [M]ankind faces a major crisis. Only a drastic change, such as is suggested by the terms rebirth, conversion, revolution, can bring deliverance. Tinkering with this or that piece of political, economic or cultural machinery will not suffice. ... War and the war system, as well as social violence, are inherent in our present politico-economic order and the prevailing materialistic culture. ...[71]

... [I]n our age, whatever may have been the case in other periods ... violence must be rejected as a means for radical social change. ... Whether ... we look at the problem of eliminating war or at the problem of radical social change (abolition of competitive nationalism, colonialism, dictatorship, feudalism, development of a non-exploitative economy, etc.) we must resort to nonviolence or we are lost. We need to build a nonviolent revolutionary movement ... rooted firmly in local and national situations ... not ... abstract cosmopolitanism ... [yet] genuinely internationalist in basis, composition and eventual structure.[72]

In India the nonviolent revolutionary approach has taken two forms, often regarded by their respective advocates as distinct. One is the "Land-Gift" (*Bhoodan*) movement and related movements led by Vinoba Bhave. The other is the emphasis on civil disobedience, most clearly espoused by Dr. Rammanohar Lohia and other Socialists.

Concerning nonviolent revolution, Dr. Lohia wrote:

Hitherto, in efforts to bring about major social changes, the world has known the sole alternatives of parliamentary and violent insurrectionary means. A reliance on only parliamentary means has often left people without any means of direct control over social decisions when Parliament was not responsive to the public will, and parliamentary means have sometimes proved incapable of bringing about genuinely fundamental changes in society when required. The reliance upon the means of violent insurrection has, however, also been proved inadequate. Even apart from considerations of the morality of violence and its chances of success, the kind of society produced by a violent insurrection does not recommend such means. Now, however, a new dimension has been added by the addition of individual and massive civil resistance as another way of bringing about major social changes. ... All those desirous of maintaining methods of nonviolence must learn to be equally loyal to revolution. ... Where such subordination of revolution to nonviolence takes place, conservative maintenance of the existing order is an inevitable result, just as chaos in the beginning and tyranny afterwards are inevitable results if nonviolence is subordinated to revolution. . . . Mankind will ever hurtle from the hands of one irresponsibility into another if it continues to seek and organize its revolutions through violence.[73]

Commenting on *Bhoodan* as a social revolution, the Indian economist Gyan Chand has written:

> From the very beginning the *Bhoodan* movement has been a movement for establishing a new social order. . . . The collection and distribution of land, it was . . . very clearly emphasized, was . . . only the first step in a succession of changes which were implicit in the concept of social revolution. Among them, a classless society, extinction of property rights and the elimination of acquisitive social relations had necessarily to be given a very high priority in the list of the new social objectives. The *gramdan* [gift of all private land in a village to village ownership] concept brings these social objectives to the fore, stresses their primacy and urgency and points to the need of making them all-embracing and the basis of the whole production organization of the community. This means that if extinction of property rights in land is realized, the very logic of the step would make its application to trade, industry and services unavoidable. . . .
>
> The movement, relying as it does exclusively on change through assent, that is, on a completely voluntary basis and by nonviolent methods, makes democracy its substance and essential feature. . . . The movement does not in any way preclude legislative action, but does not put its faith in it as the primary or the major instrument of social change. The state has no doubt the organized might of the community at its disposal, but if it is to be truly democratic it has to use this power as sparingly as possible and rely mainly on revolution from below—the upsurge and initiative of the people—for carrying out fundamental and social transformation.[74]

The incomplete nature of the ideology and program of nonviolent revolution is among the factors which have handicapped the spread of this type of principled nonviolence, especially in the West, but the general outline of its approach is sufficiently clear to justify its inclusion here, at this early stage of its development, and to indicate that it may increase in prominence in the future.

EMERGING NEW TYPE

In addition to these six types of principled nonviolence, there seems to be emerging a seventh. It appears that there is developing a new type which is characterized by a principled rejection of violence in facing social and political problems and conflicts, without necessarily rejecting violence in interpersonal relations. In this type, the rejection of violence is largely based upon the view that its application in society and politics is impractical, undesirable, and likely to lead to unwanted results, rather than the rejection being primarily moral or religious. The extreme developments in political violence and the parallel rise of nonviolent action as a practical alternative technique are the main influences contributing to this development. It thus appears to be developing from the stimulation of pragmatic rather than ideological considerations. This type, however, has not advanced sufficiently to be as yet included in this typology.

CONCLUSION

In conclusion it may be useful to note common features among certain of these six types. Five of them fall within the definition of "pacifism" presented earlier in this chapter. (That is, their adherents refuse participation in all international and civil wars and violent revolutions.) These are "nonresistance," "active reconciliation," "moral resistance," "*satyagraha*," and, generally, "nonviolent revolution." These five involve a belief in the *intrinsic* worth of nonviolent behavior. Three of the types emphasize nonviolent means as *instrumental* for achieving desired social objectives. These are: "moral resistance," "*satyagraha*," and "nonviolent revolution." There is thus an overlapping between these two groups, with "moral resistance," "*satyagraha*," and "nonviolent revolution" emphasizing both the intrinsic value of nonviolence and nonviolent behavior as a means to some social end.

"Moral resistance," "*satyagraha*," and "nonviolent revoluton" include an acceptance of nonviolent action as a substitute for political violence. On some occasions believers in the approaches classified under "active reconciliation" and "selective nonviolence" might also be under "nonviolent revolution." On rare occasions, believers in "nonresistance" might feel compelled to noncooperate with what they regard as evil, in such a way that their behavior would also come within the scope of "nonviolent action." There are, of course, many other comparisons and contrasts that might be made among the six types of principled nonviolence. Some of these will be suggested by the following chart, which indicates briefly some of the main characteristics of the types of principled nonviolence that we have discussed.

The object of this chapter has been simply to clarify, classify, and define—and to illustrate these definitions, particularly where it may have been necessary to bring a sense of reality to descriptions of often relatively little-known approaches. This typology is neither perfect nor final, but it may be helpful in clarifying the existing confusion about these phenomena and may facilitate future study, research, analysis, and evaluation of these various belief systems.

SOME MAIN CHARACTERISTICS OF THE TYPES OF PRINCIPLED NONVIOLENCE*

	Non-resist-ance	Active Recon-cilia-tion	Moral Resist-ance	Selec-tive NV	*Satya-graha*	NV Revolu-tion
1. Attitudes to self and society:						
a) "Other-worldly"	Yes	No	No	Maybe	No	No
b) "This-worldly"	No	Yes	Yes	Maybe	Yes	Yes
c) Concern with own "purity"	Yes	Yes	Yes	Maybe	Yes	Maybe
d) Support status quo in society	No	No	No	No	No	No
e) Desire to effect a particular social change only	No	No	No	No	No	No
f) Desire to effect social reforms, not basic changes	No	Maybe	Yes	No	No	No

* The characteristics attributed to each type are based largely upon the avowals of the respective groups; the section on "Attitudes toward opponents" thus refers to *avowed* attitudes toward opponents, for example.

	Non-resistance	Active Reconciliation	Moral Resistance	Selective NV	*Satyagraha*	NV Revolution
g) Desire to effect social revolution, that is, basic changes	No	Maybe	No	Maybe	Yes	Yes
2. Attitudes to "evil":						
a) Withdrawal from	Yes	Yes	Yes	Maybe	Yes	Maybe
b) Imperative to act against	No	Yes	Yes	Yes	Yes	Yes
3. Attitudes to violence (V) and nonviolence (NV):						
a) NV based on principle	Yes	Yes	Yes	No	Yes	Usually
b) NV based on expediency	No	No	No	No	No	No
c) NV based on mixed a and b	No	No	No	No	No	Maybe
d) NV regarded as intrinsically good	Yes	Yes	Yes	Maybe	Yes	Yes
e) NV regarded as a means	No	Yes	Yes	No	Yes	Yes
f) NV as a means regarded as a full substitute for V	...	Yes	Yes	...	Yes	Yes
g) NV regarded as a means which may be used in association with V	...	No	No	...	No	No
h) Personal V in general rejected	Yes	Yes	Yes	No	Yes	Usually
i) Group V in general rejected	Yes	Yes	Yes	No	Yes	Yes
j) State V in general rejected	Yes	Maybe	Maybe	No	Yes	Usually
k) War in general rejected	Yes	Yes	Yes	No	Yes	Yes
l) Only certain V rejected as a subsidiary effect of a nonpacifist principle	No	No	No	Yes	No	No
m) V regarded as more than physical V, for example, hostile attitudes	Yes	Yes	Maybe	No	Yes	Yes

	Non-resistance	Active Reconciliation	Moral Resistance	Selective NV	*Satyagraha*	NV Revolution
4. Attitude toward opponents:						
a) Hatred	No	No	No	Maybe	No	No
b) Resentment	No	No	No	Maybe	No	Maybe
c) Indifference	No	No	No	Maybe	No	Maybe
d) Respect	Maybe	Yes	Yes	Maybe	Yes	Yes
e) Good will	Yes	Yes	Yes	Maybe	Yes	Yes
f) Love	Yes	Yes	Yes	No	Yes	Maybe
5. Implementation of the approach:						
a) Acts of "self-purification"	Yes	Yes	Maybe	Maybe	Yes	Maybe
b) Personal way of living	Yes	Yes	Yes	Maybe	Yes	Maybe
c) Persistent friendliness	Yes	Yes	Yes	Maybe	Yes	Maybe
d) Acts of mercy	Yes	Yes	Yes	No	Yes	Yes
e) Exhortations	Yes	Yes	Yes	Yes	Maybe	Maybe
f) "Education"	No	Maybe	Yes	Maybe	Yes	Yes
g) Verbal persuasion	Yes	Yes	Yes	Yes	Yes	Yes
h) Use of State to effect social change	No	Maybe	Maybe	Maybe	No	Maybe
i) Use of nonstate means to effect social change	No	Yes	Yes	Maybe	Yes	Yes
j) "Constructive program"	No	No	No	No	Yes	Maybe
k) Passive forms of NV Action (NVA)	Rarely	Yes	Yes	Maybe	Yes	Yes
l) Active forms of NVA	No	Maybe	Maybe	Maybe	Yes	Yes
m) Strategy in the NVA	No	No	Rarely	No	Yes	Yes
6. Mechanisms of change intended in NVA:						
a) Conversion	. . .	Yes	Yes	Maybe	Yes	Yes
b) Accommodation	. . .	Maybe	Maybe	No	Yes	Maybe
c) Attempting conversion or accommodation, but willing to accept nonviolent coercion	. . .	No	Maybe	Maybe	Maybe	Maybe
d) Nonviolent coercion	. . .	No	No	Maybe	No	Maybe

NOTES TO CHAPTER TEN

1. H. Reichenbach, **The Rise of Scientific Philosophy** (Berkeley: University of California Press, 1951), p. 83.
2. G.F. Hershberger, "Biblical Non-resistance and Modern Pacifism," **Mennonite Quarterly Review,** 17 (July 1943), p. 116; cited by Theodore Paullin, "Introduction to Non-Violence" (pamphlet; Philadelphia: Pacifist Research Bureau, 1944), p. 5.
3. "Pacifists" here refers to persons and groups refusing participation in war on ethical, moral, or religious grounds.
4. R. Reynolds, "What Are Pacifists Doing?" **Peace News** (weekly) (London, 20 July 1956), p. 5.
5. For example, the U.S. conscription law in the 1950s provided for alternatives to military duty for those objecting to it because of religious belief and training but denied such alternatives to objectors whose pacifism arises from a personal philosophy, humanitarianism, social, economic, or political views.
6. Military conscription laws throughout the world vary concerning provisions for objectors. Many make no provisions for exemption from military duty or alternative civilian duty. Some include either or both provisions for objectors establishing their sincerity. Still others provide either or both provisions only for certain objectors, such as "religious" ones.
7. As will be indicated below, the term "nonviolence" is used in a much broader sense in this paper than it was by Gandhi.
8. *Satyagraha* will be defined later.
9. M.K. Gandhi, **An Autobiography or the Story of My Experiments with Truth** (Ahmedabad: Navajivan Publishing House, 1956), p. 318.
10. B. Kumarappa, "Editor's Note," in M.K. Gandhi, **For Pacifists** (Ahmedabad: Navajivan Publishing House, 1949), pp. v–vi.
11. C.M. Case, **Non-violent Coercion** (New York: Century, 1923), p. 287.
12. Ibid., p. 4.
13. M. Sibley, "The Political Theories of Modern Pacifism: An Analysis and Criticism" (pamphlet; Philadelphia: Pacifist Research Bureau, 1944).
14. See L. Kuper, **Passive Resistance in South Africa** (New Haven: Yale Univ. Press, 1957 and London: Jonathan Cape 1956), pp. 75–94.
15. Paullin, "Introduction to Non-Violence."
16. Ibid., p. 8.
17. Ibid., p. 9.
18. For example, nonviolent resistance with mixed motives of principle and expediency and groups rejecting international wars but not necessarily personal violence.
19. For example, including William Lloyd Garrison's approach under "*satyagraha* and nonviolent direct action."
20. "Nonviolence" for the purposes of this typology has thus a much broader meaning than that given to "nonviolence" by Gandhi and certain other votaries of nonviolence. Gandhi often referred to nonviolence as being essentially the same as love. It was *ahimsa,* which involved noninjury in thought, word, and deed to all living things. It rejected ill will and hatred as well as physical violence.

21. There is no type labeled "conscientious objection" or "war resistance," because such objection or resistance is a specific application of several of the types of nonviolence included here.

22. In this revision I have tried to offer terminology and definitions which, if adopted, might reduce future confusion in the literature. This has involved making refinements in the existing terminology while seeking to use such terms in ways harmonious with present general usage—hence the broader intermediary class of "pacifism;" hence also the use of the terms "nonresistance," "*satyagraha*," and "nonviolent revolution" in ways having clear precedents (although the first has also been widely used with varying connotations). It has seemed necessary to coin new terms, such as "principled nonviolence" and "selective nonviolence" and to give more specific meanings to "moral resistance." The writer does not regard this terminology as perfect but, in the absence of an alternative, suggests its adoption. The final solution to the terminological problem may lie in creating entirely new terms, such as Gandhi did with *satyagraha;* the difficulties in gaining their general acceptance, however, might be greater than the acceptance of terms and definitions offered in this chapter.

23. This order is inevitably somewhat arbitrary; the most active expression of one type may exceed in activity the most passive expression of the type(s) listed after it.

24. G.H. Heering, **The Fall of Christianity** (New York: Fellowship Publications, 1943), p. 33.

25. Guy F. Hershberger, "Quaker Pacifism and the Provincial Government of Pennsylvania 1682–1756" (unpublished Ph.D. thesis, State University of Iowa, 1935).

26. C.H. Smith, **The Mennonites in America,** pp. 353–354, quoted by Case, **Non-violent Coercion,** pp. 78–79.

27. Quoted in Ibid., pp. 136–137.

28. Paullin, "Introduction to Non-Violence," p. 43.

29. See Leo Tolstoy, **The Kingdom of God is Within You** (Boston: L.C. Page, 1951) and **What Then Must We Do?** (London: Oxford University Press).

30. Leo Tolstoy, "The Law of Force and the Law of Love," **The Fortnightly Review** (London: Chapman & Hall, Ltd., 1909), p. 474.

31. Leo Tolstoy, **The Kingdom of God is Within You** (London: William Heinemann, 1894), p. 160.

32. Ibid., pp. 306–307.

33. See Hershberger, "Quaker Pacifism and the Provincial Government of Pennsylvania 1682–1756."

34. **The Book of Discipline,** Part 1. "Christian Life, Faith and Thought" (London Yearly Meeting, 1920); quoted by Sidney Lucas, "The Quaker Message" (pamphlet; Wallingford: Pendle Hill, 1948), pp. 38–39.

35. Philadelphia Yearly Meeting, Arch Street, "Statements on Peace," adopted by the Yearly Meeting, 1942. Quoted by Lucas, "The Quaker Message," p.43.

36. "Friends and War: A New Statement of the Quaker Position, adopted by the World Conference of All Friends, 1920," quoted by Case, **Non-violent Coercion,** pp. 138–139.

37. These societies were often called "nonresistance" societies. This is one of the cases where a single term in this field has been used with a variety of connotations. The term "nonresistance" was also used by Tolstoy in a sense which differs from the "nonresitance" type as defined in this chapter. Adin Ballou, although using the term "nonresistance," makes it clear he advocates a moral resistance to evil.

38. **William Lloyd Garrison; the Story of his Life Told by his Children,** (New York: The Century Co., 1883), vol. II, p. 230; quoted in Fanny Garrison Villard, **William Lloyd Garrison on Non-Resistance** (New York: The Nation Press, 1924), pp. 25–28.

39. Adin Ballou, **Christian Non-Resistance, in All its Important Bearings, Illustrated and Defended** (Philadelphia: J. Miller M'Kim, 1846), p. 10.

40. **Selections from the Writings and Speeches of William Lloyd Garrison** (Boston: R.F. Wallcut, 1852), p. 88; quoted in Villard, **William Lloyd Garrison on Non-Resistance,** p. 30.

41. **William Lloyd Garrison; the Story of his Life Told by his Children,** vol. III, p. 473; quoted in Ibid., pp. 34–37.

42. "You Asked About the F.O.R." (leaflet; Nyack: Fellowship of Reconciliation, n.d.), p. 3.

43. Craig, "Preface to a Review of the Hotevilla Meeting of Religious Peoples" (MS), quoted in Sharp, "The Hopi Message of Peace for All Mankind," **Peace News** (14 Dec. 1956), pp. 6–7; see also George Yamada, ed., **The Great Resistance: A Hopi Anthology** (New York: The Editor), p. 175.

44. Some of the Socialists were objectors to all forms of social violence. Whether U.S. Socialist leader Eugene V. Debs would have used violent means for the socialist revolution is problematical. His statements on this are sometimes contradictory.

45. Quoted in Ray Ginger, **The Bending Cross: A Biography of Eugene V. Debs** (New Brunswick: Rutgers University Press, 1949), pp. 341–342.

46. Quoted in Case, **Non-violent Coercion,** p. 260.

47. R. Ginger, **The Bending Cross: A Biography of Eugene V. Debs,** p. 358.

48. Ibid., pp. 370–371.

49. Founded in 1872 by Charles Taze Russell in Allegheny, Pennsylvania. They have been known under various names, including in some countries, The International Bible Students Association. See Herbert Hewitt Stroup, **The Jehovah's Witnesses** (New York: The Columbia University Press, 1945), pp. 2–3.

50. Quoted from the official statement of belief that appears regularly in **The Watch Tower,** official publication of the Witnesses; quoted by Stroup, **The Jehovah's Witnesses,** p. 139. For a brief, but fuller, account of this conception, see the excerpt from the decision in an Appellate Court of South Africa, quoted in Stroup, **The Jehovah's Witnesses,** pp. 140–141.

51. Ibid, pp. 147–166.

52. Ibid, pp. 165–166.

53. Marion Denman Frankfurter and Gardner Jackson, eds., **The Letters of Sacco and Vanzetti** (New York: The Vanguard Press, 1930), pp. 3 and 78.

54. Ibid., p. 404.

55. Ibid., pp. 370–371.

56. In a letter to Clarence Marsh Case, Quoted in Case, **Non-violent Coercion,** pp. 261–262.

57. Case, **Non-violent Coercion,** p.261.

58. In India the term *satyagrahi* has been used both to describe the person believing in *satyagraha* as a matter of principle, and those persons participating in the resistance campaigns who were acting under a temporary discipline. Likewise, the term *satyagraha* has been used both to describe Gandhi's full belief system, and to describe resistance movements which he led or which are more or less patterned after the methods he used and advocated.

   Dr. Joan V. Bondurant, in her book **Conquest of Violence: The Gandhian Philosophy of Conflict** (Princeton: Princeton University Press, 1958), has suggested instead that the term *satyagraha* be used to describe those types of nonviolent action which have certain qualities, especially consideration for the opponent as an individual.

59. *Satyagrahis* may also lead others following a temporary nonviolent discipline in nonviolent action.

60. Gopi Nath Dhawan, **The Political Philosophy of Mahatma Gandhi,** (Bombay Popular Book Depot, 1946), pp.67–68.

61. For a fuller discussion of Gandhi's philosophy and program see, for example, R.R. Diwakar, **Satyagraha: Its Technique and History** (Bombay: Hind Kitabs, 1946); Dhawan, **The Political Philosophy of Mahatma Gandhi;** Nirmal Kumar Bose, **Studies in Gandhism** (Second ed.; Calcutta: Indian Associated Publishing Co., Inc., 1947); Gandhi, "The Constructive Programme" (Ahmedabad: Navajivan, 1948); **Non-violence in Peace and War,** vols. I and II, and **Satyagraha** (Ahmedabad: Navijivan, 1951); Krishnalal J. Shridharani, **War Without Violence** (New York: Harcourt, Brace and Co., 1939); Louis Fischer, **The Life of Mahatma Gandhi** (New York: Harper & Bros., 1950); Gandhi, **All Men Are Brothers: Life and Thoughts of Mahatma Gandhi as Told in His Own Words** (Paris: United Nations Educational, Scientific, and Cultural Organization, 1958).

62. An exception to this fourth aspect is Vinoba Bhave, who favors "gentler" forms of nonviolence than used by Gandhi in the Indian independence struggle.

63. C.M. Case, **Non-violent Coercion,** pp. 277–280, describes the beginnings of the synthesizing of the religious pacifist and the social radical approaches as early as World War I in the United States, although it is clear that this process has become socially significant only since 1945.

64. See various issues of **Chu Lieu** ("Main Current"), issued from Kowloon by the Chulieu Society, Professor Lo Meng Tze, chairman.

65. See Nikolaus Koch, **Die Moderne Revolution: Gedanken der Gewaltfreien Selbsthilfe des Deutschen Volkes** (Tübingen and Frankfurt: The Author, 1951).

66. Examples of the developing thought in the nonviolent revolutionary approach in the United States, India, and England are offered below.

67. An important step in this synthesis was made in the United States during World War II as religious pacifists and nonreligious social radicals—finding themselves thrown together in conscientious objector camps and prisons—began to expand their thinking and convictions beyond the previous limits recognized by these groups. A writer in the journal **Manas** comments on this development:

"One curious cultural synthesis which came out of the second world war was the alliance between young socialists and young religious pacifists. More than ten years ago, a writer in a small pacifist periodical, **Pacifica Views**, called attention to the new kind of 'radical' that was emerging from the war resistance movement: 'In this synthesis of extremes, we witness the birth of a New Minority. Its members are destined to remain an enigma to the public for some years to come, and they will probably be a source of confusion both to Peace Church pacifists and old line radicals. It is certain that the American Legion will not understand them at all. Who is he, this New Minority Man? . . . He is working for objectives which are both moral and practical. . . . His ends will be easily identifiable as revolutionary but his reasons for working toward them will unite moral content with critical penetration' " ("The New Man," **Manas** [Los Angeles], 9 [March 28, 1956], 7).

68. Some would view nonviolent revolution as an application of *satyagraha* to a new historical situation. Gandhi's later thinking included an emphasis on radical social, economic, and political changes. For example, in June 1942, Gandhi said that, in a free India, "The peasants would take the land. We would not have to tell them to take it" (Louis Fischer, **A Week With Gandhi** [New York: Duell, Sloan & Pearce, 1942], p. 54). Gandhi, May 1947: "There can be no *Ramarajya* [Kingdom of God] in the present state of iniquitous inequalities in which a few roll in riches and the masses do not get even enough to eat." (Gandhi, **Nonviolence in Peace and War**, vol. II, p. 255). In 1945 he said, ". . . if we have democratic *Swaraj* [Self-rule] . . . the *Kisans* [peasants] must hold power in all its phases, including political power" [Bose, **Studies in Gandhism**], p. 79).

69. Or other combinations of these, as pacifists and social revolutionaries, or *satyagrahis* and social revolutionaries. Pacifists in such cases are likely to be familiar with the methods of nonviolent action.

70. Quoted by Donald Calhoun, "The Non-violent Revolutionists," **Politics** (New York), 3 (April 1946), pp. 118–119.

71. A.J. Muste, "Build the Non-violent Revolutionary Movement—Now" (New York: The Author, 1947 [?]) (mimeographed).

72. A.J. Muste, "Problems of Non-violent Revolution," **Peacemaker** (1 March 1952), pp. 5–6.

73. Rammanohar Lohia, "Non-violence and Revolution," **Peace News** (26 April 1957), p. 2.

74. Gyan Chand, "Bhoodan as a Social Revolution," **Gandhi Marg** (Jan. 1958), pp. 44–46.

11

Ethics and Responsibility in Politics

A Critique of the Present Adequacy of Max Weber's Classification of Ethical Systems

This chapter has two objectives: (1) to demonstrate that Max Weber's classification of ethical systems into the "ethic of ultimate ends" and the "ethic of responsibility" is now inadequate and needs to be replaced, and (2) to suggest tentative lines along which a new classification might be developed.

We shall not attempt here to examine whether or not Weber's classification was ever entirely valid. That question raises fundamental problems concerning the very nature of politics and deserves serious examination. It may be, however, that it is less immediately pressing than the question of the present validity of Weber's view. This chapter will argue that *even if* Weber's classification were adequate in his own time, it is no longer so. The main reasons for this are the developments relevant to Weber's concern which have taken place since he gave his lecture "Politics as a Vocation"[1] containing this classification, in Munich in 1918. This limited analysis may raise questions relevant to a more fundamental reconsideration of Weber's classification.

Both of these tasks are important, because of the very issues he raises, because his assumptions and conclusions are widely shared in politics today, and because of Weber's considerable influence on both European and American sociological thought.

WEBER'S TWO ETHICS

First, let us summarize Weber's analysis of the "ethic of ultimate ends" and the "ethic of responsibility." According to Weber, the votary of the "ethic of ultimate ends" is concerned with being "true" to certain principles without concern with the achievement of particular immediate goals,"that is, in religious terms,"The Christian does rightly and leaves the results with the Lord'. . . ."[2]

> The believer in an ethic of ultimate ends feels "responsible" only for seeing to it that the flame of pure intentions is not quelched . . . To rekindle the flame ever anew is the purpose of his quite irrational deeds, judged in view of their possible success. They are acts that can and shall have only exemplary value.[3]

Being "true" to the ultimate ends is so important that "the absolute ethic just does not *ask* for 'consequences.' That is the decisive point."[4] Logically, this ethic "has only the possibility of rejecting all action that employs morally dangerous means. . . ."[5]

This doctrine Weber rejected, as we shall see in more detail below, and concluded:

> If. . . one chases after the ultimate good in a war of beliefs, following a pure ethic of absolute ends, then the goals may be damaged and discredited for generations, because responsibility for *consequences* is lacking, and two diabolic forces which enter the play remain unknown to the actor. These are inexorable and produce consequences for his action and even for his inner self, to which he must helplessly submit, unless he perceives them.[6]

The "ethic of responsibility," Weber said, stands in contrast to this. In it, "one has to give an account of the foreseeable results of one's action."[7]

> ... [A] man who believes in an ethic of responsibility takes account of precisely the average deficiencies of people... He does not feel in a position to burden others with the results of his own actions so far as he was able to foresee them; he will say: these results are ascribed to my action.[8]

These two ethics are, said Weber, in conflict. "We must be clear about the fact that all ethically oriented conduct may be guided by one of two fundamentally differing and irreconcilably opposed maxims: conduct can be oriented to an 'ethic of ultimate ends' or to an 'ethic of responsibility.' "[9] He describes "an abysmal contrast between conduct that follows the maxim of an ethic of ultimate ends... and conduct that follows the maxim of an ethic of responsibility. . . ."[10]

> The genius or demon of politics lives in an inner tension with the god of love, as well as with the Christian God as expressed by the church. This tension can at any time lead to an irreconcilable conflict.[11]

WEBER'S SOLUTION

Weber's solution was thus based upon the assumption that there is a distinction between responsibility and loyalty to ultimate ends. One must, Weber said in essence, choose between being responsible and making major compromises in one's ultimate ends on one hand, and, on the other, being consistent ethically but irresponsible politically. If one is true to ultimate ends, one cannot be politically responsible; if one seeks to be politically responsible, one must, in Weber's view, be willing to violate one's ultimate ends.

Weber denied "that an ethic of ultimate ends is identical with irresponsibility, or that an ethic of responsibility is identical with unprincipled opportunism. Naturally nobody says that."[12] Kurt H. Wolff, however, pointed out that there is nothing inherent in Weber's definitions which prevents this from being so.[13] Weber's denial does not remove the fact that the whole basis of his classification is the assumption that loyalty to ultimate ends and responsibility are opposite poles. Weber was able, it seems clear, to place "responsibility" and "ultimate ends" at opposite poles because he regarded them as not intrinsically a part of each other, although some kind of *modus vivendi,* a compromise of some sort, is needed between them in actual life.

Compromise, then, formed the heart of the solution of the problem for Weber, and he called politics the art of compromise. Weber found it "immensely moving when a *mature* man. . . is aware of a responsibility for the consequences of his conduct and really feels such responsibility with heart and soul. He then acts by following an ethic of responsibility and somewhere he reaches the point where he says: 'Here I stand; I can do no other.' "[14] All who are not "spiritually dead" may find themselves in that position, he continued. "In so far as this is true, an ethic of ultimate ends and an ethic of responsibility are not absolute contrasts but rather supplements, which only in unison constitute a genuine man—a man who *can* have the 'calling for politics.' "[15] But Weber offered no criteria as to how this compromise is to be reached, how one decides when to act "responsibly" and when to act because "I can do no other."

Is it unfair to put Weber's view at this point a bit more crudely in the following words? One needs to have ideals, but in politics, to be responsible, one must be ready to use essentially evil means to achieve those ideals to the degree that that is possible. But unless he is spiritually dead, the "genuine man," recognizing the tug between his ideals and political responsibility, reaches the point at which he simply cannot "stomach" any more violation of his convictions and makes his stand on the basis of his ideals. Then—without any intellectual analysis, without consideration as to the consequences, without any criteria to tell him where to draw the line—he says, "Here I stand; I can do no other." Is this apparently the best Weber is able to offer us concerning how to keep a balance between loyalty to ultimate ends and political responsibility? Surely, this is less than satisfactory.

WEBER'S ASSUMPTIONS

In an attempt to understand why Weber did not offer a better solution, let us look a bit deeper into his assumptions. The first and most obvious reason is Weber's view that "evil" means must be used to achieve "good" ends:

> No ethics in the world can dodge the fact that in numerous instances the attainment of "good" ends is bound to the fact that one must be willing to pay the price of using morally dubious means or at least dangerous ones—and facing the possibility or even the probability of evil ramifications. From no ethics in the world can it be concluded when and to what extent the ethically good purpose "justifies" the ethically dangerous means and ramifications.[16]

> The ethic of ultimate ends apparently must go to pieces on the problem of the justification of means by ends.[17]

> The proponent of an ethic of absolute ends cannot stand up under the ethical irrationality of the world. . . . If one makes any concessions at all to the principle that the end justifies the means, it is not possible to bring an ethic of ultimate ends and an ethic of responsibility under one roof or to decree ethically which end should justify which means.[18]

Weber rejected a colleague's thesis that "from good comes only good; but from evil only evil follows."[19] "In that case this whole complex of questions would not exist."[20] Rather than exploring whether there might be "good" means adequate for meeting humane social and political needs, Weber dismissed his colleague's thesis immediately, citing the justifications for violence in various religious systems and complaining that the universe is not consistent, but is "an irrational world of undeserved suffering, unpunished injustice, and hopeless stupidity."[21] For the action of the man "who lets himself in for politics," said Weber, "it is *not* true that good can follow only from good and evil only from evil, but . . . often the opposite is true. Anyone who fails to see this is, indeed, a political infant."[22] Weber accepted, almost axiomatically, the dominant view of his time and culture concerning means and ends. This helps to explain why he distinguished between responsibility and loyalty to ultimate ends, rather than seeing them as intrinsically related.

Let us now examine what underlay Weber's belief in the necessity of "evil" means to achieve "good" ends. The answer is not difficult to find. Weber made it quite explicit. It is an axiom with Weber that power plays a decisive role in politics.[23] (Here we agree.)

Weber, however, went further. (Here we do not agree.) He identified "power" with "violence." Then, as he had identified "violence" with "evil" means, he concluded that evil means were necessary in politics.

"Should it really matter so little for the ethical demands on politics," asked Weber, "that politics operates with very special means, namely, power backed up by *violence?*"[24] ". . . [T]he quite different tasks of politics can only be solved by violence."[25] "The decisive means for politics is violence."[26] "If . . . one chases after the ultimate good in a war of beliefs, following a pure ethic of absolute ends, then the goals may be damaged and discredited for generations, because responsibility for *consequences* is lacking, and two diabolic forces which enter the play remain unknown to the actor."[27] Weber said explicitly that "It is the specific means of legitimate violence as such in the hand of human associations which determines the peculiarity of all ethical problems of politics."[28] "Everything that is striven for through political action operating with violent means and following an ethic of responsibility endangers the 'starvation of the soul.' "[29] "Also the early Christians knew full well the world is governed by demons and that he who lets himself in for politics, that is, for power and force as means, contracts with diabolical powers. . . ."[30] Weber thus measured responsibility by one's willingness to use violence in politics, and violence is regarded as determining "the peculiarity of all ethical problems of politics."

Yet, this is not all. Violence was regarded by Weber as having "evil" results. The use of "morally dubious means" meant also that one must face "the possibility or even the probability of evil ramifications,"[31] and no ethic can, he said, determine when a good end "justifies" "the ethically dangerous means and ramifications."[32] "Whosoever contracts with violent means for whatever ends—and every politician does—is exposed to its specific consequences."[33]

> Whoever wants to engage in politics at all. . . must know that he is responsible for what may become of himself under the impact of these [ethical] paradoxes. I repeat, he lets himself in for the diabolic forces lurking in all violence.[34]

Weber mentioned specifically the dangers to the individual himself, but did not exclude social and political dangers. (Was Weber saying that "evil" means have *intrinsically* evil ramifications, and, if so, was he not saying that the end grows out of the means? And is this not inconsistent with the rest of Weber's discussion of ends and means?)

Weber also made it reasonably clear that the votary of an ethic of ultimate ends does not use violence. He said, for example:

> The great *virtuosi* of acosmic love of humanity and goodness, whether stemming from Nazareth or Assisi or from Indian royal castles, have not operated with the political means of violence. Their kingdom was "not of this world" and yet they worked and still work in this world.[35]

As Weber declared that it is violence which determines the peculiarity of all ethical problems in politics, it is fair to assume that the ultimate ends which are compromised by violence are essentially nonviolent ones characterized by nonviolent relationships.

Weber's view may be summarized in this way. One cannot claim responsibility in politics without willingness to influence political events. Politics operates not only with "power" but specifically with violence. Therefore, he who would influence political events must be willing to use violence. This involves willingness to use "evil" means to achieve "good" ends and, as this is the only way one can practically contribute to their achievement, this is intrinsic in the "ethic of responsibility." This is true, said Weber, despite the dangers involved in the use of such methods and the fact that this violence determines the "peculiarity of all ethical problems of politics."

The person who pursues ultimate ends consistently and refuses to use violent means in their fulfillment in politics may avoid these ethical problems, Weber continued, but is at the same time thereby irresponsible because by refusing to use violence, that person has renounced the means which could influence the actual course of political life. That person must thus renounce concern with achieving particular results and instead be satisfied with being "true" to his or her beliefs and content to "leave the results with God." In a "genuine man" these two ethics are intuitively combined, although Weber offers no criteria for this, nor any insight into how a compromise between them is to be reached.

Among Weber's assumptions basic to his analysis of the two ethics are these: (1) responsibility is determined by willingness to use violence for political ends; and (2) exclusively nonviolent behavior cannot be politically effective and hence politically responsible. The validity of Weber's classification—and of much other thinking on politics—depends on these two assumptions. It is our contention that both are today invalid.

WEBER'S ASSUMPTIONS NOW INVALID

Let us examine these assumptions individually. Our view of the first is that, whatever may or may not have been true previously, Weber's assumption that political responsibility is determined by willingness to use violence to achieve political goals is no longer valid. This is not to say, for the purposes of this analysis, that all violence for political ends is necessarily irresponsible, nor that all abstention from violence is necessarily responsible. It is to say however that the developments in technology and political organization now associated with violence for political ends have, in at least important cases, made willingness to use such violence clearly irresponsible, considering the results which may today follow from use of such means, or at the least made its responsibility questionable. Weber said that under the ethic of responsibility "one has to give an account of the foreseeable results of one's action." However, he identified this with willingness to use violence, while he said that one who insisted on "following a pure ethic of absolute ends" (that is, one who refuses to use "evil" means), was one whose behavior meant that "goals may be damaged and discredited for generations." At least in important cases today, however, it is the *use* of violence which may contribute to such damage and such violence is unlikely to be used if one takes account of "the foreseeable results of one's action." In such cases the *abstention* from such violence may be more responsible.

There are very few persons today who would argue that waging large-scale war for political ends is responsible action in an age of nuclear weapons and intercontinental rockets. Even small wars run the risk of growing into nuclear wars and hence also involve some degree of risk that the weapons of total destruction will be used, and are therefore also a questionable responsibility. Whatever case it may have been possible to present previously for the use of large-scale war for advancing or defending political and other ends on grounds of responsibility has in large degree been destroyed by modern weapons of mass destruction. In these circumstances, contrary to Weber's assumption, the use of violence may become highly irresponsible, and the refusal to use such means for political ends in international relations may become the more responsible of the alternatives.

The totalitarian State is another warning against assuming the responsibility of the use of violence for political ends. Further, effective concentration of the means of violent conflict in the hands of the State (especially the totalitarian State), means that it posesses vast military superiority over any possible popular revolt, and to the degree that the revolt thus depends upon military success, the responsibility of the revolutionaries in depending upon violence in their struggle may thus be called into question. There may be additional cases where responsibility is not associated with willingness to use violence for political ends.

The inhumanity, destruction, and death which have accompanied and followed political violence since Weber's time mean that it is no longer as simple or valid as it seemed to Weber in his 1918 lecture to identify—as people still do—political responsibility with willingness to use violence for political ends, and irresponsibility with refusal to do so. Weber recognized that violence had certain undesirable consequences. He did not, however, examine these deeply, nor did he foresee the developments in political violence which have since taken place. His assumption that responsibility is determined by willingness to use violence for political ends is now invalid, and therefore, is, perhaps the most important criterion in Weber's classification of ethical systems.

Weber's second assumption that only violent means could generate power to influence the actual course of political events, and hence produce responsibility, has also been proved false by later developments. There now exist nonviolent means of political struggle wielded as an alternative ultimate sanction (which Weber did not or could not consider seriously) capable (at least in important cases) of generating "power" to enable them to be politically effective and hence responsible, in Weber's terms. As nonviolent struggle (by such means as political noncooperation, civil disobedience campaigns, general strikes, economic boycotts, mutinies, and popular defiance) was certainly not unknown when Weber gave his lecture, he must be criticized for his assumption that political means must be violent.

This is less important, however, than the fact that since Weber's time the use of the technique of nonviolent action[36] in political conflicts has increased on a scale which would have been difficult for Weber, or anyone else, to have foreseen. India, South Africa, and the United States South are only three of the more familiar of the prominent places where this development has taken place on a large scale. Gandhi has been the most significant individual, but by no means the only one, involved in this development.[37] The technique has since been applied on a major scale also in Japan, Norway, Denmark, Hungary, East Germany, Spain, Czechoslovakia, Thailand, Iran, Nicaragua, and on a smaller scale in other places including the Soviet Union. It has been used in a variety of situations for a variety of objectives, in face of both mild and harsh repression, and with varying results.

We are not here arguing that nonviolent action is universally valid, nor that it is always successful or "responsible." (It is necessary only to establish that there are important cases where it can influence the course of political events and be "responsible" in order to establish the inadequacy of Weber's second assumption.) The contention is that nonviolent action is capable of generating sufficient power to influence the actual course of events and be politically effective, and, therefore, in Weber's sense, be responsible. The *satyagraha* campaigns led by Gandhi, the Montgomery, Alabama bus boycott, the bus boycotts and other resistance campaigns in South Africa, the general strike of the 1956–57 Hungarian Revolution, the Japanese mass agitation against the U.S. Security Pact, the eight months' Czechoslovak resistance in 1968–69, the paralysis of Iran's economic and political life by strikes and defiance in 1978–79, for example, have demonstrated that these nonviolent methods are capable of making a significant political impact.

It has often been the opponents against whom the technique has been wielded who have recognized most acutely its power. The South African Government, for example, faced in 1952 with the

Defiance Campaign, felt it necessary to take a variety of extensive measures to combat it and prepare itself to meet the possible recurrence of such nonviolent defiance on a large scale.[38] Such repression would not be necessary if nonviolent means were incapable of making a political impact and of constituting some degree of a threat to the status quo. During the 1930–31 Indian civil disobedience campaign, the British Viceroy, Lord Irwin (later Lord Halifax), in a speech to the Houses of the Legislative Assembly of India on 9 July 1930, described the nonviolent movement as "a deliberate attempt to coerce established authority by mass action," "dangerously subversive," "the application of force under another form," and declared "a Government is bound either to resist or abdicate," and "we must fight it with all our strength."[39] Quisling's fury at the nonviolent resistance of the Norwegian teachers under the Nazi occupation, the unsurmounted difficulties he faced in the popular resistance to the establishment of the Corporate State of Norway, and his charge, "You teachers have destroyed everything for me,"[40] could be cited as further evidence of the political impact of nonviolent action.

It now seems to be incontestable that nonviolent action, at least in important cases, is capable of wielding politically effective power and having a significant impact and influence on the actual course of political events, and hence is describable as "responsible." This means that, at least in important cases, contrary to Weber, it is not necessary to use "evil" (that is, violent) means to achieve "good" ends, and that one may thus remain loyal to ultimate ends while being politically responsible. (Weber, however, placed "responsibility" and loyalty to ultimate ends at opposite poles and did not conceive of the possibility of any political technique combining these qualities.) Weber's second assumption, that exclusively nonviolent behavior cannot be politically effective and hence responsible, is thus invalid.

The developments in the field of nonviolent action have opened up the possibility of bringing loyalty to ultimate ends and political responsibility under one roof and making them, not opposites, but two sides of the same coin. This possibility potentially opens the way to a solution of important ethical problems in politics.

A SUGGESTED RECLASSIFICATION

This analysis has attempted to show that two important assumptions underlying Weber's classification of ethical systems in their relation to politics are now invalid. If this analysis is itself valid, it means that Weber's classification is not adequate at present and ought therefore to be replaced. As Weber's assumptions are still widely shared, this has major implications for contemporary politics.

While claiming no finality, I would like tentatively to suggest the outlines of a possible alternative classification of political ethics. It will be recalled that in formulating his classification, Weber considered the relation of means to ends in the two ethics (and thus rather directly the question of violent and nonviolent means). This criterion is carried over into the suggested new classification.

Weber also pronounced that one ethic was "responsible" and the other suitable for "a political infant." In the new classification we shall not attempt to evaluate which ethic is "responsible" and which "irresponsible," nor which is "mature" and which suited to "infants." The question of responsibility seems to hinge on such questions as: (1) the short-term and long-term social and political consequences of the use, respectively, of violent action and non-violent action for political ends, including the relative effectiveness of these techniques against a variety of opponents and under a variety of conditions, and (2) the question of whether there is an intrinsic relationship between means used and the results achieved. Much difficult investigation and analysis is needed here if a general consensus on answers to those two questions is to be possible, as existing knowledge is relatively small, especially concerning non-violent action.

Therefore we have excluded "responsibility" as not being at present a suitable criterion (however desirable it may be that it were) for an objective classification of types of ethical systems. It is hoped that in the future considerable research will be conducted to provide the knowledge upon which an objective judgement of responsibility might be based, which would, in turn, make possible a reasonable degree of agreement concerning the relative degree of responsibility in various techniques of political action. This would then make possible a classification of ethical systems using the criterion of responsibility. At present, however, we can only suggest very briefly what appear to be five "ideal types" of ethical systems determined on the basis of their view of means and ends—the other criterion used by Weber.

(1) **Ethic of loyalty to ultimate ends and unconcern with results.** The adherents of this ethic are almost entirely concerned with being "true" or loyal to ultimate ends. Action of potential social or political significance is taken only to the extent that (a) it is forced upon them as a necessary response to the actions of others, or (b) such action results from an "imperative" which must be followed in order for them to be true to their belief system. The adherents of this ethic are not concerned in any significant way with achieving "short-run" specific social or political objectives, even by the use of means consistent with their ultimate goals. They are, rather, committed to being true to their convictions, believing that the results will follow from pursuing right actions and remaining true to basic principles.

(2) **Ethic of deliberate consistency in means and ends.** The adherents of this ethic are concerned with both ultimate ends and social and political goals, although among those who may be classified here some variation is possible in the relative intensity of the two concerns. The adherents of this ethic have deliberately chosen to work towards worldly goals only by means which are consistent with their ultimate ends, that is, by nonviolent means. They will refuse to use violent methods both on the ground that such means violate their principles and on the ground that they would thereby reduce the chances of achieving desirable social and political results. They would, however, themselves apply means consistent with their ultimate ends in working for the achievement of particular objectives, and might also provide leadership to wider groups (including persons following the third ethic below) willing to apply such nonviolent means for the achievement of particular social and political ends.

(3) **Ethic of willingness to use the "necessary" and "most suitable" means.** The adherents of this ethic are only secondarily concerned with long-term social and political goals or principles. They are interested in being "effective" politically in a relatively

immediate sense. They have reached no rigid position on means and ends, and having no principled objection to violent or nonviolent means, they are willing to use whatever means, violent or nonviolent, which may seem to be most appropriate and "necessary" in the concrete situation they face.

(4) **Ethic of "the necessary evil of violence."** Adherents of this ethic hold the view that the only, or almost only, effective power of political relevance is that which is directly or indirectly associated with violence, although they may say that judged by some ideal system this violence is regrettable. While they do not cherish violence for its own sake, seeing themselves as "realists" they are committed to using violence, directly or indirectly, to achieve their social and political objectives. While avowing certain ultimate ends, they are primarily concerned with achieving social and political objectives through furthering their relative power position, effective conduct of violent struggles, etc., as such means are regarded as a basic importance and necessity in the practical world, and other means, seen as not having such capabilities of power, are regarded as naïve and useless.

(5) **Ethic of loyalty to violence as means and end.** Adherents of this ethic have little concern with "ultimate ends." They no only hold that the real power in the world is based upon violence and that the use or threat of violence is necessary to achieve any given goal, but with them violence becomes a "positive" goal in itself. It may be a case where the means of violence is pursued with vigor while the original end is largely forgotten. The emphasis on violence is not accompanied by any serious consideration of where this leads, except perhaps an idealizing of a society characterized by violence.

This outline classification is offered only as a suggestion of one way in which a reclassification of ethical systems might be made to replace Weber's, which we have viewed as inadequate in light of events since his time. It is hoped that this chapter will make some contribution to greater clarity of thought and improved understanding of this area, and also to stimulating further examination of and rethinking about these problems.

NOTES TO CHAPTER ELEVEN

1. Max Weber, "Politics as a Vocation," in **From Max Weber: Essays in Sociology** (trans., ed. and with an Introduction by H.H. Gerth and C. Wright Mills; New York: Oxford University Press [1946], 1958, and London: Routledge & Kegan Paul, [1948] 1961), pp. 77–128.
2. Ibid., p. 120.
3. Ibid., p. 121.
4. Ibid., p. 120.
5. Ibid., p. 122.
6. Ibid., p. 126.
7. Ibid., p. 120.
8. Ibid., p. 121.
9. Ibid., p. 120.
10. Ibid.
11. Ibid., p. 126.
12. Ibid., p. 120.
13. Kurt H. Wolff, "The Means-End Scheme in Contemporary Sociology and its Relation to an Analysis of Non-Violence: A Seminar" (mimeo; Institute for Social Research, Oslo 1959), pp. 115–116. In addition to this particular point, I am deeply indebted to Dr. Wolff for his stimulating thought on this and related questions and for his general encouragement.
14. **From Max Weber,** p. 127.
15. Ibid.
16. Ibid., p. 121.
17. Ibid., p. 122.
18. Ibid.
19. Ibid.
20. Ibid.
21. Ibid.
22. Ibid., p. 123.
23. We assume that the term "politics" is not defined in a narrow sense limited to those actions directly or indirectly associated with the State, but that it applies to the general processes by which people are governed, or govern themselves, present and future social politics are determined, and conflicts over such policies are conducted and resolved.
24. Ibid., p. 119. (Italics Weber's) We understand Weber as using the term "violence" not only to mean open physical violence, such as riots, murders, violent revolutions, wars, executions, etc., but also the *threat* of such violence, and the institutions which are dependent upon such measures, including the repressive powers of the State.
25. Ibid., p. 126.
26. Ibid., p. 121.
27. Ibid., p. 126.
28. Ibid., p. 124.

29. Ibid., p. 126.
30. Ibid., p. 123.
31. Ibid., p. 121.
32. Ibid.
33. Ibid., p. 124.
34. Ibid., pp. 125–126.
35. Ibid., p. 126.
36. For a definition of "nonviolent action," see Gene Sharp, The Politics of Nonviolent Action (Boston: Porter Sargent Publisher, Inc., 1973), Chapter Two.
37. For an analysis of the significance of *satyagraha* as a technique of socio-political action for Western political practice and theory, see Joan V. Bondurant, Conquest of Violence: The Gandhian Philosophy of Conflict (Princeton, N.J.: Princeton University Press, 1958; Berkeley: University of California Press, 1965; and London: Oxford University Press, 1958), esp. pp. 189–232. See also Chapter Four in this volume, *"Satyagraha* and Political Conflict: A review of Joan V. Bondurant's Conquest of Violence."
38. For a listing of such measures, see Leo Kuper, Passive Resistance in South Africa (New Haven: Yale University Press, 1957, and London: Jonathan Cape, 1956), pp. 61–63, and 182–201.
39. Government of India, India in 1930–31: A Statement prepared for Presentation to Parliament in accordance with the requirements of the 26th Section of the Government of India Act (5 & 6) Geo. V. Chapt. 61 (Calcutta: Central Publications Branch, Government of India, 1932), pp. 80–81.
40. Sverre Amunsen, gen. ed., Kirkenesferda 1942 (Oslo: J.W. Cappelens Forlag, 1946), p. 454.

12

Morality, Politics, and Political Technique*

Believers in "Christian pacifism" and "nonviolence as a principle" have often regarded the use and advocacy of nonviolent action by nonpacifists as a practical technique as an inferior—if not actually immoral—approach to nonviolence. While some believers in principled nonviolence have encouraged and promoted the spread of the nonviolent technique of action, others have only "tolerated" this practical approach and at times have openly deprecated and opposed it, believing it would compromise their principles.

* This was originally written at Oxford for the Friends Peace Committee (Quakers) in London about 1963. This was toward the conclusion of a long and frustrating

251

This chapter has a very limited aim: to refute that view and to argue moreover that the practical "technique approach" to nonviolence is necessary to help solve both some of the world's pressing political problems (especially war and tyranny) and also at least one difficult problem in moral philosophy and moral theology.

A consideration of the relationship between "principled nonviolence" and "practical nonviolence" requires a consideration of certain aspects of the general question of how moral principles can be applied in the real political world. Inevitably involved in this is the question of the means of action by which this is attempted. The question of political technique is, therefore, inextricable from the question of a "this worldly" morality, and, as I shall argue, the technique of nonviolent action may be the "missing link" required for development of a better solution of these problems than has hitherto been possible and for the union of morality and politics.

I share a personal belief in "nonviolence as a principle" and a "philosophy of life." I also hold that such a belief may enrich the individual and the society in which one practices it. It may be a source of strength, especially in extreme difficulties when it is not possible to calculate all the practical consequences of one's actions. It may also be a useful guide in life and a stimulus to creativity and humane behavior.

But, as will be clear later, I do not accept that, when adequately understood, the "moral" and the "practical" approaches to society and politics are really different. And I vigorously deny the often accepted (but rarely expounded) doctrine that

period during which in the United States and England I attempted to work primarily within pacifist groups in efforts to persuade them to become the leaders in an effort to replace violent sanctions with nonviolent ones in society, rather than simply to continue efforts to gain individual converts to personal pacifism. When the essay appeared to have little or no impact on the committee of English Quakers for whom it was written, in order to reach pacifists throughout the world I allowed it to be published by *Reconciliation Quarterly,* then published from London by the pacifist International Fellowship of Reconciliation. Contrary to an understanding, the journal published only the middle section of the article, leaving out both the criticisms of pacifists and the plea that they had a prime responsibility to assist the development of the technique approach to nonviolent struggle. This article was my last major such effort to seek to achieve these changes within pacifist groups. Much of the analysis of this paper is, however, of interest to others, outside of pacifist and peace groups, who are concerned with political ethics. It appears here as originally written with only minor editorial changes.—G.S., 1978.

belief in a moral or religious system absolves one from the responsibility to think about its validity, and especially from responsibility to think through its implications and applications and to try to improve the lot of one's fellow human beings. Doctrine must never be a substitute for thought or action.

"OTHER WORLDLY" OR "THIS WORLDLY" NONVIOLENCE?

Of course, some belief systems which include an imperative for nonviolent behavior are primarily "other worldly" oriented. That is, their adherents do not behave nonviolently in order to improve the lot of their fellow human beings or to build a better world (which they often regard as beyond redemption). Rather, they abstain from violence in order to be "true" to their religion or creed; their nonviolence is thus primarily a contribution to their spiritual preparation for the "next world."

This approach I do not share. It is also rejected in part or in full by many Christian pacifists and most notably by the Society of Friends. The aim of these other believers in nonviolence as a moral principle, then, becomes not to withdraw from "the world" but to live in the world while following one's principles, seeking to improve both one's self and the world. This orientation to non-violence is primarily "this worldly"—although it usually includes wider philosophical or religious beliefs.

The choice to make one's orientation "this worldly" is a fundamental one with important consequences for one's approach to nonviolence. It means, among other things, that believers in a "this worldly" principled nonviolence do not seek *only* to be "faithful" or "true" in the abstract. In choosing the "this worldly" orientation, they are almost axiomatically accepting that it is inadequate merely to assert their beliefs, to follow them in their personal lives, and to urge others to repentance. Instead, they are bound by their outlook to seek to live *in* the world, which includes the effort to implement and achieve their beliefs in this world. That is, they are to seek to improve the world, to better the lot of their fellow human beings, and to influence the course of social and political events. All this, these believers are obliged to do without violating the principles themselves, if this is possible. In a world in which social and political problems are both widespread and dangerous, the believer in a "this worldly" principled nonviolence has thus accepted a responsibility to seek to contribute to the resolution of the world's problems by means compatible with his or her principles.

The acceptance of this obligation requires one to recognize the kind of a world in which one lives. This includes, among other things, the nature of the society which one is to seek to improve. It requires an acknowledgement of the qualities of society which are apparently inevitable, that is, which are part of the reality within which one must operate. These qualities include the recognition that some kind of power and some degree of conflict is inherent in the very nature of society; one cannot escape from this without giving up one's "this worldly" outlook in favor of the "other worldly" orientaton.

THE PROBLEM OF POLITICAL ACTION

The "this worldly" orientation to principled nonviolence is adventurous, challenging, and ambitious. But it also poses at once a very difficult and crucial problem: *how to act* in society in a way which is both "moral" (that is, in harmony with one's principles which include nonviolence), and also "responsible" (that is, to one's fellow human beings facing practical social and political problems). Put another way, the problem is how to respond to the real problems of this world in a way which will actively contribute to their practical solution while not violating one's avowed principles. More concisely, it is the problem of how to formulate social and political action which is both moral and practical—that is, how to form in action a working union of morality and politics.

This is not to deny that there may be no possible solution to this problem which presents absolutely no moral difficulties and which at times does not fall, at least to some degree, short of those moral principles. There would still be moral problems in the implementation of the proposal I shall discuss later in this chapter. But there are obviously *vast* differences in the degree and type of various moral difficulties. These differences are at times so vast as to be almost differences not of degree but of kind. Neither all moral nor all political problems can be completely solved all at once. One cannot, therefore, dismiss contributions to their solution which, while dealing with the most serious difficulties, leave unresolved some lesser moral and political problems. This may mean that so long as serious moral compromises are not involved, our attention should be primarily focused on the gravest moral and political problems of our world rather than upon relatively minor problems, especially those which are, in comparison to the grave ones, almost trivial, and certainly should receive lower priorities in our attention. Out of the process of solving the more serious problems may come the desire and capacity to deal with the finer points.

This approach, which I hope seems reasonable, is contrary to what sometimes takes place among certain believers in principled nonviolence. It is a source of amazement that on occasion some such persons who reluctantly find it necessary to support some type of military power internationally (as in a world government) at the same time object to some types of nonviolent action because they may be "coercive" or not based on a moral conviction or belief. Obviously, much serious fresh thought is needed on the moral problems involving principle and power in politics.

"WICKEDNESS" OR "NECESSITY"?

It is extraordinary that believers in a "this worldly" principled nonviolence have made so little effort to understand why most people are unwilling or unable to accept "nonviolence as a principle" or as "a way of life." Believers in principled nonviolence have very often assumed—implicitly or explicitly— that perversity or wickedness or blindness has been the reason why ordinary people have not accepted the "way of nonviolence." Stated nakedly this way, the assumption will often be quickly denied but if the point is pressed and the protestor's outlook, arguments, and past courses of action are examined carefully, there will nevertheless often be found substance in this interpretation.

From this attribution of wickedness to others, believers in nonviolence have often concluded that their role is to "testify" and "witness" for peace, to "speak," to "prophesy," and to urge "repentance" on their fellow human beings. This outlook has often been expressed in more sophisticated ways in pacifist and peace groups, and at times has even been passed off under the guise of political analysis. However, the essence of the outlook remains basically the same, and with it have gone grave mistakes in policy in the nonviolence and peace groups.

In my opinion, this assumption that perversity or wickedness or blindness explain why most people have not accepted nonviolence as a principle is factually wrong and lacking in sympathetic charity for others. Whatever may or may not have been true previously, most people do not today—in face of the widely recognized danger of universal extermination—accept war preparations simply because people are "evil," "blind," or "unrepentant." It is highly doubtful that this has been the case for three decades at least, although prior to that wars were often fought over avowedly less noble motives than people believe to have been the case more recently.

The more accurate explanation of the refusal to accept nonviolence as an ethic is, I suggest, both simpler and more difficult. Almost everyone—except those adhering to "other worldly" creeds —is primarily concerned to live in this world and to face and solve its problems and crises in a practical way. It is widely recognized— though not always clearly so—that conflicts are common in society; that important issues of both principle and human welfare are often at stake in these conflicts; that the exercise of power of some kind is unavoidable in such situations unless one is to abdicate responsibility for influencing the outcome of those conflicts; and finally, that ultimately such power involves and at times depends upon the application of *some* kind of sanction or means of struggle.

Most people recognizing these realities have not believed that *all* situations and crises could be faced *without* resort to the threat or use of some type of violence when other efforts had failed to solve the problem satisfactorily.

Despite the moral imperatives to nonviolence contained in widely accepted philosophies and religions, most people have been unable to accept them as universally valid because they have seen those imperatives to be impractical and inapplicable in crisis situations and in face of political dangers. Violence has thus often been deliberately chosen (or at least has been continually accepted) as an ultimate sanction and course of action because of this attitude. Most people have believed that there was no nonviolent way to face many of the difficult practical problems involved in applying a moral outlook in this world, in trying to behave responsibly toward one's fellow human beings in a world which is far from that moral outlook. Most people have believed it to be inadequate simply to "witness" to some "ultimate end" or principle. They have felt that they must act in practical ways capable of achieving immediate human objectives, or of opposing effectively the "greater evil."

It has thus been—not the wickedness or perverseness of people, but—the absence of confidence in an effectve nonviolent course of action which could in place of violence achieve or defend social and political ends as well as moral principles, which explains why most people continue to accept violence and reject the moralist nonviolent outlook. It is true, of course, that violence has often been used for antisocial objectives—such as to achieve or maintain a conquest, despotism, pillage, and exploitation. But it is also true that people have felt violence to be necessary on practical grounds to defend their principles, way of life, and society from these very threats, or, at times, to struggle for a more just society. In the present day it is almost only these "defensive" and "social" aims which remain as "justifications" for the continued use and threat of political violence.

Thus, the presumed absence of a practical technique of action which would be effective in such conflicts and crises contributes significantly to the continued acceptance of violence and the rejection of principled nonviolence. If an equally effective nonviolent technique of action applicable in such crises existed and were believed to exist, many people might gain new insights into beliefs to which they have hitherto paid only lip-service, and the most important single reason for continued acceptance of major political violence would disappear.

A QUAKER PERSPECTIVE

In the past, then, the problem of how to combine morality and politics has generally been considered on the assumption that a politically effective nonviolent technique did not exist. It is instructive to examine briefly the analyses of the problem presented by three quite different writers whose independent comments—while presented in different terminology—are all remarkably similar. They are Gerald Bailey, a prominent English Quaker, Max Weber, the important German sociologist, and E.H. Carr, a well-known English historian and writer on international affairs.

Gerald Bailey focused his analysis of this problem primarily in terms of the discussion which took place within the Society of Friends in England around 1960. The two approaches among English Quakers to the problem of applying morality in politics have been known as those of the "prophet" and the "reconciler." The terms "prophet" and "reconciler," said Bailey, are "only partly appropriate."[1] (It is perhaps instructive that these terms have been adopted even though they tend to blur certain qualities of these approaches more than the other terms of "perfectionist" and "realist" or "absolutist" and "relativist" which have also been used.)

The "prophet" was defined by W. Grigor McClelland[2] (quoted by Bailey) as one who: "devotes himself to preaching the unilateral abandonment of arms as a moral duty. He is engaged on a crusade to bring to his fellow men a consciousness that war is wrong. He calls them whether as humble citizens or as national leaders to cast away all arms, come what may."[3] In this "absolutist" or "moral" approach, the "prophet" is primarily concerned—Bailey indicated —with loyalty to his moral principles rather than the solution of immediate practical problems.

Inherent in this approach is the belief that his way of influencing society and politics involves holding true to his principles and rejecting those courses of action and policies which—in an effort to be "practical"—compromise or violate those principles. Rejecting violence and immediate policies and solutions to current problems depending upon the sanction of violence, he is willing to rely instead on producing a longer-term influence on politics and internatonal relations by his "witness."

The "reconciler"—while not abandoning his beliefs—is primarily concerned with making a more short-term contribution to the resolution of conflicts and problems. The "reconciler," said Mc-Clelland: "devotes himself to working for the establishment of conditions in which people will feel no need to rely upon arms because they do not feel threatened. He seeks to relax tensions, to promote meetings of persons and meetings of minds, to suggest acceptable solutions for divisive problems."[4] This "realistic" approach also involves the attempt to act in ways which are relevant to "temporal problems," Bailey indicated. That is, it is an attempt to influence the actual course of political and international events in the world as it exists now. The "reconciler" attempts to a large degree to reconcile the antagonists and reduce the chances of war, and the like, without demanding a radical alteration in the situation or an abandonment of reliance on violence.

The "reconciler" seeks to be immediately helpful in improving the political and international situation even though to do this he must endorse policies and courses of action which violate his principle of nonviolence and may include threats of war or reliance on an international military force. That is, such practical policies often rely upon military power and accept the necessity of such means, and these must be accepted—the "reconciler" maintains—if one is to influence the real course of events. This involves inevitable inconsistencies and compromises of principle, but it is believed that this difficult combination of moral principle and practical political action will contribute to the achievement in this world of an earthly commonwealth of liberty and peace.

WEBER'S TWO ETHICS

Max Weber used a different terminology to discuss this problem. He spoke of the two broad "solutions" to the problem of the relation between morality and politics as the "ethic of ultimate ends" and the "ethic of responsibility."* According to Weber, the votary of the "ethic of ultimate ends" is concerned with being "true" to certain principles without concern with the achievement of particular immediate goals, "that is, in religious terms, The Christian does rightly and leaves the results with the Lord'. . . ."[5]

> The believer in an ethic of ultimate ends feels "responsible" only
> for seeing to it that the flame of pure intentions is not

---

* For a fuller presentation and critique of Weber's views, see Chapter Eleven in this volume, "Ethics and Responsibility in Politics."

> quenched. . . . To rekindle the flame ever anew is the purpose of
> his quite irrational deeds, judged in view of their possible success.
> They are acts that can and shall have only exemplary value.[6]

Being "true" to the ultimate ends is so important that "the absolute
ethic just does not *ask* for 'consequences.' That is the decisive
point."[7] Logically, this ethic "has only the possibility of rejecting all
action that employs morally dangerous means. . . ."[8]

The "ethic of responsibility," said Weber, stands in contrast to
this. In it, "one has to give an account of the foreseeable results of
one's action."[9]

> . . . [A] man who believes in an ethic of responsibility takes
> account of precisely the average deficiencies of people. . . . He
> does not feel in a position to burden others with the results of his
> own actions so far he was able to foresee them; he will say: these
> results are ascribed to my action.[10]

These two ethics are, said Weber, in conflict. "We must be
clear about the fact that all ethically orientated conduct may be
guided by one of two fundamentally differing and irreconcilably
opposed maxims: conduct can be orientated to an 'ethic of ultimate
ends' or to an 'ethic of responsibility'."[11] He described: "an
abysmal contrast between conduct that follows the maxim of an
ethic of ultimate ends . . . and conduct that follows the maxim of an
ethic of responsibility. . . ."[12]

> The genius or demon of politics lives in an inner tension with the
> god of love, as well as the Christian God as expressed by the
> church. This tension can at any time lead to an irreconcilable
> conflict.[13]

CARR ON UTOPIANISM AND REALISM

E.H. Carr contrasted two approaches to politics, "utopianism" and "realism."[14] Utopianism, he argued, rejects the
existing order—whether in economics, politics, or international
relations. The utopian makes certain assumptions concerning human behavior, and on the basis of these creates in his imagination
a visionary alternative scheme of the ideal community or social
order which ought to exist in place of the present one. This goal
becomes the only relevant fact for him. The utopian concentrates
almost entirely on the end which ought to be. He elaborates the

visionary project whose simplicity and perfection endow it with a strong appeal.

The utopian sets up an ethical standard and seeks to make reality conform to it, to substitute an Utopia by an act of will, by a burst of creativity and spontaneity. His prescription is based, not upon analysis and thinking, but upon aspiration, wishing, and imagination. There is little critical analysis of the means to be used to achieve that goal, nor of the existing order as it is and as it functions. Little or no place is given in utopian thought to a consideration of causes and effects.

"Realism" stands in contrast to this. It is the reaction against utopianism. Macchiavelli, said Carr, was the first important realist in the field of politics. He pointed to the peril of ignoring the existing political facts in one's desire to create a better society. Macchiavelli's three basic tenets remain the foundation of the realist political philosophy: (1) The course of history is determined by cause and effect—*not* by the "imagination" of utopians; (2) It is practice which creates theory, not *vice versa;* (3) Ethics are a function of politics, not *vice versa;* morality is the product of power.

Other "realists"—Bodin, Hobbes, Spinoza, Hegel, Marx, etc. —followed Macchiavelli, but these principles remain. Morality and ethics are thus seen to be determined by politics and the search for an independent ethical norm outside politics is thus futile. The facts are described, analyzed, and consideration is given to their cause and consequences. Explicitly or implicitly the "realists" maintain that one is powerless to influence or change the established course of events. The existing forces possess irresistible strength, in his view, and existing tendencies are inevitable.

One must, says the realist, accept these facts *and adapt oneself to them.* What *should be* is thus deduced from *what is.* Theory becomes the codification of practice, and there is no direction or standard for political behavior except conformity to the existing forces. There becomes no other good except to understand and accept reality.

THE TRADITIONAL "SOLUTIONS"

Although there are important differences in the descriptions by these three writers, the similarities are even more important and often the descriptions supplement each other. They are so complimentary that we might speak of the two broad existing approaches to the problem of morality in politics as the "prophet-ultimate ends-utopian" approach and the "reconciler-responsibility-realist" approach.

The first of these is predominantly characterized by a desire to remain faithful to principles which one deeply believes to be eternally true. Compromise and betrayal of them in an effort to produce short-term social or political ends are therefore believed both immoral and, in the politics of eternity, unable to achieve a lasting earthly implementation and realization of these principles. Instead, this is replaced in efforts to achieve social and political change by indifference to the social and political reality while creating in one's imagination a new order which is believed will somehow come into being—without major attempts to bring it about.

The second approach is predominantly characterized by the desire to solve practical problems in a practical way here in the real human world. Considerable attention is then given to ways to do this. There is also a recognition of the assumed necessity of means —especially violence—to achieve short-term social and political goals, although these means may violate one's principles. The degree to which the adherent of this approach is uneasy about this inconsistency varies widely.

I have devoted considerable attention to outlining these two approaches to the relationship between morality and politics because they are, roughly, the alternative "solutions" between which it has long been accepted that one must choose, or work out an uneasy compromise. This is true even of those who have failed to think consciously about this relationship or to articulate the assumptions on which they have acted. If we are to have the chance of reaching a more satisfactory solution to this problem than has thus far been developed, we must understand the existing outlooks in order to be able to examine their qualities and their assumptions.

BOTH "SOLUTIONS" INADEQUATE

It is my conviction that both the "prophet-ultimate ends-utopian" and the "reconciler-responsibility-realist" approaches are partly correct, but that in the present form each is an inadequate solution, to both the moral and the political aspects of the problem of how to relate morality and politics.

In practice, the *first* of these approaches runs the severe danger —with the rejection of morally tainted means (especially violence) —of leading, not to the realization of morality in human society and to the removal of social and political evil, but to *inaction*. That is, the first often leads to a failure to face real problems, and hence to a capitulation to social and political evil, thus contributing to a continuation of unprincipled inhumanity in political society. This cannot be regarded as an adequate resolution of the moral problems, and it can, not unfairly, be characterized as irresponsible to one's fellow human beings.

On the other hand, the *second* of these two usual positions is certainly not more adequate. The active attempt to influence the real course of social and political events and to oppose in action the most blatant evils is there. But because of the means—involving political violence—accepted for this task, the principles themselves are not only violated, but also one adds oneself, to the accumulation of inhumanity and violence in human political society and puts still further into the distance the rebuilding of human society in harmony with those moral principles.

It is highly significant that none of the three writers we have cited is entirely satisfied with the alternatives he sees before him and has himself presented. The writers vary, however in the degree to which they think one must choose clearly between them or whether the two ethics or approaches to politics can in some way be combined.

It has been widely accepted among Quakers—including Bailey —that the "prophet" and the "reconciler" are both necessary and that each plays an important role. Bailey argued, however, that (contrary to the opinions of some) these two approaches cannot be combined in the same persons, primarily because one approach requires the rejection of violence while the other accepts violence as inevitable in politics and therefore necessary. Bailey, however, recorded that he has come to this conclusion "reluctantly and not without much exercise of spirit," and recognized that it has "implications deep and far-reaching and that they face me with dilemmas hardly less acute than those I claim to have resolved."[15]

Weber, on the other hand, argued that to be politically responsible—that is, responsible to one's fellow human beings and to influence the course of political events—one must be willing to violate one's ultimate ends. However, he also felt that that same person must at times be willing to draw the line and (without any criteria and without consideration to the consequences) say "Here I stand: I can do no other." Weber favored some sort of a working compromise between the two ethics, although he offered no criteria for reaching that compromise.

Carr, similarly, found flaws in both the "utopian" and the "realist" approaches and was unwilling to accept either of them as they exist. There must, he argued, be a working compromise between the two approaches, including both morality and power. The solution lies, he argued, in developing this compromise and in reliance on means of "peaceful change" (which includes threats of war!). The solution of peaceful change must, Carr said, be based on that "uneasy compromise between power and morality, which is the foundation of all political life."[16] In specific cases, he argued, morality must be sacrificed to power, and power to morality, for international as well as national politics is a meeting place for ethics and power. They are closely intertwined, and it is fatal to ignore either, he emphasized.

It is a natural reaction for people who see the moral and political inadequacies of either of these approaches alone to suggest (as Weber and Carr did) that what is *really* needed is a working compromise between these, or (as some Quakers quakerly do) to suggest that *both* are needed and in the long run each in its own way helps to improve the human condition.

If, however, we are acutely aware of the inadequacies of each of the two approaches and of the severe practical difficulties in combining power and morality under present political and technological conditions, we cannot be satisfied with these superficial "solutions" of our basic problem. Such efforts at "compromising" or "harmonizing" the incompatible can only mean that the second approach—with its acceptance of violence in politics—becomes dominant with all the severe moral and practical political problems which that produces. This is especially the case today as the means of political violence in both war and tyranny have grown, increasing both human suffering and the problems of political morality. Is there not possible some more adequate resolution of the problem of morality in politics?

THE PRESUMED NECESSITY OF VIOLENCE

One is naturally tempted to ask if there is not some fundamental error underlying both these established "solutions" to the problem of how to relate morality and politics. This error is not difficult to find. All three writers rightly, in my opinion, assumed that to be politically effective and "responsible," to be able to influence the course of social and political events, to be able to cope with regimes and forces whose aims and policies are regarded as most undesirable, it is necessary at some stage to wield power. This power may sometimes be effective merely by the possession of the capacity to wield it, and at times it must be applied in open struggle, but it must be present. How to wield power is a crucial problem, one which many exponents of principled "this-worldly" nonviolence persistently dodge—in contrast to Gerald Bailey who faces it squarely.

This recognition of power and the need for it is not, however, the error. The error lies in the assumptions which are usually made about the nature of power. All three writers assume that if power is to be politically effective, and hence responsible, it must, to a significant degree, be power which in the last analysis rests on the willingness and the capacity to use some type of political violence, especially military struggle. Bailey, very uneasy about this, reluctantly found it to be necessary, as he identified in his lecture on "The Prophet and the Reconciler" "power" and "force" with violence and military means, assuming that there is no politically-effective nonviolent power or force.

Weber was not so uneasy, although he recognized the "possibility or even probability of evil ramifications" for the society as well as the individual which follow from the use of "morally dubious means" which include violence.[17] "Should it really matter so little for the ethical demands on politics," asked Weber,"that politics operates with very special means, namely, power backed up by *violence?*"[18] Furthermore, he admitted—and for our discussion here this is crucial—"It is the specific means of legitimate violence as such in the hands of human associations which determines the peculiarity of all ethical problems in politics."[19] "Everything that is striven for through political action operating with violent means and following an ethic of responsibility endangers the 'salvation of the soul'."[20]

Carr made essentially the same assumption. He spoke of "that uneasy compromise between power and morality which is the foundation of all political life."[21] ". . . [W]e can neither moralise power nor expel power from politics. . . ." "Every political situation contains mutually incompatible elements of utopia and reality, or morality and power."[22] Carr assumed that only individuals—not groups—are capable of moral behavior. He also assumed that "power" must be power wielded by or at the disposal of the State, that this inevitably involves power depending on military sanctions, and that peaceful behavior is incapable of generating politically relevant power.

POLITICAL MORALITY AND POLITICAL TECHNIQUE

Thus, all three of these writers who recognized the moral difficulties of combining morality and politics found that these difficulties have their roots in the presumed necessity to rely upon violence in politics if one is not to abdicate responsibility for influencing the course of political events. Put another way, the departure in politics from strict adherence to nonviolent beliefs, and the consequent major moral difficulties, are seen to arise from the presumed necessity of using a technique of violent action to wield power and to deal with crises.

It is the presumed absence of an effective power-wielding technique of nonviolent action in politics which thus "requires" the departure from the religious and moral norms requiring abstention from violence, and thus produces the moral difficulties and dilemmas.

Both the "prophet-ultimate ends-utopian" approach and the "reconciler-responsibility-realist" approach are in different ways therefore inadequate because *both* have accepted that politically effective power must in the last analysis include violence, and *neither* has seriously explored the existence or development of politically effective nonviolent power.

In other words, the question of political technique is at the heart of all discussion of political morality. In my opinion, then, all efforts to discuss the application of a "this-worldly" morality without consideration of its application in politics, and all efforts to discuss morality in politics without discussion of political technique are sterile and escapist. These are the most crucial problems confronting us today in moral philosophy and moral theology as well as in practical politics. They are the problems to which attention is urgently demanded—especially by those who believe they share a moral outlook relevant to all of life.

NONVIOLENT TECHNIQUE

The existence of a nonviolent technique of action—capable of wielding and meeting power effectively in times of crisis in defense and in furtherance of moral principles, ways of life, democratic societies, freedom, justice, and the like, so that reliance on violence would no longer be necessary to achieve political effectiveness— would thus pave the way for the union of morality and politics, the union of action with moral principles and the union of nonviolence and political effectiveness.

It has been my contention for some years that such a technique of action exists and has been for several decades in the process of refinement and increasing application under a wide variety of political and historical circumstances. It is true that our knowledge still is highly limited. It is true that there are immense practical difficulties still involved in the possible substitution of this type of action for violence (as war and violent revolution) in difficult political and international circumstances. It is also true, so basic has the role of violence been to politics and international relations as we have known them, that it is not an easy matter to replace such violence with nonviolent sanctions and means of struggle. A rethinking of politics and international relations is clearly required along with experimentation and research.

But despite all these difficulties, there is already sufficient knowledge of the technique of nonviolent action to make possible the challenging of the categorical assumptions about the necessity of violence in politics (violence is today often clearly impractical and irresponsible and nonviolent action often clearly has practical advantages). A more detailed discussion of the technique of non-violent action and its political potentialities is not possible in this chapter. However, it is important to emphasize once again that it has in a large degree been the erroneously presumed nonexistence of an effective power-wielding technique of nonviolent action which has been responsible for the rejection in politics of moral imperatives to nonviolence and for the separation of morality and politics.

In this light, it is both amazing and disturbing that believers in "this worldly" philosophies of nonviolence have often been indifferent and even hostile to the development of nonviolent action as a practical technique of political action. Sometimes the very same people who have found that this "practical" approach to nonviolence compromised their principles have themselves supported political and international policies and actions which relied ultimately upon the threat or use of military power. One can sympathize with the person who, in the presumed absence of other effective means of achieving or preserving peace or some other objective in politics, may reluctantly find it necessary to support such measures involving violence. But for the same person then to be indifferent or hostile to the exploration or development of the practical potentialities of nonviolent action as a possible substitute for violence on the basis that it violates his or her moral principles is difficult to understand or justify.

MORALITY AND PRACTICALITY

Part of the source of this widespread reluctance may be the reverse reason for the reluctance of most politically-oriented persons to be concerned with this nonviolent technique. That is, there has been a predispositon, regardless of thought or events, to look upon the "moral" or "principle-oriented" approach to life as being quite distinct and separate from the "practical" or "political-oriented" approach to life. When pressed, adherents of both approaches will usually admit that the other is also important, but despite this there usually continues a reluctance to see the "moral" and the "practical" approaches to life as fully compatible.

Yet, on the one hand, the approach to life through belief in a moral principle (or moral system), and on the other hand, the practical approach to life through an attempt to understand and learn from the experience of living, are both approaches to "reality." They are both efforts to understand and act upon the nature of existence, especially as related to the experience and role of human beings. These are thus potentially compatible—and not intrinsically opposed—approaches to life.

If so, there is no necessary reason why the "practical" person should categorically reject a "moral" approach or course of action simply because it is "moral." Conversely, there is also no reason why a "moral" person should categorically reject a "practical" approach or course of action because it has been developed or adopted from consideration of "practical" reasons. Does the "moral" person not believe that his or her system of morality and principles are in harmony with the nature of reality and life? And if they are, is not the practical approach—when deeply understood—fully consistent with the moral approach, just as moral behavior in society is often believed to be ultimately the highest form of practicality?*

Is there, then, any reason why the believer in a principled approach to nonviolence should be hostile to the practical approach to the same phenomena? This question is especially crucial when only a minority of people today are likely to adopt a doctrine of nonviolence which they believe to be impractical.

Yet, if humanity is to survive, people must quickly give up reliance on violence to solve conflicts. Millions of people must be willing to do this who will never become believers in nonviolence as a moral principle, but who could well come to see the practical advantages of a substitute technique to use in place of violent revolution and war. (This I have argued elsewhere and shall therefore not develop the point in detail here.)†

In this situation, for believers in a "this worldly" principled nonviolence to decline to do all within their power to further the development of the technique of nonviolent action—by action, and thought, research and analysis—seems to me to involve both human irresponsibility and moral abdication.

---

* This perspective is developed more fully in Chapter Thirteen. "Nonviolence: Moral Principle or Political Technique?"

† See Sharp, "Developing a Substitute for War" and other chapters in Sharp, **Social Power and Political Freedom** (Boston: Porter Sargent Publishers, Inc., 1979).

In the face of our crisis with the dual threats of extermination and tyranny, the requirements of a moral course of action and of the practical solution to the problems of the human conditions today both point to the need to remove violence from politics and international relations, while developing and applying alternative nonviolent means of defending and advancing human dignity, freedom, and international peace.

Thus, in this analysis, both the consideration of the role of a technique of action in political morality and the consideration of the need to resolve the dangerous practical problems facing us, point to the importance of a nonviolent technique of action capable of resolving our moral *and* practical problems. It is to this task of removing violence from politics that we must address ourselves. This primarily requires a technique of action which will make it possible to implement moral principles effectively in the practical political world in which we live.

NOTES TO CHAPTER TWELVE

1. Gerald Bailey, "The Politics of Peace: The Lilly Lectures in Religion" (pamphlet; Richmond, Indiana: Earlham College Press, 1963), p. 1.
2. W. Grigor McClelland, "The Prophet and the Reconciler" (pamphlet; London: Friends' Peace Committee, 1960).
3. Bailey, "The Politics of Peace," p. 2.
4. Ibid.
5. Max Weber, "Politics as a Vocation," in **From Max Weber: Essays in Sociology** (trans., ed., and with an introduction by H.H. Gerth and C. Wright Mills; New York: Oxford University Press [1946], 1958, and London: Routledge & Kegan Paul [1948], 1961), p. 120.
6. Ibid., p. 121.
7. Ibid., p. 120.
8. Ibid., p. 122.
9. Ibid., p. 120.
10. Ibid., p. 121.
11. Ibid., p. 120.
12. Ibid.
13. Ibid., p. 126.
14. E.H. Carr, **The Twenty Years Crisis 1918–1939: An Introduction to International Relations** (Rev. ed. London: Macmillan & Co., [1942] 1946). This summary of his views is based on various parts of the book.
15. Bailey, "The Politics of Peace," p. 7.
16. Carr, **The Twenty Years Crisis 1918–1939**, p. 220.

17. Weber, "Politics as a Vocation," p. 221.
18. Ibid., p. 119. Weber's italics.
19. Ibid., p. 124.
20. Ibid., p. 126.
21. Carr, **The Twenty Years Crisis 1918–1939**, p. 230.
22. Ibid., p. 100.

13

Nonviolence: Moral Principle or Political Technique?

Clues from Gandhi's Thought and Experience[1]

As soon as one tries to apply a nonviolent approach in politics, as Gandhi did, one runs into problems. One of the most important of these problems is whether or not nonviolent action as a political technique is separable from belief systems which stress nonviolence as a moral principle. Or, does the acceptance of nonviolent action in politics require the acceptance of the norms of principled nonviolence, either as a precondition or a corollary of the non-violent technique? These questions have both a philosophical and a political significance. The practical importance of such questions is readily illustrated.

If the technique and the norms are indeed inseparable, and we try to separate them, or acquiesce in their separation, then the consequence of an attempt to apply the technique alone in political conflicts is likely to be failure. It is sometimes suggested that without a belief in nonviolence as an ethical imperative it will be difficult or impossible to maintain the necessary nonviolent discipline in face of repression, or that nonviolent actionists will lack necessary courage, or that the practitioners' low quality nonviolent action will lead to undesirable social consequences. The result of such use, some people suggest, could be increased conflicts, hostilities, bitterness, chaos, and finally an increased reliance on physical violence. Partially because of such reasons, many believers in several types of principled nonviolence[2] have been cool or hostile to the development and use of nonviolent action by people not sharing their beliefs. This opposition is also partially rooted in the believers' preference for giving first place to principles, beliefs, or dogmas.

Others argue, however, that the technique of nonviolent action and the belief system *are* separable. Therefore, they believe, the insistance that they are not is itself likely to lead to a quite different series of undesirable consequences. Most importantly, arguments claiming that the technique and the belief systems are inseparable will confirm the widespread uninformed prejudice that only pacifists can give up violence for nonviolent means. That confirmation will discourage the substitution of nonviolent action for war and other types of political violence, and thus help their perpetuation.

There are, of course, important variations on these two broad positions on the relation of the technique to the belief systems, and these vary in the degree of their consideration of the complex ethical and political factors involved.

Despite the obvious importance of the question whether or not the technique and the belief system are separable, and of what results are likely to follow from their separation or nonseparation, remarkably little attention has been given to this problem. Usually persons holding views on it have made little serious effort to justify those views with rational analysis. This may be in part due to the close relation between this question and one's basic convictions (either the determination to be "true" to one's belief in nonviolence as an ethic, or the determination *not* to believe in it as an universal ethic). Others who have wrestled with the problem, such as Gandhi, have tended, or appeared, to shift from one position to another. Although Gandhi discussed the problem repeatedly, he never attempted to provide a systematic analysis of the factors and influences involved in it. Nevertheless, because Gandhi was an important practitioner of the application of nonviolent action to politics and also one of the most revered exponents of nonviolence as a moral principle, it may be helpful to examine his opinions of the subject. His philosophical and political insights may aid us in seeking a solution to our problem.

The core of Gandhi's contribution to the possible solution of the relation between the principle of nonviolence and the technique of nonviolent action lies in his insights into the relationship between ethical standards and practical behavior. Some, however, believe that Gandhi's contribution to the resolution of this problem lies primarily in his presumed final conclusion that only nonviolence practiced out of inner conviction (identified as the "nonviolence of the brave") was worthwhile, and that the Indian practice of nonviolent struggle had been a complete failure. It is, therefore, necessary to examine briefly at least his views on the "nonviolence of the brave" and the "nonviolence of the weak," and review here his evaluation of the Indian experiments in nonviolent action, which were presented more fully in Chapter Six. It is true that Gandhi's insights and opinions on these subjects are very relevant to the relationship between nonviolence as an ethic and nonviolent action as a practical technique. However, these views are by no means simple ones, nor do they in themselves offer a complete solution to the problem upon which our attention is focused.

INSIGHTS FROM GANDHI

While Gandhi believed in nonviolence as a moral principle and that "pure" individuals could wield immense power which could make organized mass nonviolent struggle unnecessary, he was also convinced that the community as a whole should learn to use nonviolent action and thereby become able to solve its problems by its own efforts. This led to difficult questions for which Gandhi claimed no final answers.*

The popular version of Gandhi's changing views on the relationship between the principle and the technique is roughly this: In the early stages of his career Gandhi advocated the adoption of nonviolent action as a practical means of struggle to achieve certain objectives by people who might otherwise use violence or submit to injustice. This expedient nonviolence Gandhi often called the "nonviolence of the weak." Later, however, especially from the 1930s on, Gandhi became dissatisfied with the results of this and instead emphasized the importance of accepting nonviolence as a comprehensive principle, which he often called "the nonviolence of the brave" or "the nonviolence of the strong." It seems quite simple. It is, therefore, often concluded that Gandhi's final view of how to resolve the problem of how to relate nonviolence as a moral principle to its application in politics was roughly approximate to that of Western pacifists, with the proviso that believers in principled nonviolence ought to seek actively to improve their society.

But such a conclusion is quite in error; Gandhi's views of the problem are far less simple than the above version would suggest. Gandhi's whole approach differed radically from Western pacifism. He also firmly rejected passivity and inaction in face of severe political problems as the worst possible course.[3] Gandhi neither demanded perfect nonviolence nor thought that it was possible.[4] Although imperfection and inconsistencies were inevitable, Gandhi insisted, one's duty was to strive constantly toward the least imperfection and the least inconsistency.[5] Thus the exponent of nonviolence would have to operate in the ordinary world of human beings, choosing as best he or she could, the most appropriate means to serve one's fellow human beings and fulfill one's ethical principles, while always operating with a certain degree of inconsistency and imperfection. This difficulty was even more severe for Gandhi than for exponents of other types of principled nonviolence, because nonviolence for him was not only personal but also social and political. Even in his moments of sharpest anguish he never altered this view.[6]

* Here it is necessary in the next few pages to summarize, and even repeat, certain passages from Chapter Six, "Gandhi's Evaluation of Indian Nonviolent Action," pp. 91–116, along with additional analyses and citations of Gandhi's views.

It is instructive to note that Gandhi's insistance that his important contribution was to offer people a technique with which they could cope themselves with their social and political problems[7] was not reversed when he became dissatisfied with the Indian practice of nonviolent action and when he increasingly emphasized the importance of the "nonviolence of the brave." In fact Gandhi explicitly refuted the view that the riots which occurred in India in 1947 brought into question "the efficacy of non-violence in matters political."[8] In facing the difficulties and dilemmas of how to apply nonviolent means in the political world, Gandhi declined to follow those who believed in certain types of principled nonviolence by withdrawing from political life. Instead he confirmed his confidence in the role of collective nonviolent popular action to solve problems.

Not only was Gandhi convinced that people *ought* to be able to help themselves by using the technique of *satyagraha,* but he also believed that the masses of people were *capable* of doing so.[9] His desire for an improved quality of nonviolence did not mean the rejection of mass nonviolent action.

MORAL PROBLEMS OF INACTION AND ACTION

Gandhi did not, of course, begin his political career with a fully developed outlook or political program. Both his political philosophy and his political technique were, to a considerable degree, worked out and developed in response to immediate social needs and in the fire of political struggle. Thus the technique of *satyagraha* was born in the midst of the conflict between the Indian minority and the South African government.

The problem of how to apply nonviolence in human life was to Gandhi—and this is crucial—not simply a bilateral relationship between an ethical principle and the individual seeking to live according to that principle. *There were also the other dimensions of the individual's obligations and responsibilities.* These included the individual's relationship to the society and the political order, and the relationship of the nonviolent ethic to the sanctions and means of struggle which could be used for social and political objectives. With passivity and submissiveness in face of injustice and oppression rejected by Gandhi as immoral,[10] the problem then became how to act in the existing situation in which serious human needs and significant conflicts were often present.

One was confronted not only with the ethical problems of *acting* in such situations, but also the ethical problems of *not* acting. Gandhi in such instances resolved that he must act, that the victims of the injustice or oppression ought to be offered means of action by which they could potentially right the wrong, and that such means on ethical and practical grounds ought to be nonviolent. Nor could Gandhi wait until he had converted the oppressed group, or even a significant section of it, to a belief in nonviolence as a moral principle.

His approach could be described as opposing spiritual strength to physical might, Gandhi believed. But presented solely in those terms it would gain few adherents.

> However, being a practical man, I do not wait till India recognizes the practicability of the spiritual life in the political world. India considers herself to be powerless and paralysed before the machine-guns, the tanks and the aeroplanes of the English, and takes up non-cooperation out of her weakness. It must still serve the same purpose, namely, bring her delivery from the crushing weight of British injustice, if a sufficient number of people practise it, [he wrote in 1920].[11]

Sometimes Gandhi explained his advocacy of limited nonviolence for achieving political objectives in those terms, and at other times, he explained it in part in terms of his own spiritual imperfections.[12]

He called this political use of nonviolent action by nonpacifists "non-violence as a policy."

> The non-violence that I have preached from Congress platforms is non-violence as a policy. . . Non-violence being a policy means that it can upon due notice be given up when it proves unsuccessful or ineffective.[13]

> A policy may be changed, a creed cannot. But either is as good as the other whilst it is held.[14]

While it was maintained as a policy, Gandhi insisted the nonviolent approach had to be applied consistently and honestly—and with full confidence in the *policy itself.* "I cannot get rid of the conviction, that the greatest obstacle to our progress towards Swaraj [self-rule] is our want of faith in our policy.[15]

It is usually understood that Gandhi's later strong deprecations of the Indian practice of nonviolent action mean that he saw the root cause of the difficulties in the attempt to practice nonviolent action as a policy, rather than having made the effort to promote it as a creed for the whole of life. The above statement, however, raises the question as to whether he saw the difficulties to be rooted, in part at least, in inadequacies in the application of nonviolent action *within the context of nonviolent action as a policy.* This interpretation is supported by at least one statement on the validity of nonviolent action as a policy, made long after he came to emphasize the "nonviolence of the brave." In a voluminous letter to the British Government of India, refuting charges against himself and the Congress based on the events of 1942 and 1943, Gandhi wrote:

> I admit at once that there is "a doubtful proportion of full believers" in my "theory of non-violence." But it should not be forgotten that I have also said that for my movement I do not at all need believers in the theory of non-violence, full or imperfect. It is enough if people carry out the rules of non-violent action.[16]

This was as late as July 1943.

In applying nonviolent action as a practical technique for limited objectives, however, Gandhi always insisted that the application had to be honest, the maintenance of nonviolence had to be thorough, and the policy had to be well implemented.[17] Otherwise, it should be rejected. For example, members of the Indian National Congress who did not really believe in the organization's policy of nonviolent means ought either to have the policy changed or resign.

IMPERFECT BUT STORMPROOF

Gandhi presented *satyagraha* both in South Africa and in India as a practical technique of action, and it was accepted as such.

> People followed my advice and took to non-violent resistance against the British Government, because they wanted to offer some sort of resistance.[18]

> The people had followed him then, because they knew they could not face the might of British arms in any other way.[19]

There is little doubt about the accuracy of this explanation. It radically challenges the common Western view that the use of nonviolent, instead of violent, means in India was due to special religious or psychological qualities of the Indian people. In this situation, in order to maintain the highest possible standards of nonviolence, and hence the greatest effectiveness, and the required coherence and direction in the movement, Gandhi instituted a system of strong leadership in the initial stages of such campaigns, and also required effective discipline among the actionists.

Not being inclined to systematic analysis and being occupied with immediate difficulties just before and after independence, especially the riots, Gandhi never attempted a carefully balanced evaluation of the Indian experiments with nonviolent struggle. He did, however, in a variety of articles and speeches offer a whole series of observations, evaluations, and comments.* These sometimes seemed to vary with his mood, being more self-critical in times of depression over events in India. Because these comments are often flatly contradictory, the recapitulation of, say, only his harsher judgements will give a quite distorted impression.[20] Late in his career, especially, Gandhi saw the Indians' expedient use of the nonviolent technique in an unfavorable light.

> But their non-violence, I must confess, was born of their help-lessness. Therefore, it was the weapon of the weak.[21]

Gandhi even came to the point where he repeatedly described the Indian practice by the derogatory term "passive resistance"—which in Gandhi's view had such connotations as weakness, passitivity, hatred, and willingness to use violence when it seemed to have a chance of success.[22]

By focusing only on Gandhi's deprecation of the Indian practice of nonviolent action, it would be easy to conclude that Gandhi must have regretted having advocated and led the expedient use of nonviolent action in South Africa and India. Such a conclusion, however, would be quite inaccurate. "Yes, I adhere to my opinion that I did well to present to the Congress non-violence as an expedient," he wrote in 1942.

---

* For more details, see Chapter Six, "Gandhi's Evaluation of Indian Nonviolent Action."

I could not have done otherwise, if I was to introduce it into politics. In South Africa too I introduced it as an expedient. It was successful. . . . I have no sense of disappointment in me over the results obtained. If I had started with men who accepted non-violence as a creed, I might have ended with myself. Imperfect as I am, I started with imperfect men and women and sailed on an uncharted ocean. Thank God that, though the boat has not reached its haven, it has proved fairly stormproof.[23]

Gandhi told students in late 1947 that:

He had all along laboured under an illusion. But he was never sorry for it. He realized that if his vision were not covered by that illusion, India would never have reached the point which it had today.[24]

The use of nonviolent action had resulted in a considerable strengthening both of the Indian National Congress and of the people as a whole.[25]

India's experience in the application of nonviolent struggle had been "a very imperfect experiment" in the use of the technique by the masses of mankind, but still useful. "We may not be perfect in our use of it, but we definitely discard the use of violence, and grow from failure to success."[26] Keeping in mind both the achievements and the inadequacies in the new situation, one should press on with the political application of nonviolent action. "It was the duty of Free India to perfect the instrument of non-violence for dissolving collective conflicts, if its freedom was going to be really worth while."[27]

NONVIOLENCE OF THE BRAVE AND OF THE WEAK

Repeatedly, over a long period of years and especially in his last few, Gandhi prescribed the "nonviolence of the brave" as the type which avoided the weaknesses he saw in the Indian practice. The impression is widespread that this type of nonviolence simply meant that one believed in "principled nonviolence," or in adherence to nonviolence and rejection of violence, because of ethical, moral, or religious beliefs. This would provide, if accepted, a simple, one-sided, solution to the question of whether the nonviolent political technique is separable from an ethical system

enjoining nonviolence. An examination of Gandhi's own descriptions of the "nonviolence of the brave" does not confirm the
prevalent simple interpretation, however. Because of this, and
because of serious problems in the concept of the "nonviolence of
the weak" (and in the term itself), it is not possible to seek a
solution to our problem within the simple categories of nonviolence
out of conviction and nonviolence out of practicality.

The frequent complexity of Gandhi's views extends to the
"nonviolence of the brave" and the "nonviolence of the weak." It
is true that one of the important qualities of the first, is that it is a
"creed" and not a "policy," that is it is a permanent approach to all
of life including the problems of society and politics.[28] This type of
nonviolence Gandhi also called "the enlightened non-violence of
resourcefulness,"[29] which indicates another of its qualities. Belief in
the nonviolent ethic was *not* by itself, in Gandhi's view, sufficient to
qualify one as a votary of the nonviolence of the brave. Creativity
and the use of the intellect were also needed in the application of
nonviolence in meeting the problems of personal and social life.

> A mere belief in *ahimsa* [nonviolence] . . . will not do. It should be
> intelligent and creative. If intellect plays a large part in the field of
> violence, I hold that it plays a larger part in the field of non-
> violence.[30]

The "nonviolence of the brave" was also called by Gandhi the
"nonviolence of the strong"[31] and the "nonviolence of the stout of
heart."[32] These three terms together describe two other qualities of
this type of nonviolence as Gandhi saw it. First, the *satyagrahi* with
such confidence in the nonviolent course would be both willing to
act, and nonviolently to persist in the action, in very difficult
circumstances and in face of severe repression and danger.[33] Had
the Indian practice of nonviolent action been the "nonviolence of
the brave," the social and political consequences would, in
Gandhi's opinion, have been quite different. There would have
been no riots, and Indian internal democracy and Indian society
would have been greatly improved and inwardly strengthened.[34]
Gandhi believed that the quality of the nonviolent action was also
relevant for its world-wide acceptance.[35]

Despite Gandhi's depression, disappointment, and lack of
ready-made answers, he maintained his determination to press on

with the development of a nonviolent way out of the difficulties faced by India and the world.[36] He confessed that his effort to discover how to cultivate the "nonviolence of the brave" had been rather "desultory." "I have not concentrated upon it, or given it the weight I might have."[37] Even if the problem of how to develop this type of nonviolence were adequately solved, there would remain the related but different problem of how to apply this type of nonviolence. Although there is a strong tendency in Gandhi's discussions of these problems to revert to a greater reliance on individuals and small groups, only some few weeks before his assassination he explicitly rejected any interpretation which limited nonviolence to personal, and not group or political relationships:

> That non-violence which only an individual can use is not much use in terms of society. Man is a social being. His accomplishments to be of use must be such as any person with sufficient diligence can attain. That which can be exercised only among friends is of value only as a spark of non-violence. It cannot merit the appelation of *ahimsa*.[38]

WEAKNESS OR STRENGTH?

An invalid preconception seems to be built into the terminology which Gandhi used in discussing the relationship of the principle and the technique which, if uncritically accepted, may interfere with reasonable and objective analysis. The term which seems to be causing difficulties is "the nonviolence of the weak." At times he associated undesirable results with this use of nonviolent action, saying, " . . . when it becomes a cloak for our weakness, it emasculates us."[39]

A series of questions are relevant here which require answers before one can assume that the matter stands simply as Gandhi at times described it. One of these is: *When* does nonviolence become a cloak for weakness? Is it *any* time people use nonviolent action as an expedient? Or, is it when they plead reasons of nonviolence to justify *inaction* in crisis situations? Or when? Quite different conclusions follow from such alternative answers.

To the degree that Gandhi indentified the "nonviolence of the weak" with the use of nonviolent action as an expedient technique, the question arises as to why, as a generalization, one can describe such use as based upon weakness. In at least two passages Gandhi identified the source of this "weakness." In one case he said that "their non-violence . . . was born of their helplessness. Therefore, it was the weapon of the weak."[40] In the other, Gandhi said that the Indian use of the technique was "passive resistance which only the weak offer because they are unable, not unwilling, to offer armed resistance."[41]

If these are really Gandhi's reasons for choosing the term the "nonviolence of the weak," then it is a highly questionable term. It not only has strong emotional overtones but seems to be based on two *non sequitors*. For example, if people in a difficult situation have felt helpless, and then attempt to act by resorting to non-violent action, is not the earlier condition of helplessness changed? It is indeed one of the basic characteristics of nonviolent action in both theory and practice that by resort to the technique people become able to cease being the helpless victims of forces beyond their control, and act to influence the course of their own lives and society. This view was firmly supported by Gandhi. But if, then, the condition of helplessness is ended through the use of nonviolent action and replaced by a condition of self-help and self-reliance by corporate action to change the course of events, then Gandhi's above statement that "their non-violence . . . was born of their helplessness" does not hold. Their earlier inaction and passivity, instead, were born of their helplessness. But their later nonviolent action was instead born of a new determination and ability to influence their own fate. Therefore, it would *not* follow that their expedient nonviolent action "was the weapon of the weak".

In the second passage cited above, Gandhi related the alleged weakness in nonviolent action to the inability, not the unwillingness, to use "armed resistance." Here too, there are a number of unasked questions: Why should a condition of *military* weakness be reason to describe the substituted nonviolent action as "weak"? It would seem that the condition of military weakness is quite different from a condition of weakness in nonviolent action, due to the radical differences in the two techniques. Also, Gandhi himself repeatedly said that the Indian use of nonviolent action as an expedient had considerably strengthened both the Indian people as a whole and the Indian National Congress. He said among other things that "the fact remains that under non-violence we have progressed from strength to strength even through our apparent failures and setbacks."[42] In 1925 he wrote:

> The non-violence I teach is active non-violence of the strongest. But the weakest can partake in it without becoming weaker. They can only be the stronger for having been in it. The masses are far bolder today than they ever were.[43]

There seems little justification here either for labeling an expedient use of nonviolent action as the "nonviolence of the weak." Gandhi's choice of terminology in this particular case seems therefore to be inaccurate and likely, if not replaced, to contribute to distortions in perception and analysis.

Gandhi's occasional deprecation of others for the use of nonviolent action as simply a substitute for political violence in conflicts seems very unreasonable when it was to a very significant degree precisely the substitute which Gandhi had himself advocated, developed, and urged others to adopt. It is evident that on different occasions Gandhi applied different criteria in his evaluation of what was needed and in his criticism of what had taken place. Seen in the perspective of his whole outlook and program, these criteria were not necessarily ultimately inconsistent with each other. However, Gandhi did not always make the interrelationships between them clear, and the result often is apparent flat contradictions between certain of his own views, often held simultaneously, on the same subject.

POLITICAL ACTION REAFFIRMED

Although the solution to the problem of the relationship between the nonviolent ethic and the technique does not lie in these aspects of Gandhi's thought, he does contribute in a significant way to its resolution. There is a great deal in his thinking which points to a possible answer to the problem with which we began: is nonviolent action as a political technique separable from belief systems which stress nonviolence as a moral principle? Some of Gandhi's basic views which we deem to be relevant in seeking a solution to this problem may be briefly summarized. First, Gandhi rejected passivity and inaction in face of political problems as the worst possible course. He also affirmed emphatically, long after his dissatisfaction with the Indian practice, that nonviolence must be applied in politics. This was based both on his general philosophy and on his view of the needs of political life. In Gandhi's philosophy, moral principles and religion could not be separated from social and political life.

> I claim that human mind or human society is not divided into watertight compartments called social, political and religious. All act and react upon one another.[44]

> I do not believe that the spiritual law works on a field of its own. On the contrary, it expresses itself only through the ordinary activities of life. It thus affects the economic, the social and the political fields.[45]

In a series of statements, made as late as 1940 to the end of 1947 during the period of Gandhi's greatest depression over the course of events in India, he categorically affirmed the relevance of nonviolence to society as a whole, and to politics in particular. In fact at a meeting of the All-India Congress Committee in January 1942 (at which the proposal that the Congress offer the British support in the war in exchange for independence was discussed), Gandhi insisted with no regrets on the political nature of nonviolent action as he had presented it to India and rejected the views of those who would dismiss his policy as being "religious."

> I placed it before the Congress as a political method, to be employed for the solution of the political questions. It may be it is a novel method, but it does not on that account lose its political character ... As a political method, it can always be changed, modified, altered, and even given up in preference to another. If, therefore, I say to you that our policy should not be given up today, I am talking political wisdom. It is political insight. It has served us in the past, it has enabled us to cover many stages toward independence, and it is as a politician that I suggest to you that it is a grave mistake to contemplate its abandonment. If I have carried the Congress with me all these years, it is in my capacity as a politician. It is hardly fair to describe my method as religious, because it is new.[46]

Despite Gandhi's dissatisfaction with the Indian practice of nonviolent action, he did not revert to a "fellowship of true believers" who would save the world, but instead affirmed the importance of corporate and mass action by which people could themselves achieve a sense of their own strength and power and thereby correct the particular problem they were facing. A "perfect" *satyagrahi* was not possible, and in any case was not the desirable means of solving political problems. Instead, Gandhi presented the means by which "millions" could act in order to "solve their own difficulties." This emphasis on the political relevance of nonviolent action, and the desirability of mass action, clearly excluded in Gandhi's thinking any retirement into purism as a way of meeting the problem of how to combine the nonviolent ethic with the technique of action. The question is then, how, within the context of social and political action (which must necessarily include people who do not believe in nonviolence as a moral principle), the ethic and the technique are related.

THE "ETHICAL" AND THE "PRACTICAL"

As we have seen, Gandhi did not pretend to have solved this problem. It is possible, however, that there lies within his own thinking some insights which may significantly contribute to a possible solution to the problem of the relationship of the ethic and the technique. Some of these insights from Gandhi belong more properly in the field of philosophy, and others in the field of practical politics. But they are in Gandhi's thinking interrelated and are both stimulating and suggestive of a possible resolution of the problem.

Behind the usual formulation of the tension between the "ethical" and the "practical" is the assumption that they are not necessarily identical, and even may be opposed to each other. In the usual type of politics this assumption is often traced to the belief that violence is necessary as the ultimate sanction in politics in order for power to be effectively applied in defense or the furtherance of ethically desirable principles and objectives.[47] But in Gandhi's thinking this is not the case.[48] Furthermore, as we have seen, Gandhi rejected any withdrawal from the "practical" problems or from political action in an effort to solve the "ethical" dilemma. Yet, despite the rejection by Gandhi of both violence and purism, the problem of relating the "ethical" and the "practical" still remains. In discussions by others of this problem within the context of nonviolent means it seems often still to be assumed that the ethically most desirable course is not always the politically most practical course.

However, Gandhi's view of the relationship between ethical action and practical action is that when fully understood the two types of actions are in the long-run identical. This view, if accepted, opens the way for a different solution to the problem.

The very term *"satyagraha"* has connotations of the union of ethical and practical action. *"Agraha"* means "holding fast," "adherence," or "insistance." *"Sat"* or *"Satya,"* also from the Sanscrit, means "Truth," but Truth here connotes "essence of being." Thus *"satyagraha"* may be interpreted as clinging to, holding fast to, adherence to, or insistance upon "Truth." With "Truth" having connotations of essence of being, *"satyagraha"* means that in one's action one holds to the essence of being or ultimate reality. Action thus in harmony with the nature of existence and reality must in the final analysis be action which "works" and is "practical."

Within this framework of thought it would be inconceivable that action in order to "work" had to go contrary to the nature of existence and the "laws" of life. The principles or "laws" of "God" or "Truth" were believed by Gandhi to be universally valid and operative: ". . . He and His Law abide everywhere and govern everything."[49] Gandhi's secretary Mahadev Desai explained Gandhi's views on the relationship of such principles or "laws" to human affairs:

> . . . Gandhiji has dared to experiment [with] the method of Non-violence on the mundane plane . . . because . . . [he] refuses to make any distinction between the mundane and the "other-wordly" plane so far as the moral and physical laws which govern them are concerned. For him the outside universe is but a reflection of the inside universe . . . .

Furthermore, Gandhi held "the conviction that moral principles have no meaning unless they can be made to serve as guides of conduct in the daily affairs of men."[50] Gandhi similarly wrote:

> Religion which takes no account of practical affairs and does not help to solve them, is no religion. And that is why I am putting a religious matter before you in a practical form.[51]

Gandhi himself sometimes formulated this assumed relationship between the "ethical" and the "practical" course of action in clear terms, and in other statements simply assumed the relationship.

> I am not "a statesman in the garb of a saint." But since Truth is the highest wisdom, sometimes my acts appear to be consistent with the highest statesmanship. But I hope I have no policy in me save the policy of truth and *ahimsa*. I will not sacrifice truth and ahimsa even for the deliverance of my country or religion. This is as much as to say that neither can be so delivered.[52]

It was thus in the context both of this general outlook and of the political situation that Gandhi insisted that "Satyagraha is, as a matter of fact and in the long run, the most expeditious course."[53] Gandhi again touched on the point when writing of the characteristics of a leader of a *satyagraha* campaign during the 1928 Bardoli struggle:

> The leader depends not on his own strength but on that of God. He acts as the Voice within guides him. Very often, therefore, what are practical politics so called are unrealities to him, though in the end his proved to be the most practical politics.[54]

Over a decade later, Gandhi wrote:

> If any action of mine claimed to be spiritual is proved to be unpractical it must be pronounced to be a failure. I do believe that the most spiritual act is the most practical in the true sense of the term.[55]

MEANS AND ENDS

Gandhi's view of the ultimate identity of the ethical and the practical is interrelated with his view of the relationship between means and ends in social and political action. "Means and end are convertible terms in my philosophy of life," he wrote.[56] In Gandhi's view the end which is actually achieved grows out of means which are used in the effort to achieve the intended goal. "The means may be likened to a seed, the end to a tree; and there is just the same inviolable connection between the means and the end as there is between the seed and the tree."[57] He termed the common view that there is no connection between the means and the end "a great mistake."

> Through that mistake even men who have been considered religious have committed grievous crimes. Your reasoning is the same as saying that we can get a rose through planting a noxious weed. If I want to cross the ocean, I can do so only by means of a vessel; if I were to use a cart for that purpose, both the cart and I would soon find the bottom.[58]

Gandhi accepted the importance of determining the goal, but emphasized that simple repetition of the goal or spelling it out in great detail would not take one toward it if one does not know and apply the means of achieving it.

> I have therefore, concerned myself principally with the conservation of the means and their progressive use. I know if we can take care of them attainment of the goal is assured. I feel too that our progress towards the goal will be in exact proportion to the purity of our means. This method may appear to be long, perhaps too long, but I am convinced that it is the shortest.[59]

It was therefore in Gandhi's view reasonable to maintain that "if one takes care of the means, the end will take care of itself."[60] Gandhi rejected the view that "means are after all means," arguing instead that "means are after all everything."

> As the means so the end. There is no wall of separation between means and end. Indeed the Creator has given us control (and that too very limited) over means, none over the end. Realization of the goal is in exact proportion to that of the means. This is a proposition that admits of no exception.[61]

This view of the relationship of means to ends led Gandhi to reject violent means to achieve desirable goals. The view that "violent or unjust" means were justified if the end were good was "pernicious." "Many movements had come to grief by reliance on doubtful means."[62] "Two wrongs will not make one right."[63] "We reap exactly as we sow."[64] " . . . [F]air means alone can produce fair results. . . ."[65]

Gandhi's view of the means as instrumental, that is, as causally related to the ends achieved, led him to concentrate on the immediate and intermediate steps toward a goal, instead of attempting to plan in detail the whole series of actions until final achievement of the ultimate goal.[66] Because of his view of the instrumental nature of means in political action, Gandhi emphasized the importance of using only nonviolent means. The use of violent and unjust means in an effort to "hurry up" the achievement of a certain goal would in his view prove disastrous and prevent the achievement of the desired end in a recognizable form. One of the ways in which Gandhi sought to reduce the tempatation to use such self-defeating means was to emphasize "faith in a good deed producing only a good result: that, in any opinion, is the Gita doctrine of work without attachment."[67] He said in 1940 that "for over 50 years I have trained myself never to be concerned about the result. What I should be concerned about is the means. . . ."[68] Much earlier, he had related nonattachment to the intended goal with his view of the relationship of means and ends.

> . . . [T]o be detached from fruits of actions is not to be ignorant of them, or to disregard or disown them. To be detached is never to abandon action because the contemplated result may not follow. On the contrary, it is proof of immovable faith in the certainty of the contemplated result following in due course.[69]

Thus Gandhi drew on the Hindu concept of "nonattached action," going back at least as far as the *Bhagavad Gita,* and sought to apply it in politics. He maintained that action which is determined on the basis of ethical or moral standards turns out in the final analysis to be the more practical course than that determined by short-term expediency for achieving the desired goal.

THE "PRACTICAL" AND THE "ETHICAL"

Gandhi's view of the ultimate identity of the "ethical" and the "practical" in social and political action may provide a key which may open the way to consideration of a relatively neglected possible solution to the problem of the relationship between the nonviolent ethic and the nonviolent technique of action.

Reasoning from the assumed identity of the "ethical" and the "practical," Gandhi concluded, as we have seen, that if one determined one's political actions on the basis of their consistency with the moral principle, one's actions would finally be proved to be the most practical ones. Such actions would contribute instrumentally to the achievement of a result harmonious with the nonviolent means and one's original humanitarian goal. This conclusion would be accepted by all believers in a "this-worldly" oriented type of principled nonviolence. They see their moral principles to be universally valid and in accordance with "reality." Reasoning from universal principles to particular problems, they conclude that human actions based on those principles in the long run are "practical" and "work" in terms of achieving humanitarian objectives and a society more in harmony with the ethical principles. For these believers, therefore, the way is open for an identification of the ethical behavior and practical action, and therefore for a combination of the moral principle with the political technique, provided that they can see a way to apply the technique which does not threaten to violate the principle. There should therefore be no intrinsic reason why they should object to courses of action presented as the most practical ones when the action is consistent with their nonviolent ethic.

Can we, however, go further than this in seeking a resolution of the problem? It should be noted that both Gandhi's discussion of "nonattached action" and the above view of believers in principled nonviolence are based upon one-way reasoning, from the ethic to the practicality of the action. This reasoning is, therefore, likely to appeal only to persons who already accept a belief system which prohibits violence and enjoins nonviolence. Such persons are, of course, a very small section of the population, and (although at times they may have a disproportionate influence), their views will not predominate when the overwhelming majority of nonbelievers is of the opinion that in fact the prescribed "ethical" course of action is not at all identical with the "practical" course. This majority is unable to accept the universal validity of moral principles as part of what they believe to be abstract philosophical or religious systems. To them, the question of whether particular social policies are valid or not cannot be judged solely by whether they are consistent with such moral principles. They believe, instead, that the achievement of moral principles in human society, imperfect as it is, requires the willingness at times to take actions which they believe contribute to the defeat of forces which blatantly violate such moral principles, even though the action itself when viewed in isolation is inconsistent with those principles. In other words, these people decide on what actions must be taken on the basis of whether they can see a reasonable likelihood that these acts are practical and will "work" in opposing forces of "greater evil" and in achieving in society those principles which they hold to be fundamental. These are generally the same ultimate principles as those held by believers in principled nonviolence.

"TWO-WAY" REASONING?

Gandhi's basic view of the ultimate identity of the "ethical" and the "practical" does not by its nature restrict one to the "one-way" reasoning from the ethical to the practical which he and others have used. It is, theoretically at least, just as possible (though it may be much more difficult) to determine first what is ultimately the most practical course of behavior which "works" in the long-run to achieve desirable humanitarian goals, and then to conclude that this must therefore be in harmony with "reality" or "the nature of things." That course of behavior would be finally identifiable as the "ethical" or "moral" course of social or political action. If the ethical equals the practical, it is, to say it another way, theoretically just as possible to begin at either end of the equation and work toward the other end. This was implied at least once by Gandhi (as we noted) when he wrote that an action which proved "impractical" failed to fulfill the characteristics of a spiritual action. If one could begin at either end of the equation, this would, as we shall see, have important implications for the relationship between the nonviolent norm and the technique of nonviolent action.

One could take some examples of how this approach to the ethical through the practical might operate for the moment within the context of the use of nonviolent action. Believers in principled nonviolence who have sought to practice nonviolent action have firmly insisted that there must be no physical violence used by or on behalf of the nonviolent actionists. Often they have also urged avoidance of expressions of hostility and feelings of hatred, and at times they have pleaded for "love" of the opponents. Given a belief in the nonviolent ethic it is very easy to conclude that both physical violence and expressions of personal hostility should be eschewed in the use of nonviolent action. But it is quite possible to conclude that physical violence must be excluded from the behavior of the nonviolent actionists because such behavior seriously disrupts the working of the technique. Physical violence introduces forces and processes which operate contrary to the technique's mechanisms of change, and finally contribute not to victory but to defeat.[70] (Such practical arguments against the use of violence as part of a nonviolent struggle, or parallel with it, were in fact often voiced by Gandhi.)

An understanding of past experience in specific cases of nonviolent struggle and of the general dynamics and mechanisms of the technique may thus make one aware that such use of physical violence against the opponent instead of weakening him may in fact strengthen him and weaken the resisters. This violence is likely to serve as an excuse and "justification" for severe repression, to reduce the sympathy and support for the nonviolent actionists from "third parties," to increase the loyalty and obedience of the opponent's own troops, agents, and general home population, and to alienate support for, and participation in the nonviolent struggle from the population of potential resisters. The resisters' violence, therefore, is likely not only *not* to weaken the opponent but may reverse the operation of the process of "political *jui-jitsu*" which nonviolent action introduces and thereby strengthen the opponent while weakening the resisters.

By such examination of the nature of nonviolent action (including its requirements for successful operation, its dynamics, and mechanisms) one can reach the same point of rejecting physical violence during the use of nonviolent action as one would reach by arguing from the nonviolent ethic. It is conceivable that a similar analysis of the influence of expressions of hostility and hatred on the operation of the mechanisms of change in nonviolent action might, under at least certain circumstances, lead to a similar conclusion.

IDENTICAL REQUIREMENTS

It would be possible to offer other examples in addition to the maintenance of nonviolent behavior to illustrate the frequent approximation or identity of the demands of the nonviolent ethic and the "practical" requirements for the successful application of the technique of nonviolent action. One further example here may suffice to illustrate the general point: the necessity for nonviolent actionists to persist in their chosen course despite the punishment and repression inflicted upon them by the opponent. Gandhi usually described this as the role of "self-suffering" which he often associated with Hindu religious concept of *tapasya,* meaning (roughly) penance. But this can be represented not as penance or self-suffering for the cause of Truth, but as a necessary requirement for the successful operation of the psychological, sociological and political mechanisms of nonviolent action. Just as in military campaigns there is a chance of success only if the soldiers stand firm, risking suffering or death rather than fleeing from the danger, so too in nonviolent campaigns a comparable risk is required from the nonviolent soldiers. The practical requirements for the successful operation of the technique once again are identical with the demands imposed by the ethical or religious principles.

Of course, it is often easier to reason from a universal principle to the specific application of the principle, than it is to determine that behavior identical with that enjoined by the principle is required on the basis of detailed knowledge of the nature, requirements, and consequences of nonviolent action as a political technique. But at least this is a possible contribution to the process whereby the behavior of nonviolent actionists who believe in principled nonviolence and the behavior of those who use the technique as an effective means to a given end become virtually identical. Thereby a significant degree of the tension between principle and practicality within the context of the use of nonviolent action is drastically reduced or even removed. If this interpretation and understanding are correct, the way is open for the intelligent and informed use of the technique even by persons not believing in a universal nonviolent ethic to be as consistent and reliable as the use of the technique by believers in the universal principle. The development of this type of approach would of course require much greater research and analysis on nonviolent action in order to broaden and deepen the knowledge and understanding of the nature and operation of the technique, so that evaluations of the likely consequences of alternative courses of action could be soundly based.

The above discussion has been an exploration of the possible relevance of Gandhi's view of the ultimate identity of the "ethical" and the "practical" for the resolution of the frequent tensions between these two approaches within the context in which reliance has already been placed on the nonviolent technique. It is possible that the Gandhian view of the ultimate identity of the "ethical" and the "practical" may have another at least equally significant contribution to make.

MAINTAINING REQUIRED STANDARDS

Gandhi himself of course often urged his followers to pursue on grounds of practicality the standards of behavior in *satyagraha* as political struggle which were also demanded by his system of norms. It is highly significant for the problems of relating the nonviolent ethic to the nonviolent political technique that, despite his criticisms of the inadequacy of the Indian practice, Gandhi did not conclude that he had been wrong to recommend nonviolent action as a practical political technique for use by people who did not believe in principled nonviolence. Such statements as those made in 1942, 1946, and 1947, [71] were repeated long after he became dissatisfied with the Indian practice. Rather than concluding that the fault with the Indian use of nonviolent action lay simply in the absence of belief in the moral principle, Gandhi suggested that the Indian difficulties could be rooted in inadequacies in the application of the technique *within the context of nonviolent action as a policy.* The most emphatic of such judgements was made in 1931, but he made statements which supported that view as late as 1940 and 1943.[72]

It has been argued by some, as we noted, that without a belief in principled nonviolence, it will be most difficult or impossible to maintain the necessary degree of courage, nonviolent discipline, or absence of ill will and hatred among the nonviolent actionists. Such reduced standards of behavior would of course introduce extreme difficulties into the operation of nonviolent action. It is instructive to look at these three points in light of Gandhi's conclusions and the Indian experiments.

The view that people who do not believe in principled non-violence will lack the necessary courage to use nonviolent action is not supported by the evidence. First, courage is not monopolized by believers in principled nonviolence. Great courage has been demonstrated by users of violence, and on the other hand believers in principled nonviolence have not without exception possessed this quality in every situation. Second, while it is often maintained that the "religious" or "other-worldly" beliefs often associated with belief in principled nonviolence give a greater tenacity than that of nonbelievers, it has been demonstrated that avowed atheists and materialists have in extreme situations been equally tenacious and heroic. Last, in the context of nonviolent action itself, there is a whole series of instances in which nonviolent actionists, who did not believe in nonviolence as an universal moral principle, nevertheless practiced the technique with great persistance and heroism in the face of severe suffering and even death. Such examples of course have occurred in the West as well as in the Indian campaigns. Gandhi recognized this, and cited the 1930-31 campaign in particular:

> Did not thousands of men and women brave hardships during the salt campaign equal to any that soldiers are called upon to bear? No different capacity is required from what has been already evinced, if India has to contend against an invader.[73]

Gandhi opposed the view that nonpacifists could not maintain the necessary nonviolent discipline under time of stress,[74] and emphasized the importance of confidence in the policy, qualified leadership, confidence in the leaders, discipline, and appropriate attitudes. Since Gandhi's time there have been cases in which expedient nonviolent action has been used with adequate maintenance of nonviolent discipline.

Even when it comes to the question of the attitudes of the nonviolent actionists toward the members of the opponent group, the issue is not clearly in favor of the critics of expedient nonviolent action. In the first place, there is no necessary connection between emotions and attitudes on the one hand and beliefs on the other. Anyone with considerable association with pacifist groups will know that some of the most hostile and aggressive people simultaneously are opponents of violence and believers in principled nonviolence. Similarly, anyone with significant contact with military personnel will know that many exponents of violent means can be, in their personalities and attitudes, far less hostile and far more sympathetic than some pacifists. Second, while Gandhi did charge that Indian nonviolent actionists had frequently continued to harbor "violence in the breast" (hence producing undesirable results),[75] he also, as late as November 1939, refuted the view that the masses could not practice nonviolent action because of proneness to "anger, hate [and] ill-will," citing two cases in which nonviolent actionists who did not believe in the nonviolent ethic had acted without ill will.[76] There have since been other Western experiences which confirm that this is possible; indeed some English practitioners of expedient nonviolent action have reported that during and following such actions they have experienced a reduction of personal hostilities both toward members of the opponent group and in their personal lives. Since Gandhi affirmed the possibility of practitioners of expedient nonviolent action maintaining the recommended attitudes and emotions toward members of the opponent group, and also on another occasion identified the "nonviolence of the weak" as "non-violence of the mere body without the cooperation of the mind,"[77] even the view that all expedient nonviolent action falls within his classification of the "nonviolence of the weak" is cast into doubt.

If, then, the appropriate standards of behavior can in fact be maintained by nonviolent actionists using the technique as a practical means toward the achievement of certain social or political objectives, it is further evidence that it may be possible to develop a more adequate solution to the problem of the relationship between the nonviolent ethic and the nonviolent technique of action.

NONVIOLENT GOALS AND NONVIOLENT MEANS

If some doubt then is cast on the usual understanding of the nature of the "nonviolence of the weak" as Gandhi understood it (as well as on the validity of the term itself), the usual understanding of the "nonviolence of the brave" as being equated with "principled nonviolence" is emphatically refuted as inadequate by a close look at its characteristics as described by Gandhi.[78] As we saw in Chapter Six, and recounted earlier in this chapter, Gandhi listed five qualities of the "nonviolence of the brave": (1) it was a "creed", which meant (a) that it would not be given up in favor of violence in difficult times, and (b) that nonviolence would be applied in all areas of life; (2) it required resourcefulness; (3) creativity in its application was needed; (4) the use of the intellect was required; and (5) bravery and courage were needed (so that the nonviolent actionists would be able to suffer without retaliation even in face of severe provocation and against great odds).

Only the *first* of these qualities is clearly connected with principled nonviolence. The other qualities are either not at all, or not necessarily, associated with the nonviolent ethic. Believers in principled nonviolence can, for example, be very uncreative and unresourceful. They can act largely intuitively or emotionally without a significant use of the intellect, and they may not all, without exception, possess great courage. There is even evidence that some practitioners of expedient nonviolent action, perhaps feeling less sure of themselves or less self-satisfied may be more likely to be creative and to use the intellect to a greater degree in applying nonviolent action. It is quite clear that Gandhi did not regard simple belief in the nonviolent ethic or nonviolence as a "creed" as adequate, just as he did not regard a crude application of expedient nonviolent action as acceptable.

It is possible to press the matter even further, focusing on the first characteristic: nonviolence as a "creed." The two qualities which Gandhi cited as characteristics of the "creed" are: first, that the nonviolence is maintained in spite of apparent defeats or lack of success, and not then given up, as might be the case with those following nonviolent action as a policy, and, second, the believer in nonviolence as a "creed" will seek to apply it to all areas of his or her life. Let us now look at these two qualities in the light of Gandhi's view of the ultimate identity of the "ethical" and the "practical" courses of action.

As Gandhi's belief in the nonviolent principle was "this–worldly" oriented, it is valid to examine what such a belief means in terms of personal and social life. Broadly speaking, its significance could be divided into goals (or desired conditions) and means (or ways of action). This implies, of course, a somewhat rationalist way of looking at the realities, and people frequently approach life less rationally relying largely on intuition and feelings. This does not, however, by itself invalidate the discussion of goals and means in personal or social action. There are, of course, persons and groups who adhere to goals which are inherently antisocial and associated with violence, injustice, and oppression and hence cannot be regarded as harmonious with the nonviolent ethic. But most people in most societies desire goals which are harmonious with the nonviolent ethic. For example, in extremely broad terms they desire a peaceful world, a just, free society which respects the human dignity and develops the capacities of its individual members, and they cherish personal and family relationships free from violence and hatred, and filled with affection and love. For most people on the level of goals there is little or no difficulty which prevents them from accepting the nonviolent ethic. Indeed, virtually all religions and most political outlooks place significant emphasis on the desirability of goals and future conditions which are harmonious with principled nonviolence.

The difficulty has generally arisen when people have not felt able to put the moral injunctions unconditionally into practice, and have seen it as either impossible or impracticable to behave in the present situation as one would like all behavior to be in an improved future condition of society. Sometimes this inability has been rooted in such difficult and hostile past experiences that the individual or the group simply has not known how to behave in a way which, if examined, would be recognized as harmonious with the nonviolent ethic. But more frequently, people have believed that possible nonviolent ways of acting would not be practicable, that is, that they would not be effective means of action in the current situation to achieve desirable personal, social, or political goals. In other words, people have often believed that nonviolent courses of action would not "work" in the face of current obstacles.

But to say that the nonviolent means would not "work," and violence therefore becomes necessary in at least certain circumstances, is the same as to deny the universal validity of the nonviolent ethic. In other words, the distrust of the practicality of nonviolent means of action prevents people from accepting the nonviolent ethic as an universally binding moral principle. (It may survive, and has done so, of course, as an ultimate ideal toward which one works, but to which at present various exceptions must regrettably be made. But that is a very different matter from seeing it as an universal principle.) On the other hand, if people perceived nonviolent means as capable of "working" in even the difficult circumstances, that is, saw them to be practical, they would see themselves able to form their behavior on the basis of the same standards as those required by the moral principle—regardless of whether or not they formally stressed their "belief" in the principle.

Gandhi himself had seen something of this relationship between the practical technique and the moral principle. It was partly on the basis of this that he had justified his advocacy and leadership of nonviolent struggle by masses of people who did not believe in the ethic. He had thought that as people saw the working and power of nonviolent action, they would realize that it could be applied instead of violence in other conflicts also and this would make them more able to accept *ahimsa* as a moral principle for all of life. Thus, for example, Gandhi had spoken of the need of an "occular demonstration" of successful nonviolent action in India before he could, as he was asked, take his recommended course of action to Afro-Americans.[79] He had also believed that as nonviolent struggle was applied in India against the British *Raj* Congressmen would come to appreciate "the logical result" of that experience and become ready to accept similar means for defending independent India against possible aggressors.[80]

PRACTICAL BARRIERS TO MORAL CONVICTIONS

But when the Congress Party assumed governmental responsibilities, first in the interim government and then after India became independent, Gandhi's hope was dashed that his colleagues and fellow countrymen would demonstrate an acceptance of the universal validity of the nonviolent ethic by rejecting military defense against international dangers and adopt instead defense by nonviolent resistance.

It is instructive to note that Indian political leaders often explained their rejection of Gandhi's pleas for India to follow the nonviolent way here also, on the grounds that they did not believe that it would "work." Gandhi himself frequently reported this explanation. For example in late 1939 he wrote: "So far as I can read the Working Committee's mind after a fairly full discussion, the members think that congressmen are unprepared for nonviolent defence against armed invasion."[81] After further discussion in mid-1940 with the Working Committee, Gandhi reported similar reactions to his repeated pleas to meet both internal disorders and possible invasion with "the force of non-violence":

> But the members of the Working Committee felt that congressmen would not be able to act up to it. It would be a new experience for them. They were never before called upon to deal with such a crisis. The attempt made by me to form peace brigades to deal with communal riots and the like had wholly failed. Therefore they could not hope for the action contemplated.[82]

A few days later Gandhi wrote: "The Congress Working Committee were of opinion that, while it might be possible for us to exercise *ahimsa* in internal disturbances, India has not the strength to exercise *ahimsa* against the invasion of a foreign foe."[83]

The Congress President Maulana Abul Kalam Azad, in his summary of the discussions, told the July 1940 meeting of the All-India Congress Committee:

> There is not a soul in the Congress who is not anxious to go the whole length with Mahatma Gandhi, if he can help it; but we cannot close our eyes to hard facts. We know that arms and ammunitions have not been able to save the freedom of France, Holland, Belgium and Norway but we also know that human nature even after realizing the futility of armed resistance is not prepared to give up force. We had not the courage to declare that we shall organize a State in this country without an armed force. If we did it would be wrong on our part.[84]

Though not limited to the question of India's defense policy, the explanation of Congress President J.B. Kripalani as to why he could no longer follow Gandhi's recommendations follows in a similar vein. In his concluding speech at the All-India Congress Committee on June 15, 1947, Kripalani said:

> I have been with Gandhiji for the last thirty years. I joined him in Champaran. I have never swayed in my loyalty to him. It is not a personal but a political loyalty. Even when I have differed from him I have considered his political instinct to be more correct than my elaborately reasoned attitudes. Today also I feel that he with his supreme fearlessness is correct and my stand is defective.

Why then am I not with him now? It is because I feel that he has as yet found no way of tackling the problem on a mass basis. When he taught us non-violent non-co-operation, he showed us a definite method which we had at least mechanically followed. Today he himself is groping in the dark. He was in Noakhali [in an effort to stop the Hindu-Muslim riots]. His efforts eased the situation. Now he is in Bihar. And the situation is again eased. But this does not solve in any way the flare-up in the Punjab. He says he is solving the problem of Hindu-Muslim unity for the whole of India in Bihar. May be. But it is difficult to see how that is being done. There are no definite steps, as in non-violent non-co-operation, that lead to the desired goal. And then unfortunately for us today though he can enunciate policies, they have in the main to be carried out by others and these others are not converted to his way of thinking. It is under these painful circumstances that I have accepted the division of India.[85]

Unable to see Gandhi's recommended general policy as capable of practical application with concrete forms of action in difficult circumstances, it was therefore out of the question for these men and millions of others to accept the nonviolent ethic as a comprehensive principle of life. Gandhi explained that his description of himself as "groping in the dark" meant that "he did not know how to make the people see his view-point."[86]

STEP BY STEP TOWARD A RESOLUTION

It is possible that a great part of the answer to this specific difficulty and to the wider problem of the relationship between the ethic and the technique lay in various statements made by Gandhi and his colleagues and in the events of the independence struggle. As Gandhi himself acknowledged, if he had simply done as many previous exponents of principled nonviolence had done, and preached the virtues of the morality of nonviolence, it is most likely that he would have had little influence on the course of political events and would have at most influenced the personal lives of a group of admirers and disciples. But he did not do that, and never concluded that he ought to have done so. The acceptance of nonviolent means in political struggle was possible because the technique of nonviolent action was presented as a practical course of action. Gandhi had been able to outline in sufficient detail the means of implementation, and on particular occasions to demonstrate the effectiveness of the technique in struggle, so that people who otherwise would have used violence accepted the political wisdom of Gandhi's alternative course.

So long as they were able to remain convinced of the practicality of his policy, they continued to support it. But when other problems and situations arose in which Gandhi still believed his nonviolent technique was relevant but in which he offered only generalizations and not comparable detailed courses of action which could be seen to be practicable, his political colleagues went their own way and rejected Gandhi's recommendations. Unable to spell out in detail an effective nonviolent course of action for the new, and often more difficult, situations, Gandhi fell back upon his faith that nonviolence was the morally right way of behaving (and therefore to him ultimately the most practical way). But his general expressions of faith and his religious terminology in such political situations did little to convince his colleagues that the course Gandhi recommended in general terms could in fact be applied as the most practical policy in concrete situations. Hence they rejected both his general policy and his universal ethic.

Gandhi's assumption that people having once seen and experienced the practicality of the nonviolent technique in one situation would easily accept the universality of the ethic and the political technique was demonstrated not to be correct. This does not mean, however, that the practical development and demonstration of the technique was of no help in the wider efforts to remove political violence and to gain acceptance for the nonviolent ethic. It is more likely that this particular case means simply that the carry-over is not automatic, and that specific policies and courses of action must be worked out which are practicable, and are seen to be practicable, for a whole variety of specific social and political situations where reliance is now placed upon violence as the ultimate sanction. This is, of course, a more difficult task than any one person could achieve alone, and Gandhi can by no means be regarded as a failure because he was able to take this development only to a certain point before his assassination.

Gandhi's spirit of experimentation and constant search for the most valid way of applying his principles in human society, however, suggest that this type of step-by-step development of the potentialities of the nonviolent approach, drawing partly upon practical experimentation in conflicts, partly upon intuition, and to a considerable degree upon intellectual efforts would have been the sort of approach which Gandhi himself might have encouraged and continued to develop. It was indeed the approach which he had pursued from his first experiments in South Africa, through the variety of local campaigns in India, and several national struggles toward self-rule for the Indian people. However, it is admittedly conceivable that without equally detailed answers to the new problems Gandhi might in discouragement have retired from political life into an emphasis upon a more narrowly religious approach to nonviolence. But it is doubtful, for he wrote in late 1947 that it was independent India's duty to perfect the nonviolent technique for dissolving collective conflicts.[87] He also spoke in terms of a step-by-step development in 1940, when he said that despite imperfection in the use of nonviolence in politics, it was possible to discard the use of violence, and by using nonviolent means, to grow from failure to success.[88]

In light of these various insights from Gandhi, it is possible that the usual formulations of the problem of the relationship of the nonviolent moral principle and the nonviolent political technique often distort their real relationship and therefore hinder rather than assist finding a solution. If, as Gandhi believed, the ethical course of action and the practical course of action are ultimately identical, then the "believer" in the nonviolent ethic must be involved with the practical development of the political technique, and the "practical politician" can explore the possibility of substituting effective nonviolent means in place of violence in one specific problem area after another.* If such a stage-by-stage substitution proves viable, the behavior of the practical politician would in the end become virtually indistinguishable from that of those who profess their belief in the universal moral principle. (If, however, this development did not prove practicable, it would suggest that nonviolence is not valid as an universal ethic.) If the universal ethic is in fact valid, the progressive development of the practical

---

* For further discussion of this conception of social change, see Gene Sharp, "Perpetual Dissent or Fundamental Change," in G. Sharp, *Social Power and Political Freedom* (Boston: Porter Sargent Publishers, Inc., 1979).

application of nonviolent means in social and political life may thus finally proceed to the point at which the supposed conflict between loyalty to the nonviolent ethic and political practicality is dissolved into a more advanced synthesis.

NOTES TO CHAPTER THIRTEEN

1. This is a revision of a paper of the same title which was written and issued in duplicated form while the author was at the Institute of Philosophy and the History of Ideas of the University of Oslo, Norway, in 1965; this version was prepared at Harvard University's Center for International Affairs, in 1968.
2. For a classification and description of such belief systems, see Chapter Ten, "Types of Principled Nonviolence."
3. See Chapter Eight, "Gandhi's Defense Policy."
4. Harijan (hereafter cited as H.), 21 July 1940; M.K. Gandhi, Non-Violence in Peace and War (hereafter cited as NVPW), 2 vols. Ahmedabad: Navajivan, 1948–1949), vol. I, p. 292. The original source and date given, in addition to the book in which it is reprinted.
5. M.K. Gandhi, Speeches and Writings of Mahatma Gandhi (Madras: 1922), p. 301; Gopi Nath Dhawan, The Political Philosophy of Mahatma Gandhi (Third rev. ed.; Ahmedabad: Navajivan, 1962), p. 107. See also H., 14 Oct. 1939; Dhawan, The Political Philosophy of Mahatma Gandhi, pp. 107–108.
6. H., 29 Sept. 1940; Dhawan, The Political Philosophy of Mahatma Gandhi, p. 165.
7. H., 12 Jan. 1947; NVPW, II, p. 190. H., 14 Dec. 1947; NVPW II, p. 339. Sarvodaya (Hindi), April 1948; Dhawan, The Political Philosophy of Mahatma Gandhi, pp. 165–166. H., 8 Sept. 1949; Dhawan, The Political Philosophy of Mahatma Gandhi, p. 166. H., 7 Apr. 1946; Dhawan, The Political Philosophy of Mahatma Gandhi, p. 166. H., 28 June 1942; M.K. Gandhi, In Search of the Supreme (ed. by V.B. Kher; 3 vols. Ahmedabad: Navajivan, 1961, 1961, and 1962), vol. II, p. 42.
8. H., 2 Nov. 1947; NVPW, II, p. 329.
9. H., 4 Nov. 1939; NVPW, I, p. 245.
10. For some of Gandhi's statements on this, see Chapter Eight, "Gandhi's Defense Policy."
11. Young India (hereafter cited as YI), 11 Aug. 1920; NVPW, I, p. 3.
12. YI, 7 May 1925; NVPW, I, p. 28.
13. YI, 30 July 1931; Nirmal Kumar Bose, Selections from Gandhi (hereafter cited as Bose, Selections) (Ahmedabad: Navajivan, 1948), p. 123.
14. YI, 30 July 1931; Bose, Selections, p. 124.
15. Ibid. It is clear from the context that Gandhi indeed meant policy here, both from the distinction in the previous quotation between policy and creed, and from his putting "policy" in italics two sentences prior to that.
16. M.K. Gandhi, Correspondence with the Government 1942–1944 (Second ed.; Ahmedabad: Navajivan, 1957).

17. See: YI, 31 July 1931; Bose, Selections, p. 124. H., 29 Sept. 1940; NVPW, I, p. 353. YI, 2 March 1922; Bose, Selections, pp. 123–124. H., 29 Sept. 1940; NVPW, I, p. 353. YI, 2 April 1931; Bose, Selections, p. 154.
18. H., 4 Aug. 1946; NVPW, II, p. 132.
19. H., 29 June 1947; NVPW, II, p. 266.
20. See: H., 2 Nov. 1947 (NVPW, II, p. 328); H., 3 Aug. 1947 (NVPW, II, p. 279); H., 24 Feb. 1946 (NVPW, II, p. 30); H., 28 Apr. 1946 (NVPW, II, p. 84); H., 6 Oct. 1946 (NVPW, II, p. 153); H., 26 March 1938 (NVPW, I, pp. 133–135); H., 2 Apr. 1938 (NVPW, I, p. 136); H., 8 June 1947 (NVPW, II, p. 258); H., 3 Aug. 1947 (NVPW, II, p. 279); H., 27 July 1947 (NVPW, II, p. 277) H., 31 Aug. 1947 (NVPW, II, p. 289); H., 11 Jan. 1948 (NVPW, II, pp. 327–328); H., 6 Oct. 1946 (NVPW, II, pp. 153–154); H., 13 July 1947 (NVPW, II, p. 272); H., 27 July 1947 (NVPW, II, p. 281); H., 9 Dec. 1939 (NVPW, I, p. 250); H., 9 Dec. 1939 (NVPW, I, p. 250); H., 30 Sept. 1939 (NVPW, I, p. 230). For statements by Gandhi that he had deliberately sought to develop a practical nonviolent alternative for use in place of violence, see Chapter Eight, "Gandhi's Defense Policy."
21. H., 4 Aug. 1946; NVPW, II, p. 132. See also: H., 27 July 1947; NVPW, II, p. 281. H., 29 June 1947; NVPW, II, p. 266. Dhawan, The Political Philosophy of Mahatma Gandhi, p. 72.
22. On Gandhi's view of the nature of passive resistance, see M.K. Gandhi, Satyagraha in South Africa (Second rev. ed.; Ahmedabad: Navajivan, 1950), and M.K. Gandhi, An Autobiography or the Story of My Experiments with Truth (Ahmedabad: Navajivan, 1956 [1927]), p. 318. On his view of the Indian practice as passive resistance, see H., 27 July 1947 (NVPW, II, p. 276); H., 31 Aug. 1947 (NVPW, II, p. 289); H., 11 Jan. 1948 (NVPW, II, pp. 327–328); H., 14 Oct. 1939 (NVPW, I, p. 235); H., 9 Dec. 1939 (NVPW, I, p. 250); H., 13 July 1947 (NVPW, II, p. 272); H., 16 Nov. 1947 (NVPW, II, p. 323); M.K. Gandhi, Delhi Diary (Ahmedabad: Navajivan, 1948) p. 280, and D.G. Tendulkar, Mahatma: Life of Mohandas Karamchand Gandhi (New ed., Delhi: Publications Divisions, Ministry of Information and Broadcasting, Government of India, 1961), vol. IV, p. 253.
23. H., 12 Apr. 1942; NVPW, I, p. 396. See also H., 27 July 1947; NVPW, II, p. 277.
24. H., 31 Aug. 1947; NVPW, II, p. 290. See also H., 21 July 1946; NVPW, II, p. 109.
25. See H., 26 Mar. 1938; NVPW, I, p. 133. H., 14 Oct. 1939; NVPW, I, p. 236. H., 10 Feb. 1946; NVPW, II, p. 2. H., 24 Feb. 1946; NVPW, II, p. 30. H., 21 July 1946; NVPW, II, p. 109.
26. H., 21 July 1940; NVPW, I, p. 292.
27. H., 31 Aug. 1947; NVPW, II, p. 290.
28. H., 29 June 1940; NVPW, I, pp. 275–276. H., 27 July 1947; NVPW, II, p. 280.
29. Dhawan, The Political Philosophy of Mahatma Gandhi, p. 70.
30. H., 21 July 1940; NVPW, I, pp. 290–291.
31. H., 12 May 1946; NVPW, II, p. 91.
32. H., 31 Aug. 1947; NVPW, II, p. 289.
33. See H., 7 Apr. 1946; NVPW, II, p. 57. H., 8 Sept. 1946; NVPW, II, p. 146. H., 21 July 1946; NVPW, II, p. 109. H., 12 May 1946; NVPW, II, p. 91.

34. See H., 27 July 1947 (NVPW, II, p. 281); H., 9 Apr. 1938 (NVPW, I, p. 140); H., 2 Apr. 1938 (NVPW, I, p. 137); H., 29 June 1947 (NVPW, II, p. 265); H., 31 Aug. 1947 (NVPW, II, p. 289); H., 27 July 1947 (NVPW, II, p. 276); Bose, Selections, pp. 42–43; Bose, **Studies in Gandhism** (hereafter cited as Bose, **Studies**) (Calcutta: Indian Associated Publishing Co., 1947), pp. 15, 65, and 71. Tendulkar, **Mahatma**, VI, p. 41; H., 22 Sept. 1940 (NVPW, I, p. 470); H., 24 Dec. 1938 (NVPW, I, p. 327); H., 2 Mar. 1947 (NVPW, II, p. 218); and Dhawan, **The Political Philosophy of Mahatma Gandhi**, p. 130.

35. H., 4 May 1940; NVPW, I, p. 267. H., 29 June 1940; NVPW, I, p. 277.

36. H., 10 Feb. 1946; NVPW, II, p. 3.

37. H., 21 July 1940; NVPW, I, p. 300. See also: H., 6 Jan. 1940; NVPW, I, p. 253. H., 21 July 1947; NVPW, I, p. 302. H., 15 Sept. 1946; NVPW, II, p. 136. H., 29 June 1947; NVPW, II, p. 267. Bose, Selections, pp. 3–7. H., 29 June 1947; NVPW, II, p. 267. And Ranganath R. Diwakar, **Satyagraha: Its Technique and History** (Bombay: Hind Kitabs, 1946), pp. 73–74.

38. H., 14 Dec. 1947; NVPW, II, p. 339. See also H., 12 Jan. 1947; NVPW, II, p. 196. H., 24 June 1939; Gandhi, **Satyagraha** (hereafter cited as S.) (Ahmedabad: Navajivan, 1951), p. 296.

39. H., 2 Apr. 1938; NVPW, I, p. 136.

40. Above n. 21.

41. H., 27 July 1947; NVPW, II, p. 281.

42. H., 10 Feb. 1946; NVPW, II, p. 2.

43. YI, 12 Feb. 1926; Bose, Selections, p. 160.

44. YI, 2 Mar. 1922; Bose, Selections, p. 26.

45. YI, 3 Sept. 1925; Bose, Selections, p. 26.

46. Tendulkar, **Mahatma**, VI, pp. 40–41.

47. For discussion of this point in the views of Max Weber, see Chapter Eleven, "Ethics and Responsibility in Politics: A critique of the Present Adequacy of Max Weber's Classification of Ethical Systems."

48. See the discussion of Gandhi's views on violence in Chapter Eight, "Gandhi's Defense Policy."

49. H., 23 Mar. 1940; Bose, Selections, p. 6. See also H., 25 Apr. 1936; Bose, Selections, p. 3.

50. Mahadev Desai, "Nonviolence in Evolution," in NVPW, I, p. v.

51. YI, 7 May 1925; Bose, Selections, p. 224.

52. Gandhi, **Young India**, (Triplicane, Madras: S. Ganesan, 1935) vol. III, 1927–1928, p. 43.

53. YI, 19 Sept. 1924; S., p. 189.

54. YI, 2 Aug. 1928; S., p. 216.

55. YI, 1 July 1939; Bose, Selections, p. 224.

56. YI, 26 Dec. 1924; Bose, Selections, p. 13.

57. M.K. Gandhi, "Hind Swaraj or Indian Home Rule," (pamphlet; Ahmedabad: Navajivan, [1938, written 1908] 1958), p. 71.

58. Ibid.

59. **The Amrita Bazar Patrika**, 17 Sept. 1933; Bose, Selections, p. 38.

60. H., 11 Feb. 1939; Dhawan, **The Political Philosophy of Mahatma Gandhi**, p. 54.

61. YI, 17 July 1924; Bose, Selections, p. 37.

62. H., 23 Feb. 1947; NVPW, II, p. 215.
63. H., 1 June 1947; NVPW, II, p. 255.
64. Gandhi, "Hind Swaraj," p. 71.
65. Ibid., p. 75.
66. YI, 26 Dec. 1924; Bose, Selections, p. 11. H., 20 Apr. 1934; Bose, Selections, p. 11.
67. YI, 29 Dec. 1920; NVPW, I, p. 4.
68. H., 22 Sept. 1940; NVPW, I, p. 461.
69. YI, 15 Mar. 1928; NVPW, I, p. 72. For Gandhi's interpretation of the relevant passages from the *Bhagavad Gita* concerning nonattached action, see Mahadev Desai, **The Gospel of Selfless Action or the Gita According to Gandhi** (Ahmedabad: Navajivan, 1951 [1946]), pp. 161–162, 175, 181, 183–185, 197–198, 200–203, 323, 333, 361, 364, and 376–380.
70. For such analyses of the dynamics and mechanisms of nonviolent action, which clearly point to the negative effects of violence, see Part Three of Gene Sharp, **The Politics of Nonviolent Action** (Boston: Porter Sargent Publisher, Inc., 1973).
71. See statements cited above in n. 23 and n. 24.
72. See statements cited above in n. 14, n. 15, n. 16, and also H., 29 Sept. 1940; NVPW, I, p. 353.
73. H., 14 Oct. 1939; NVPW, I, p. 236.
74. **The Amrita Bazar Patrika,** 3 Aug. 1934; Bose, **Selections,** pp. 195–196. H., 4 Nov. 1939; NVPW, I, p. 245.
75. H., 24 Feb. 1946; NVPW, II, p. 30.
76. H., 4 Nov. 1939; NVPW, I, p. 245. The cases he cited of mass action without ill will were women collecting illegal salt during the 1930–31 campaign, and the behavior of the peasants in Champaran in 1917.
77. YI, 2 Apr. 1931; Bose, **Selections,** p. 154.
78. Above pp. 282–283.
79. H., 14 Mar. 1936; NVPW, I, p. 116.
80. H., 14 Oct. 1939; NVPW, I, p. 235.
81. Ibid.
82. H., 29 June 1940; NVPW, I, p. 275.
83. H., 13 July 1940; NVPW, I, p. 285.
84. **Congress Bulletin,** 7 Sept. 1940; Bose, **Studies,** pp. 310–311.
85. Tendulkar, **Mahatma,** VIII, p. 19. See also H., 29 June 1947; NVPW, II, p. 266. Pyarelal, **Mahatma Gandhi: The Last Phase** (2 vols. Ahmedabad: Navajivan, 1958), vol. II, pp. 255–256.
86. H., 29 June 1947; NVPW, II, p. 266.
87. Above n. 27.
88. Above n. 26.

But I must warn you against carrying the impression with you that mine is the final word on non-violence. I know my own limitations. I am but a humble seeker after truth. And all I claim is that every experiment of mine has deepened my faith in non-violence as the greatest force at the disposal of mankind.

M.K. Gandhi

Appendices

Appendix A

Shridharani's Contribution to the Study of Gandhi's Technique

Krishnalal Shridharani's *War Without Violence** remains after all the years since its original publication in 1939, one of the most important books on Gandhi and his approach to struggle which have been written. Shridharani understood that Gandhi's personal qualities, including his reception as a mahatma, were all subordinate in significance to the technique of struggle which Gandhi wielded and urged others to wield. Shridharani also perceived the dangers of naiveté in politics and international relations, the bankruptcy and dangers of violence and war, and the failure of Western pacifism to remove injustices, tyranny, and war. Gandhi's technique of fighting—*satyagraha*—stood in contrast to all three of these. It remained however closest to war, for it too was a final means of struggle, except that in this case the fighting was conducted without physical violence. Gandhi's technique was best described, then, as "war without violence."

Shridharani was not alone in the 1930s in presenting and advocating this approach. For example, in the Netherlands Barthélemy de Ligt stressed the political relevance of nonviolent struggle and authored several studies including *The Conquest of Violence: An Essay in War and Revolution* (New York: E.P. Dutton, 1938; reprint ed., New York: Garland Publishing, 1972); in Denmark a German and two Danes produced a study with a similar

---

* Krishnalal Shridharani, *War Without Violence: A Study of Gandhi's Method and Its Accomplishments*. 351 pp. New York: Harcourt, Brace, and Co., 1939. London: Victor Gollancz, 1939. Reprinted with this essay as an Introduction, New York: Garland, 1972. Revised edition, 299 pp. Bombay, Bharatiya Vidya Bhavan, 1962.

theme, *Kamp Uden Vaaben: Ikke-vold som Kampmiddel mod Krig og Undertrykkelse* (Struggle without Weapons: Nonviolence as a means of struggle against war and oppression [Copenhagen: Levin & Munksgaard, Ejnar Munksgaard, 1937]). There were also others developing this approach including in the United States Richard Gregg with his *Power of Nonviolence* which first appeared in 1934 (Revised edition, New York: Schocken, 1960); Gregg, however, with his extreme emphasis on conversion of the opponent was far closer to religious pacifism than any of the authors of the other three books.

Despite these important studies of the 1930s this "technique approach" to nonviolent struggle did not continue to be developed in the literature and in new thinking during the next two decades. It appears however, to have had a distinct influence on the development of nonviolent direct action in protest and resistance groups, such as the early Congress of Racial Equality. Much of the later studies of Gandhi and the Indian experiments in nonviolent struggle instead emphasized Gandhi as a mahatma, a charasmatic leader, his ethical commitment to nonviolence, and the like, with the political utilization of the nonviolent technique often viewed as subordinate to, and dependent upon, these personal qualities and his ethical commitment. Sometimes Gandhi's own statements encouraged those interpretations, while Gandhi's contrary views and judgements were ignored. An examination of Gandhi's early speeches and writings in South Africa makes it clear, perhaps for the first time, that *before* Gandhi's first participation in nonviolent action as group struggle he was familiar with both the concept of the nonviolent technique of struggle separated from the ethical element, and also with specific cases from Russia, China, Bengal, England, Ireland, and elsewhere.* That discovery adds strong support to the technique approach which Shridharani utilized in his study. The recent burst of interest in the potential of prepared nonviolent resistance for national defense purposes—a line of development which Shridharani briefly discussed in 1939 in *War Without Violence*—also adds support to the merits of the technique approach, as distinct from emphasis on moral arguments.

* See Chapter Two, "Origins of Gandhi's Use of Nonviolent Struggle."

Krishnalal Shridharani was born in 1911 in Bhavnagar (Saurashtra), India. While very young he published six books of poetry and plays in the Gujarati language. He was a participant in the famous Salt March to the sea led by Gandhi in early 1930, in order at its conclusion to commit civil disobedience of the Salt Acts, and thus launch the nationwide 1930–1931 civil disobedience independence struggle. He graduated from Rabindranath Tagore's school Shanti Niketan in 1934, and then became a newspaper correspondent. Then he undertook graduate study in the United States at New York University and Columbia University, from which he received his Ph.D. in sociology with his thesis "War Without Violence" which became the present book. Shridharani also lectured widely and published other books in the United States, *My India, My America,* and *Warning to the West.* His 1960 revision of *War Without Violence* brought the book up to date with new material from the later period of British rule, World War II, independence, the riots, Gandhi's death, and briefly later developments of nonviolent action in India. The substance of the book remained, however, unchanged. He died at the age of forty-nine.

If there are weaknesses in the book which are not explained solely by the limitations which fall on pioneering books, they are few. The author mentions nonviolent struggles in other parts of the world so briefly that it is easy to get the impression that the Indian struggles are more unique than they in fact were. The discussion of the role of suffering, and the "folklore of non-violence" may both be useful, but they may also unintentionally tie *satyagraha* more closely to ethical and religious systems than the author seems to have intended. The most serious gap in the book is an absence of a power analysis, showing that in fact all governments are dependent for their existence upon the cooperation, obedience, and submission of the people they rule, and that consequently noncooperation, disobedience, and defiance through the nonviolent technique may not only be able to coerce despotic governments but also to destroy them.

Shridharani recognized that the nonviolent technique might have a greater acceptance in the West than in India itself. That judgement may have seemed naive or brash to readers at the time. However, my own studies of cases of nonviolent action in Western countries have convinced me also that this technique is at least as Western as it is Indian or Eastern, and probably much more so.

There is a new interest in this basic technique approach to nonviolent struggle. In retrospect, it now seems we might have been further ahead in the effort to abolish war while achieving or maintaining freedom and justice if more attention had been paid to Shridharani's approach during the intervening years. How much my own thought has been influenced by Shridharani's study over the years is hard to say, but it was striking in going back over the book which I had not read as a whole for many years, how familiar his various basic arguments sounded to ones which have long since been incorporated into my own thought. My major study *The Politics of Nonviolent Action* (Boston: Porter Sargent Publisher, 1973) is a fuller study based on this technique approach. I certainly agree with Shridharani that "Conflict, competition, strife and struggle . . . are not the 'enemy' we are after." ". . . [W]e want a new form of war which can be waged without inflicting violence in retaliation." Telling people what *not* to do in a severe crisis almost never works. Instead, we need to be able to present a nonviolent alternative technique of action and struggle which people can utilize in place of rioting, civil war, terrorism, and international war. There are increasing signs that this approach can be successful in the development of this nonviolent alternative form of struggle. Shridharani merits not only acknowledgment as a pioneer but his book deserves continued study.

Appendix B

The War in 1942

In 1942 Gandhi was willing to accept that an independent India allow Allied use of India as a military base for carrying on the war against the Axis Powers, and he personally approved of non-military types of aid for the Allied cause. He also recognized that an independent Indian Government which did not share his views on nonviolence would very probably also provide military aid to the Allies. This has been interpreted (incorrectly in my opinion) as a significant alteration in Gandhi's position. Therefore, although it is beyond the scope of Chapter Eight itself to offer a detailed account of Gandhi's discussion of World War II, it is necessary in this appendix to summarize his views briefly and to refer the reader to the original statements.*

For a series of Gandhi's 1940 statements on the war, see *NVPW*, I, pp. 275, 280–282, 314–316, 348–349, 351, 357–358, 361, 445–447, 454–455, 457, 464–465, 469, and 474–476. For two relevant statements from early 1942 see pp. 374 and 397–399. For a convenient account with extensive texts of Gandhi's views later in 1942, see D.G. Tendulkar, *Mahatma* (Delhi: Government of India, 1962), vol. VI, esp. pp. 60–168, to which the following page references refer.

Gandhi in accordance with his general position was opposed to international aggression and Nazism, and hence clearly preferred the cause of the Allies. He did not wish the Axis powers to win, favoring instead an Allied victory (pp. 94, 102, and 104–105). Gandhi therefore gave the Allies his general moral support as indicated in the section "Fighting Nazism by War" in Chapter Eight; his statements concerning China and Russia were especially

---

* I am grateful to Adam Roberts for urging the inclusion of a description of Gandhi's 1942 views.

clear (pp. 86, 100, and 110). This support for the Allies was not, however, uncritical, as especially some statements about Britain (p. 86). This general moral support did not mean that he approved of the Allies' use of violence, although he regarded passivity and acceptance of evil as morally worse (see the main body of Chapter Eight).

The Japanese military advance toward India raised in an acute form the question of the relation of India's political subjection to the chances of victory for the Allied cause. Gandhi concluded that the Allied cause was weakened by the obvious hypocrisy of talk of defending freedom while continuing the subjection of India. (Churchill had made a speech saying the Atlantic Charter did not apply to India). It followed in Gandhi's view that if Britain gave India independence during the war, this would on the moral level greatly strengthen the Allies' war effort (pp. 95, 109, 113, and 126). Gandhi in fact believed that Indian independence was necessary if the Allies were to win the war (pp. 125 and 179).

The nearness of Japanese troops to India also raised urgently the question of India's reaction to the possible invasion. Although Gandhi had no really detailed plan of action, he favored nonviolent resistance to a Japanese (or possibly a Nazi) invasion (pp. 69, 76–77, 79, 81, 84, 85, 88, 103, 135, and 137). He opposed a "scorched earth" policy (pp. 67, 68, and 85). But on the basis of the example of Burma especially, Gandhi believed that a subjected people would not only *not* resist the Japanese invasion and would behave passively; he feared that major sections of the population would welcome the Japanese (pp. 127, 140, and 144). Gandhi, however, not only opposed Axis aggression in general; he had no desire for India to accept a new foreign master in place of the old one (p. 114). Gandhi therefore believed that for Indians to resist, they must be free (pp. 127 and 144), and India should "play her natural role" in her own defense (p. 114).

Therefore, believing Indian independence would help the Allied cause, and give Indians the necessary motivation to resist a Japanese invasion, Gandhi urged, and the Congress adopted, the "Quit India" program (pp. 75–76, 78–83, 94–95, 100, and 113).

While Gandhi would have preferred the British, Chinese, Russians, and others to use nonviolent resistance against the Nazis, he recognized that they would not do so. Under those circumstances he had no desire to disrupt their conduct of the war by obstructionism and similar behavior (pp. 93, 104–105, 116). Nor did he wish that India's independence (and the demand for it) be interpreted as welcoming Japanese invasion (pp. 108, 136, and 172).

If the British would relinquish political control of India, two problems would arise. The first was to whom would the State apparatus be turned over, especially in light of communal conflicts in India. Gandhi said that even chaos was preferable to denial of independence, for out of the chaos nonviolence and order could arise (pp. 83, 95, 107, 137 and 178).

The second problem was how would India freed from the British Empire resist a Japanese invasion and aid the Allies. Gandhi expected that in a freed India the British Indian Army would have been disbanded (pp. 102 and 107). However, he recognized the virtual certainty that independent India not sharing his own views would adopt military means of defense (pp. 129 and 145–146). (It is most important to recognize the distinction which Gandhi himself pointed out between his personal views and those of the Congress and its leaders (pp. 77, 79, 96, and 115) which had never accepted Gandhi's idea of nonviolent means of defense for independent India.)

Gandhi believed that the granting of immediate independence to India would contribute to the Allied war effort also by increasing the spirit of resistance in India against a Japanese invasion (pp. 127, 141, and 144). This would, for example, help keep India from falling to the Japanese and thereby help China which was also fighting Japanese invaders (pp. 100–101, 110, 113, 115, 129, 159, 167–168, and 179).

But Gandhi recognized the importance of further assistance to the Allies (p. 125). He was often vague about the forms of such aid (p. 110), but said that Britian should trust India to help the Allies (p. 144). Independence was a prerequisite to Indian help in the war, and would "let a free India make her full contribution to the war effort" (p. 89). Without independence, "Those of us who would fight for a cause, for India and China, with armed forces or with non-violence, cannot, under the foreign heel, function as they want to" (p. 115). It is important to remember that Gandhi was at this point cooperating with the Congress on a common policy to achieve the shortrange political objective of Indian independence, after which the policies of Gandhi and the Congress would again diverge on the question of defense policy. It is thus necessary to look carefully at his statements (especially when he is replying to questions) to determine whether he is expressing his own personal views, or saying what he expects will actually happen, or giving a statement in general terms on which he and the Congress agreed.

Gandhi favored that an *independent* India would conclude an alliance with the Allies for defensive operations (pp. 102 and 106). India should declare that she did not need troops for her own defense, but that under the circumstances she ought not to put China or the Allies in jeopardy by denying Allied military bases in India (pp. 111–112). Gandhi was ready to recommend personally that independent India, by a treaty containing certain specified conditions, allow the Allies to use India as a military base for the war effort. Such use would require India to provide certain other necessary conditions, including the use of the railways and ports and an absence of riots (pp. 94–95, 104–105, 108, 115, and 131). Gandhi specifically mentioned the granting of such bases as a means of helping China (pp. 111–112, 117, 119, and 122). It was clear, however, that Gandhi himself did not believe this should extend to military help (p. 102), and did not believe that such an alliance required, for example, a declaration of war (p. 106). India could still then choose either the military or the nonviolent way (p. 125). He continued to favor moral and nonviolent support and not military support (pp. 120, 125, and 129).

Gandhi, however, recognized that an independent India would not follow the course he recommended on national defense by nonviolent resistance but would adopt conventional military defense instead (pp. 115, 129, and 145–146). In line with his views on democracy, he recognized the right of the majority to make that choice, although he favored a different policy. This majority decision would mean that in all likelihood an independent India would also help the Allies militarily (pp. 98, 129, and 148–149). Gandhi's recognition of the likely course of events did not imply approval of it, except that India must be free to make her own choice.

In line with Gandhi's policy of cooperating with political nonviolent action for limited objectives, Gandhi and the Congress cooperated on the development of the "Quit India" demand and plans. Gandhi did not see this as committing him to personal approval of Indian military aid to the Allied war effort at a later date if India were granted independence, although he would not oppose that democratic decision (p. 125). Nor was Gandhi in any way attempting to trade Indian military support for the war for independence: he had earlier split with the Congress over such an attempt.

Gandhi did not, however, see that a treaty of alliance between independent India and the Allies would necessarily require Indian military help. He spoke instead in general terms of nonviolent types of help and of means by which nonviolent measures could affect the fortunes of the war (pp. 120, 124–125, and 129). Gandhi also spoke of the possible contribution of free India to the resolution of the world crisis (p. 108), and said that there was no change in his views concerning nonviolence (pp. 145–146 and 152).

Appendix C

Glossary of Indian Terms

Ahimsa: Noninjury in thought, word, and deed to all forms of life. Roughly, "nonviolence."

All-India Congress Committee: During the nationalist struggle, the deliberative standing committee of the Indian National Congress (see), elected by delegates to its annual meeting.

Ashram: A hermitage; a residence for community living, spiritual retirement, study, and religious discipline, often the home of a spiritual teacher; frequently the residence of a group devoted to social, religious, or political service, who live under certain rules or discipline.

Bahadur: Brave; brave people; sometimes Englishmen. See asterisked note on p. 46.

Bhagavad Gita: An important Hindu scripture; part of the great epic *Mahabharata,* in which Krishna is the divine hero. Its violent aspects were interpreted symbolically by Gandhi, who was convinced that it recommended nonattached action, that is, that one should act because one had a duty to do so whether or not there was any chance of succeeding. Popularly known as the *Gita.*

Bhang: An intoxicating beverage made from a type of hemp.

Bhoodan: Land-gift; a movement for redistribution of the ownership of land begun after Gandhi's death by Vinoba Bhave to be achieved solely by persuading owners to give a portion of their holdings to the landless.

Congress: The Indian National Congress (see).

Congressmen: Members, especially leaders, of the Indian National Congress (see).

324

Crore: A unit of measurement equal to ten million.

Dacoit: Bandit.

Gandhiji: "Gandhi" with the suffix "-ji" added, which denotes respect.

Gita: Popular term for the *Bhagavad Gita* (see).

Goondaism: Hooliganism.

Gramdan: Village-gift; a development from the *Bhoodan* (see) movement, in which all owners of land in a village were asked to transfer ownership voluntarily to the whole village.

Harijan: Gandhi's name for the untouchables; literally, people of God; also the name of the weekly paper founded by Gandhi in February 1933.

Hartal: A stoppage of work and business, usually for one day or rarely a few days, for self-purification, expression of mourning, protest, and arousing the imagination of the population and the opponent in a conflict.

Himsa: Violence.

Indian National Congress: The Indian nationalist political party with which Gandhi often worked, which led the independence struggle, and later became the governing party of independent India.

Jallianwala Bagh: The place of the 1919 massacre in Amritsar, the Punjab, where troops under orders of General Dyer killed without warning at least 379 people and wounded at least 1,137 others, who had been attending a peaceful meeting and were unarmed.

-ji: A suffix to the name of a person denoting respect.

Khadi: Hand-spun, hand-woven cloth.

Lathi: A heavy bamboo rod, often with an iron or steel-covered end, used by police or troops for beating people to control crowds and disperse demonstrations.

Maharaja: A king or ruler.

Mahatma: A great soul; great-souled one.

Muslim: Moslem; a believer in Islam.

Mussalman: Muslim.

Navajivan: Literally, new life; the name of a weekly in the Gujarati language edited by Gandhi, and also of the publishing house he founded.

Panchayat: A village council of five members which hears and resolves local disputes without use of the State court system.

Raj: Rule, or government, as the British *Raj.*

Raja: King.

Satyagraha: (1) Gandhi's type of nonviolent struggle, which emphasizes both militant action and concern for the opponent, seeking conversion where possible but also change by altering power relationships. (2) The type of principled nonviolence developed by M.K. Gandhi enjoining believers to improve their own lives, combat social evils by nonviolent action, and build a better social order by constructive program work. (3) A particular nonviolent action campaign, as the Bardoli *satyagraha.*

Satyagrahi: (1) One who participates in a *satyagraha* campaign. (2) One who believes in *satyagraha* as a comprehensive philosophy.

Sarvodaya: Literally, uplift of all; used to describe an ideal "nonviolent society."

Shanti Sena: Peace army; peace brigade; an organization of volunteers pledged to nonviolent discipline with the task of keeping internal peace, stopping riots, and resisting foreign invasions.

Swadeshi: Indigenous product; the principle of using goods grown or made locally or in one's country, in preference to foreign products.

Swaraj: Self-rule, independence. *Poorna swaraj* refers to "full" or "complete" independence, exceeding in its qualities simple political independence of the government from foreign control and referring instead to self-rule on a decentralized basis of the general population.

Tapasya: Religious penance; sacrifice; austerity.

Vande Mataram: Literally, "Hail Mother," that is, Mother India, the refrain of the Indian national anthem "Vande Mataram."

Working Committee: The committee of the Indian National Congress (see) during the independence struggles which functioned for the All-Indian Congress Committee (see) between its meetings.

Young India: Gandhi's weekly paper in English from 1919 to 1922.

Zulum: Oppression.

Appendix D

Sources for Further Study

ON NONVIOLENT STRUGGLE AS A POLITICAL TECHNIQUE

Sharp, Gene, **The Politics of Nonviolent Action.** 902 pp. Boston: Porter Sargent, 1973. Paperback edition in three volumes: I, **Power and Struggle,** 114 pp.; II, **The Methods of Nonviolent Action,** 348 pp.; III, **The Dynamics of Nonviolent Action,** 466 pp. Boston: Porter Sargent, 1974

BIOGRAPHIES OF GANDHI

Ashe, Geoffrey, **Gandhi.** 404 pp. New York: Stein & Day, 1968. (Bibliography. Illustrations.)

Dalal, C.B., **Gandhi: 1915–1948: A Detailed Chronology.** 210 pp. New Delhi: Gandhi Peace Foundation, 1971, and Bombay: Bharatiya Vidya Bhavan, 1961. (Bibliography. Appendices.)

Doke, Joseph J., **M.K. Gandhi: An Indian Patriot in South Africa.** 97 pp. London: London Indian Chronicle, 1909.

Erikson, Erik, **Gandhi's Truth: On the Origins of Militant Nonviolence.** 474 pp. New York: W.W. Norton, 1969 and London: Faber & Faber, 1970. (A psycho-historical study focused especially on his early life and the Ahmedabad labor strike and fast.)

Fischer, Louis, **Gandhi: His Life and Message for the World.** 192 pp. New York: Mentor, New American Library, 1954.

———————, **The Life of Mahatma Gandhi.** 593 pp. New York: Harper & Bros., 1950, and London: Jonathan Cape, 1951. New

York: Collier Books, Macmillan, (1962) 1969, and Toronto: Collier-Macmillan Canada, 1969.

Gandhi, Manubahen, **The Lonely Pilgrim (Gandhiji's Noakhali Pilgrimage)**. 273 pp. Ahmedabad: Navajivan, 1964. (Account of Gandhi's efforts to stop Hindu-Muslim riots in Noakhali, Bengal, Dec. 1946–Mar. 1947.)

Gandhi, Mohandas K., **An Autobiography or the Story of My Experiments With Truth**. 640 pp. Ahmedabad: Navajivan, 1948 (1927), Washington: Public Affairs Press, 1954, and Boston: Beacon Press, 1957. (Emphasizes Gandhi's ascetic, psychological, and religious concerns. Not recommended as an introduction.)

Jack, Homer A., ed., **The Gandhi Reader: A Source Book of his Life and Writings**. 532 pp. Bloomington, Ind.: Indiana University Press, 1956. (Includes some biographical chapters.)

Kytle, Calvin, **Gandhi, Soldier of Nonviolence: His Effect on India and the World Today**. 194 pp. New York: Grosset & Dunlap, 1969. (For young people. Many illustrations.)

Moon, Penderel, **Gandhi and Modern India**. 312 pp. New York: W. W. Norton & Co., 1969. (Glossary. Bibliography.)

Nanda, Bal R., **Mahatma Gandhi: A Biography**. 542 pp. Boston: Beacon Press, 1958, and London: George Allen and Unwin, 1958. (Glossary. Select bibliography.)

——————, **Mahatma Gandhi** (abridged). 272 pp. Woodbury, N.Y.: Barron, 1969.

Payne, Robert, **The Life and Death of Mahatma Gandhi**. 703 pp. New York: Dutton, 1969, and London: The Bodley Head, 1969.

Polak, Henry S. L., Brailsford, Henry N., and Lord Pethick-Lawrence, **Mahatma Gandhi**. 320 pp. London: Odhams Press, 1949. (Illustrations.)

Pyarelal (Nair), **Mahatma Gandhi: The Early Phase**. Vol. I, 854 pp. Ahmedabad: Navajivan, 1965. (Describes the early life of Gandhi. Vol. II has not yet been published.)

——————, **Mahatma Gandhi: The Last Phase**. In two volumes, I, May 1944-May 1947, 750 pp.; II, March 1947-Jan. 1948, 887 pp. Ahmedabad: Navajivan, 1956 and 1958. (Glossary. Photographs.)

—————————, A Pilgrimage for Peace: Gandhi Among N.W.F. Pathans. 216 pp. Ahmedabad: Navajivan, 1950. (Gandhi's 1938 visit to the Pathans of the North-West Frontier Province with Khan Abdul Ghaffar Khan.)

Tendulkar, Dinanath G., Mahatma: Life of Mohandas Karamchand Gandhi. In eight volumes, I (1869–1920) 338 pp.; II (1920–1929), 394 pp.; III (1930–1934) 327 pp.; IV (1934–1938) 330 pp.; V (1938–1940) 355 pp.; VI (1940–1945) 315 pp.; VII (1945–1947) 426 pp.; VIII (1947–1948) 336 pp. New Delhi: Publications Division, Ministry of Information and Broadcasting, Government of India, 1960–1963 (1951–1954). (Many illustrations.)

Walker, Roy, Sword of Gold: A Life of Mahatma Gandhi. 200 pp. London: Indian Independence Union, 1945.

ANALYSES AND INTERPRETATIONS

Agarwal, Shriman Narayan, Relevance of Gandhian Economics. 256 pp. Ahmedabad: Navajivan, 1970. (Includes discussion of decentralization, Gandhian socialism, *sarvodaya,* and Marxism.) *For other studies on Gandhian economics, see the various entries in the bibliographies listed in an earlier section; for example:* Indian Council of Social Science Research, Mohandas Karamchand Gandhi: A bibliography, entry nos. 487–535 and 723–729, and index pp. 224–225.

Bandyopahyaya, Jayantanuja, Social and Political Thought of Gandhi. 415 pp. Bombay, New York, and London: Allied Publishers, 1969. (A social scientist's critical analysis of Gandhi's thought in the context of the growth of State power and military weaponry.)

Battacharyya, Buddhadeva, Evolution of the Political Philosophy. 601 pp. Foreword by Nirmal Kumar Bose. Calcutta: Calcutta Book House, 1969. (A serious Marxist examination of Gandhi's thought, including his views on human nature, history, society, economics, *satyagraha,* and political theory.)

Bondurant, Joan V., Conquest of Violence: The Gandhian Philosophy of Conflict. 269 pp. Princeton, N.J.: Princeton University Press, 1958, and Berkeley, Calif.: University of California Press, 1965. (Especially recommended.)

Bose, Nirmal Kumar, **Studies in Gandhism.** 358 pp. Calcutta: Indian Associated Publishing Co., 1947. (Essays on economics and politics.)

ㄨ Dhawan, Gopi Nath, **The Political Philosophy of Mahatma Gandhi.** Third revised ed. 354 pp. Ahmedabad: Navajivan, 1962. (Bibliography.)

Diwakar, Ranganath R., **Saga of Satyagraha.** New Delhi: Gandhi Peace Foundation, and Bombay: Baratiya Vidya Bhavan, 1969.

⸻, **Satyagraha: Its Technique and History.** 202 pp. Bombay: Hind Kitabs, 1946. Abridged U.S. edition: **Satyagraha: The Power of Truth.** 108 pp. Hinsdale, Ill.: Henry Regnery, 1948. (Appendices. Bibliography. Glossary.)

Erikson, Erik, **Gandhi's Truth: On the Origins of Militant Nonviolence.** 474 pp. New York: W. W. Norton, 1969, and London: Faber & Faber, 1970. (Focuses on psychological elements in Gandhi's application of nonviolent struggle in the famous Ahmedabad strike.)

Horsburg, H.J.N., **Non-violence and Aggression: A Study of Gandhi's Moral Equivalent of War.** 207 pp. London: Oxford University Press, 1968.

Iyer, Raghavan N., **The Moral and Political Thought of Mahatma Gandhi.** 449 pp. New York: Oxford University Press, 1973. (A scholarly examination of basic components of Gandhi's philosophy. Bibliography. Glossary.)

Kripalani, Jiwatram Bhagwandas, **Gandhian Thought.** 281 pp. New Delhi: Gandhi Smarak Nidhi, and Bombay: Orient Longmans, 1961. (Includes essays from the 1930s written during controversies about Gandhi's approach and Marxism.)

Lewis, Martin Deming, ed., **Gandhi: Maker of Modern India.** 113 pp. Lexington, Mass.: D. C. Heath, 1965. (Diverse commentaries from Quaker to Communist on Gandhi's social and political significance. Bibliography.)

Lohia, Rammanohar, **Marx, Gandhi and Socialism.** 550 pp. Hyderabad: Nava Hind Publications, 1963. (Analysis of the potential beneficial influence of Gandhi's approach on the future development of socialism.)

Mukerjee, Hiren, **Gandhiji: A Study.** Second edition, revised. 225 pp. New Delhi: People's Publishing House, 1960. (A Communist analysis of Gandhi's political career. Bibliography.)

Murthi. See Ramana Murthi.

Næss, Arne, **Gandhi and Group Conflict: An Exploration of Satya-graha.** 172 pp. Oslo: Universitetsforlaget, 1974. (Concentrates on the metaphysics and norms of Gandhi's philosophy. Appendices.)

——————, **Gandhi and the Nuclear Age.** 149 pp. Totowa, N. J.: Bedminster Press, 1965. (Discusses Gandhi's political ethics and compares them to those of Luther, Hobbes, Nietzsche, and Tolstoy. Bibliography.)

Pattabhi Sitaramayya, Bhograju, **Gandhi and Gandhism (A Study),** In two volumes, I, 267 pp.; II, cont. to p. 520. Allahabad: Kitabistan, 1942.

——————, **Socialism and Gandhism.** 244 pp. Rajahmundry, Andra: Hindustan Publishing Co., 1938.

Power, Paul F. ed., **The Meanings of Gandhi.** 199 pp. Honolulu: University Press of Hawaii, 1971.

Ramachandran, G., and Mahadevan, T. K., eds., **Gandhi: His Relevance for Our Times.** Revised edition. 393 pp. New Delhi: Gandhi Peace Foundation, 1967. Berkeley, Calif.: World Without War Council, 1970.

Ramana Murthi, V. V., **Non-Violence in Politics: A Study of Gandhian Techniques and Thinking.** 246 pp. New Delhi: Frank Bros. & Co., 1958. (An introductory study of the nonviolent struggles in India. Bibliography. Appendices.)

Rao, M. B., ed., **Mahatma: A Marxist Symposium.** 136 pp. Bombay: People's Publishing House, 1969. (Essays from a Communist Party of India symposium.)

Rattan, Ram, **Gandhi's Concept of Political Obligation.** 346 pp. Calcutta: Minerva Associates, 1972. (Appendices. Select bibliography.)

Ray, Sibnarayan, ed., **Gandhi, India and the World: An International Symposium.** 384 pp. Bombay: Nachiketa Publications, 1970.

Sharma, Bishan Sarup, **Gandhi as a Political Thinker.** 164 pp. Allahabad: Indian Press, 1956. (Focuses on Gandhi's political philosophy and views on social and political structure. Bibliography.)

Shridharani, Krishnalal, **War Without Violence: A Study of Gandhi's Method and Its Accomplishments.** 351 pp. New York:

Harcourt, Brace, 1939. Revised updated edition, 299 pp.
Bombay: Bharatiya Vidya Bhavan, 1962. Reprint of the 1939
edition: New York and London: Garland Publishing, 1972.
(Discusses the technique of *satyagraha,* its application, origins,
and compares it to war. Selected bibliography. Recommended.)
Sitaramayya. See Pattabhi Sitaramayya.

GANDHI'S CAMPAIGNS AND THE INDIAN INDEPENDENCE STRUGGLES

Azad, Maulana A. K., **India Wins Freedom: An Autobiographical
Narrative.** 252 pp. Bombay, Calcutta, and Madras: Orient
Longmans, 1959. (Covers 1935–1948. Appendix. By an impor-
tant Muslim Congress leader, later President of India.)

Bose, Subhas Chandra, **The Indian Struggle, 1920–1942.** 476 pp.
New York: Asia Publishing House, 1964. (By a pro-violence
popular nationalist leader.)

Brailsford, H. N., **Rebel India.** 262 pp. New York: New Republic,
Inc., 1931. (1930–31 campaign.)

Brown, Judith M., **Gandhi and Civil Disobedience: The Mahatma in
Indian Politics, 1928–1934.** 414 pp. Cambridge, Eng.: Cambridge University Press, 1977. (Analysis of the salt *satyagraha.*)

——————, **Gandhi's Rise To Power: Indian Politics, 1915–1922.**
384 pp. Cambridge, Eng.: Cambridge University Press, 1972.
(Analyzes the first noncooperation campaign of 1920–22. Recommended. Bibliography.)

Coupland, Reginald, **Report on the Constitutional Problem in India,**
Part I, **The Indian Problem, 1833–1935,** 160 pp.; Part II, **Indian
Politics, 1936–1942,** 344 pp. London, New York, and Bombay:
Oxford University Press, 1943–1944.

Desai, Mahadev, **The Epic of Travancore.** 251 pp. Ahmedabad:
Navajivan Karyalaya, 1937. (The Vykom *satyagraha* of
1924–1925 to lift discrimination against untouchables with
writings by Gandhi from 1925–1937.)

—————— **The Story of Bardoli: Being a History of the Bardoli
Satyagraha of 1928 and Its Sequel.** 249 pp. Ahmedabad:
Navajivan, 1957 (1929).

Doke, Joseph J., **M. K. Gandhi: An Indian Patriot in South Africa.** 97 pp. London: London Indian Chronicle, 1909.

Edwardes, Michael, **The Last Years of British India.** 250 pp. London: Cassell, 1963. (Covers 1914–1947.)

Furneaux, Rupert, **Massacre at Amritsar.** 183 pp. London: George Allen & Unwin, 1963. (Bibliography. Illustrations.)

Gandhi, Mohandas K., **Satyagraha in South Africa.** 351 pp. Ahmedabad: Navajivan, 1950 (1928).

Gopal, Ram, **How India Struggled for Freedom: A Political History.** 469 pp. Bombay: Book Centre, 1967. (Includes accounts of various struggles, from the 1906 Bengal boycott movement to the 1940s.)

Gopal, S., **The Viceroyalty of Lord Irwin, 1926–1931.** 152 pp. Oxford: Clarendon Press, 1957. (Includes the 1928 Bardoli campaign and the 1930–31 civil disobedience campaign.)

Government Of India, **India in 1930–31: A Statement Prepared for Presentation to Parliament.** 752 pp. Calcutta: Government of India Central Publication Branch, 1932. (See Chapter 2, and Appendices 2–4 on the civil disobedience campaign.)

Hancock, William K., **Smuts: The Sanguine Years, 1870–1919.** 619 pp. London and New York: Cambridge University Press, 1962. (See pp. 321–348 about Smuts and Gandhi and the South African conflict.)

Hutchins, Francis G., **India's Revolution: Gandhi and the Quit India Movement.** Cambridge, Mass.: Harvard University Press, 1973. (A study of the 1942 struggle. Bibliography.)

Huttenback, Robert A., **Gandhi in South Africa: British Imperialism and the Indian Questions, 1860–1914.** 368 pp. Ithaca, N.Y. and London: Cornell University Press, 1971. (A history of the civil rights campaigns 1893 to 1914, including the 1907–1910 Transvaal *satyagraha.* Selected bibliography. Appendix. Photographs.)

Irwin, Lord (later Lord Halifax), **Indian Problems: Speeches by Lord Irwin.** 376 pp. London: George Allen & Unwin, 1932. (See pp. 74–115, 290–301, and 321–325 on the 1930–31 campaign.)

Krishnadas, **Seven Months With Mahatma Gandhi: Being an Inside View of the Non-Co-operation Movement (1921–1922).** Two vols.: I, 449 pp. Triplicane, Madras: S. Ganesan, 1928; II, 505 pp. Dighwara, Bihar: Rambinode Sinha, 1928. (Appendices.)

Kumar, R., ed., **Essays on Gandhian Politics: The Rowlatt Satya-graha of 1919.** 347 pp. London: Oxford University Press, 1971. (Consists of a series of case studies of the regions responding to Gandhi's call in March, 1919.)

Masani, R.P., **Britain in India: An Account of British Rule in the Indian Subcontinent.** 278 pp. London, New York, and Bombay: Oxford University Press, 1960. (See Chapters 6–20, covering 1858–1948. Illustrations.)

Miller, Webb, **I Found No Peace: The Journal of a Foreign Correspondent.** 332 pp. New York: Simon and Schuster, 1936. (See Chapters 16–19 and 21.)

Nehru, Jawaharlal, **An Autobiography.** London: John Lane, 1936. New York: Paragon Press, 1965. (By a very important leader of the Indian National Congress, later Prime Minister of India.)

——————, **The Discovery of India.** 595 pp. New York: John Day, 1946. (See pp. 358–505 on the Indian National Congress and British policies.)

——————, **Toward Freedom: The Autobiography of Jawaharlal Nehru.** 440 pp. New York: John Day, 1941, and Boston: Beacon Press, 1958. (Abridgement of Nehru's Autobiography.)

Panter-Brick, Simone, **Gandhi Against Machiavellism: Nonviolence in Politics.** 240 pp. Bombay, London, New York, *et al.:* Asia Publishing Co., 1966.

Pattabhi Sitamarayya, Bhogaraju, **The History of the Indian National Congress, 1885–1935.** Vol. I, Madras: Working Committee of the Congress, 1935. (Important. More complete than later edition.)

Prasad, Rajendra, **Satyagraha in Champaran.** (Second Revised Edition), 224 pp. Ahmedabad: Navajivan, 1949. (The 1917 Champaran campaign. By Gandhi's co-worker, later President of India. Appendices.)

Pyarelal (Nair), **The Epic Fast.** 327 pp. Ahmedabad: Mohanlal Maganlal Bhatt, 1932. (Gandhi's "fast unto death" in 1932 about the status of untouchables.)

Ram, Raja, **The Jallianwala Bagh Massacre: A Premeditated Plan.** 208 pp. Chandigarh, India: Punjab University Publication Bureau, 1969. (Bibliography. Appendices.)

Sharp, Gene, **Gandhi Wields the Weapon of Moral Power: Three Case Histories.** 316 pp. Ahmedabad: Navajivan, 1960. Foreword by Albert Einstein. (Gopal's account of the 1930–31 struggle should be read with the account here. Also contains Champaran campaign and the 1948 Delhi fast.)

Swinson, Arthur, **Six Minutes to Sunset: The Story of General Dyer and the Amritsar Affair.** 216 pp. London: Peter Davies, 1964. (Bibliography.)

Sykes, Sir Frederick, **From Many Angles: An Autobiography.** 592 pp. London, Toronto, and Bombay: George G. Harrap & Co., 1942. (See Chapters 13–20 on the years 1928–1942.)

Tendulkar, Dinanath G., **Gandhi in Champaran.** 115 pp. New Delhi: Publications Division, Ministry of Information and Broadcasting, Government of India, 1957.

> Check also Erikson's *Gandhi's Truth* on the Ahmedabad strike, biographies of Gandhi for sketches of various campaigns, and, for longer accounts as beginnings for historical studies: D. G. Tendulkar, *Mahatma: Life of Mohandas Karamchand Gandhi* (eight volumes), New Delhi: Ministry of Information and Broadcasting, 1962.

NONVIOLENT STRUGGLE BY INDIAN NATIONALISTS BEFORE GANDHI

Datta, Kalinkinkar, **Renaissance, Nationalism and Social Changes in Modern India.** 144 pp. Calcutta: Bookland, 1965. (See pp. 23–35.)

Gopal, Ram, **How India Struggled for Freedom: A Political History.** 469 pp. Bombay: Book Centre, 1967.

Karunakaran, K. P., **Continuity and Change in Indian Politics: A Study of the Political Philosophy of the Indian National Movement, 1885–1921.** 204 pp. New Delhi: People's Publishing House, 1964. (See pp. 56–91.)

Majumdra, Ramesa Chandra, **The History and Culture of the Indian People.** Vol. XI. Bombay: Bharatiya Vidya Bhavan, 1969. (See pp. 253–260.)

Pattabhi Sitaramayya, Bhogaraju, **The History of the Indian National Congress.** Vol. I (1885–1935). 1038 pp. Bombay: Padna Publications, 1946 (1935). (See pp. 130–150.)

GANDHI'S WRITINGS

Bose, Nirmal Kumar, ed., **Selections from Gandhi.** 311 pp. Ahmedabad: Navajivan, 1948.
Gandhi, Mohandas K., **All Men Are Brothers.** Compiled and edited by Krishna Kripalani. 253 pp. Paris: United Nations Educational, Scientific and Cultural Organization, and New York: Columbia University Press, 1958. Ahmedabad: Navajivan, 1960. Chicago: World Without War Publications, 1972. (Bibliography.)
——————, **An Autobiography or the Story of My Experiments With Truth.** 640 pp. Ahmedabad: Navajivan, (1927) 1948, Washington: Public Affairs Press, 1954, and Boston: Beacon Press, 1957. (Emphasizes Gandhi's ascetic, psychological, and religious concerns. Not recommended as an introduction.)
——————, **The Collected Works of Mahatma Gandhi,** Series incomplete. **1** (1884-1896) 343 pp.; **2** (1896-1897) 413 pp.; **3** (1898–1903) 498 pp.; **4** (1903–1905) 520 pp.; **5** (1905–1906) 520 pp.; **6** (1906–1907) 560 pp.; **7** (Jn.-Dec. 1907) 576 pp.; **8** (Jan.-Aug. 1908) 603 pp.; **9** (Sept. 1908–Nov. 1909) 668 pp.; **10** (Nov. 1909-Mar. 1911) 580 pp.; **11** (Apr. 1911-Mar. 1913) 666 pp.; **12** (Apr. 1913-Dec. 1914) 700 pp.; **13** (Jan. 1915-Oct. 1917) 646 pp.; **14** (Oct. 1917-Jl. 1918) 580 pp.; **15** (Aug. 1918-Jl. 1919) 538 pp.; **16** (Aug. 1919-Jan. 1920) 581 pp.; **17** (Feb.-Jn. 1920) 616 pp.; **18** (Jl.-Nov. 1920) 515 pp.; **19** (Nov. 1920-Apr. 1921) 604 pp.; **20** (Apr.-Aug. 1921) 567 pp.; **21** (Aug.-Dec. 1921) 603 pp.; **22** (Dec. 1921-Mar. 1922) 544 pp.; **23** (Mar. 1922-May 1924) 606 pp.; **24** (May-Aug. 1924) 615 pp.; **25** (Aug. 1924-Jan. 1925) 640 pp.; **26** (Jan.-Apr. 1925) 607 pp.; **27** (May-Jl. 1925) 492 pp.; **28** (Aug.-Nov. 1925) 508 pp.; **29** (Nov. 1925-Feb. 1926) 482 pp.; **30** (Feb.-Jn. 1926) 618 pp.; **31** (Jn.-Nov. 1926) 594 pp.; **32** (Nov. 1926-Jan. 1927) 631 pp.; **33** (Jan.-Jn. 1927) 517 pp.; **34** (Jn.-Sept. 1927) 579 pp.; **35** (Sept. 1927-Jan. 1928) 575 pp.; **36** (Feb.-Jn. 1928) 503 pp.; **37** (Jl.-Oct. 1928) 453 pp.; **38** (Nov. 1928-Feb. 1929) 464 pp.; **39** (Feb. 1929) 563 pp.; **40** (Feb.-May 1929) 462 pp.; **41** (Jn.-Oct. 1929) 605 pp.; **42** (Oct. 1929-Feb. 1930) 554 pp.; **43** (Mar.-Jn. 1930) 480 pp.; **44** (Jl.-Dec. 1930) 497 pp.; **45** (Dec. 1930-Apr. 1931) 494 pp.; **46** (16 Apr.-17 Jn. 1931) 451 pp.; **47** (Jn.-Sept. 1931) 478 pp.; **48** (Sept. 1931-Jan. 1932) 542 pp.; **49** (Jan.-

May 1932) 577 pp.; **50** (Jn.-Aug. 1932) 499 pp.; **51** (1 Sept.-15 Nov. 1932) 505 pp.; **52** (Nov. 1932-Jan. 1933) 483 pp.; **53** (Jan.-Mar. 1933) 538 pp.; **54** (6 Mar.-22 Apr. 1933) 527 pp.; **55** (23 Apr.-15 Sept. 1933) 494 pp.; **56** (16 Sept. 1933-15 Jan. 1934) 550 pp.; **57** (16 Jan.-17 May 1934) 540 pp.; **58** (18 May-15 Sept 1934) 496 pp.; **59** (16 Sept.-15 Dec. 1934) 490 pp.; **60** (16 Dec. 1934-24 Apr. 1935) 505 pp.; **61** (25 Apr.-30 Sept. 1935) 506 pp.; **62** (1 Oct. 1935-31 May 1936) 507 pp.; **63** (1 Jn.-2 Nov. 1936) 450 pp.; **64** (3 Nov. 1936-14 Mar. 1937) 478 pp.; **65** 15 Mar.-31 Jl. 1937) 506 pp.; **66** (1 Aug. 1937-31 Mar. 1938) 510 pp.; **67** (1 Apr.-14 Oct. 1938) 478 pp.; **68** (15 Oct. 1938-28 Feb. 1939) 518 pp.; **69** (1 Mar.-15 Jl. 1939) 501 pp.; **70** (16 Jl.-30 Nov. 1939) 464 pp. New Delhi: Publications Division, Ministry of Information and Broadcasting, Government of India, 1960–1978.

――――――――, "Constructive Programme: Its Meaning and Place."(pamphlet; second edition; 32 pp. Ahmedabad: Navajivan, 1945).

――――――――, **For Pacifists**. 106 pp. Ahmedabad: Navajivan, 1949.

――――――――, **Gandhiji's Correspondence with the Government, 1942–44**. 360 pp. Ahmedabad: Navajivan, 1945.

――――――――, **Gandhiji's Correspondence With the Government, 1944–47**. Edited by Pyarelal (Nair). 375 pp. Ahmedabad: Navajivan, 1959.

――――――――, "Hind Swaraj or Indian Home Rule." (pamphlet; 80 pp. Ahmedabad: Navajivan, (1908) 1938).

――――――――, **Non-violence in Peace and War**. Vol. I, 512 pp. Vol. II, 403 pp. Ahmedabad: Navajivan, (1942) 1948 and 1949. (Collected writings and talks on nonviolent responses to diverse Indian and international problems. Recommended.)

――――――――, **Non-violent Resistance**. New York: Schocken Books, 1967. Indian edition entitled: **Satyagraha**. Ahmedabad: Navajivan, 1951, 406 pp. (Collected articles and summaries of speeches on the nonviolent technique.)

――――――――, **Satyagraha in South Africa**. Ahmedabad: Navajivan, (1928) 1951.

――――――――, **Young India, 1919–1922**. 1199 pp. Triplicane, Madras: S. Ganesan, 1922.

――――――――, **Young India, 1922–1924**. 1286 pp. Triplicane, Madras: S. Ganesan, 1924.

—————————, Young India, 1924–1926. 984 pp. New York: Viking Press, 1927.

Jack, Homer A. ed., **The Gandhi Reader: A Source Book of His Life and Writings.** 532 pp. Bloomington, Ind.: Indiana University Press, 1956.

Merton, Thomas, ed. **Gandhi on Non-violence: Selected Texts from Gandhi's Non-violence in Peace and War.** New York: New Directions, 1965.

Nag, Kalidas, **Tolstoy and Gandhi,** 136 pp. Patna: Pustak Bhandar, 1950. (The Gandhi-Tolstoy correspondence plus relevant writings.)

Prabhu, R.K., and Rao, U.R. eds. **The Mind of Mahatma Gandhi.** 226 pp. London: Oxford University Press, 1945. (Compiled brief quotations.)

MEMOIRS ABOUT GANDHI

Birla, Ghanshyam D., **In the Shadow of the Mahatma: A Personal Memoir,** 337 pp. Bombay: Orient Longmans, 1953. (Appendix.)

Chandiwala, Brijkrishna, **At the Feet of Bapu.** 345 pp. Ahmedabad: Navajivan, 1954. (Reminiscences of an aide to Gandhi, especially during his later years.)

Desai, Mahadev H., **Day-to-Day With Gandhi (Secretary's Diary).** In four vols.: I (Nov. 1917-Mar. 1919) 400 pp.; II (Apr. 1919-Oct. 1920) 400 pp.; III (Oct. 1920-Jan. 1924) 400 pp.; IV (Jan. 1924-Nov. 1924) 388 pp. Varanasi: Sarva Seva Sangh Prakashan, 1968-1969.

Krishnadas, **Seven Months with Mahatma Gandhi: Being an Inside View of the Non-Co-Operation Movement (1921–1922).** In two vols.: I, 449 pp. Triplicane, Madras: S. Ganesan, 1928; II, 505 pp. Dighwara (Bihar): Rambinode Sinha, 1928. (Appendices.)

Nehru, Jawaharlal, **Nehru'on Gandhi: A Selection, Arranged in the Order of Events, From the Writings and Speeches of Jawaharlal Nehru.** 150 pp. New York: John Day, 1941.

Watson, Francis, **Talking of Gandhiji: Four Programmes for Radio First Broadcast by the British Broadcasting Corporation.** 141 pp. London, New York, and Toronto: Longmans, Green and Co., 1957.

KHAN ABDUL GHAFFAR KHAN AND THE MUSLIM KHUDAI KHIDMATGAR "SERVANTS OF GOD" NONVIOLENT STRUGGLE MOVEMENT

Andrews, C.F., The Challenge of the North-West Frontier. London: Allen & Unwin, 1937.

Bondurant, Joan V., Conquest of Violence: The Gandhian Philosophy of Conflict. 269 pp. Princeton, N.J.: Princeton University Press, 1958, and Berkeley, Calif.: University of California Press, 1965. (See pp. 131–144. Glossary. Bibliography.)

Pyarelal (Nair), Thrown to the Wolves. Calcutta: Eastlight Book House, 1966.

Spain, James W. The Way of the Pathans. London: Robert Hale, 1962.

Tendulkar, D.G. Abdul Ghaffar Khan: Faith Is a Battle. 550 pp. Bombay: Popular Prakashan, for the Gandhi Peace Foundation, 1967.

Yunus, Mohammad, Frontier Speaks. Bombay: Hind Kitabs, 1947.

BIBLIOGRAPHIES ON GANDHI

Despande, Pandurang Ganesh, compiler, Gandhiana: A Bibliography of Gandhian Literature. 239 pp. Ahmedabad: Navajivan, 1948.

Indian Council of Social Science Research, Mohandas Karamchand Gandhi: A Bibliography. 379 pp. New Delhi: Orient Longman, 1974. (Classified and annotated bibliography of English language books on Gandhi published before December 1972. Includes subject, author, and title indexes, and each entry offers full table of contents and other information.)

Kovalsky, Susan J., "Mahatma Gandhi and his Political Influence in South Africa, 1893–1914." (mimeo) 27 pp. Johannesburg: University of the Witwatersrand, 1971. (A selective bibliography issued by the Department of Bibliography, Librarianship and Typography.)

Sharma, Jagdish S., **Mahatma Gandhi: A Descriptive Bibliography,
Book One and Two.** 650 pp. New Delhi: S. Chand & Co., 1968
(1955).
Vir, Dharma, **Gandhi Bibliography.** 575 pp. Chandigarh: Gandhi
Smarak Nidhi, 1967.

GANDHI BOOKS AVAILABLE IN
THE UNITED STATES

A large variety of books by and about Gandhi which are
published in India, including many of those listed in this appendix
and others, are available in stock in the United States from
Greenleaf Books.

Those seriously interested may write for their "Special List of
Gandhian Literature." Enquiries on availability of particular items
may also be sent to:

Greenleaf Books
Weare
New Hampshire 03218

Appendix E

Recommendations for Course Usage

This book as a whole, or individual chapters, may be used, in conjunction with other resources, in a variety of college and university courses, as well as in courses for advanced high school students, and in adult study groups and continuing education courses. For the following subjects, the chapters listed under each heading are especially recommended for consideration by the instructor or coordinator.

CIVILIAN-BASED DEFENSE *

One	Gandhi's Political Significance
Three	Gandhi on the Theory of Voluntary Servitude
Seven	India's Lesson for the Peace Movement
Eight	Gandhi's Defense Policy
Nine	Gandhi as a National Defense Strategist

GANDHI

One	Gandhi's Political Significance
Two	Origins of Gandhi's Use of Nonviolent Struggle: A Review-Essay on Erik Erikson's *Gandhi's Truth*
Three	Gandhi on the Theory of Voluntary Servitude
Four	*Satyagraha* and Political Conflict: A Review of Joan V. Bondurant's *Conquest of Violence*
Five	The Theory of Gandhi's Constructive Program
Six	Gandhi's Evaluation of Indian Nonviolent Action
Seven	India's Lesson for the Peace Movement

---

*A national defense policy of prepared nonviolent noncooperation and defiance against foreign occupations and *coups d'état*.

PACIFISM

PEACE AND WAR

POLITICAL ETHICS

POLITICAL THEORY

POWER

PRINCIPLED NONVIOLENCE

SOCIAL MOVEMENTS

STRATEGY

WAR AND PEACE

Appendix F

Suggestions for Preparing Courses on Gandhi *

Some people may wish to focus a full course, or a section of a broader course, seminar, or study group on Gandhi, his thought, and his activities. These may vary in their concentration, depending on the origin of the interest in Gandhi and those aspects or problems which seem most important to the group. Some of those are suggested by the headings in both Appendices D and E. In planning a course one should choose one or a few of these only; it is impossible to cover all aspects.

Since no single course plan can be suitable for every interest and situation, it is better if the group or individual responsible develop an individual plan, rather than imitate a single blueprint which might be offered in a book. The development of such a plan is necessarily difficult at best, even if one has had considerable experience in such courses and broad familiarity with the available literature. Even then, all is unlikely to go smoothly. One may, for example, discover at the last minute that one of the chosen books for reading has just gone out of print! Despite the difficulties, however, it is possible to make some broad suggestions here which may be useful in planning a course, seminar, or study group.

A number of variables are always present: the number of students, their interests and backgrounds, whether or not the group members and the coordinator or instructor facilitate a rich participating educational experience, and others.

---

* This Appendix is designed for persons and groups which have never before planned a course or study group on Gandhi. The suggestions here are often very elementary and unnecessary for persons with experience in such preparation.

It is necessary in the planning to give maximum attention to those aspects over which we have the most control. Such careful planning may in turn indirectly influence other variables over which direct control is difficult or impossible.

We need first of all to note the broader context, subject, or problem area in which Gandhi is seen to be relevant. We then need to know how to lead the group from that broader interest to the specific aspect or aspects of Gandhi on which the study is to be focused.

At times, the bulk of the course—perhaps even nine-tenths of it—will be devoted to that broader field, whether social movements, international relations, resistance and revolution, social ethics, or whatever. That would only leave the possibility of limited reading and limited time on Gandhi. In such a case, careful planning and selection is even more important. At other times, such a broader course will permit a quarter or even a third of the readings and time to be focused on aspects of Gandhi. The inclusion of the broader field in readings and discussion is not usually a problem in such courses, for they constitute the main content of the course: it is important, however, in such cases to make clear the connection between the broader field and the specific attention to aspects of Gandhi, so that the study of those aspects both is, and is seen to be, relevant to the course as a whole.

In courses which are primarily or almost exclusively about some aspect of Gandhi, his thought, or actions, it is essential to provide some carefully selected brief survey of the broader area, subject, or problem, within which attention is primarily to be given to Gandhi. Depending on the situation, this may be done by reading a book or an article, or a brief lecture, or a group discussion based upon some familiarity with the broader field.

Several other basic factors need to be taken into consideration in advance planning. These include the educational, academic, or intellectual level of the group, the probable number of participants, whether it is to be a formal course in an institution or an informal study group, the level and amount of reading which can be expected of group members, the availability or otherwise of a resource person, coordinator, or instructor with expertise on the subject (as distinct from beliefs and opinions), and the number of weeks the course is to last. It is usually better to plan initially for a limited course which can be extended or supplemented with a new one if needed, rather than a course too long or ambitious, which may not keep the active involvement of the group.

If a genuine authority who is not domineering is available as an instructor, coordinator, or resource person, that can be helpful. However, the absence of such an "expert" is no reason not to begin. In fact, that absence may be an advantage: the "expertise" may be in fact limited; there will be less of a tendency to defer judgement and questions to a single person; and the whole group may then work together more effectively in thinking through the problems, and searching for knowledge and understanding.

Good reading material for all such courses, seminars, and study groups is essential. It must be wisely selected, and group members must be expected to study between sessions. Sound opinions and judgements need to be based on knowledge and understanding, which can often be significantly increased by careful study of quality books written by people whose experience, research, analysis, or other qualifications have given them the understanding and knowledge which they share with others through their books. Films about Gandhi and the Indian nationalist struggles may also be helpful, but they cannot replace good books.

Since no single course can cover all aspects of Gandhi's life, thought, and actions, and since only certain aspects of those may be relevant to a course with a broader orientation, a selection must be made. Where the broader field of the course narrows the focus of attention to only one or two particular aspects—for instance, strategy, or political ethics, or national security studies—then readings need to be selected from the available resources suitable for the particular group and course. Appendix D "Sources for Further Study" and Appendix E "Recommendations for Course Usage" of chapters of this book may be helpful in that identification and selection, along with studies which may have been published at a later date. It will be necessary to determine whether the books are in print, by consulting *Books in Print* or *Paperback Books in Print,* examining publishers' catalogues, writing to publishers, or (in the case of Indian books) enquiring of Greenleaf Books, Weare, New Hampshire, 03218.

For courses largely or entirely on Gandhi, more possibilities exist, but it is still necessary to select only a few of the range of subjects, such as those listed as headings in Appendix E and the subject headings of Appendix D. In general, it may be useful in most cases to include a good biography of Gandhi; so one should examine those listed in Appendix D under the biography section which might be suitable, such as those by Fischer, Nanda, Payne, or others, and determine whether they are currently in print, available, at what price, and the like. Then, depending on the general field and orientation of the course, its duration, level, amount of reading which can be expected, and the like, one might select one or more substantive areas (as the headings in Appendices D and E) as the main focus or foci of study and exploration.

The books and chapters listed under those headings may then be considered for possible use, along with any ones more recently published than this book. Joan V. Bondurant's *Conquest of Violence: The Gandhian Philosophy of Conflict* is important enough to be considered in a variety of such courses. If one is focusing on the dynamics of nonviolent struggle, then Part Three of Gene Sharp's *The Politics of Nonviolent Action* is relevant as it quotes Gandhi's insights and uses examples from the Indian struggles extensively. Other resources in the various substantive areas are listed in those appendices.

A great variety of possible courses can be created by selection of one or more of these substantive areas: studies of the Gandhian campaigns of nonviolent struggle, problems of political obligation, Gandhi's social psychology, Gandhi as a charismatic leader, Gandhi's principles of strategy, Gandhi's alternative conceptions of nationalism, internationalism, and defense, relationships between social structure and State power, and on and on.

A careful selection of reading matter for these is necessary; simply because a book is listed in these appendices does not necessarily mean that it is suitable for a particular course or group of students. Some items are far more, and far less, suitable than others; the most likely, and available, possibilities need to be carefully examined and considered in comparison to the other options.

Beyond the selection of the focus of the course, and the choice of books for study, many important decisions remain. These include, for example, whether or not also to have participants prepare research papers, whether to use films, whether to have lectures or to avoid them, whether to involve the students actively

in the day-to-day running of the course, and others. Intrinsic to the
subject matter, of course, is the encouragement of different view-
points, opinions, and perspectives; the search for knowledge and
understanding, or for truth if one prefers, is a constant one, never
completed.

Appendix G

Original Publication Sources

The chapters of this book have been edited or revised from essays and chapters which have appeared in a variety of publications in India, England, Norway, and the United States. In some cases the chapters appear here with slightly different titles than in earlier publications, and in some cases the chapter has been previously revised one time or more. This appendix supplies the record of the publication background of each chapter.

One   Gandhi's Political Significance
Original title: "Gandhi's Political Significance Today." G. Ramachandran and T. K. Mahadevan, eds., *Gandhi: His Relevance for Our Times.* Bombay: Bharatiya Vidya Bhavan, 1964. Revised edition: New Delhi: Gandhi Peace Foundation, 1967, and Berkeley, Calif.: World Without War Council, 1971.

Two   Origins of Gandhi's Use of Nonviolent Struggle: A Review-Essay on Erik Erikson's *Gandhi's Truth*
Original title: "The Origins of Gandhi's Nonviolent Militancy." *Harvard Political Review,* vol. II, no. 1 (May 1970).

Three   Gandhi on the Theory of Voluntary Servitude
Gandhi Marg (New Delhi), vol. VI, no. 4 (October 1962).

Four   *Satyagraha* and Political Conflict: A Review of Joan V. Bondurant's *Conquest of Violence*
Original title: "A Review of Joan V. Bondurant, *Conquest of Violence: The Gandhian Philosophy of Conflict. Journal of Conflict Resolution,* vol. III, no. 4 (December 1959).

Five   The Theory of Gandhi's Constructive Program
Selected and edited from "The Constructive Programme." *Mankind* (Hyderabad), vol. I, no. 12 (July 1957).

Six   Gandhi's Evaluation of Indian Nonviolent Action
Political Science Review (Jaipur, Rajasthan), vol. 9, nos. 1 and 2 (January and June 1970).

Seven   India's Lesson for the Peace Movement
Peace News (London), 15 November 1963. Revised and reprinted from *The Pacifist* (London), October-November 1963.

Eight   Gandhi's Defense Policy
Gandhi Marg, vol. X, nos. 3 and 4 (July and October 1966). Also: T. K. Mahadevan, Adam Roberts, and Gene Sharp, eds., *Civilian Defense: An Introduction.* Introductory statement by President Sarvepalli Radhakrishnan. Bombay: Bharatiya Vidya Bhavan, and New Delhi: Gandhi Peace Foundation. 1967.

Nine   Gandhi as a National Defense Strategist
Gandhi Marg, vol. XIV, no. 3 (July 1970).

Ten   Types of Principled Nonviolence
A. Paul Hare and Herbert H. Blumberg, eds., *Nonviolent Direct Action: American Cases: Social-Psychological Analyses.* Washington, D. C.: Corpus Books, 1969. That was a major revision of two previous versions: "A Study of the Meanings of Nonviolence." *Gandhi Marg,* vol. III, no. 4 (October 1959) and vol. IV, nos. 1, 2, and 3 (January, April, and July, 1960); and, "The Meanings of Nonviolence: A Typology (revised)," *Journal of Conflict Resolution,* vol. III, no. 1 (March 1959). For the earlier development of this typology, see the first footnote to the March 1959 version.

Eleven   Ethics and Responsibility in Politics: A Critique of the Present Adequacy of Max Weber's Classification of Ethical Systems
Inquiry (Oslo), vol. VII, no. 3 (Autumn 1964).

Twelve   Morality, Politics, and Political Technique
Mimeo; London: Friends Peace Committee, 1963. In part, *Reconciliation Quarterly* (London), First Quarter, 1965, no. 108.

Thirteen   Nonviolence: Moral Principle or Political Technique? Clues from Gandhi's Thought and Experience
Indian Political Science Review (New Delhi), vol. IV, no. 1 (October 1969).

Appendix A   Shridharani's Contribution to the Study of Gandhi's Technique

Original title: "Introduction." Krishnalal Shridharani, *War Without Violence: A Study of Gandhi's Method and Its Accomplishments.* Reprint of the 1939 edition by the Garland Library of War and Peace. New York: Garland Publishing Co., 1972.

Appendix B   The War in 1942

The same as Chapter Eight, to which it was joined.

Appendix H

Copyright Acknowledgements

"A Review of Joan V. Bondurant, **Conquest of Violence: The Gandhian Philosophy of Conflict,**" published in the **Journal of Conflict Resolution,** vol. III, no. 4 (July 1959), was copyrighted by that Journal: © by the Editorial Board, **Journal of Conflict Resolution,** 1959. It is reprinted here by permission of Sage Publications, Inc., present publisher of that Journal.

"Introduction" to Krishnalal Shridharani, **War Without Violence: A Study of Gandhi's Method and Its Accomplishments** was published in the reprint of the 1939 edition issued by the Garland Library of War and Peace. New York: Garland Publishing Co., 1972. It was copyrighted by that publishing house: © Garland Publishing Co., 1972. It is reprinted here by permission of Garland Publishing Co.

The other previously published chapters and appendix were variously published with notice of copyright reserved to Gene Sharp, with a copyright notice in the name of Gene Sharp, or without copyright notice.

All previously published material by the author appears here with some degree of editorial changes, revisions, and in some cases additions or deletions, or both.

While Gandhi's own writings and speeches were mostly not originally copyrighted, many of them have been issued in new editions or collections by Navajivan Publishing House, some of them copyrighted by Navajivan Trust. I am grateful to Navajivan Trust and Navajivan Publishing House for making these available.

I am also grateful to the University of California Press for permission to use the quotations from Joan V. Bondurant's **Conquest of Violence: The Gandhian Philosophy of Conflict** (copyright,